THE LURE
OF WHITEHEAD

THE LURE OF WHITEHEAD

NICHOLAS GASKILL
and A. J. NOCEK, Editors

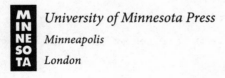

University of Minnesota Press
Minneapolis
London

Chapter 1 was previously published as "A Constructivist Reading of *Process and Reality*," *Theory, Culture & Society* 25, no. 4 (July 2008): 91–110; reprinted by permission of SAGE Publications. Chapter 3 was previously published as *What Is the Style of Matters of Concern?* (Assen, Netherlands: Van Gorcum, 2008).

Published by the University of Minnesota Press
111 Third Avenue South, Suite 290
Minneapolis, MN 55401–2520
http://www.upress.umn.edu

Library of Congress Cataloging-in-Publication Data
The lure of Whitehead / Nicholas Gaskill and A. J. Nocek, editors.
Includes bibliographical references and index.
ISBN 978-0-8166-7995-9 (hc : alk. paper)
ISBN 978-0-8166-7996-6 (pb : alk. paper)
1. Whitehead, Alfred North, 1861–1947. I. Gaskill, Nicholas, b. 1981, editor.
B1674.W354L87 2014
192—dc23
2014002119

Printed in the United States of America on acid-free paper

20 19 18 17 16 15 14   10 9 8 7 6 5 4 3 2 1

Contents

Acknowledgments

Whitehead's philosophy of organism tells us that nothing is what it is outside of the relations it holds to a wider environment. This idea has been made even more vivid for us in the process of editing this book. From start to finish, we benefited from the advice, enthusiasm, provocations, and generosity of a host of friends and colleagues, without whom *The Lure of Whitehead* would not be what it is. Gregory Flaxman deserves special recognition; without his prompting, we never would have met one another let alone pursued his suggestion of editing a volume on Whitehead. We are deeply grateful for his guidance and friendship. Douglas Armato has been a supportive and energetic editor from the moment we approached him about the book, and Danielle Kasprzak provided quick and essential advice on practical matters without ever showing exasperation at our many questions and emails. The readers for the University of Minnesota Press offered encouraging and helpful suggestions on how to develop the volume. Because of their reports, the final collection is a stronger and more comprehensive account of the new interest in Whitehead than the one we initially proposed. We are grateful to Gwendolen Muren, who assisted in the early stages of formatting and proofreading, as well as to Katherine Hunt and Kyla Schuller, whose late-stage edits sharpened our Introduction. Each of us would also like to thank the institutions that provided us with the time and resources to develop this project: Nicholas thanks the Society of Fellows at the University of Chicago and the Department of English at Rutgers University; Adam thanks the Comparative History of Ideas Program and the comparative literature department at the University of Washington.

One of the most exciting aspects of assembling this volume has been delving into the adventure of Whiteheadian thought. In this enterprise, each of us benefited greatly from conversations and engagements with our colleagues. Nicholas would especially like to thank Michael Thomas for his diligence and insight during a year of reading through Whitehead's works, as well as the short-lived "Occasionalists" group at the University of North Carolina for meeting Whitehead's strange philosophy with patience and curiosity. Colin Jager and Margaret Ronda, at Rutgers, and the members of the Society of Fellows at the University of Chicago all offered a helpful mix of interest and skepticism as we framed our Introduction. Adam would like to thank both Gregory Flaxman and Gregg Lambert for their continued support and guidance during the writing and revising process. He also thanks Phillip Thurtle, whose friendship and mentorship proved invaluable for thinking about Whitehead and biology outside preestablished frameworks. And without fellowship assistance from the "Biological Futures in a Globalized World" initiative, jointly sponsored by the Fred Hutchison Cancer Research Center and the Simpson Center for the Humanities at the University of Washington, the time and energy required for this project would never have been possible.

Finally, Nicholas thanks his ever-supportive family for their ongoing encouragement and love. He also thanks William T. Myers for introducing him to Whitehead's philosophy more than a decade ago; without that initial lure, this volume could not possibly have taken the form that it has. Adam would like to offer a special thanks to his loving wife, Stacey, for her encouragement, guidance, and never-ending belief in his ability to succeed, along with his two girls, Fiona and Ivy, for the love and laughter they bring into his life.

Abbreviations

AI	*Adventures of Ideas* (New York: The Free Press, 1967 [1933])
CN	*The Concept of Nature* (Cambridge: Cambridge University Press, 1964 [1920])
FR	*The Function of Reason* (Princeton, N.J.: Princeton University Press, 1929)
MT	*Modes of Thought* (New York: The Free Press, 1968 [1938])
PR	*Process and Reality: Corrected Edition*, ed. D. R. Griffin and D. W. Sherburne (New York: The Free Press, 1978 [1927–28])
RM	*Religion in the Making* (New York: Fordham University Press, 1996 [1926])
S	*Symbolism: Its Meaning and Effect* (New York: Fordham University Press, 1985 [1927])
SMW	*Science and the Modern World* (New York: The Free Press, 1967 [1925])

INTRODUCTION

An Adventure of Thought

Nicholas Gaskill and A. J. Nocek

> The vitality of thought is in adventure. *Ideas won't keep.*
> Something must be done about them.
> —Alfred North Whitehead,
> *The Dialogues of Alfred North Whitehead*

Rarely have a philosopher's fortunes changed so drastically—and in so short a time—as those of Alfred North Whitehead (1861–1947). Not fifteen years ago, his speculative metaphysics stood at the margins of contemporary thought, dismissed as a baroque exercise in an outworn philosophical mode. But since the turn of the last century, his work has attracted the attention not only of a variety of philosophers but also of sociologists, new-media theorists, artists, and literary critics, all of whom have found it useful for addressing problems particular to their fields. As a result, one is now just as likely to see Whitehead invoked in discussions of artificial life or digital art as in theoretical debates about consciousness or subjectivity. This resurgence of interest has unfolded with such speed and from so many directions, however, that the full measure of Whitehead's relevance for contemporary thought has yet to be taken. Why, after such a long period of neglect, is Whitehead suddenly generating so much enthusiasm? What problems and concerns have called his propositions out of obscurity and put them to work in novel contexts?

To address such questions, this volume assembles writers working within an array of disciplines to bring the concepts and techniques of Whiteheadian philosophy to bear on contemporary thought. The paths these thinkers have taken to and from Whitehead have no doubt been myriad, yet together they suggest some of the intellectual currents drawing new readers to Whitehead's work: among them, a dissatisfaction with the epistemological and anthropocentric limitations of "critique"; an effort to engage the unique efficacies of nonhuman forces; and an approach to conceptual construction that avoids both the correspondence model of truth and the free-for-all of relativism. In light of these concerns, Whitehead's capacious metaphysical scheme, understood both as the result of a rigorous speculative method and as a description of the world in terms of constructive processes, has emerged as a genuine alternative to twentieth-century attempts to move beyond Kant. For whereas almost all such attempts proceed by turning from the transcendental subject to the wider conditions of human experience (such as being-in-the-world, history, or discourse), they nonetheless remain anthropocentric in their scope and "critical" in their methods. Whitehead's philosophy, from this vantage point, has come to seem less a historical oddity and more a resource for reformulating many of the fundamental assumptions and approaches shaping humanistic and social scientific inquiry.[1]

The Lure of Whitehead seeks to clarify this renewed relevance and to stimulate its further development. To do so, it groups a range of engagements with Whitehead's work according to three primary tasks: offering a coherent description of experience against the divisions and judgments of modern philosophy; articulating a conceptual scheme capable of affirming genuine novelty; and proposing an ecological and nonanthropocentric framework for analysis. Under these broad headings the contributions below investigate a variety of topics, spanning debates about realism, technology, and the social, as well as experiments in education, computer science, and biology. This collection thus differs from previous "revivals" of Whitehead, which have been isolated instances launched within a specific tradition of scholarship, by channeling a groundswell of interest touching a variety of fields both inside and outside professional philosophy.[2] The first section of our introduction will contextualize this developing interest by surveying Whitehead's reception in relation to the course of twentieth-century philosophy and to the concerns of the present. In the sections that follow, we will demonstrate the importance of Whitehead's speculative technique by drawing attention both to his manner of thinking and to the particular conceptual tools he offers his readers, ending finally with a brief overview of the essays included below. Throughout, we will argue that the growing interest in Whitehead's work should not be treated as a "return" but as a way forward, a way through and around the impasses of contemporary thought. And as a corollary to this, we will show that once Whitehead's "philosophy of organism" is brought into contact with contemporary intellectual practices, both the philosophy and the practices are transformed.

Whitehead began his career as a mathematician, and it was in this capacity that he coauthored the three-volume *Principia Mathematica* (1910, 1912,

1913) with his former student Bertrand Russell. This work continues to stand as one of the landmarks of mathematical logic, a pillar of the attempt "to show that all pure mathematics follows from purely logical premises and uses only concepts definable in logical terms."[3] Yet Whitehead soon parted ways with the logical procedure that preoccupied Russell and his analytical colleagues and turned his attention to explaining how the entities of mathematical and scientific discourse (such as points, instants, and lines) achieve their practical relevance within the conceptual terrain introduced by relativity theory and quantum mechanics. He pursued this topic in his early works on the philosophy of science and, in particular, on the challenges relativity posed to the "container" notion of space inherited from Newton.[4] Then, in *The Concept of Nature* (1920), Whitehead hit upon a formulation that would eventually propel him into cosmological speculation. In that work he presents the modern tendency to confuse the abstract entities of science with the concrete events of the universe as effecting a "bifurcation of nature" into two distinct realms—the really real world of primary qualities, molecules, and energy fields, and the only apparently real world of secondary qualities and sensory experiences, the embellishments our minds make upon the world. Whitehead protested against this division as untenable and spent the rest of his career framing a system of thought capable of putting every aspect of experience—from the insights of science to the intimations of the poets—"in the same boat" (*CN*, 148). This task eventually led him beyond the interests of the philosophy of science and into the realm of metaphysics, first in *Science and the Modern World* (1925) and then, most spectacularly, in *Process and Reality* (1929). In this latter work, Whitehead elaborated a speculative scheme aimed at transforming the habits of thought that supported the modern epoch's "complex of bifurcations," offering in the process powerful reformulations of nature, life, perception, and consciousness (*PR*, 290). Finally, in *Adventures of Ideas* (1933) and *Modes of Thought* (1938), he extended his metaphysical project—what he referred to as the philosophy of organism—into issues specific to human experience, with the result of prompting further revisions and elucidations of his broader system.

Whitehead developed his metaphysics while working in Harvard's philosophy department, which he joined after leaving University College London in 1924. But despite his wide popularity in the 1920s and 1930s, his influence came to an abrupt halt around the time of his death in 1947. At Harvard, philosophers in the emerging analytic tradition balked at the unabashed metaphysics of their former colleague's late work, even as they took up the (Russellian) contributions of the *Principia* in their aspirations to scientific precision. More broadly, Wittgenstein's influence tilted professional philosophy in England and America toward concerns with language and the philosophy of mind, and from this perspective Whitehead's work appeared as dubious speculation based on naïve neglect of the linguistic and epistemological structuring of experience.[5] Likewise, after the Second World War, European philosophers abandoned the once-popular metaphysics of Bergson to pursue the phenomenology of Husserl and ultimately Heidegger. The latter figure towers over the tradition of what became known as "continental philosophy," and though his dismissal of substance ontology in favor of the relational constitution of the world certainly resonates with Whitehead's similar interventions, Heidegger's suspicion of both metaphysics and science as ontic abstractions made possible by a more primordial lived experience *(Dasein)* turned key constituents of Whitehead's work into objects of derision.[6] As a result, Whitehead remained largely unexamined by the postwar phenomenologists (Merleau-Ponty, Levinas, Nancy) and by the poststructuralists (Lacan, Derrida, Foucault), all of whom worked within a tradition wary of both metaphysical speculation and scientific certainty and concerned primarily with identifying the structuring conditions of human experience, be they epistemological, intentional, linguistic, or political.

Given such a climate, it is no wonder that Whitehead fell by the wayside. He was too scientific for the "continentals," not scientific enough for the "analytics," and too metaphysical—which is to say *uncritical*—for them both. But we should note that these assessments were made from within the condition of modern thought that Whitehead spent his career combatting: phenomenology, scientism, and all forms of critique parse the world into two halves—the "real" causal half and the "apparent" effected half. When approached through such critical disjunctions, a philosophy committed to the task of "coherence" and "sheer disclosure" could only appear naïve.

But to say that Whitehead has been neglected since his death is to ignore his significant impact on American theology—an impact that, though in many ways productive, has done as much harm as good for the broader reception of his thought. Indeed, until recently, Whitehead was known more for his descriptions of God than for his criticisms of Kant and epistemology. For the proponents of "process theology"—from Charles Hartshorne to John Cobb and David Ray Griffin—Whitehead's emphasis on becoming and his description of God as being in constitutive relation with the evolving world offered a new way of framing the age-old problems of theodicy and the meaning of God's love. Yet the particular appropriations of Whitehead's thought are less important here than the *style* of Whiteheadian scholarship that took shape among the theologians: a scholastic approach that emphasized textual explication and cast Whitehead as a rationalist system-builder. Thus, by the end of the century, Whitehead was known—if he was known—first and foremost as a theologian with an intimidatingly technical philosophy. The full sweep of his contribution and its relevance were left undeveloped.

Now, however, we are in the midst of a series of philosophical shifts that allow us to approach Whitehead's work anew. At the most general level, these shifts follow from a dissatisfaction with the critical tradition inaugurated by Kant and developed, in different ways, by phenomenology, structuralism and poststructuralism, and literary and cultural theory, each of which limits philosophy to an elucidation of the conditions of knowledge or experience (in the transcendental subject, in our intentional orientation to a world, or in linguistic and historical constructions). Quentin Meillassoux groups these approaches under the banner of "correlationism"—"the idea according to which we only ever have access to the correlation between thought and being, and never to either term considered apart from the other"—and his criticism of post-Kantianism in *After Finitude* has provided a rallying cry for writers interested in overcoming the "correlationist circle."[7] Though the thinkers referred to as "speculative realists," "object-oriented ontologists," and "new materalists" hold divergent positions, they arguably share the goal of thinking the world as it exists apart from human cognition, often to the end of describing material forces unregistered by previous forms of social critique and yet essential for addressing our own era of ecological crisis.[8] In this task, many have found a rich resource in Whitehead's metaphysics. "Of all the great philosophers of the past century," writes Graham Harman, "it is Whitehead who has done the most to free us from the constraints of the philosophy of human *access* to the world."[9]

Similarly, within science studies, the brands of "constructivism" articulated by Isabelle Stengers, Bruno Latour, and Donna Haraway—all of whom have been energized by an encounter with Whitehead—have long pursued the overcoming of Kantianism that Meillassoux advocates, but they have done so through a focus on the material practices of experimentation rather than on rationalist procedures. Accordingly, these scholars use Whitehead to account for the status of scientific knowledge as simultaneously "constructed" and "objective," and in so doing, they have developed a powerful counterexample to the tradition of critique.[10] Rather than demystify "constructions"—be they cultural, linguistic, historical, or psychological—Whitehead affirms them, not as hoaxes or pernicious plots, but as achievements that invent a particular way of engaging an environment.[11] Stengers in particular has shown how this approach promises to foster an "ecology of practices" within which the productions of the sciences—as well as of the humanities and other disciplines—might come to rely on one another, even nurture one another, without claiming for themselves exclusive access to reality.

Even more than in her philosophy of science, Stengers has reinvigorated the contemporary understanding of Whitehead's appeal with her monumental study *Penser avec Whitehead* (2002; translated as *Thinking with Whitehead* in 2011), a work that dramatizes the originality of Whitehead's philosophical constructions and reads him alongside Gilles Deleuze, Michel Foucault, and Étienne Souriau. This book has energized a long-standing but only recently pursued recognition of Deleuze's own affinity for Whitehead, which he expressed by aligning his philosophy with "the two characteristics by which Whitehead defined empiricism: the abstract does not explain but must itself be explained; and the aim is not to discover the eternal or the universal, but to find the conditions under which something new is produced."[12] The renewed inquiries into this philosophical friendship have not only brought continental styles of reading and thinking to Whitehead's work but have also introduced Whiteheadian concepts (such as "prehensions" and "concern") into affect theory and posthumanism, fields widely influenced by Deleuze and Guattari. We are only now beginning to register the difference that Whitehead might make in these inquiries.[13] This volume seeks to facilitate such developments by moving away from the earlier moment of enthusiastic comparison—a moment that produced important books connecting Whitehead to continental thinkers—and toward a focused investigation into Whitehead's unique contributions and the interdisciplinary range of their relevance.[14]

In *Process and Reality,* Whitehead defines a proposition as a "lure for feeling": not a statement about the world to be judged true or false, not a tool for unveiling the truth behind appearances, but a possibility that draws those who entertain it into a different way of feeling their world (*PR,* 85). As such, he remarked more than once that "it is more important that a proposition be interesting than that it be true"—more important that it energize and direct feeling than that it conform to some already established pattern in the data (*PR,* 259; see also *AI,* 244). What the above sketch of Whitehead's reception shows us, then, is that after a period of long obscurity, his propositions have suddenly become interesting: they are acting as a lure for a range of thinkers seeking a path beyond anthropocentrism and toward a mode of thought sensitive to the wider environments in which humans are entwined. And we can be certain that as Whitehead's work has been embraced by these new readers and addressed to these new problems, our very sense of his philosophical contribution has been altered—for as Whitehead noted, a proposition does not determine but lure, and its actualization inevitably modifies its proposal. In this spirit, *The Lure of Whitehead* seeks to render vivid the allure of this astounding thinker and, by bringing his methods and concepts to a wider readership, to foster unforeseen expansions and applications of this thought—new enticements, new transformations.

Whitehead's Speculative Propositions

More so than any one of his concepts, it is Whitehead's unique way of doing philosophy that promises a new direction for contemporary thought. Before turning to his conceptual scheme, then, or to the uses of his approach in the essays below, we will investigate the distinctive features of his philosophical technique. Whitehead characterizes his method of speculative philosophy as "descriptive generalization" (*AI,* 234). But his descriptions are not meant to reveal some hitherto unnoticed element, as with the physicist's particle or Bergson's *durée,* each of which indicates a new vision of the universe, a "view-from-nowhere." Rather, they are imaginative constructions aimed at transforming our modes of thought, the habits of attention and interest that shape our engagements with the world. As such, Whitehead's propositions address our manner of thinking "in the way a tool addresses our modes of action," adjusting the relation between "those who act and . . . that on which they act, by redistributing what is proposed as doable or not doable."[15] No wonder, then, that for Whitehead "philosophy is akin to poetry": its descriptions are carefully constructed utterances *(poesis)* "requiring a leap of the imagination"—lures for feeling, and by extension for thought and action, rather than dogmatic statements of the world as it must be (*PR,* 13).

How, then, does Whitehead go about building his concepts? In *Process and Reality,* he famously likens the "true method of discovery" in philosophy to "the flight of an aeroplane": "It starts from the ground of particular observation; it makes a flight in the thin air of imaginative generalization; and it again lands for renewed observation rendered acute by rational interpretation" (*PR,* 5). This approach stands in stark opposition to the techniques of introspection, positivistic observation, or any methodology that asks us to put aside theory or abstraction and see the world directly. For as Whitehead remarks, "we habitually observe by the method of difference"; that is, we notice what is not always there and base our observations on an unobserved yet operative set of selections (*PR*, 4). Metaphysics breaks this habit through "the method of imaginative rationalization" whereby "thought supplies the differences which direct observation lacks" and so enables "factors which are constantly present" to "yet be observed" (*PR*, 5). Rather than eliminate abstractions in order to attain direct access to the world, Whitehead contributes new concepts to draw our attention to what is exemplified in all experiences. The notions that Whitehead invents are therefore general notions—which is to say they are generic. They do not derive their authority from privileged cases—such as scientific observation or subjective experience—but are inclusive to the point that "we can never catch the actual world taking a holiday from their sway" (*PR*, 4).

But this process of imaginative additions is never complete; indeed Whitehead insists that "in philosophical discussion, the merest hint of dogmatic certainty as to finality of statement is an exhibition of folly" (*PR*, xiv). However, fallibilism does not preclude progress, and Whitehead presents his efforts as an ongoing adventure of speculative creation and subsequent adjustment made in light of the airplane's "landing" in experience. "Every science must devise its own instruments," he writes, and since the "tool required for philosophy is language," "philosophy redesigns language in the same way that, in a physical science, pre-existing appliances are redesigned" (*PR*, 11). The method of imaginative rationalization thus provides conceptual and linguistic lenses aimed at introducing new "differences" invisible to our habitual ways of observing, new contrasts that modify our sense of what matters. Philosophy (as akin to poetry) involves inventing and continually adjusting these lenses.

Already we should note a crucial difference between Whitehead's approach and the Kantian and post-Kantian traditions, captured in the distinction between a transcendental condition and a problematic constraint. Even though Whitehead repeatedly acknowledges the limitations of language—describing it as "elliptical," "incomplete and fragmentary"—he never despairs that the linguistic medium poses insurmountable barriers to what philosophy can investigate (*PR*, 13; *AI*, 226). He instead treats language as a tool capable of recalibration, just as our conventional modes of perception are adjusted through speculative construction. Whitehead thus calls for philosophers to experiment with their linguistic expressions, knowing full well that metaphysical statements will tax even our most ingrained commonsense notions and the grammatical habits that support them.[16]

Likewise, Whitehead refuses to countenance any absolute barrier to thought, any transcendental condition that would render certain features of experience intrinsically beyond our intellectual horizon. For him, as Stengers explains in her chapter on *Process and Reality,* rationality and consciousness are adventures of hope and not "the sad tale of discovering our limitations and illusions." And yet this lack of an *absolute* limit conditioning our philosophical speculation does not imply that there are *no* limits or constraints on metaphysical construction: it is just that these constraints are specific to particular problems, not features of thought as such. They are tied to the task at hand. Thus, directly after describing the airplane's flight, Whitehead insists that "the conditions for the success of imaginative construction must be rigidly adhered to"—not out of reverence for our finite conditions but out of a commitment to particular problems (*PR,* 5).[17]

We will soon consider the nature of the constraints on Whitehead's metaphysical construction, noting both their empirical and rationalist components, but first we must examine what allows these constraints to be specified at all: the formulation of a problem. Indeed, this is a fundamental tenet of Whitehead's approach and one of the primary lures he offers for contemporary thought: that no claim to knowledge be separated from the problem it attempts to solve and the means invented to solve it. This doctrine, as it is developed and enacted in his metaphysical writing, will guide our own interpretation of Whitehead's propositions as themselves forged in relation to a particular problem—namely, that posed by the modern habit of allowing certain knowledge-claims to step beyond their relevant domains and thereby eliminate the real values and achievements available in other modes of experience. Such is the habit that produces the "bifurcation of nature" protested in *The Concept of Nature* and that is identified as "the fallacy of misplaced concreteness" in *Science and the Modern World.* To grasp the nature of Whitehead's constructions, then, we must first consider his description of the problems they address.

When Whitehead diagnoses the fallacy of misplaced concreteness as "the expression of more concrete facts under the guise of very abstract logical constructions," he does not lament it as a necessary effect of our cognitive operations; instead, he treats it as an "accidental error," a *fallacy* that we might learn to avoid (*SMW,* 51). And as the method of imaginative rationalization suggests, the way to avoid this error is not to *subtract* thought, thereby arriving at the concrete via more intuitive routes, but rather to *add* abstractions that can account for the abstracting process by which thought arrives at its claims. "You cannot think without abstractions," Whitehead explains; "accordingly, it is of the utmost importance to be vigilant in critically revising your *modes* of abstraction." As "the critic of abstractions," then, philosophy's task is not to attack abstractions but to manage them, even care for them, by preventing any one of them from being mistaken as more concrete or exhaustive than it is (*SMW*, 59). The problem, in other words, comes when what has been *drawn out* (an abstraction) is treated as what has *grown together* (the concrete), rather than as the result of a selective process. The evidence of such errors abounds. For instance, in Whitehead's own day, the descriptions proposed by Euclid and Newton, once thought to be exhaustive of their respective domains, were shown to apply only to a rather limited set of phenomena. Or, to take an example still very much with us, when the abstractions suitable for describing physical systems are used to account for our qualitative and purposive lives, all that fails to fit within the materialist abstractions is treated as epiphenomenal. ("Scientists animated by the purpose of proving that they are purposeless constitute an interesting subject for study," Whitehead once wrote [*FR*, 12].) In each case, the point is not to replace one abstraction with another but instead to learn how to *guard* the abstractions we inevitably use: "Newton's formulae were not false," Whitehead remarks; "they were unguardedly stated" (*FR*, 42–43). For this reason, "the criticism of a theory does not start from the question, True or false? It consists in noting its scope of useful application and its failure beyond that scope." Before being criticized, each theory "is an unguarded statement of a partial truth" (*AI*, 221; see also *SMW*, 17).

Whitehead worried that our educational methods only exacerbated the mix of narrowed vision and hubristic assertion associated with misplaced concreteness. In particular, he lamented the "method of training professionals" whereby advanced students are trained "to specialize in particular regions of thought" dealing with "a certain type of facts, abstracted from the complete circumstances in which they occur" (*SMW*, 196, 17). Already a prevalent trend in Whitehead's day, this segmentation of knowledge-production has increased significantly with the emergence of technoscience in the last fifty years. And though it has produced impressive results—witness the achievements of the ever-proliferating range of technological and scientific subfields in recent decades—the general effect on our intellectual climate has been deleterious. In particular, this mode of training "produces minds in a groove," inattentive to all that lies outside of that groove. When a professional sticks to his or her set of abstractions, "the remainder of life is treated superficially, with the imperfect categories of thought derived from one profession" (*SMW*, 197). In some ways, we might see the "science wars" of the 1990s as a sad illustration of this professional situation.[18] Each side had its groove, and because they both used their own abstractions to dismiss those of the other, the achievements of each practice were pitted against one another, offered as an either/or, rather than guarded within an "'ecology' of abstraction" (*TWW*, 141). Thankfully, the battle cries of that war are mostly behind us; indeed, if anything, twenty-first century humanists seem as excited about scientific achievements as their late-twentieth-century counterparts were suspicious.[19] But such a reversal can nonetheless be an instance of the same general mistake, and Whitehead's injunction to guard our abstractions is just as relevant for the emerging debates around the digital humanities and cognitive or evolutionary approaches to culture as it was for the arguments of an earlier generation.

The modern mode of abstraction and the institutional formations that sustain it thus form the problem that guides Whitehead in his articulation of the requirements constraining metaphysical construction. His goal in *Process and Reality* is to create conceptual tools that both facilitate and exemplify a new manner of thought, one that avoids the "chief error in philosophy" ("overstatement") and the "chief danger to philosophy" ("narrowness in the selection of evidence") by constructing a fully general habit of mind (*PR*, 7, 337). Whitehead calls this "condition for the success of imaginative construction" the "requirement of coherence": nothing in experience can be ignored, no achievement reduced to the explanations provided by the abstractions of an unrelated groove (*PR*, 6). This of course does not mean that an abstraction from one field may not prove useful for another, only that when such a transference is accomplished, the abstraction must be actively related to the problems and constraints of the new practice and not simply imposed as a verdict from on high. By respecting the requirement of coherence, philosophy thus performs its service as the critic of abstractions, facilitating mobility among specialized practices by generalizing under specific constraints: "An active school of philosophy is quite as important for the locomotion of ideas," Whitehead writes, "as is an active school of railway engineers for the locomotion of fuel" (*SMW*, 59). To build connections among practices rather than to treat one practice as the "express train" to Reality is the goal of coherence, and to accomplish this goal, philosophy must guard against the exaggerations associated with misplaced concreteness by considering all of the evidence given in experience. Whitehead's inclusiveness is often astounding: "Philosophy may not neglect the multifariousness of the world—the fairies dance, and Christ is nailed to the cross" (*PR*, 338).

A world in which the fairies dance is not a world familiar to those who pursue the powerful intellectual operations known as "critique." Indeed,

Whitehead offers this vivid injunction as a challenge to those who would too quickly parse the world into really real causes (say, the biological, psychological, or sociological determinants of religious experience) and their secondary effects. Here we can note the sharp difference in tone between critical and constructivist approaches: where the former proceeds by unveiling and demystifying, pulling away the epiphenomenal surface to expose the real forces beneath, the latter constructs concepts that draw our attention to how particular experiences are produced and maintained, to how and when they matter. One subtracts, the other adds. And though these two methods share a number of general techniques, their difference—critique as denunciatory and suspicious, constructivism as creative and affirmative—nonetheless produces a variance in procedure: for a constructivist approach resists the temptation to describe a construction in its own familiar terms (the terms of its particular "groove") and thereby dismiss the particular values attainable outside of its sphere. Instead, it introduces a new contrast between experiences that makes their divergence from one another a matter of interest and concern, something to be explored by articulating "the means invented" and the "authorities invoked" to produce particular constructions.[20] When thinking with Whitehead, the goal is to guard, not to disregard, our abstractions. And for this reason, Whitehead insists, "philosophy destroys its usefulness when it indulges in brilliant feats of explaining away" (*PR*, 17).[21]

Consider this example: according to Whitehead, one of the most persistent and pernicious instances of misplaced concreteness in modern philosophy has been the mistake of treating our clear and distinct perceptual experience as the best means for disclosing the fundamental nature of reality (*MT*, 132–33). The troubles multiply when the perceiving subject is conceived on the model of Aristotelian subject-predicate logic, as it is by Descartes; in that case, the subject needs only itself to exist, and all modifications (including the deliverances of sense-perception) come through the mediation of universals. The result is that what one sees (colors, shapes, etc.) must be linked to the world outside of the subject through an act of judgment that in turn must be secured, usually through the beneficence of God or, for Hume, the introduction of habit. "We find ourselves in a buzzing world, amid a democracy of fellow creatures," Whitehead remarks; "whereas, under some disguise or other, orthodox philosophy can only introduce us to solitary substances, each enjoying illusory experience: 'O Bottom, thou art changed! what do I see on thee?'" (*PR*, 50). To wake from this midsummer night's dream, and so to restore a sense of reality in our perceptual experience, Whitehead protests the exclusive reliance on sense-perception and follows William James (whose image of the "buzzing world" he invokes above) in calling for "the re-instatement of the vague to its proper place in our mental life."[22] And like James, Whitehead does not seek simply to overturn clarity by putting vagueness in its place; instead, he introduces a new contrast between "perception in the mode of presentational immediacy" (i.e., the sensa) and "perception in the mode of causal efficacy" (the vaguely felt process by which the past enters into the constitution of the present) meant to turn our attention to how these modes diverge, combine, and gain relevance in relation to particular questions about knowledge and experience.[23] When addressing the exaggerations of past philosophers, then, Whitehead does not dismiss their concepts without trying first to find their proper sphere of application, guarding them by placing them within a wider conceptual scheme.

As this example suggests, metaphysical construction requires more than the rationalist constraints of logic and coherence (in this case, the need to include both the distinct and the vague in a noncontradictory way); the speculative flight must always return to experience, tested through the difference it makes for particular practices. Without such a check, philosophic generalization runs the risk of exaggerating, of explaining away experiences it fails to consider. A system is therefore coherent only to the extent that it is also "applicable" and "adequate": the former demands that any given experience be interpretable in terms of the scheme, and the latter requires that "all related experience must exhibit the same texture" (*PR*, 4). Whitehead thus insists on the "interplay of thought and practice"—the rhythm of philosophical creation and verification—as "the test by which the charlatanism of speculation is restrained." "The supreme authority of the speculative flight is that it issues in the establishment of a practical technique for well-attested ends," Whitehead writes, adding that the "speculative system" must also provide "the elucidation of that technique" (*FR*, 64–65). Verification here concerns the scheme's ability to modify a practice, to change the habits of thought involved in our interpretation of experience. For this reason it does *not* refer to an extraphilosophical method of detection whereby one of Whitehead's descriptions might be "proven," as if they were the matters-of-fact proposed by scientific practice rather than metaphysical generalities. Put simply, the only way that Whitehead's scheme could be verified by science would be if individual scientists, in adopting the scheme, began to interpret their own activities and productions differently—for instance, if they refrained from claiming exclusive access to reality and instead experimented with the efficacy of their abstractions as abstractions, guarded within their spheres of relevance.

Keeping in mind both the entwined rationalist and empiricist constraints and the harmful habit of thought to which they respond, we can now return to Whitehead's insistence that "it is more important that a proposition be interesting than that it be true" (*PR*, 259). In fact, Whitehead holds that "any scheme of philosophic categories" considered "as one complex assertion" and held to the "logician's alternative, true or false," will always be found false. "The scheme is true with unformulated qualifications, exceptions, limitations, and new interpretations in terms of more general notions"; it is a tentative presentation, as yet insufficiently guarded. But this in no way detracts from its efficacy, since the scheme is not meant to conform to a world "out there" but instead to provide "a matrix from which true propositions applicable to our particular circumstances can be derived" (*PR*, 8). The ambition of imaginative generalization is to discover "new generalities" that "add to the fruitfulness of those already known" and thus "lifts into view . . . new possibilities of combination" (*AI*, 235; see also *PR*, 17).

To modify the familiar language of logic, then, we might say that for a speculative proposition, the form is not "S is P" but rather "S *could be* P": it is a lure for feeling that, if entertained in "our particular circumstances," creates new possibilities for thought and action. The togetherness of "S and P" is thus proposed as realizable—a set of "particular facts [S] in a potential pattern [P]"—and the function of such propositions is to introduce the space for entertaining alternatives in experience (*PR*, 194). With regard to metaphysical propositions, which must be general, the potential pattern must relate "any and every set of logical subjects" in such a way that its truth-value is *uniform*—that is, "identical with the truth-value of each of the singular propositions to be obtained by restricting the application of the predicate to any one set of logical subjects" (*PR*, 197). What matters, then, is the *uniformity* of the pattern, and not whether it conforms to the world as disclosed through our habitual modes of observation (the method of difference). Thus, for Whitehead, philosophy balances "speculative boldness" with humility before the unfathomable richness of experience to provide "a restraint upon specialists, and also an enlargement of their imaginations" (*PR*, 17). His propositions lure us, not into the kind of hubris authorized by a totalizing worldview, but instead toward a different way of being interested in, of paying attention to, and of engaging with what experience offers.

Lures for Feeling: Whitehead's Categoreal Scheme

Whitehead presents his metaphysical categories as "tentative formulations of the ultimate generalities," not as "dogmatic statements of the obvious" (*PR,* 8). Indeed, one of the peculiar features of *Process and Reality*—something that threatens to deter so many first-time readers—is that it begins with a cryptically condensed "scheme" of concepts that Whitehead then tests against the evidence of experience, reformulating and adding as he goes (*PR,* xii).[24] The essays in this volume continue the work of experimenting with these concepts, altering and adapting them to address particular problems, often in areas Whitehead could not have foreseen. Yet before we follow the modifications of the scheme prompted by these new inquiries, we must first present the generalizations Whitehead offers in *Process and Reality,* along with an account of how he came to formulate them. For although his concepts may seem strange—and certainly counter to what passes as common sense—they were created in an effort to revise our most fundamental intellectual dispositions.

Whitehead begins his scheme by naming *creativity* as the "Category of the Ultimate." An "ultimate" here does not signify a permanent horizon for thought, a barrier beyond which our intelligence cannot penetrate; nor does it refer to an eminent reality. Rather, it specifies the exact nature of the problem that spurs Whitehead to philosophical construction, and it signals, at the very start, the obligations that will constrain his thinking. As we have already noted, the problem proper to an empirical metaphysics is that of describing the generalities exemplified in every experience; it is the problem of putting everything "in the same boat," against the bifurcations of the modern epoch. In *Process and Reality,* Whitehead approaches this problem by designating as the "ultimate metaphysical principle" the creative activity that transforms the disjunctive "many" of the universe (the multiplicity of existing entities) into one novel entity (those many in conjunction) that is then added to the disjunctive many. Through creativity, then, Whitehead transforms a long-standing philosophical dualism into the very rhythm of the universe: "The many become one, and are increased by one" (*PR,* 21). And when this rhythm is affirmed, all that exists must be approached as creatures of creativity, which synthesize the many in their various and specific ways. In this manner, Whitehead attempts a fully general proposition that transforms metaphysical description into the specification of *how* each entity exemplifies creativity, a task that will be applied equally to all we encounter in experience. *How* and not *why:* for as the ultimate, creativity cannot be questioned without changing the problem (see *TWW,* 254–59).

As the "ultimate notion of the highest generality at the base of actuality," creativity "cannot be characterized, because all characters are more special than itself" (*PR*, 31). In fact, it is only actual "in virtue of its accidents," the actual occasions that express how the many are composed into *this* novel one (*PR*, 7). To describe how this highest metaphysical generality functions, then, Whitehead populates his scheme with an almost baffling array of "more special" categories, including eight Categories of Existence, twenty-seven Categories of Explanation, and nine Categoreal Obligations, all of which presuppose the Category of the Ultimate. In particular, he requires concepts for the process by which the many become one *(concrescence)* and for the singular entities that are both the process and the product of this creative activity *(actual entities)*. And he must also describe the bonds that assemble the many into the one *(prehensions)*, the potential forms of definiteness that are actualized in this process *(eternal objects)*, the real modes of togetherness that constitute the enduring objects of our experience *(nexūs, societies)*, and the feature of actuality that accounts for how the disjunctive many can form not only a new unity but a relevant and orderly one *(God)*. What's more, all of these notions, and many others besides, must mutually presuppose one another if the system is to be coherent (*PR*, 3).

As the "accidents" of creativity's rhythms, *actual entities* (or *actual occasions*) are "drops of experience, complex and interdependent": singular units of creative process that require reference to the "many" they synthesize to be understood as the "ones" that they are (*PR*, 18). With this concept, Whitehead aims to lure his readers away from the entrenched habit of imagining the fundamental realities as self-sufficient substances undergoing adventures of change and qualification. He thus offers as "the final facts" entities that (a) are what they are by virtue of the way they relate to all the other entities in their world and (b) do not change but rather become and exist through the conditions they lay on successive becomings (temporal atomicity) (*PR*, 18). To think with actual occasions, then, means to leave behind all of our commonsense notions of individuality, especially those that would treat the final facts as the abstractions of physical science, as the lifeless stuff of a material universe. For the activity through which an actual occasion forms its determinate bonds with the many is that of *feeling* or, more precisely, *prehension*, and such a bond is, through and through, purposeful and emotional. As such, the most general description of an actual occasion is that it is *a feeling of its world*, where "feeling" is deployed in its full ambiguity as denoting both a process and a product. And this feeling, understood in all of its relations and manners of relating, is a fully concrete fact that stands as its own reason, its own source of value: "there is no going behind actual entities to find anything more real" (*PR,* 18). To "search for a *reason,*" then, "is to search for one or more actual entities," and Whitehead terms this insistence that "actual entities are the only *reasons,*" the *ontological principle* (*PR,* 24; see also *PR,* 19).

An actual entity can be analyzed in terms of its component *prehensions,* acts of appropriating the disjunctive many into the self-constitution of the concrescent occasion (*PR,* 23, 219). Prehensions thus perform a crucial role in the philosophy of organism's revision of individuality: they specify the "concrete facts of relatedness" through which one actual occasion is *in* another (see *PR,* 7, 48–49, 56). These relations are properly metaphysical—that is, they apply to every occasion of experience. Therefore, they cannot be conceived on the model of a conscious perception but must instead be understood as a general activity that may, given the specific manner of appropriation in a particular occasion, be labeled conscious, intellectual, affective, sensory, and so on. Whitehead lists three components of all prehensions: an object felt, a subject feeling, and a manner of feeling (called the *subjective form*), all of which are functional aspects of the prehension rather than hard ontological categories (see *PR,* 23). The subject of one prehension will, by the rhythm of creativity, be an object of another. Furthermore, the subject does not preexist the feeling but, paradoxically, is produced by the feelings: "the feelings aim at the feeler" and "the feeler is the unity emergent from its own feelings" (*PR,* 222, 88).[25] On the other hand, the objectified actual entity *does* preexist the feeling—and for this reason conditions the feeling through its provocative power—but the prehension appropriates only a limited perspective of the past entity, not the entity in its full concreteness. This last point is crucial for Whitehead's realism: if one occasion is really in another, then the perspective objectified is that of the object, not of the subject. It is a perspective of, not on, the object. But we must not confuse the conditioning power of the object with the power to determine. Every prehension feels its object with a particular subjective form that ensures that the manner of appropriation refers to the decision of the subject and not merely the force of the object (*PR,* 47, 85–86). In this way, Whitehead seeks to invert the Kantian account of experience as a constructive functioning productive of the objective world: "For Kant, the world emerges from the subject; for the philosophy of organism, the subject emerges from the world" (*PR,* 88). Thus, "the philosophy of organism aspires to construct a critique of pure feeling, in the philosophical position in which Kant put his *Critique of Pure Reason*" (*PR,* 113; see also *PR,* 154–56).[26]

The subjective form of a prehension specifies the particular manner of feeling in *this* occasion by selecting from an infinite range of potential ways of feeling, from the "forms of definiteness" available for actualization. Whitehead calls these "Pure Potentials for the Specific Determination of Fact," or *eternal objects,* in order to emphasize that their existence is not exhaustively defined in terms of their realizations in temporal entities (*PR,* 22). The redness of a rose, the circularity of a circle, the bravery of an act: these are potentialities that characterize many actual occasions without being exclusively tied to any one of them. In Whitehead's processual cosmos, these "forms" are not adjectives appended to Being, but rather adverbs qualifying the activity of the universe: they express *how* one occasion functions in another (*PR,* 50). When an actual occasion realizes an eternal object in its prehension of a datum—either physically, when the eternal object has been realized in a past occasion, or conceptually, when the eternal object remains unrealized—Whitehead says that the eternal object has *ingression* in that occasion. Yet we must be careful here, for although actual experience testifies to the ingression of eternal objects, these forms of definiteness cannot be said to appear in experience as such. Our experience is of actuality; it is of *this* feeling or *that* occasion. Eternal objects, on the other hand, are pure potentials; they refer to *any* experience or *some* feelings (*PR,* 114; see also *TWW,* 412). Therefore, the efficacy of eternal objects does not depend on our "discovering" them in their naked state; rather, it turns on their success in luring us toward a coherent description of and engagement with the actual world, apart from which eternal objects do not exist.[27]

Using the concepts of the actual entity, prehensions, and eternal objects, we can now provide a more exact description of the *concrescence,* or the growing-together of a concrete occasion that synthesizes the disjunctive many into a novel one. Though this process is atomic—actual occasions come "totally or not at all," to borrow a phrase from William James—Whitehead distinguishes a series of "phases" through which a concrescence might be analyzed; in this way, he suggests how the generic process of creativity gives rise to such a bewildering variety of creatures.[28] Each new occasion gets its start by prehending the provocations of past occasions. These primary feelings—which are *conformal* in relation to what is felt—generate a vague and important sense of the occasion's inheritance from the past and, as such, provide the basis for our intuition of causality. They constitute the *physical pole* of an occasion, and they are met, in successive phases of concrescence, by the *conceptual prehensions* that make up the *mental pole.* "Conceptual" here does not imply consciousness (*PR,* 85).

Rather, a conceptual prehension has an eternal object as its datum, and so the mental pole consists in the definition of *how* the confused inheritance of the past will be integrated as *this* occasion. As Whitehead writes, "each actuality is essentially bipolar, physical and mental, and the physical inheritance is essentially accompanied by a conceptual reaction partly conformed to it, and partly introductory of a relevant novel contrast, but always introducing emphasis, valuation, and purpose" (*PR*, 108). The additions of the mental pole can propose any number of strategies for unifying the physical data: discordant feelings may be relegated to the background, weakened in intensity, cancelled out, or subsumed under a coordinating contrast. It is in the integration of the two poles that the occasion forms its determinate bonds with the many and thus becomes what it is: a complex feeling, or *satisfaction*, that takes its place among the conditioning multiplicity and contributes to the *transition* provoking yet another occasion.[29]

Each satisfaction, as a creature of creativity, is a *novel* synthesis; its mental reaction effects the creation of a new concrete fact. But if conceptual prehensions have eternal objects as their data, and if there is an infinity of eternal objects, then how does the occasion manage to sort through "unfathomable possibility" to realize a form of definiteness that is not just novel but *relevant*, one that will extend and contribute to the intensity it finds in the universe (*SWM*, 174)? Whitehead insists that everything has to be somewhere in the actual world; according to the ontological principle, "there is nothing which floats into the world from nowhere," and so everything that exists is either an actual occasion or one of its components (*PR*, 244). Thus, if there is an unrealized possibility that becomes relevant in a concrescence, then it must be part of the internal constitution of a nontemporal actuality (*PR*, 32). Whitehead terms this nontemporal actuality *the primordial nature of God*. Far from suggesting a transcendent deity, Whitehead's God thus names an immanent characteristic of the cosmos that allows us to describe the self-evident facts of order and novelty that characterize our experience without appealing to a force outside of actuality.[30] The details of this controversial concept—and of Whitehead's adventure in constructing it—will be examined in some of the essays in this book. For now, we need only to emphasize that God's primordial valuation of eternal objects does not predetermine what an occasion will be. Instead, it proposes an *initial subjective aim* as a lure for conceptual prehension, leaving to the decision of the concrescent occasion how it will modify this aim in the course of its becoming. God contributes an *aim*, not a fate or even a plan. Moreover, because "God is not to be treated as an exception to all metaphysical principles" but instead as "their chief exemplification," Whitehead must offer an account of God's own concrescence such that it situates both God and the World as coherently integrated aspects of the scheme (*PR*, 343). Whitehead accomplishes this by characterizing divine experience in terms of a pole reversal: where occasions begin through physical feelings that are modified through the introduction of conceptual feelings, God begins as a primordial valuation of eternal objects and is modified by his physical feelings of the world. That is, just as the occasion physically prehends God's conceptual experience, so too, as Whitehead specifies in the fifth part of *Process and Reality*, does God physically prehend the conceptual complex of the achieved satisfaction. God's physical experience is termed his *consequent nature*, and it enables Whitehead to put God and the World in mutual requirement, as twinned expressions of "the ultimate metaphysical ground, the creative advance into novelty" (*PR*, 349).

So far we have spoken of the atomic units of creativity and the entities constructed to analyze them. But if Whitehead hopes to transform our experience through its coherent interpretation, then he cannot rest satisfied with metaphysical redescription (e.g., the claim that the universe is populated with actual occasions instead of subjects and objects); he must also account for how actual occasions provide sufficient reason for what it is we encounter in our experience. Otherwise, he would not only fail with respect to the ontological principle (which insists that "actual entities are the only *reasons*"), but would also render his system incoherent, since the enduring objects of our perception would then be "explain[ed] away," and philosophy would have once again "destroy[ed] its usefulness" (*PR*, 19). To this end, Whitehead offers the related concepts of *nexūs* and *societies*. "Actual occasions," he explains, "involve each other by reason of their prehensions of each other," and thus there are "real facts of togetherness of actual entities," which Whitehead terms *nexūs* (*PR*, 20). In the concrescence of a new occasion, these facts of togetherness constitute the orderliness in the subject's actual world and conditions what that occasion can or cannot become. This order, in turn, is necessary for the realization of intensity in the satisfaction, where intensity is understood as involving a balance between order and disorder, width and depth of feeling.[31] By Whitehead's account, the most general characterization of an actual entity's aim is its singular attempt to achieve in concrescence the maximum amount of intensity available to it. In fact, the drive of the universe is toward such intensity, and God's lure for each occasion, as well as the Categoreal Obligations of concrescence, are Whitehead's ways of including this cosmological tendency in his scheme.

The aim at intensity, with its corollary emphasis on degrees of order and disorder in the actual world, sets the stage for Whitehead's notion of a *society*, a notion that accounts for the particular mode of togetherness that characterizes the objects of our perception. When the occasions in a nexus share a common characteristic (i.e., a complex eternal object) by virtue of their prehensions of one another, then the nexus is said to have social order. A social environment is thus generated out of the transmission of a shared eternal object among each occasion in a nexus, which serves the function of knitting those entities together through "positive feelings" of a "common element" (see *PR*, 34, 90). Social order persists so long as the members continue to impose this transmission on one another.[32] These mutual prehensions create the conditions for greater intensity as they coordinate the narrow depth facilitated by the shared eternal object with the variety provided by the many different occasions involved.[33] As such, Whitehead's rich description of societies does not impose another bifurcation—one between "really real" actual occasions and merely apparent societies—because societies arise immanently from the bonds that occasions impose upon each other in order to generate greater intensity of satisfaction for themselves and for the future. Both constructions, occasions and societies, are required if the constraint of creativity is to be capable of modifying how we regard our experience.

The components of Whitehead's metaphysical scheme cannot be separated from the speculative method that produced them, both because Whitehead's constructivism demands that the products be tied to the process and because his description of experience includes within it the means to account for the construction of that scheme. In this regard, it is significant that Whitehead includes *propositions* among the Categories of Existence, not as their linguistic expression—Whitehead insists that linguistic formulations never exhaustively convey their propositions—but as hybrid entities linking a set of actual occasions with a complex eternal object, a datum for feeling that introduces a space of hesitation, a possibility for feeling the world otherwise. What this means is that highly complex, human propositions, such as metaphysical propositions, are grounded in a much wider account of the conditions for being lured by possible, and not necessarily actual, values in perceptual experience. And if the motivation behind Whitehead's propositions is, as we have seen, to address our modes of abstraction, then it is worth noting how thoroughly the metaphysical categories just described revise our notions of the concrete, the abstract, and the relation between them. To begin, Whitehead treats them as *phases of process:* just as the universe pulses from object to subject to object (as the many become one and are increased by one), so, too, does it swing from the abstract to the concrete and back to abstraction. This is because the very definition of the concrescence, or the becoming-concrete, involves the process of abstraction, whereby one occasion is objectified in another. As Whitehead writes in *Symbolism,* "'objectification' itself is abstraction; since no actual thing is 'objectified' in its 'formal' completeness" (*S*, 25). This means that the concrete is always being produced; it is not something stable or eminently real from which the abstract processes of thinking (or of building a speculative scheme) separate us. To the contrary, the role of abstraction/objectification in the concrescence assures us that our thinking is a part of nature rather than an alien entity: "Abstraction expresses nature's mode of interaction and is not merely mental. When it abstracts, thought is merely conforming to nature—or rather, it is exhibiting itself as an element in nature" (*S*, 25). Our thinking becomes concrete when it assembles the data with as many constructive contrasts and relations as possible. And so Whitehead's aim of coherence is embedded in the very scheme: his speculative adventure seeks not to *recover* concreteness but to *achieve* it, by adjusting our modes of abstraction.

Speculation beyond the Bifurcation

The essays included in this volume continue the ongoing work of speculative construction, launching further into the heights of imaginative rationalization and pulling down the concepts to be tested in experience. They are divided into three sections, each of which addresses a particular set of challenges that prompt the verification, clarification, and sometimes modification of the categoreal scheme. The first takes up Whitehead's task of thinking beyond the modern bifurcations of actuality to propose a coherent and concrete description of experience. The second examines the metaphysics of novelty presented in the philosophy of organism, tracking both the conceptual constituents of this commitment to the new and the consequences it has for our specialized investigations. The final section follows Whitehead's revision of individuality into its implications both for our notions of society, life, and the place of the human in a wider ecology and for the sciences that engage these notions.

In "A Constructivist Reading of *Process and Reality,*" the essay that opens our volume, Isabelle Stengers identifies Whitehead's response to the problem of modern incoherence as one that entails a radical constructivism: against the habit of granting exaggerated power to our abstractions, allowing them to step outside of their pertinent social orders, Whitehead insists that every knowledge-production be tied to the problem it attempts to answer, including the demands it must fulfill and the means it invents to fulfill them. As a consequence, Stengers warns, his philosophy will be misunderstood if treated as yet another "conception of the world" or put forth as "neutral statement" unrelated to a specific problem. In fact, Whitehead designs his scheme as a lure addressed precisely to those whose mental habits would elevate a particular set of abstractions to the status of a "vision of the world," and everything from the content of his concepts to the style of his writing aims at this end. Yet this approach does not consign us to relativism; "constructivism" certainly does *not* mean "social constructivism," nor should it induce in us what Stengers has elsewhere called "the monotonous refrain 'it *is only* a construction,' as if an all-powerful truth were at stake, apparently the only one to escape the relativity it proclaims."[34] The difference is that the "qualified" constructivisms most familiar in the humanities (linguistic, social, cultural, transcendental) always introduce another bifurcation between the merely constructed and an implied mute reality, but Whiteheadian constructivism insists that reality itself is a *constructive process*. With this shift, the entire problem changes: the task is not to hunt down and denounce the fact of construction but rather to inquire into the specific tasks and procedures to which a construction responds. It is no longer "a question of criticizing our specialized abstractions, or of dictating limitations" but of "presenting our abstractions as important achievements with a price."

Where Stengers illustrates this distinctive philosophical approach by putting us close beside Whitehead as he constructs the actual occasion, Jeffrey A. Bell's "Scientism and the Modern World" situates Whitehead's creation within a wider philosophical tradition stretching from Hume to Husserl to Deleuze. Each of these thinkers sought to "account for the emergence of order and identity without presupposing order and identity," and it is in light of this imperative—here termed the "Humean problematic"—that Bell emphasizes the actual occasion's "characteristic of self-causation" (*PR*, 222). While Kant and Husserl assume order and unity in their explanations of the constitution of experience, Whitehead (like Deleuze after him) insists on locating the genesis of all such regularities within the processes of particular concrescences. Particular orders cannot be given in advance; they refer instead to the decisions of actual occasions, whereby the "indeterminate substantive multiplicity" of eternal objects is prehended to produce a genuinely novel unity. Whitehead describes this account of the self-constitution of an occasion as "extending and rigidly applying Hume's principle, that ideas of reflection are derived from actual facts"

(*PR*, 40). In the end, Bell's essay does more than provide a broad intellectual context for Whitehead's resurrection of *causa sui*: as its title suggests, it also traces a counternarrative to the exaggerations of scientific reductionism that threaten to do away with the unique domain of philosophy altogether.

Bruno Latour takes up this task of resisting reductionism, here characterized as an effect of the bifurcation of nature, in the two lectures presented below as "What Is the Style of Matters of Concern?" In the first of these, Latour sets Whitehead alongside Gabriel Tarde to replace the "bridge-building" projects of the moderns (the hopeless attempts to jump directly from nature to the social, matter to mind, facts to values, where each is considered as independent) with a method of "kayaking" among the processual elements of experience (where new relations between interconnected entities are always being created). Following Tarde, he redefines "society" not as involving any particular social stuff but rather as indicating a general feature of the objects of our experience: that they must "associate with others in order to remain in existence." The resulting metaphysics avoids the intractable bifurcations of the moderns by replacing "I am" with "I have"; for whereas "I am" gives you only the thinker, "I have" provides the object had and the manner of having to boot. (Recall that Whitehead offered his concept of a prehension, with its components of a subject, object, and a subjective form, as a "protest" against "the bifurcation of actualities" [*PR*, 289].)

In the second lecture, Latour draws on both science studies and art history to account for how the modern mode of abstraction, with its own unique styles and procedures, came to be mistaken for the very content of reality. He thus adds greater historical texture to Whitehead's own account, in *Science and the Modern World*, of how the modern mindset emerged, offering the "humble mediators" of painting and artistic representation as essential ingredients in "the confusion between ontology and visualization strategies" that supports the bifurcation of nature. Having identified the "aesthetics of matters of fact" as a particular historical style, Latour then challenges us to develop an "aesthetic of matters of concern" that—like Stengers's constructivism—includes the whole machinery involved in staging matters of fact as a necessary component of its knowledge claims.

In "The Technics of Prehension: On the Photography of Nicolas Baier," Nathan Brown provides a vivid account of what such an aesthetic might look like. Yet he does so in a distinctly different key, for where Latour suspects the digital of exacerbating our bifurcating habits, Brown locates in Baier's new media art an exacting attention to the "technical conditions" of digitization and formalization involved in the procedures of empirical science. In particular, through close engagements with installations and individual works by Baier (including one titled "Prehension"), Brown develops a theory of what he calls "the technics of prehension," a concept that combines the work of Whitehead, Bernard Stiegler, and Gaston Bachelard to articulate the specific processes of recording and transmission that constitute scientific knowledge as "both *objective* and *constructed*." He thus shows how empiricism and rationalism—against their displacement in Kant's transcendental philosophy—are mediated through local acts of technical construction, inscription, and formalization, all understood as specialized instances of the general category of *prehensions*, their unification in *concrescence*, and their repetition and transformation in *transition*. In the process, Brown not only identifies the "epistemological terrain of science" as that of "the technics of prehension" but also demonstrates how this terrain is investigated and staged in the digital arts.

The essays in this section all take Whitehead as a point of departure for speculating beyond the divisions and limitations that have dominated modernist philosophy. Each adopts Whiteheadian concepts and techniques as tools for transforming our modes of analysis, and each extends the speculative hope that the impasses of previous centuries might be transformed into novel contrasts. For this reason, all of these writers assume a universe of genuine novelty, one whose very operations support our philosophical efforts to change our habits of thought. Indeed, this emphasis on novelty is yet another of the variations of interest the actual occasion is meant to produce, as each actual occasion is always a new occasion. As Stengers points out in her essay, Whitehead came to consider novelty as the "ultimate challenge that his demand for coherence had to satisfy." And so it is to the problem of novelty that we now turn.

The Metaphysics of Creativity

For those accustomed to associating metaphysics with eternal verities—descriptions of reality as it is, has been, and must be—the title of our second section will inevitably puzzle. Why would metaphysics be creative, as opposed to precise or revelatory or, above all, referentially true? We have already seen how Whitehead understood his project of producing imaginative generalizations as itself an inventive one, as a kind of creative metaphysics; yet this emphasis on philosophical creation also testifies to his deeper commitment to a *fully general* notion of creativity, a notion that encompasses each new synthesis of the many into one, from those comprising the social orders of a plant to those involved in the highly complex orders characteristic of metaphysical speculation. It is this general notion of creativity as "the principle of novelty" that our next group of essays explores (*PR*, 21).[35] In doing so, many of them engage the controversial concepts that Whitehead constructed to give a more fine-grained explanation of the actual occasion as an accident of creativity: eternal objects and God. Many of them also test the affiliation between Whitehead and that more recent metaphysician of the new, Gilles Deleuze. But in all cases, their aim is to demonstrate what is at stake in Whitehead's presentation of creativity as his "ultimate" and to ask whether his philosophy takes us far enough—or perhaps too far—toward a genuine metaphysics of the new.

In "Whitehead's Involution of an Outside Chance," Peter Canning links the clinical concern of Whitehead's philosophy—the address to our modes of abstraction discussed in the previous section—with his distinctive challenge to mechanistic thought: the imperative to *"take the perspective of life itself,"* to incorporate the powers of creation and chance into our descriptions of the world. After demonstrating how the notions of law and mechanism seduced modern thinkers into dismissing life as mere "accident," Canning insists that "[a] true science of life must be able to distinguish between *being* a machine and *building* a machine, between *being controlled by* a program and *designing* a program." Our acts of creation must be "counted in"; any other approach would allow incoherence to reign, as creativity would be treated not as an ultimate but as the "accidental" character of certain advanced forms of life. Canning thus embraces Whitehead's injunction to think "nature alive" by including anticipation and other real relations to an unpredictable future within his description of an actual occasion. Yet he worries that Whitehead's split between real and pure potentiality, along with his concomitant insistence that eternal objects are not created and that God is required for relevant novelty, presents a "stumbling block" to confronting this problem. To overcome this obstacle, he turns to Spinoza and Mallarmé to show how chance "accomplishes its own Idea" and thus how possibility itself "evolves and emerges."

Canning is not alone in hesitating before the lure of Whitehead's God. Others have questioned the efficacy of the concept—and indeed, the name alone threatens to deter some readers.[36] For this reason, Roland Faber reorients the discussion around the Whiteheadian divine by asking us to consider why the task of conceptualizing genuine novelty in a world of becoming prompted not only Whitehead but also Deleuze to employ mystical language, either in the form of God or of an "absolute consciousness." More precisely, in "Multiplicity and Mysticism: Toward a New Mystagogy of Becoming," Faber analyzes the way that these respective invocations of mystical traditions function within the broader metaphysical project of theorizing novelty such that it avoids the twin traps of chaotic change, on the one hand, and the "eternal repetition of the same," on the other. "If novelty is to be neither change nor repetition," he writes, "it must be about attainment of worth in the midst of change that is not eternally pre-given." Following a brief discussion of Whitehead's eternal objects as performing an analogous function to Deleuze's virtualities, he then develops this claim by juxtaposing two late essays—Whitehead's "Immortality" and Deleuze's "Immanence: A Life"—that sharpen our sense of how the "mystical inclination" in these philosophers unfolds in parallel yet divergent ways.

The next essay, Keith Robinson's "The Event and the Occasion: Deleuze, Whitehead, and Creativity," continues the work of reading Whitehead alongside Deleuze, this time with an emphasis on their distinct accounts of temporality. In particular, Robinson argues that the two philosophers "valorize different modalities of time in the structure of creativity" and that these different modalities bespeak conflicting assumptions about "the values of transformation, mutation, and the creativity of the new." Robinson elaborates these divergent accounts under the names of the *occasion* and the *event,* each of which describes creativity as a single process with two "dissymmetrical" yet fully articulated aspects (transition/concrescence, actual/virtual). The structure of the occasion emphasizes "the origination of the present in conformity with the 'power' of the past," where the past's "power" refers to the conditions that concrete occasions lay on creativity (*PR,* 210). By this model, "the creativity of the occasion" involves the "integrating and unifying work of the temporal relation between past and present." Yet, as Robinson makes clear, this account differs drastically from the Deleuzean event, where the conditions for novelty involve first and foremost an "unknown and unknowable future that has ontological priority in disrupting and fracturing the present." Robinson's essay develops these accounts of creativity in detail and uses aspects of each to challenge and supplement the other.

Where Faber and Robinson see interesting divergences in the otherwise analogous projects of Whitehead and Deleuze, Graham Harman sees an absolute rift. In "Whitehead and Schools X, Y, and Z," he argues that even though both philosophers share a commitment to process, understood here as the emphasis of "change over stasis," Whitehead affirms "a world made up entirely of distinct individuals" while Deleuze treats such entities as "derivative outcroppings of some deeper pre-individual becoming." To further specify the divergence of these two thinkers, and to provide a larger map to the landscape of contemporary philosophy, Harman distinguishes among three schools according to their respective positions on process, becoming, and relations: the schools of Whitehead and Latour (X), of Deleuze, Bergson, Simondon, and other philosophers of becoming (Y), and of object-oriented philosophy (Z). As he parses the philosophical field, Harman emphasizes Whitehead's "compellingly ambiguous status" for School Z by indicating two "gaps" that Whitehead's account notices but fails to solve. The first, the discontinuity between individual entities, raises the question of mediation that Harman suggests should be central to contemporary philosophical debate; the second, which treats the problem of how fully relational entities might persist in time, he dismisses as a false problem created by Whitehead's system. The challenge that these issues pose, Harman concludes, must be met with a "new *anti-process philosophy,*" one that incorporates features of Whitehead's thought but that will inevitably depart from many of its commitments.

The final two essays in this section return from the imaginative flights and logical tests just described to investigate how two specialized practices—education and computer program design—might be transformed through the concepts Whitehead elaborates in his commitment to creativity. James Williams begins these inquiries by reading Whitehead's educational writings, collected in *The Aims of Education* (1929), against the backdrop of the accounts of time and the event developed in his metaphysics. Whitehead honed his thoughts on education through decades of teaching and years of administrative work, and his suggestions for progressive reform demonstrate a keen awareness of the demands and constraints on educators.[37] Williams argues that we are best able to recognize the promise of these suggestions—and thus to imagine how Whitehead's philosophy addresses present-day threats to education—if we understand the "rhythms of education" in terms of the relational structure of the event, especially as it gathers the past and anticipates a future. In this way, his essay illuminates a claim, made late in *Process and Reality*, that the "contrast between order as the condition for excellence, and order as stifling the freshness of living . . . is met with in the theory of education" (*PR*, 338). Throughout, Williams considers not only the "profound reflection on time and practice" presented in Whitehead's theory but also the practical challenges facing education reform now, alongside the conceptual lures that might help to overcome them.

So far, the inquiry into creativity conducted by these essays has focused primarily on time. Yet as Luciana Parisi reminds us, temporal advance is an abstraction from a more fundamental notion of *extension,* which Whitehead carefully refined from his 1916 essay on "La theorie relationiste de l'espace" through to the fourth part of *Process and Reality* ("The Theory of Extension").[38] "Extension," Whitehead explains, when considered "apart from its spatialization and temporalization," names "that general scheme of relationships providing the capacity that many objects can be welded into the real unity of one experience." Otherwise called the "extensive continuum," it is "the most general scheme of real potentiality" required for creativity (*PR*, 67). In "Cutting Away from Smooth Space: Alfred North Whitehead's Extensive Continuum in Parametric Software," Parisi uses this theory of extension to articulate the different conception of space required to grasp the "computational power of parametric software" and the role it plays in architectural design. In particular, she argues that spatial programming "does not simply involve the design of space according to given sets or geometrical points" but rather generates it through the use of "variables open to change in real time." Space, in these terms, concerns the "mereotopological relations between parts and wholes" through which novelty-defining relations are added to the extensive continuum. In her discussions of objects, part-whole relations, and the extensive continuum in relation to software design, Parisi thus concludes this section's inquiry into creativity and the new by showing how Whitehead's general notions assume a new relevance when activated in specific fields.

Process Ecology

By affirming a general concept of creativity, one that holds for all that exists and thus responds to the requirement of coherence against the bifurcations of modern thought, Whitehead makes possible a philosophy unbounded by the anthropocentrism of previous metaphysics. This is not to say that Whitehead does away with the category of the human altogether. Rather, he concretizes it, setting human experience in constitutive relation with a wider ecology of experiences and using his metaphysical scheme to slow down the usual ways we parse subject and object in the analysis of an event. The essays in our last section detail the theoretical constituents capable of transforming our anthropocentric bias without therefore washing away human practice and knowledge in a monolithic flux. As we have seen, Whitehead always adds more articulations, more nuance; he is never satisfied with less. After a series of essays analyzing the concepts required to renew the general concepts guiding our practice, then this section turns to discussions of how individual disciplines might be reimagined and advanced through Whitehead's conceptual lures.

The task of breaking with the anthropocentric limitations of modern philosophy requires first and foremost a revised notion of the subject, what Whitehead calls a "reformed subjectivist principle." In "Possessive Subjects: A Speculative Interpretation of Nonhumans," Didier Debaise demonstrates how this principle provides the basis for a radically pluralist philosophy of nature, one capable of moving away from the critical or phenomenological interpretations of the subject and toward a more capacious notion of "subjects of nature." Such a subject emerges as an act of *feeling* its world into a unified feeling-composition; it is an act of aesthetic synthesis, wherein the aesthetic refers to a generalized process of prehension rather than a specific theory of art. To specify this complex relation between a subject and feeling, Debaise traces Whitehead's combination of two philosophical approaches to the subject: one in which the subject (as *subjectum*) grounds a feeling, and another in which the subject (as *superjacio*) exists as a tendency, a virtual subject "thrown above" the productive feelings. For Whitehead, these dual aspects—as the subject-superject—describe "two moments of a feeling" that, when linked, "can be taken in a renewed thought of subjects detached from all exclusively anthropological inscription." In particular, Debaise argues that Whitehead's subjects of nature challenge us to adopt a "universal mannerism" in which "[b]eing and the manner of being are indistinguishable": feeling-as-noun and feeling-as-activity join to "form the conditions of existence for all subjects, human and non-human."

Debaise's call for a universal mannerism emphasizes the relational nature of the Whiteheadian subject, and as Whitehead stresses in *Adventures of Ideas,* this relation is not that of knowledge but that of *concern,* a term he borrows from the Quakers: "the occasion as subject has a 'concern' for the object," and "the 'concern' at once places the object as a component in the experience of the subject, with an affective tone drawn from this object and directed toward it" (*AI,* 176). In "Another Regard," Erin Manning combines this notion of concern with the practice of counterpoint in dance to "[rework] the dichotomy of subject and object, reinserting them in the event" to develop a framework for approaching interspecies relations without presupposing their terms. Taking the encounters between Dawn Prince-Hughes, an autistic woman, and Kanzi, a captive gorilla, as her primary example, Manning uses concern to insist that "human" and "animal" should not be understood as starting points of the relation but instead as speciations that emerge in the movement of the event's unfolding as "rhythmic activations of a body-morphing that never precede the event of their coming-into-relation." Manning offers this model as an alternative to identity politics in the theorization of gender, the animal, and disability, considering by way of conclusion accounts of "autistic perception" that promise to loosen habitual ways of arranging the perceptual field.

Whitehead's revision of the subject-object dichotomy, central to the two previous essays, unfolded in relation to his broader notion of *togetherness,* of how different entities—including a knower and a known object—are together in experience. In "Of 'Experiential Togetherness': Toward a More Robust Empiricism," Steven Meyer presents the intellectual context within which Whitehead developed this notion, assembling a rich array of early twentieth-century thinkers and debates to dramatize the historical arena within which Whitehead became a philosopher. In particular, he discusses competing senses of "togetherness" from the work of William James, F. H. Bradley, Samuel Alexander, Frederick Cornwallis Conybeare, and J. Ellis McTaggart, to name just a few, and tracks the way that Whitehead's use of the term emerged from this conversation in ways both subtle and direct. Through this approach, Meyer not only offers insights into the formation of a central concept in the philosophy of organism, but also identifies a manner of intellectual engagement that marks Whitehead, like James, as a "robust empiricist."

By emphasizing the relation between togetherness and process in their redescriptions of nature, the authors of the first three essays in this section all draw attention to the adverbial, to the *how* of activity rather than the *what* of substance. Likewise, in "The Order of Nature and the Creation of Societies," Michael Halewood draws on Whitehead's discussion of societies both to resist any hard metaphysical separation between the realm of nature and the realm of the social and, subsequently, to use Whitehead's generalized notions to reorient the specific practice of sociology. He begins by carefully following Whitehead's presentation of societies as it develops from a discussion of the "order of nature," where order always refers to a specific ordering that holds a particular relation to disorder. He thus shows how "social order" is a function of nature, a function characteristic of all of the enduring objects of our experience and not just of human groups. These orders, Halewood argues, must be approached as adverbial—as characterized by "the shared manner in which their constituents regard each other"—rather than as "noun-like," that is, "as having some inner core of which qualities are predicated." Yet this unsettling of the traditional nature/social divide is not meant to deny all differences between the orders exhibited in human societies and those expressed in nonhumans. Instead, the redescription prompts us to attend to those distinctions and specificities differently: as Halewood explains, a Whiteheadian sociology would eschew fixed assumptions about what humans are and instead seek out "*how* humans are, and have been, made human." Where a "search for 'what' makes us human" may "fall into essentialism," the "search for a 'how' will provide a fuller grasp of what we have become and what we might yet be."[39]

Similarly, A. J. Nocek draws on Whitehead's concept of life as "the origination of conceptual novelty" that "lurks in the interstices of each living cell" to describe the practices of wet-life synthesis or bottom-up synthetic biology, practices that challenge any notion of life as involving a specific *what* rather than a complex *how* (*PR,* 102, 105–6). In particular, Nocek traces the parallels between the attempt to synthesize life from inorganic materials (life *de novo)* and Deleuze and Guattari's "prodigious idea of nonorganic life" to articulate the conditions under which an ostensibly "royal science" may testify to a concept of life as immanent in matter. Nocek then defends this neovitalist thesis against the criticisms of "subjectivist metaphysics" in recent continental philosophy, including those from Quentin Meillassoux, Eugene Thacker, and Francois Laruelle, not to endorse Deleuze and Guattari per se, but to discover the conditions under which the inorganic materials of wet-life synthesis might require a notion of nonorganic life. Ultimately, Nocek proposes that in order to avoid the idealization of the Real, we need Whitehead's speculative pragmatics of life, which, far from representing a thought-independent state of affairs, brings into being the experience of the nonorganic life of matter.

The five essays in this final section thus provide a compelling account of how Whitehead's metaphysical notions might be embraced as tools for thinking capable of transforming the thinker's relationship to his or her specific tasks and problems. In this case, the transformation especially concerns the anthropocentric habits that have shaped previous philosophical analyses of animals, human societies, nature, and life.[40] Yet the lesson of these inquiries extends even further than the efforts to frame an ecological and nonanthropocentric notion of existence, as they demonstrate just what it means to be lured by Whitehead's philosophy while thinking about topics and technologies that he left unexplored.

At the end of *Modes of Thought,* Whitehead modifies an old Platonic saw: "Philosophy begins in wonder," he writes, "[a]nd, at the end, when philosophic thought has done its best, the wonder remains" (*MT,* 168). Our goal in *The Lure of Whitehead* is not to provide the final interpretation of the philosopher's thought; nor is it simply to showcase the range of applications and richness of possibilities available through his ideas. In the end, we hope to incite a renewed wonder toward both the philosopher and his conceptual constructions. And as the essays collected here make clear, the relevance of these concepts extends beyond the three tasks under which we have grouped them—overcoming the bifurcation of actuality; affirming novelty; and thinking nature outside of anthropocentrism—into productive encounters with a range of other fields and concerns: for instance, art and aesthetics (Latour, Brown, Debaise, Williams), the nature of the social (Halewood, Latour, Manning), scientific practice (Bell, Canning, Nocek), the specificity of the digital (Brown, Parisi), the ontology of objects (Harman, Parisi), the distinctive task of philosophy (Stengers, Bell, Canning, Faber), and Whitehead's relation to other philosophers (Bell, Meyer, Robinson). We hope that readers not only will be drawn to find other connections among these essays but will also use these links as starting points for work that continues Whitehead's speculative adventure, both its imaginative flights and empirical landings. Only with such engagement can Whitehead's philosophy be verified; only with wonder can we be so lured.

Notes

1. This renewed interest in Whitehead is evidenced in no small part by the many special issues and forums devoted to his thought in recent journals: e.g., Steven Meyer and Elizabeth Wilson, eds., "Whitehead Now," special issue, *Configurations* 13, no. 1 (Winter 2005); Michael Halewood, ed., "A. N. Whitehead," special section, *Theory, Culture and Society* 25, no. 4 (July 2008): 1–117; Keith Robinson, ed., "Deleuze, Whitehead and Process," forum, *Deleuze Studies* 4 (March 2010). Furthermore, there have been numerous conferences convened in Europe and North America to explore Whitehead's work, not to mention monographs and edited volumes.

2. For earlier attempts to revive Whitehead, see George Lucas's *The Rehabilitation of Whitehead: An Analytical and Historical Assessment of Process Philosophy* (Albany: State University of New York Press, 1989) and David Ray Griffin's *Whitehead's Radically Different Postmodernism: An Argument for Its Contemporary Relevance* (Albany: State University of New York Press, 2007).

3. Bertrand Russell, *My Philosophical Development* (London: George Allen and Unwin, 1959), 74.

4. Alfred North Whitehead, *An Enquiry Concerning the Principles of Natural Knowledge* (Cambridge: Cambridge University Press, 1919); and Alfred North Whitehead, *The Principle of Relativity with Applications to Physical Science* (Cambridge: Cambridge University Press, 1922).

5. Lewis S. Ford, George Lucas, and, most recently, Michael Weber and Anderson Weekes all offer accounts of how Whitehead became a marginal figure during the rise

of analytic philosophy. See Lewis S. Ford, "Afterward: A Sampling of Other Interpretations," in *Explorations in Whitehead's Philosophy*, ed. Lewis S. Ford and George L. Kline (New York: Fordham University Press, 1983); George Lucas, *The Rehabilitation of Whitehead;* and Michael Weber and Anderson Weekes, "Whitehead as a Neglected Figure of Twentieth-Century Philosophy," in *Process Approaches to Consciousness in Psychology, Neuroscience, and Philosophy of Mind*, ed. Michael Weber and Anderson Weekes (Albany: State University of New York Press, 2009), 57–72.

6. For a sustained account of the affinities between these two philosophers, see Ron L. Cooper, *Heidegger and Whitehead: A Phenomenological Examination into the Intelligibility of Experience* (Athens: Ohio University Press, 1993). Among other points of comparison, Cooper discusses the similarities between Heidegger's notion of "care" and Whitehead's concept of "concern"; their shared rejection of epistemology as first philosophy; and their insistence on the relational structuring of existence. But although Cooper performs a helpful service in drawing these connections, there are good reasons to resist turning Whitehead into a phenomenologist (as Cooper ultimately does). For instance, Whitehead's capacious notion of experience offers an alternative to Heidegger's narrow focus on *Dasein* and human existence. This contrast partly explains Whitehead's appeal to those working in animal studies and posthumanism; see Erin Manning's essay in this volume. That said, Graham Harman has offered a reading of Heidegger that promises to bring him closer to Whitehead. Thus, in *Tool-Being: Heidegger and the Metaphysics of Objects* (Peru, Ill.: Open Court Publishing, 2002), he radicalizes Heidegger's famous "tool analysis" to show that the distinction between ready-to-hand and present-at-hand applies to every entity—and thus that *Dasein* is dethroned from its status as the privileged Being among beings. In contrast to Harman, Steven Shaviro brings Whitehead and Heidegger together to delineate their differences rather than to draw out similarities; see the "philosophical fantasy"—of a world in which "Whitehead, instead of Heidegger, had set the agenda for postmodern thought"—that opens *Without Criteria: Kant, Whitehead, Deleuze, and Aesthetics* (Cambridge, Mass.: MIT Press, 2009), viii–xiii.

7. Quentin Meillassoux, *After Finitude: An Essay on the Necessity of Contingency*, trans. Ray Brassier (London: Continuum, 2008), 5.

8. For a sustained attempt to change our ways of thinking about matter—and, by extension, our ways of interacting with nonhuman nature—see Jane Bennett's *Vibrant Matter: A Political Ecology of Things* (Durham, N.C.: Duke University Press, 2010) and Timothy Morton's *Ecology without Nature: Rethinking Environmental Aesthetics* (Cambridge, Mass.: Harvard University Press, 2007) and *The Ecological Thought* (Cambridge, Mass.: Harvard University Press, 2010).

9. Graham Harman, *Tool-Being*, 232. The diversity of positions within the "speculative realist" movement is on display in Levi Bryant, Nick Srnicek, and Graham Harman, eds., *The Speculative Turn: Continental Materialism and Realism* (Victoria, Australia: re.press, 2011). For more examples of the new realism, see Diana Cole and Samantha Frost, eds., *New Materialisms: Ontology, Agency, and Politics* (Durham, N.C.: Duke University Press, 2010) and Stacy Alaimo and Susan Hekman, eds., *Material Feminisms* (Bloomington, Ind.: Indiana University Press, 2008).

10. Stengers and Latour have each devoted considerable efforts to escaping the limitations of critique and scientific certainty. See, for example, Stengers' account of the paradoxical mode of existence of the scientists' "factishes"—such as the neutrino, the

atom, DNA, etc.—that are once fabricated and fabricate us in *Cosmopolitics I* (Minneapolis: University of Minnesota Press, 2010), 19–23; and Bruno Latour's *On the Modern Cult of the Factish Gods* (Durham, N.C.: Duke University Press, 2010). In a less explicit though no less decisive mode, Donna Haraway characterizes her project in *Modest_Witness @Second_Millennium. FemaleMan© Meets OncoMouse™* (New York: Routledge, 1997) as "a commitment to avoiding what Whitehead called 'the fallacy of misplaced concreteness'" (269).

11. For this reason, Whitehead's role in science studies offers a potential model for the growing number of literary and cultural critics searching for an alternative to critique. One has only to note the impressive amount of citations of Latour's "Why Has Critique Run Out of Steam? From Matters of Fact to Matters of Concern"—an essay that borrows from Whitehead to frame its provocations—to recognize the enthusiasm for an alternative to the rhetorical stance (if not the specific operations) of critique. Bruno Latour, "Why Has Critique Run Out of Steam? From Matters of Fact to Matters of Concern," *Critical Inquiry* 30 (Winter 2004): 225–48. For key illustrations of these trends in literary and cultural studies, see Eve Kosofsky Sedgwick's "Paranoid Reading and Reparative Reading, Or, You're So Paranoid You Probably Think This Essay Is about You," from *Touching Feeling: Affect, Pedagogy, Performativity* (Durham, N.C.: Duke University Press, 2003); Stephen Best and Sharon Marcus's "Surface Reading: An Introduction," *Representations* 108, no. 1 (Fall 2009), 1–21; Heather Love's "Close But Not Deep: Literary Ethics and the Descriptive Turn," *New Literary History* 41, no. 2 (Spring 2010): 371–91; and Rita Felski's "Suspicious Minds," *Poetics Today* 32, no. 2 (2011): 215–34.

12. Gilles Deleuze and Claire Parnet, *Dialogues* (New York: Columbia University Press, 1977), vii. Deleuze also remarks on his affinity for Whitehead both in *Difference and Repetition,* where he celebrates Whitehead's distinctive use of philosophical categories, and in *The Fold,* where he situates Whitehead in a lineage of philosophers devoted to answering the question, "What is an event?" See Gilles Deleuze, *Difference and Repetition* (New York: Columbia University Press, 1994), 284–85, and Gilles Deleuze, *The Fold: Leibniz and the Baroque* (Minneapolis: University of Minnesota Press 1993), 76.

13. Steven Shaviro, Brian Massumi, and Erin Manning have each begun to theorize affect through Whiteheadian concepts, but in many cases—for instance, in the recent exchange about affect between Ruth Leys and William Connolly in *Critical Inquiry*—Whitehead's name is invoked without any sustained attention to how his concepts differ from those of Deleuze. Yet if Whitehead can contribute anything to affect theory, surely it is his general concept of "prehension" that encompasses both what we usually call "thought" and what we call "feeling," gathering this opposition into a constructive contrast and sharpening our sense of when and where affect, as an explanatory term, is helpful. Brian Massumi, *Semblance and Event: Activist Philosophy and the Occurrent Arts* (Cambridge, Mass.: MIT Press, 2011); Erin Manning, *Relationscapes: Movement, Art, Philosophy* (Cambridge, Mass.: MIT Press, 2009); Ruth Leys, "The Turn to Affect: A Critique," *Critical Inquiry* 37 (Spring 2011): 434–72; William E. Connolly, "The Complexity of Intention," *Critical Inquiry* 37 (Summer 2011): 791–98; Ruth Leys, "Affect and Intention: A Reply to William E. Connolly," *Critical Inquiry* 37 (Summer 2011): 799–805.

14. For a selection of the volumes bringing Whitehead into relation with continental thought, see Roland Faber, Michael Halewood, and Deena M. Lin, eds., *Butler on*

Whitehead: On the Occasion (New York: Lexicon, 2012); Keith Robinson, ed., *Deleuze, Whitehead, Bergson: Rhizomatic Connections* (London: Palgrave Macmillan, 2009); Roland Faber, Henry Kripps, and Daniel Pettus, eds., *Event and Decision: Ontology and Politics in Badiou, Deleuze, and Whitehead* (Cambridge: Cambridge Scholars Publishing, 2010); Katherine Keller and Anne Daniell, eds., *Process and Difference: Between Cosmological and Poststructuralist Postmodernisms* (Albany: State University of New York Press, 2002). One exception to these comparative volumes is Isabelle Stengers, ed., *L'Effet Whitehead* (Paris: Vrin, 1994).

15. Isabelle Stengers, *Thinking with Whitehead: A Free and Wild Creation of Concepts,* trans. Michael Chase (Cambridge, Mass.: Harvard University Press, 2011), 23–24. Hereafter cited parenthetically as *TWW.*

16. As these sentences suggest, Whitehead's notion that new linguistic forms might create new modes of perception not only glosses his sense of philosophy's affinity with poetry, but also, and more importantly for Whitehead's contemporary relevance, indicates possible avenues for literary studies. Steven Meyer and Joan Richardson have already begun this work, the former through a study of Gertrude Stein's radical empirical experiments in and with language that directly considers her friendship with Whitehead; the latter through an investigation of the habit of mind that came to be called "pragmatism" and that is exhibited as a way of writing in authors from Jonathan Edwards to Wallace Stevens. Steven Meyer, *Irresistible Dictation: Gertrude Stein and the Correlations of Writing and Science* (Stanford, Calif.: Stanford University Press, 2003); Joan Richardson, *A Natural History of Pragmatism: The Fact of Feeling from Jonathan Edwards to Gertrude Stein* (Cambridge: Cambridge University Press, 2007). See also Joan Richardson, "Recombinant ANW: Appetites of Words," *Configurations* 13, no. 1 (2005): 117–33, for a more sustained engagement with Whitehead than Richardson provides in her book.

17. Isabelle Stengers makes this distinction between conditions and constraints both in her discussion of Whitehead and in her own speculative propositions in *Cosmopolitics*: "Unlike conditions, which are always relative to a given existent that needs to be explained, established, or legitimized, constraint provides no explanation, no foundation, no legitimacy. A constraint must be satisfied, but the way it is satisfied remains, by definition, an open question." Isabelle Stengers, *Cosmopolitics I,* 43. See also her discussion of prerequisites and conditions in "Beyond Conversation: The Risks of Peace" in Keller and Daniell, *Process and Difference,* 242.

18. See Andrew Ross, ed., *Science Wars* (Durham, N.C.: Duke University Press, 1996) for a compelling collection of essays by science studies scholars responding to the climate of debate during the "science wars." Isabelle Stengers offers a vivid account of the "minds in a groove" that produced the standoff between "relativist sociologists" and "technoscientistific rationalists" in the first chapter of *The Invention of Modern Science,* trans. Daniel W. Smith (Minneapolis: University of Minnesota Press, 2000).

19. The growing importance of the sciences for humanistic studies is evident in much of the critical literature issuing from speculative realism, radical empiricism, actor-network theory, new material feminism, and materialist studies of media. This is so much the case that complexity science (with its allied concepts of emergence, self-organization, and distributed systems) now provides a nearly ubiquitous framework for accounting for novelty at multiple human and nonhuman scales (biological, literary, social, informatic, physical, etc.). See, for instance, Manuel Delanda, *Intensive Science*

and Virtual Philosophy (London: Continuum, 2002); N. Katherine Hayles, *How We Became Posthuman: Virtual Bodies in Cybernetics* (Chicago, Ill.: The University of Chicago Press, 1999); and John Protevi, *Political Affect: Connecting the Social and the Somatic* (Minneapolis: University of Minnesota Press, 2009).

20. Stengers, *Cosmopolitics I,* 38.

21. Much has been written lately in object-oriented ontology about how Whitehead offers an alternative to what Meillassoux identifies as the correlationism issuing from Kant's critical philosophy and extending into twenty-first century philosophy. Importantly, Meillassoux resurrects the doctrine of primary (in-itself) and secondary (for-us) qualities as the basis for overturning the correlational circle in *After Finitude*: "the theory of primary and secondary qualities seems to belong to an irremediably obsolete philosophical past. It is time it was rehabilitated" (1). And yet, in Whitehead's perspective, the rejection of correlationism based on the in-itself and for-us distinction is underwritten by the same logic as critique: both aim at the critique of particular abstractions. Given this, it would seem that the debates around Whitehead's status as an "honorary" speculative realist are misguided, since in Whitehead's view the challenge is to guard against the tendency to affirm a Real nature, or what is "in-itself" as separate from what is *merely* "for-us." To produce the in-itself and for-us distinction is to produce a bifurcation. Cf. Bryant, Srnicek, and Harman, *The Speculative Turn.*

22. William James, *Principles of Psychology* (New York: Henry Holt and Co., 1918), 1:254.

23. Importantly, neither of these modes is ever experienced in its "pure" state. They generally enter our experience in a mixed mode that Whitehead calls "symbolic reference." As such, the point of the contrast is not to parse our perceptual experience into tidy packages that might be recognized as having always been there but rather to induce variations in how we attend to our perceptual experience (see *PR,* 168–83).

24. Lewis Ford's study of the revisions and additions Whitehead made to the manuscripts of *Science and the Modern World* and *Process and Reality* provides a captivating account of the philosopher's compositional process that makes explicit the conceptual fine-tuning that is often understated in the final texts. See Lewis S. Ford, *The Emergence of Whitehead's Metaphysics, 1925–1929* (Albany: State University of New York Press, 1984).

25. Prehensions considered apart from the subject at which they aim—a subject that only emerges when the actual occasion is fully determinate—are thus abstract. This is why actual occasions are the final real things and yet can be analyzed into component parts which, while concrete in the occasion, are abstract in themselves.

26. Importantly, though, Whitehead is not merely critical of Kant's constructivism. He fully acknowledges his debt to Kant, calling him "the great philosopher who first, fully and explicitly, introduced into philosophy the conception of an act of experience as a constructive functioning" (*PR,* 156). For a thorough and illuminating account of Whitehead's relation to Kant (and to Deleuze), see Steven Shaviro's *Without Criteria.*

27. Whitehead repeatedly insists that though actual occasions and eternal objects may be separated in analysis, in reality there are no eternal objects apart from actual occasions. The notions require one another. See *SMW,* 159; *PR,* 42–43, 244, 256; *MT,* 69.

28. William James, *Some Problems in Philosophy* (New York: Longmans, Green, and Co., 1911), 155. Whitehead presents his most elaborate account of concrescence in part 3 of *Process and Reality*, "The Theory of Prehensions."

29. In *Process and Reality*, Whitehead names two types of process that are best understood as different perspectives or aspects of the ultimate creativity: concrescence, which names the process of self-constitution (process seen from the perspective of the subject); and transition, which names the process whereby past satisfactions provoke a new occasion (process seen from the perspective of the superject). The "classical" tradition of Whiteheadian scholarship, including the important exegetical work by Christian, Leclerc, and Ford, is characterized by an emphasis on concrescence, to the detriment of the reality of satisfied occasions. The "ecstatic" school of interpretation, including the more recent work of Judith Jones, Elizabeth M. Kraus, Jorge Luis Nobo, and Brian Henning, seeks to correct this bias and therefore emphasizes the neglected importance of transition. The central text for reinstating transition and extension in our understanding of Whitehead's work remains Nobo's *Whitehead's Metaphysics of Extension and Solidarity* (Albany: State University of New York Press, 1986).

30. It is in this regard that we can answer the charge of those who would eliminate God and eternal objects from the philosophy of organism, replacing them with a theory of "emergence" whereby new eternal objects are created in actual experience and have their relevance decided by past occasions and the categoreal obligations (see George Allan's "A Functionalist Reinterpretation of Whitehead's Metaphysics," *The Review of Metaphysics* 62, no. 2 [December 2008]: 327–54, for the most forceful example of this criticism in recent years; versions of the general complaint stretch back all the way to Everett W. Hall's "Of What Use Are Whitehead's Eternal Objects?" *The Journal of Philosophy* 27, no. 2 [January 1930]: 29–44.) In short, we see Whitehead's full schema as providing a more nuanced vocabulary for describing precisely the operations foregrounded by the emergentists without falling into the trap of a lurking determinism. Whitehead's distinction between real potentiality and general or pure potentiality (along with its corollary concepts of eternal objects and the primordial and consequent natures of God) was meant to describe the emergence of real potentials in actual experience in such a way that they could not be reduced either to their social environment, the past occasions, or some scheme of potentiality whereby universal qualities (or eternal objects) have their own intrinsic order and thus suggest the possibility of going "behind" actuality to find something more real (cf. *TWW*, 361).

31. See Judith A. Jones, *Intensity: An Essay in Whiteheadian Ontology* (Nashville, Tenn.: Vanderbilt University Press, 1998), 84–131.

32. All societies are finite; moreover, there are no "self-contained" societies, only requiring themselves for reproduction. Every society is embedded within larger societal environments that provide the requisite stability for the endurance of more specialized ones (e.g., molecules, cells, organs).

33. We should note that order and disorder always exist relative to a particular occasion. Furthermore, disorder does not exist in a negative relation to social order but is rather a necessary condition for intense satisfactions among members genetically propagating order.

34. Stengers, *Cosmopolitics I*, 38. Stengers also addresses Whitehead's constructivism in the introduction to *Thinking with Whitehead* and in "Beyond Conversation," in Keller and Daniell, *Process and Difference*.

35. Steven Meyer discusses the general nature of the concept of creativity—and its distinction from artistic innovation and the Romantic imagination—in his introduction to the special issue of *Configurations* on Whitehead (1–33). See also Isabelle Stengers, *Thinking with Whitehead,* ch. 16.

36. Most recently, George Allan has argued that God is a superfluous component of Whitehead's scheme and, furthermore, that Whitehead himself signaled the concept as extraneous by leaving it largely unexamined in his work after *Process and Reality.* See George Allan, "A Functionalist Reinterpretation of Whitehead's Metaphysics." Graham Harman, in this volume, also opposes the concept of God as an unnecessary and potentially harmful addendum to Whitehead's otherwise helpful description of actual entities. Others, however (and Roland Faber is prominent among them), have attempted to make Whitehead's divine legible to a wider audience by reading it alongside analogous notions from postwar European philosophy. For instance, in "God, or the Body without Organs," Steven Shaviro argues that Whitehead's God and the body without organs, though not identical, "are structurally parallel" in that they perform similar roles in their respective systems. Shaviro, *Without Criteria,* 129. Other work at the intersection of continental philosophy and Whitehead's God includes Roland Faber's "De-Ontologizing God: Levinas, Deleuze, and Whitehead," in Keller and Daniell, *Process and Difference,* 209–39; Tim Clark, "A Whiteheadian Chaosmos: Process Philosophy from a Deleuzian Perspective," *Process Studies* 28, nos. 3–4 (Fall–Winter 1999): 179–94; and James Williams, "Immanence and Transcendence as Inseparable Processes: On the Relevance of Arguments from Whitehead to Deleuze Interpretation," *Deleuze Studies* 4 (2010): 94–106. Of course, the most sustained discussion of Whitehead's God has taken place in the context of "process theology," and surely one of the tasks for future research in this area will involve bringing the insights of this school to bear on the recent work cited above. See in particular the work of Charles Hartshorne, John Cobb Jr., David Ray Griffin, and Marjorie Suchocki.

37. For an account of Whitehead's educational writings in the context of his work at University College London and Imperial College London, see the second volume of Victor Lowe's biography of Whitehead, *Alfred North Whitehead: The Man and His Work,* ed. J. B. Schneewind, vol. 2, *1910–1947* (Baltimore, Md.: Johns Hopkins University Press, 1990), ch. 5. Moreover, there is a wide body of scholarship on Whitehead's theory of education. For instance, see George Allan, *Higher Education in the Making: Pragmatism, Whitehead, and the Canon* (Albany: State University of New York Press, 2004); George Allan, *Modes of Learning: Whitehead's Metaphysics and the Stages of Education* (Albany: State University of New York Press, 2012); Harold B. Dunkel, *Whitehead on Education* (Columbus: Ohio State University Press, 1965); Malcolm D. Evans, *Whitehead and Philosophy of Education: A Seamless Coat of Learning* (Amsterdam: Rodopi, 1998); Adam Christian Scarfe, ed. *The Adventure of Education: Process Philosophers on Learning, Teaching, and Research* (Amsterdam: Rodopi, 2009).

38. Whitehead initially delivered his account of a relational theory of space at the First Congress of Mathematical Philosophy, held in Paris in 1914—thus the French text. P. J. Hurley translated the resulting article as "The Relational Theory of Space" in 1979; see Lowe, *Alfred North Whitehead,* vol. 2, ch. 1. Whitehead began generating his account of space while working on the planned fourth volume of *Principia Mathematica,* and he devoted many chapters to the topic in his early philosophy of science, eventually revising his approach in the fourth part of *Process and Reality.*

39. For a more extensive treatment of how Whitehead might change the way we approach specific problems in social theory, see Michael Halewood, *A. N. Whitehead and Social Theory: Tracing a Culture of Thought* (London: Anthem Press, 2011).

40. For a discussion of how this Whiteheadian project contributes to contemporary debates about environmental philosophy, see Brian Henning's insightful study, *The Ethics of Creativity: Beauty, Morality, and Nature in a Processive Cosmos* (Pittsburgh, Pa.: University of Pittsburgh Press, 2005).

Part I

SPECULATION BEYOND THE BIFURCATION

ONE

A Constructivist Reading of *Process and Reality*

Isabelle Stengers

The problem that I want to address in this essay is how to tackle *Process and Reality.* This is a text whose obscurity has put off many readers, but one that I wish to defend against a particular way of being read.

It is perfectly possible to suggest that *Process and Reality* offers a new "conception of the world," the master themes of which are complexity, emergence, self-organization, and so on. And, given that such themes form part of contemporary science and contribute to what is sometimes called the "postmodern" science of a creative universe, it may be further maintained that we can and should recognize Whitehead's intuition of the centrality of creativity, but get rid of the redundant philosophical jargon that makes his text so hard to understand.

Such approaches replicate the rather classical stance wherein philosophy is viewed as the forerunner of science. Science simply confirms some of philosophy's ideas and consigns that which it cannot make sense of to the bin. However, in the case of *Process and Reality,* the problem is that rather a lot is left for the bin. For, within the text, not only does creativity never appear as an actor, or a power, or a tendency, or a force, but strange concepts, such as eternal objects or God, seem to stand in the way of any intuitive understanding of the world in terms of a creative, spontaneous becoming. Furthermore, Whitehead's need for these strange concepts is linked to a principle that itself seems to inherit the great rationalist tradition—namely, the "ontological principle." This principle states that "there is nothing which floats into the world from nowhere" (*PR,* 244)—that is, that whatever happens must be related to reasons. And creativity is not a reason, for "actual entities are the only reasons" (*PR,* 24).

In this essay I intend to distance Whitehead's speculative philosophy from the role it is given as a forerunner of a new, "enlightened," scientifically grounded conception of the world. I will argue that such a distribution of roles insults both science and philosophy. For the notion of a "conception of the world" entails that sciences forget the constraints that mobilize them, and that philosophy forgets the difference between philosophical concepts and mere generalities that appear to explain the world. I will use the term "constructivist" to refer to my approach as it emphasizes the need to actively and explicitly relate any knowledge-production to the question that it tries to answer, and refuses to transform knowledge into the kind of neutral statement that comes from nowhere and that could be called a "conception of the world."

Before proceeding to experiment[1] a constructivist approach to *Process and Reality,* I will first differentiate this conception of constructivism from those that may be generally characterized as "debunking"; I will then relate my version of constructivism to Whitehead's own definition of the task of philosophy.

Constructivisms

Debunking, or "deconstructive" conceptions of constructivism usually address only the value of truth associated with our judgments in order to denounce it: the question of adequacy to some preexisting matter of fact must be debunked. But why does the claim to adequacy act as such a red rag to some theorists? How could a police investigation into a murder, for instance, be described without accepting that adequacy matters? The simple point is that a claim should be related to the demands that it has to fulfill. In terms of a police inquiry, its value refers to an adequate "whodunit solution" and should highlight the importance of specific and challenging questions, such as: "does this solution bring together all the relevant facts?" and "does it resist relevant doubts?" In other words, the kind of achievement that "adequacy" implies must be specified, and a definition provided for "preexisting matters of fact."

This is especially important when we address scientific, and more particularly experimental, claims that are the usual targets of deconstruction. In contrast to the success of a careful and intricate police investigation, some deconstruction, or debunking, is indeed needed in face of the tales of "objectivity as the opposite of subjective opinion" that have been part of scientific propaganda since Galileo. Such stories induce the fairy-tale idea that science gains access to "objective matters of fact" rather like the heroic prince who overcomes the entangled forest of our illusions and discovers Sleeping Beauty's castle, lying there, clear and obvious, under the sun. Criticizing science's claim that nature can be discovered and described as independent of the perceiving mind or human language or culture, or as a mirror of nature, has been an easy sport for many philosophers since Kant, and they are now followed by a new brand of critical protagonists. Despite the variety of critiques, the conclusion is always that objective knowledge is conditioned. The philosopher, cultural theorist, or sociologist will then tell the scientist: "you believe that you enjoy some kind of a direct access to reality; you are wrong, and the value of the realism you associate with your description is mistaken."

It may well be that this value is mistaken, but I would part company with those critiques that focus solely on the idea that knowledge is always subject to some form of conditioning, be it transcendental, cultural, linguistic, social, or even neurophysiological, and thus leads to the denial of any particular relation between science and "reality." Each time "constructivism" gains a qualifying adjective (transcendental, cultural, etc.), it produces a contrast between those who believe they have direct access to reality and those who know that reality remains mute because they know what is really speaking instead. On this view, it is not the fairy tales surrounding sciences that are to be criticized but the very idea that there is something special about scientific knowledge. The qualifying adjective implies that the claimed "access" is nothing but a construction that can be explicated in terms of the conditioning power designated by the adjective. In order to resist science's fairy tales, however, there is no need to deny Galileo's achievement. Rather, the task is to characterize the achievement—that is, to specify the rather singular and specific demands it succeeded in satisfying.

I will be brief here, as I have developed this argument more fully elsewhere in *The Invention of Modern Science.*[2] In physics, and in any experimental science (I exclude sciences that just mimic experimentation), objectivity is indeed the name for an achievement, the very specific value of which permeates both the concern of the experimenter and the achievement's verification[3] by his or her competent colleagues. What must be verified is that a scientist has achieved a very peculiar feat: he or she has constructed an experimental situation that allowed what was questioned to make an actual, decidable difference. This is why the difference between artifacts and reliable facts is at the center of experimenters' attention. It is a difference they have to *make*, and it is not a difference between mirroring and constructing but between what they define as a successful construction and what they define as a failure.

Divorcing constructivism from deconstruction also means that we must not interpret the difference between achievement and failure simply in terms of some kind of "social construction." Where experimental achievement is concerned, the verification of this difference demands that there is a community that can question and test both the strength of the path leading from facts to interpretation and the design and redesigning of the minute aspects of the technical devices that produced those facts, in order to verify the claim that reliable access has indeed been constructed—that is, that the responsibility for the results can be related to what the scientist was trying to get access to. It is certainly possible to deconstruct a particular scientific achievement into a set of more general, socially entertained conditions, leaving behind (and ignoring) a kind of mute being with which no reliable relation has been produced. But whoever succeeds in doing this has only played the very important scientific role of diagnosing an artifact.

If the experimental sciences do not have an interesting relation with the production of "conceptions of the world" or with an adequacy to some "preexisting matters of fact," it is because the production of the matter of fact that could operate as a reliable witness for the "adequacy" of an interpretation is always an experimental achievement. As long as this achievement remains a matter of controversy, the putative matter of fact will remain a matter of collective, and demanding, concern.

Whitehead on Philosophy

We can now turn to Whitehead, and the way he defined his philosophical task:

> Every science must devise its own instruments. The tool required for philosophy is language. Thus philosophy redesigns language in the same way that, in physical science, pre-existing appliances are redesigned. It is exactly at this point that the appeal to facts is a difficult operation. This appeal is not solely to the expression of the facts in the current verbal statements. The adequacy of such sentences is the main question at issue. (*PR*, 11)

Here, again, adequacy is a matter of concern, but the concern is different. The main point at issue for Whitehead is that our current verbal statements, as well as the way we take our perceptions into account, are all highly selective. They involve discarding what does not matter and, more particularly, what there is no need to notice because it is always present.

> We habitually observe by the method of difference. Sometimes we see an elephant, and sometimes we do not. The result is that an elephant, when present, is noticed. Facility of observation depends on the fact that the object observed is important when present, and sometimes is absent. (*PR*, 4)

While experimental demonstration relies on transforming the "method of difference" into a "suspense drama"—it is the difference between this and that possible observation that makes the difference—the problem for philosophy is the selective aspect of both what we perceive as a matter of fact and the way in which we describe it.

Adequacy is a trap for philosophy as soon as it concerns matters of fact in the terms that we usually characterize it. If philosophers start with apparently simple situations such as "I see here a grey stone," they start from something already shaped by perceptive and linguistic interpretation. The point, however, is not to start from an experience devoid of interpretation. Whitehead famously remarked that if you wish to locate an experience devoid of interpretation, you may as well ask a stone to record its autobiography (see *PR*, 15). And, I would add, it would be better still that such a demand be made of Galileo's carefully polished round balls, rolling down an equally carefully smoothed, inclined plane. Indeed the whole aim of the experimental activity of polishing and smoothing is that the autobiography of the rolling ball would tell nothing about the ball, as such, in order for the speed it gains to reliably testify to what we now call terrestrial attraction (gravity). The intricate adventure that we call friction must not be recorded. When friction matters, the motion of the ball no longer illustrates one particular solution to an abstract, anonymous differential equation. What happens, in such a case, demands a level of attention that today's engineers and physicists, who specialize in surface effects, still laboriously learn how to pay.

In contrast, the kind of achievement that Whitehead aimed at could be described as a maximization of friction, recovering what has been obscured by specialized selection. This applies not only to Galileo's selection (the smoothing away of friction), but more generally to all the selections produced by consciousness and language—for example, the very important and successful abstractions that put emphasis on what matters in our many specialized practices, including that of surviving.

If Whitehead can be characterized as a constructivist philosopher, it is because by "disclosing," he does not mean gaining access to some concrete truth hidden by our specialized abstractions. If no experience is devoid of interpretation, then what is prohibited from the start is that we should retain some nostalgic memory of what we previously believed we genuinely knew about nature, and entertain the possibility of a more authentic experience. Whitehead's speculative philosophy is not about trying to recover concrete experience against its falsification by abstract interpretation. He recognized his indebtedness to Henri Bergson, and also to William James and John Dewey, but he stated that one of his preoccupations "has been to rescue their type of thought from the charge of anti-intellectualism, which rightly or wrongly has been associated with it" (*PR*, xii).

For Whitehead, we cannot think without abstractions, but this does not mean that we are irretrievably separated from that which we try to address. Abstractions, for Whitehead, are not "abstract forms" that determine what we feel, perceive, and think; nor are they "abstracted from" something more concrete; and, finally, they are not generalizations. Whitehead was a mathematician, and no mathematician would endorse such definitions. But most of them would endorse Whitehead's idea that abstractions act as "lures," luring attention toward "something that matters," vectorizing concrete experience. Just think of the difference between the mute perplexity and disarray of anybody who faces a mathematical proposition or equation as a meaningless sequence of signs, as opposed to someone who looks at this same sequence and immediately knows how to deal with it or is passionately aware that a new possibility for doing mathematics may be present.

In order to think abstractions in Whitehead's sense, we need to forget about nouns like "a table" or "a human being," and to think rather about a mathematical circle. Such a circle is not abstracted from concrete circular forms; its mode of abstraction is related to its functioning as a lure for mathematical thought: it lures mathematicians into adventures that produce new aspects of what it means to be a circle into a mathematical mode of existence.

This is why Whitehead could write, in *Modes of Thought*, that "the aim of philosophy is sheer disclosure" (*MT*, 49), while also defining its task as that of redesigning language, and indeed redesigning it in such a way that it has produced the mute perplexity and disarray of all those readers who wonder how they can, using such a language, ever hope to define a table or a human being. The aim of the abstractions that Whitehead designed is not to produce new definitions of what we consensually perceive and name, but to induce empirically felt variations in the way our experience matters. In *Modes of Thought*, Whitehead wrote that the basic expression of this value experience is: "Have a care, here is something that matters! Yes—that is the best phrase—the primary glimmering of consciousness reveals something that matters" (*MT*, 116). For Whitehead, consciousness was an ongoing adventure, not the sad tale of discovering our limitations and illusions.

There is a great difference between the adventures of mathematics and philosophy, however. The mathematician may well redesign mathematical tools, but may also trust them, while the philosopher must distrust both language and the facts as they are expressed in current verbal statements. This is why the analogy with physics' experimental "appliances" is so interesting. Indeed, the idea that experimentation appeals to facts as they are observed by means of experimental appliances only refers to the stabilized end product of a difficult operation. As Andrew Pickering marvelously characterized it, in his *The Mangle of Practice*,[4] experimenters may well know in advance what they want to achieve—what, for instance, their appliance should detect. However, a long process of tuning will nevertheless be needed, within which nothing will be trusted, neither the human hypothesis nor the observations made. Indeed, the process of tuning works both ways, on human as well as on nonhuman agency, constitutively intertwining a double process of emergence, of a disciplined human agency and of a captured material agency.

It is interesting to note that this intertwined process of co-emergence may clarify a controversy among Whiteheadian scholars. On the one side, Lewis Ford has promoted a compositional analysis of *Science and the Modern World* and of *Process and Reality* that emphasizes the radical nature of the discontinuities that occur in these texts. Indeed, it may seem on many occasions that a new philosopher enters the scene and, as Leibniz would say, leads readers back toward the wide sea while they thought themselves safely in a harbor. On the other side, some refuse the idea of a Whitehead who changes his mind and his philosophy, time and time again, and they insist on the continuity of one and the same philosophy always being expressed, under different emphases.

I would claim that we may trace in the compositional adventure of *Process and Reality,* as Lewis Ford has tentatively reconstituted it, what Pickering calls the "dance of agency," with the practitioner tentatively constructing a device, then adopting a passive role in order to follow the consequences of its functioning, then intervening again. The adventure of the creation of a conceptual agency cannot be disentangled from the experiential adventure of the philosopher experimenting disclosure. We can speak here of "experimenting" because the disclosure is part of a process that can be described as conceptually "lured." Each concept has to be designed and redesigned, as the point is not of adequacy to some kind of preexistent matter of fact but, rather, that of two questions that are always at work together: Is the conceptual agency succeeding in doing what the philosopher wants it to do, and are those aims an adequate expression of the challenge he or she has decided to confront?

We come here to a second feature of constructivism. Not only is construction to be understood in terms of achievement and failure, with adequacy being in some cases only implied and defined by the achievement, but also, we do not construct in general. A construction is an answer to a challenging situation, which produces both its felt necessity and its meaning. For Whitehead, philosophy indeed had necessity and meaning:

> You cannot think without abstractions; accordingly it is of the utmost importance to be vigilant in critically revising your modes of abstraction. . . . An active school of philosophy is quite as important for the locomotion of ideas as is an active school of railways engineers for the locomotion of fuel. (*SMW,* 59)

By comparing philosophy with engineering and viewing it as charged with the necessary revisions of our modes of abstractions, Whitehead implies that if we are not prisoners of our abstractions, then we may well become prisoners of the false problems they are bound to create if we extend, outside their specialized domain, the trust they deserve only inside this domain. For example, as soon as the abstractions relevant for the interpretation of "physicality" (whether they are derived from classical physics or contemporary physics) are given free rein to rule under the form of "conceptions of the world," we are faced with what Whitehead famously called the "fallacy of misplaced concreteness."

Whitehead maintained that the challenge for philosophy was to resist this fallacy—that is, to resist the concrete character that our modern epoch has attributed to its most powerful abstractions. But the originality of his answer, and of the mode of abstraction he designed, was that the aim was not simply to critique specialized abstractions but to produce different abstractions that would act as lures for an aesthetic appreciation of our diverging, specialized abstractions, for they are well worth the same kind of attention, care, and lucidity that engineers devote to technical equipment.

With the fallacy of misplaced concreteness no compromise is possible; Whitehead's construction started with a resounding "no." We have first to feel the absurdity of the consequences of the power we give to our modern abstractions and more specifically the absurdity of the "bifurcation of nature" that they produce. Nature bifurcates when we assert that there exists on one side a causal, objective nature—for instance, the molecular mechanisms explaining the functioning of neurons and the interactions between neurons—and on the other side a perceived nature full of sounds, odors, enjoyments, and values—all these so-called secondary properties being subjective ones, attributed to nature by the perceiving subject. This entails, Whitehead comments, that nature usually

> get[s] credit which should in truth be reserved for ourselves: the rose for its scent; the nightingale for his song; and the sun for its radiance. The poets are entirely mistaken. They should address their lyrics to themselves, and turn them into odes of self-congratulation on the excellency of the human mind. (*SMW,* 54)

It might be claimed that Whitehead's whole speculative enterprise started from his diagnosis of the bifurcation of nature as a case of radical incoherence that literally plagues modern thought. This incoherence is an ever-renewed source of problems of our own making—problems that stem from the clash between those abstractions associated with the success of the so-called laws of nature on the one side and, on the other, those abstractions organized around human perception, freedom, intentionality, or responsibility. A contemporary example of such problems is the definition of the so-called naturalization of consciousness as the remaining "hard problem" to be solved by the progress of objective science.

Many critical philosophers, including empirical philosophers, followers of Kant, or phenomenologists, would certainly agree that this hard problem is in fact a false problem. If consciousness, conscious perception, or human intentionality is required by any objective knowledge, then they are what objective knowledge presupposes and thus cannot objectify. Whitehead, however, rejected escaping the bifurcation of nature at the price of defacing scientific achievements by turning the requirement into a condition that would solve the problem, for objective, causal nature would then be a production of the human mind—just like the beauty of the nightingale's song. Already, by the time of *The Concept of Nature,* he had clearly stated that

> For natural philosophy everything perceived is in nature. . . . In making this demand I conceive myself as adopting our immediate instinctive attitude towards perceptual knowledge which is only abandoned under the influence of theory. We are instinctively willing to believe that, by due attention, more can be found in nature than that which is observed at first sight. But we will not be content with less. (*CN,* 29)

Quite what it means to be "in" nature will be a matter for philosophical construction but, whatever the manner of this construction, whatever interpretation is made of what we come to perceive, if the way we pay attention changes, then the challenge remains that neither the poet singing the beauty or sadness of nature, nor the physicist building a new detector, can be called to task or made to bow down in front of general conditions that explain away what mattered for them in the first place. Due attention means becoming able to add, not subtract; it means learning how to get relevant access, not renouncing the possibility of any such access.

Adding, not deconstructing: this is a crucial point where constructivism is concerned. However, it is impossible simply to "add" the beauty of the song to matter hurrying blindly by. The crucial importance of constructivism, as I present it here, is to relate the mode of existence to the mode of achievement. We may well say that electrons "truly exist" as opposed to their being mere fictions—that is, products of free, human interpretation—because the whole of experimental practice aims at dramatizing this alternative. The mode of existence of the electron must, primarily, be irreducible to a question of mere interpretation. But the crucial point for Whitehead is that this alternative, if generalized, would despoil interpretation. Our modes of interpretation matter. The experimental opposition between "mere fiction" and "truly existing" is to be understood as giving its value and importance to a very particular and demanding mode of interpretation. What can and should be generalized is that no mode of existence can be disentangled from the way in which it matters. Interpretation is a serious, vital business, never to be reduced to "mere interpretation."

A constructivist approach implies that any new, creative construction testifies explicitly not only to a matter of concern, but also to a commitment. Matters of concern no more command the way that they should be taken into account than "reality" does. Engineers usually know what they are committed to achieving. Whitehead's own matter of concern was that the incoherence associated with the bifurcation of nature has been proudly accepted by modern thought and even identified as evidence of us overcoming our childish illusions. This may explain that his commitment, and the task that his whole enterprise in *Process and Reality* had to satisfy, was to achieve coherence. The mode of existence of Whitehead's conceptual abstractions cannot be separated from this mode of achievement to which he committed himself.

Coherence entails that we become able to interpret conjointly (that is, without opposition, hierarchy, or disconnection) what we usually describe in mutually contradictory terms—for example, freedom and determination, cause and reason, fiction and reality, or mind and matter. However, it is crucial to remember that the point is not to go beyond these contradictions towards some kind of an inspired or transcendent vision that is mysteriously able to discover a unified reality. Philosophy, as a kind of engineering, is about designing, not transcending, and this is why Whitehead deliberately formulated the kind of satisfaction that his demand for coherence would have to fulfill. The divide manifested by the bifurcation of nature must not be repaired or tamed. Any strategy of explaining away, of reducing some aspects of our experience to others has to be resisted. Everything that we experience must matter.

Again, it is not a question of criticizing our specialized abstractions or of dictating limitations. Rather, it is a question of presenting our abstractions as important achievements with a price. As I have already remarked, friction must be maximized in order to produce both a restraint upon specialists and an enlargement of their imagination (see *PR*, 17). Limitation produces nostalgia, dreams of the forbidden possibility for your abstractions to rule undisputed, while enlargement of the imagination means appreciating the importance and value of abstractions as such.

It is time now to stop speaking "about" Whitehead as a constructivist thinker and to enter into the construction. I will certainly not try to summarize Whitehead's conceptual scheme. This would contradict the very idea of a constructivist reading, which cannot be separated from the efficacy of concepts encountered therein. For the value of concepts is to lure new feelings, to induce "sheer disclosure" as a new way for experience to come to matter. I want to try to give you a taste of this kind of efficacy by following the change of emphasis that a particular question may go through from its first starting point, when it begins to matter, to its Whiteheadian, conceptual unfolding.

Reading *Process and Reality*

Victor Lowe reports that after Whitehead gave his first lecture at Harvard (which is also the first philosophy lecture that Whitehead ever attended), his students were "in despair about the course," but "all in love with Whitehead as a person, for somehow the overwhelming magic of his being had shown through."[5] The philosopher who had been assigned to be his assistant remembered that when Whitehead concluded his lecture, "the angels were singing."[6] In contrast, when we are reading *Process and Reality,* angels are not singing. Instead of this kind of immediate enjoyment, the reader experiences constant perplexity. Is the sentence I have just read to be taken seriously? Is it rather badly written poetry? Is it sheer nonsense?

The difference between listening to Whitehead and reading him could be explained away in terms of the opposition between the transitory effect that nonsense statements and charismatic tricks may produce and the stable understanding associated with statements with an objective content, the faithful transmission of which can be verified. Whitehead's charismatic presence would then have been responsible for the effect he produced, suggesting to the poor students that he was exploring deep intuitions while, in fact, he was uttering sheer nonsense.

Such an opposition, and terms such as "charismatic presence" or "suggestion" that amplify this opposition without adding anything to it, may certainly be important. But it is also a highly specialized opposition and one that designates specific practices, the value of which rely on the faithful transmission of well-defined information. Its generalization, namely, the feeling that this opposition is generally important, may rely on the habit that we have of asking, "what is responsible for what?" For example: "Is it the singer or the song?" Am I moved because what I experience is moving, or do I feel it as moving because I am emotionally excited? But this idea of responsibility is also part of those very abstractions that govern special modes of thought, the domination of which, according to Whitehead, it is the task of philosophy to restrain. It is the same problem as the elephant (noted above, and in *PR,* 4): responsibility matters because sometimes you are responsible and sometimes you are not. What would it feel like to restrain the importance that we associate with judgments that assign responsibility?

The crucial point is that this restraint must result not from a renunciation but from what Whitehead calls an enlargement of the imagination. We have to learn to wonder about what we take for granted. We must leave the settled, frictionless ground where all that matters is the question of what is responsible for a misunderstanding, yet leaves frictionless understanding as taken for granted. Sometimes we misunderstand but usually we understand.

In order to wonder, it is important to realize that understanding and misunderstanding designate a secondary contrast, a matter of occasional verification: "Did I understand correctly?" Whitehead writes that "Spoken language is merely a series of squeaks" (*PR,* 264). What matters, first of all, is that these "squeaks" make some sense: this is a matter of wonder. It is what Whitehead calls, in *Religion in the Making,* the one fundamental sacrament—the sacrament of expression. "There is a community of intuition by reason of the sacrament of expression proffered by one and received by the other. But the expressive sign is more than interpretable. It is creative. It elicits the intuition which interprets it" (*RM*, 131–32).

How are we to understand the use of this unusual word, "sacrament"? Do we have to take seriously, literally, the community of intuition it elicits, and view it as a religious rite? Or is it just a fuzzy metaphor? I would suggest that it is simply a starting point, which produces a double challenge. One is addressed to the reader: to use the word "sacrament" is to ask the reader to wonder, to slow down and accept that the expressivity of the sign that we usually take for granted is indeed a wonder. The other is addressed to the conceptual construction that will proceed from it, and it indicates the kind of risk that Whitehead has decided to take.

In *Modes of Thought,* Whitehead wrote: "Philosophy begins in wonder. And, at the end, when philosophic thought has done its best, the wonder remains" (*MT,* 168). At the end, when Whitehead has done his best, the wonder will remain. The conceptual construction is not meant to think wonder away but to fully develop how it puts our usual generalizations and explanations at risk. Indeed, in the Catholic doctrine, which we know Whitehead had carefully examined, sacramental efficacy cannot be reduced to anything else, to something more general, and, in particular, not to some catch-all explanation such as "human subjectivity." To use the expression "the sacrament of the sign" thus commits Whitehead as a problem commits a mathematician; whatever we mean by human subjectivity, it will presuppose the efficacy of the sign—it will not explain it.

This certainly does not mean that such efficacy exhibits a "supernatural" power, as it does in Catholic sacraments. Rather, it asks us not to be satisfied with what we might, by contrast, call a "natural" explanation. Whatever explanations we are tempted to provide for the fact that meaning is elicited from the squeaks of spoken language, such explanations are bound, one way or another, to bypass what Whitehead wants us to dwell upon. For example, if we were to think of some kind of a selective process that, after a long period of biological evolution, has made it possible for us to understand each other—in whatever way we characterize this process—it must presuppose and celebrate the sacrament of expression, not explain it away.

Here, however, we face a critical point. To celebrate the efficacy of the sign as unique could well lead to a particular version of the bifurcation of nature, through the linguistic turn for instance. One way or another, all our experiences, all our explanations, would then be characterized as conditioned by linguistic expressivity. Also, if the importance of a "community of intuition" were to be exaggerated, this would merely reinstate consciousness to center stage, with the nightingales or the fragrant roses as accessories. This is why it is so important to emphasize that conceptual construction has not begun at this point. It will start only with the demand for coherence. That is, it is only when Whitehead's position with regard to modern abstractions (especially abstractions that overemphasize the divide between the conscious subject and the known object) receives a positive formulation that the challenge that conceptual construction must satisfy is made explicit. The task of philosophy is not only to produce concepts that put in "sheer disclosure" the wonderful efficacy of the expressive sign as that which primordially matters for us as conscious beings. The task of philosophy is also to elucidate those aspects of experience that do not matter in the same way, for instance because they are always there, even when the community of intuition breaks down and you stop understanding what somebody says to you.

In *Concept of Nature,* Whitehead emphasized that what he called, "roughly speaking," "bodily life" (*CN,* 107) was an integral part of our experience, and in *Process and Reality,* he called this "causal efficacy" the experience of our own body. The loss of this experience has been described by the psychiatrist Oliver Sacks as the worst catastrophe that we can experience.[7] Indeed, he describes the loss of this feeling of the body as entailing the loss of the very enjoyment, the "withness," of the world. We enjoy a world, including the feeling of our own body, even if we are not usually conscious of it, even if we have only vague words for it. Such words must be carefully fabricated if the elucidation of our experience is not to stop with the wonderful efficacy of the sign.

However, if such enjoyment is restricted to human embodied experience, we return, again, to the bifurcation of nature. The poet enjoys the beauty of the nightingale's song but the nightingale enjoys nothing. We may decide to attribute this enjoyment to some select animal species, including the singing nightingale, but we would then have to ask biological evolution to explain how such enjoyment came to exist only for certain living species. At this point we might invoke some level of cerebral complexity, but here, again, nature will bifurcate with, on one side, those beings whose functioning is to be explained by causal, objective mechanisms and, on the other, those beings who (and that which falls under the term "who" could be correlatively extended) *enjoy,* that is, those beings endowed with experience.

It is here, at last, that the demand for coherence produces its positive challenge. It is experience that must be affirmed. Not "experience" in terms of knowledge, consciousness, or perception, but experience in terms of creative self-determination with respect to something else. And such experience must be affirmed for everything that exists; if not, then incoherence will rule. As Whitehead wrote, "apart from the experience of subjects there is nothing, nothing, nothing, bare nothingness" (*PR*, 167).

The wonder that starts with the wonderful efficacy of expressive signs is now generalized. Signs may elicit intuition but what matters now is "efficacy" itself—that is, the subjective, value-producing process of self-determination that is the coming into existence of everything that actually exists. A Whiteheadian subject is not something that simply exists and then happens to enjoy this or that; and it is not something that shares or does not share a community of intuition as elicited by a sign. What Whitehead calls a subject is the very process of the becoming together, of becoming one and being enjoyed as one, of a many that are initially given as stemming from elsewhere. In other words, the sacrament associated with the sign was just a beginning. Whatever we call a cause, even a physical interaction, has no power to cause independently of the way in which it will be grasped in a subjective process of self-production. This subjective process of self-production is the self-production of what Whitehead called the "concrescence of an actual occasion."

I will not go into the full conceptual construction of actual occasions here. But I do want to avoid a certain conceptual trap—namely, the idea that the proposition "actual occasions exist" is something Whitehead wanted his reader to accept as a matter of fact, as physicists have done with such propositions about atoms. Rather, I want to try to generate a feeling of the kind of efficacy that these fantastic metaphysical existents that he named "actual occasions" can produce, in terms of their being speculative abstractions. That which decides between their failure and success is indeed the transformation of emphasis that they must be able to produce with regard to the powerful and pragmatically justified abstractions that lure and sometimes dominate our experiences. The demand for coherence means that Whitehead's speculative abstractions will be a failure if the kind of emphasis they produce maintains the privileges of those abstractions.

It is in this way that we can understand the most surprising feature of Whitehead's actual occasions—that is, that they are indeed "occasions," that is, temporally atomic. When the process of subjective self-determination of that which was initially given has been fulfilled, when the occasion has achieved its own specific individual being—its satisfaction—when the initial many have become one, the many are increased by one. The occasion has attained what Whitehead calls "objective immortality." It will feel no longer, it will experience no longer, but it will be that which has to be felt by other subsequent occasions. Thus, actual occasions imply that discontinuity is primordial, while continuity and, thereby, all our usual perceptual habits, causal explanations, and the experience of ourselves as continuous identities have lost their claim and power to explain.

Whitehead is not claiming thereby that physics is wrong when it explains change in terms of physical entities continuously interacting with each other, and he is not asking us to avoid any interpretation of ourselves as living, intentional continuities. The role of actual occasions entails restraining the authority of explanations that take for granted any continuous endurance and turn into interesting contrasts the oppositions that such explanations produce (freedom or consciousness as continuously "ours," as against causality implying the action of something upon something else). This is why endurance will have to be conceptually explained, and it will be explained by what Whitehead characterizes as social order. What we call an electron, or ourselves as feeling endowed with a continuing life of its own, are societies, complex routes of occasions exhibiting some level of conformity as each reproduces and confirms a way of feeling, of achieving its own identity, as proposed by the particular social environment it inherits.

But the temporal discontinuity of actual occasions is not simply a means to construct the one plane on which all that confronts us is to be described and characterized as societies. What also matters is that each occasion is, as such, a new occasion. When Whitehead first described the bifurcation of nature, his main concerns were perception and explanation, and he did not include the problem of novelty in his challenge. It is an important part of his conceptual adventure that he came to identify this problem as the ultimate challenge that his demand for coherence had to satisfy. It is no longer the enjoyment of the nightingale's song that matters, but also the very hope and trust that suffuses the thinker, namely, that he or she will be able to produce new, relevant propositions.

The possibility of a breaking of social continuity by some new, nonconformal occasional mode of becoming one is why actual occasions matter. But novelty, defined as unpredictability, is not sufficient for coherence to be achieved. And it is also not sufficient to view conformity and nonconformity as opposed in the same way that "yes" and "no" are opposed. To belong to a society is, in a way, to answer "yes"—but the "no" of nonconformity is not the opposite of such an affirmative response. For Whitehead "no" is the germ of consciousness; it needs a very special social environment and cannot characterize novelty as such. What we need, conceptually speaking, is the possibility of "relevant" novelty or what Whitehead calls "originality." If this possibility is not a primary conceptual feature, it will never be obtained without a bifurcation of nature, with the nightingale's and our own social habits on the one hand, and, on the other, the very fact you are reading this essay with the faint hope that, maybe, I will provide the occasion for some new idea relevant to your own problems.

One of the challenges at work during the composition of *Process and Reality* was the implementation of the possibility of relevant novelty and the tuning of Whitehead's conceptual agency until it was able to enhance and unfold into disclosure what originality demands. It does not mean that Whitehead has discovered the true nature of originality, but that the question of originality obliged him to put to the test and revise his concepts. And this is the very role of the "ontological principle" that I alluded to at the start of this essay. For the "ontological principle" demands reasons and prohibits any easy appeal to creativity as explaining novelty. It thus confers upon novelty the power to compel thought.

To summarize, Whitehead produced a strict distinction between data as things that have to be felt, and the open, yet-to-be-determined question of how they will be felt (how they will become an ingredient in the superjective, final unification). This distinction between what we feel and how we feel it seems simple enough—philosophy is sheer disclosure. However, to make this distinction irreducible and to escape the possibility that experience, any experience, is reduced to a function that can be explained in terms of some kind of continuity necessitated Whitehead's famous, but so easily misunderstood, "eternal objects." The determination of the "how" of becoming cannot be derived from data because any determination involves the ingression of an eternal object. But this concept of ingression also entailed Whitehead's God without which no unrealized eternal object could ingress—that is, without which no new relevant novelty marked by a new "how" or new contrast would be possible. "Apart from the intervention of God, there could be nothing new in the world, and no order in the world. The course of creation would be a dead level of ineffectiveness, with all balance and intensity progressively excluded by the cross-currents of incompatibility" (*PR*, 247).

A constructivist stance is essential for this word "God" not to elicit a communion of scandalized intuition. Whitehead did not need God in order to answer an emotional or religious need, and the way he designed and redesigned this particular conceptual appliance makes it quite clear how strongly he felt the need to tune it precisely. In particular, God is not to be the source of social order, be it one that is exemplified by physical laws or by moral habits. God's functioning has to do with actual occasions alone or, more precisely, with the envisaging of each occasion as an opportunity for a slightly non-conformal, original feeling.

The fact that order needs novelty is not evident in physics since the relevance of the laws of physics depends on the possibility of the definition of their specific social order being organized around conservation and functional conformity. But for Whitehead, the fact that order needs novelty is evident in biology, in the very inconspicuous kind of novelty that is the capacity of any living being to adapt to a changing environment.

As always with Whitehead, the question of originality has been generalized into a wonder about what it is rather easy to take for granted or to explain away by natural, ad hoc explanations. For Whitehead, the fact that there is a certain originality in the response of a cell to an external stimulus does not have to be explained in social terms but is to be celebrated through the distinction between living societies and "Life." "Life is a bid for freedom" (*PR*, 104), he wrote, not to be confused with the enduring order of living societies. Life "lurks in the interstices of every cell" (*PR*, 104–5), shaking off the shackles of the reiteration of the past.

As I have already stated, the primary value of Whitehead's argument is to experiment how the demand for coherence, when systematically and constructively enacted, may modify our relations to our own experience. This can only be verified concretely, and in order to verify it, I will at last come back to the efficacy of the sign as eliciting a community of intuition. It was the starting point, the initial wonder, but it is now witness to a social achievement, as dominated by the settled ground of common understanding and anticipation. As Whitehead remarked in *Religion in the Making:*

> The sign cannot elicit what is not there. A note on a tuning fork can elicit a response from the piano. But the piano has already in it the string tuned to the same note. In the same way the expressive sign elicits the existent intuition which would not otherwise emerge into individual distinctiveness. (*RM*, 133)

However, not all intuitions can be characterized in the same manner; there is a difference between "having understood" and those occasions when you feel the precariousness of your grasp, its readiness to disintegrate, or the beginning of a new intuition, or something that was not there before. And you can hear "angels sing" while listening to Whitehead and be afterwards in despair about understanding the course.

To hear angels sing is an experience akin to what poetry may achieve, at least when novelty in the use of words is not experienced as such but immediately elicits a novel and original communion of intuition. Furthermore, the fact that for most students the experience faded away like a dream would not be seen as an obvious failure for poetry. But it certainly is a failure for philosophy. Achievement, for a philosopher, surely implies the transmission of concepts as the abstractions that they are, as appliances whose effectiveness will be verified by new, original modes of thought. Using Whitehead's own concepts in order to describe this failure, one could say that the experience did not achieve socialization. The students' habitual thought patterns endured, whilst the interstices, where the possibility of original, new lures for feeling lurked, closed down.

Whitehead clearly recognized the legitimacy of this response from his students when they turned his philosophical propositions into something like an art performance; they did not accept this experience as their own but attributed it to something that they would never be—singing angels: "we are no angels, we return to the settled ground." Whitehead knew that it was not a simple matter of the reception of ideas that was at stake, but becoming, the students' own becoming.

Such is the power of what Whitehead called propositions, luring abstractions that are not to be confused with sentences (which eventually serve as their vehicles), that their acceptance into experience may disrupt social order. "When a non-conformal proposition is admitted into feeling . . . a novelty has emerged into creation. The novelty may promote or destroy order; it may be good or bad. But it is new, a new type of individual, and not merely a new intensity of individual feeling" (*PR*, 187). Thought patterns, as with everything that endures, are societies that succeed in holding together and in maintaining themselves, or they collapse. No transcendental legitimacy can authorize criticizing the students whose thought patterns resisted collapse. Indeed the students' refusal may have been a saving one since it can be that a new, non-conformal actuality appears in "the wrong society amid which its claims to efficacy act mainly as inhibitions" (*PR*, 223). For Whitehead, "insistence on birth at the wrong season is the trick of evil" (*PR*, 223).

Now, it is a clear empirical fact that, when reading *Process and Reality*, we do not hear angels sing but have to face and experiment the challenge to our usual thought patterns. This is not a failure in Whitehead's terms, as the elucidation of experience that he wished to induce was not to be a matter of immediate enjoyment but was to induce disclosure about the task of philosophy, that is, engineering relevant abstractions. And it may be that the very strange experience of reading *Process and Reality* exhibits and dramatizes an aspect of the very problem that Whitehead wanted to address. Indeed, beyond the incoherence of our dominant modern abstractions there is another problem, that of the way in which we accept the domination of abstractions—that is, the way in which we consent to forget or neglect what we are aware of when it cannot be formulated in a clear, self-contained way.

Whitehead was not a Bergsonian; this domination was not, for him, a result of the weakness of the human mind against which the philosopher has to struggle. Rather, Whitehead linked it with an historical event, that of writing taking a dominant position in our intellectual life. In *Modes of Thought,* he states that speech is as old as human nature, it could even be said to be human nature itself, whilst writing is comparable to the steam engine. It is important, modern, and artificial (*MT,* 37). Writing gave us increased powers of thought, of analysis, of recollection, and of conjecture, but an ideal of self-sufficiency associated with writing (though not compelled by writing) also came historically to govern, or misgovern, our understanding of the function of language. Before the advent of writing, Whitehead guesses that speech could not be separated from the interfusion of emotional expression and signaling and always entailed an immediate situation. "Whether it was signal or expression, above all things it was this reaction to that situation in this environment" (*MT,* 38). But when we talk now, we entertain the ideal that we can abstract the meanings of the words that we use from the presupposition of any particular environment. "We cannot congratulate ourselves too warmly on the fact that we are born among people who can talk about green in abstraction from springtime. But at this point we must remember the warning—Nothing too much" (*MT,* 38).

To "civilize" abstractions, which was Whitehead's aim, means to engineer the kind of new, relevant abstractions that would not overcome the specific, mutually incompatible partiality of our usual abstractions but would transform the drama of their contradiction into a feeling of the divergence between their respective, specific, social definitions of what matters. And it also means to elicit into sheer disclosure the exaggerated trust we have in our own abstractions. Whitehead did not want to have readers merely being told about abstractions that are able to civilize modern, proud incoherence. He wanted to actually transform the experience of his readers with regard to the role of abstractions that writing has promoted.

Whitehead states at the very beginning of *Process and Reality* that the "fundamental ideas" that he will propose all presuppose each other, but not as words do in a dictionary, where each is definable in terms of the others. Instead, what he meant by this was that what was indefinable in one idea could not be abstracted from its relevance to the others. In other words, Whitehead was going to use writing and the increased powers of thought, of analysis, of recollection, and of conjecture that writing makes possible in order to provide the environment needed for his abstractions to counteract the very kind of trust in our abstractions that an authoritative use of writing has induced—namely, the idea that abstractions have a meaning that is independent of their context: the idea, for instance, that we know very well what is green in abstraction from our experience of springtime. In *Process and Reality,* despite the definitions that Whitehead gives, we cannot but feel that the definition does not provide the settled ground that permits the communion of intuition that we call meaning. Each abstraction is mutely appealing for an imaginative leap, and it is this very leap that cannot be abstracted from its relevance to other abstractions that are also calling for an imaginative leap.

This is why you cannot read *Process and Reality* from the first to the last page, in a linear manner, but must zigzag, using the index, being lured to come back to something you recollect but that had remained mute and now takes on a new importance, taking the leap that you have just felt is possible. And it may also be why Whitehead's writing zigzagged as well, why he abstained from a careful rewriting of the whole text each time he redesigned his own concepts. Each new insertion, each new addition was to be understood as a partially explicit definition of what had, until then, been indefinable for him. And it may be, finally, that the very fact that his text does not run smoothly like a steam engine that has to avoid clashes or bumps is as important as the content of the book. It demonstrates how Whitehead was working against the kind of ideal, self-contained abstractions that writing induces, the definition of which is that of direct access, or of "double click" as Bruno Latour calls it. We may well complain that this does not make for an easy read, but we cannot say that Whitehead betrayed the urgent challenge that he set as the task of modern philosophy: to make the ideal of coherence matter.

Notes

I warmly thank Didier Debaise for his critical and constructive comments and Michael Halewood for his careful editing of this text.

1. The verb "to experiment" is here used in a sense akin to "to experience," that is, without "on" or "with," which would induce the idea of a separation between the experimenter and what she is experimenting on or with. It is thus a (French-inspired) neologism meant to signal a practice of active, open, demanding attention paid to the experience as we experience it. For instance, a cook would be said to experiment the taste of a new dish. In French, there is no clear distinction between the terms "experience" and "experiment" as there is in English. This neologism, when used throughout

this essay, signals Whitehead's particular empiricist stance that philosophy exhibits experience as experiment and vice versa.

2. Isabelle Stengers, *The Invention of Modern Science,* trans. Daniel W. Smith (Minneapolis: University of Minnesota Press, 2000).

3. "Verification" refers here to an art of consequences—if he or she is right, then we should obtain that result in other, modified conditions—not a simple repetition. Verification is both testing and extending.

4. Andrew Pickering, *The Mangle of Practice* (Chicago, Ill.: Chicago University Press, 1995).

5. Victor Lowe, *Alfred North Whitehead: The Man and His Work* (Baltimore, Md.: Johns Hopkins University Press, 1990), 142.

6. Ibid.

7. Oliver Sacks, *The Man Who Mistook His Wife for a Hat: And Other Clinical Tales* (New York: Touchstone, 1998).

TWO

Scientism and the Modern World

Jeffrey A. Bell

An important debate among contemporary philosophers concerns the very role of philosophy itself, and especially the nature of its relationship to science. James Ladyman and David Ross, for example, have recently argued that it is not philosophy but rather science, and more precisely physics, that best provides the answers philosophers have long asked about the nature of reality. The famous physicist Stephen Hawking states the point even more blithely in his latest book, concluding that "philosophy is dead."[1] Ladyman and Ross may not go this far, but according to the "scientism" they endorse, they would indeed argue that philosophy's only meaningful role as metaphysics is to show how the various sciences relate to one another, and more importantly how all the special sciences ultimately derive from fundamental physics. In short, with Ladyman and Ross, we have a form of scientific reductionism.

The Deleuzian position to be put forth in this essay will resist placing philosophy into a subservient role to the sciences, as the sciences' handmaiden so to speak. The position to be argued for here can be traced to Husserl and Heidegger, and especially to the trajectory Deleuze's thought takes with respect to their philosophies. Deleuze argues, for instance, as did Husserl and Heidegger before him, that the task of philosophy is to address problems that are irreducible to scientific treatment—namely, those problems associated with *life,* or what Husserl discussed as problems integral to the *lebenswelt.*

In addition to the importance of Husserl and Heidegger to understanding the Deleuzian position concerning the nature of philosophy to be argued for here, this essay will posit that there are two key sources that are even more significant in their influence—namely, Hume and Whitehead. This might be surprising since Hume is often credited with laying the philosophical foundations for scientific positivism, and by derivation the scientism of Ladyman and Ross; and Whitehead may be thought to be too strongly connected with Bertrand Russell, with whom he wrote *Principia Mathematica,* and thus with Russell's efforts to develop a "scientific philosophy."[2] Both Hume and Whitehead might thus seem to be ill-chosen figures from whom to draw so much significance in arguing for the independence of philosophy. That this might be thought to be the case is a reflection, I shall argue, of the hegemonic status the scientific paradigm of philosophy has today, and it is precisely this paradigm that I shall challenge.

To begin to make the case, it will be helpful to turn first to Ladyman and Ross's reading of the Husserlian/Heideggerean legacy to see how they place it within an understanding of the history of philosophy. Put bluntly, Ladyman and Ross argue that both Husserl and Heidegger are ultimately engaging in a form of "philosophical anthropology" that is not "interested in objective truth." In other words, the efforts of Husserl and Heidegger may be illuminating with respect to our human experience of the world, but they are not, in the end, capable of revealing the true, objective nature of reality; only the sciences, Ladyman and Ross argue, and physics in particular, can do that. Their argument is not with Heidegger in particular but, as they put it, "with philosophers who claim to share this interest [in objective truth], but then fail properly to pay attention to our basic source of information about objective reality"— namely, as Ladyman and Ross will go on to argue, the findings of our best contemporary physics.[3] The Husserl-based argument will be resumed shortly, when beginning to build a Deleuzian case in defense of philosophy, but it should first be noted that there are others who are arriving, albeit by different means, at similar conclusions to those reached here. For example, Michael Della Rocca, L. A. Paul, Eric Schliesser, and others have all argued that philosophy has a role that is quite distinct from science and a role that is essential to science without being subservient to it.[4] In the argument to be made here, following Deleuze, it is philosophy's distinctive task to create concepts for addressing the problematic, indeterminate nature of reality and thus to provide the resources for thinking through aspects of reality that are not available to those who rely strictly on the resources of the natural sciences. Philosophy may well draw from the resources of the sciences, as I have argued elsewhere,[5] but the philosophical concepts, problems, and efforts to which such resources contribute are irreducible to the work of the natural sciences. This distinctive role for philosophy becomes especially evident at times when established ways of thinking about reality, or when established scientific as well as moral practices, are in flux, and both Hume and Whitehead provide indispensable resources for thinking through such times.

There is a historical narrative that is frequently told in order to support the claim that philosophy has nothing special or distinctive to say about reality and that ultimately it is and ought to be subordinate to the sciences, which does have something legitimate to say. This history is in many ways the history of the modern world—the world, as the standard narrative tells us, that turned in the beginning of the seventeenth century away from the sacred and the speculative toward the secular and the empirical. Although moving at times in fits and starts, this turn was definitive and inexorable, and one result has been that philosophy has come to be seen as inextricably tied to science. Ladyman and Ross place their book, *Every Thing Must Go,* within this historical narrative, and they place Hume at the center of their narrative!

> This book is not hostile to metaphysics; indeed, it is an exercise in metaphysics. However, we think that the kind of intellectual atmosphere that led Hume, and later Russell, the Vienna Circle, and Reichenbach, to denounce whole leading branches of the philosophy of their times as scholastic have arisen again [*sic*]. It seems, inductively, that such moments recur endemically in the discipline.[6]

Since the time of Descartes's efforts to align philosophy with the natural sciences, philosophy frequently and endemically loses its way and gets lost within the echo chamber of philosophers arguing with one another while forgetting that there "is an important source of opinion besides rational arguments."[7] Hence the need for the philosophical heroes of this modernist narrative: Hume, Russell, Carnap, and Reichenbach.

In the case of Hume, again as the modernist narrative tells us, it was the rationalist "intellectual atmosphere," and its presumption to attain a priori knowledge about the world, that led Hume to attempt, in his *Treatise,* to employ the experimental methods of science as exemplified in the work of Newton. For Russell, it was the predominance of idealist philosophy at the turn of the twentieth century, and in particular the philosophy of Bradley, that led both Russell and G. E. Moore to advocate, respectively, a realist and common-sense philosophy that was better attuned to the findings and methods of science. Carnap and the Vienna Circle emerged as a reaction against the then-perceived dominance within German philosophy of Husserlian phenomenology, and Heidegger in particular. (Carnap's oft-cited critique of Heidegger is frequently offered as evidence of the nonsensical, misguided path of Heidegger.)[8]

This essay lacks the space to explore the recent findings that complicate the historical narrative within which Ladyman and Ross place their book. But it is worth mentioning that the reactions of Russell and Carnap, for example, to the "atmosphere" of their day are much more complex than the modernist narrative would lead one to believe. Michael Della Rocca, for one, has shown how the Russellian move against Bradley was problematic because it rejects the principle of sufficient reason, and moreover this Russellian move is not wholly endorsed by the analytic tradition itself (Della Rocca argues that Quine's arguments against the analytic-synthetic distinction have a Bradleyan flavor to them in that they rely on the principle of sufficient reason).[9] In the case of Carnap's rejection of the philosophy of Heidegger (and the late Husserl and by extension the continental tradition of philosophy as a whole), Abraham Stone has shown that the famous critique of Heidegger's passages from his *Introduction to Metaphysics,* especially the "nothing that nihilates" passage, were not simply cursory dismissals of Heidegger's project. To the contrary, Stone shows, the criticism is a conclusion Carnap reaches after a very deep engagement with problems Carnap saw as common to himself and Heidegger, with Carnap ultimately disagreeing only with the manner in which these problems were addressed.[10]

Both Della Rocca's and Stone's historical accounts of the reaction of Russell and Carnap against the "intellectual atmosphere" of their day show that Russell and Carnap both continued in many ways to work through the problems that were central to that very "intellectual atmosphere." For Russell and Bradley, as Della Rocca tells it, this was the problem of accounting for relations. For Bradley, the relation between thought and the object of thought cannot be justified or given sufficient reason, and therefore he does away with this relation, whereas Russell maintains the relation, but to do so, he does away with the principle of sufficient reason. For Carnap and Heidegger, the problem is to maintain the spirit of Kant's project while doing away with some of its problematic notions, such as the *Ding an sich,* and as they develop their respective approaches, the difference between them boils down to the problem of determining "what constitutes a responsible and therefore clear and significant use of language."[11]

As one unpacks the historical details of the problems that motivated the heroes of the modernist narrative, one finds that while it may be accurate to say that the reaction to the "intellectual atmosphere" of the day did entail a "return" to the ways of natural science, accompanying this return was an active philosophical engagement with problems that motivated approaches that were then left behind by the turn to science. What was left behind was the philosophical engagement with problems that are irreducible to the methodologies and practices of the sciences. A consequence of this philosophical engagement is the creation of concepts that address concerns that are distinctively philosophical and thus give to philosophy a task that is both independent from and ultimately essential to science.

To begin clarifying the distinctive nature of philosophy, it will be useful to turn to the first of the heroes listed in Ladyman and Ross's modernist narrative—Hume. By returning to Hume we will find Hume tackling a problem that will be shared, I argue, by those who argue for scientism and by those who call for the independence of philosophy. In short, Hume's problematic, or what I will call, following Husserl, the *constitutional problem,* is precisely what makes possible the contestable difference between a philosophy that is the subservient handmaiden to science and a philosophy that is not, and it is this difference that underlies much of post-Kantian philosophy. By returning to Hume, therefore, I will argue that scientism is a neo-Kantian solution to a Humean philosophical problem, and by exploring alternative approaches to this problem—namely, those of Husserl, Whitehead, and Deleuze—I will show that there is an equally important role for philosophy—namely, that of being a creator of concepts—that is irreducible to science and yet essential to our understanding of reality and hence to science itself.

Beginning with Husserl may seem to be an unlikely place to establish a connection with Hume. After all, Husserl sought to establish a transcendental philosophy that would provide a secure foundation for the sciences, and his neo-Kantian move to base this philosophy on the pure "transcendental ego" would seem to be moving in a diametrically opposite direction from Hume. Moreover, to connect Hume and Husserl would appear to conflate Husserl's *philosophical* task, especially given the metaphysical status of the pure transcendental ego for Husserl (or the *lebenswelt* in his late writings), with Hume's *scientific,* experimental efforts. Such a conflation, when it comes to Husserl, is common, however, and has been noted from the beginning when Dorion Cairns, for example, who was one of Husserl's prominent students in the 1920s, criticized Sidney Hook's account of Husserl's project for being guilty of such conflation.[12]

Cairns's critique of Hook is significant for a number of reasons. First and foremost among them is that Cairns was intimately connected to the historical context discussed above—namely, the resurgence of realism as a counter to the then-dominant atmosphere of idealism as found in the work of Bradley. When Dorion Cairns entered Harvard University as an undergraduate in 1919, he became a protégé of Raphael Demos, who was close friends with Bertrand Russell and a proponent of Russell's form of realism. The chair of the department, Ralph Barton Perry, was also a strong proponent of the new realism and was one of six signatories to the important 1910 "Program and First Platform of Six Realists,"[13] which was the manifesto for the new realists and anticipated in many ways the manifesto of the Vienna Circle.[14] Key to the "program" and "platform" of the six realists was the desire to align philosophy with the methodological approach of the sciences, or, as they stated it, the "hope [is] to develop a common technique, a common terminology, and so finally a common doctrine which will enjoy some measure of authority which the natural sciences possess."[15] While a student, Cairns had heard Husserl mentioned favorably as being among the realist philosophers, and a philosopher Russell particularly liked.[16] With his interest piqued, Cairns pursued graduate study with Husserl from 1924 to 1926, and again in 1931; this work resulted in his 1933 dissertation and was subsequently published as *The Philosophy of Edmund Husserl* (Harvard University Press, 1933).

When Cairns offered his assessment of Hook's 1930 "impression" of German philosophy, and of Husserl in particular, it was as a Husserl expert. Cairns begins his response by citing a long passage in which Hook argues, among other things, that Husserl's phenomenological call for researchers to "keep their eyes on the object" results in phenomenology being "the strongest analytical group in Germany and closest to the English and American school of neo-realism."[17] Hook, in other words, accepted Husserl as a neorealist, as someone in line with Russell's and the American neorealists' positions. Husserl, on Hook's account, would be one of the heroes of scientism. While Cairns, like Hook, had initially been told that Husserl was a realist, years of studying with Husserl had led Cairns to a very different conclusion about Husserl.

Cairns argues that Hook's neorealist formulation, "keeping one's eyes on the object," is a bad definition of the phenomenological method, for it is not "the mere object, but the subjective act with its intentional correlate as such [the *noematic correlate* as it comes to be called by Husserl], which is the fundamental datum."[18] Hook thus conflates Husserl's phenomenological project with that of the natural sciences; Cairns accuses Hook of treating Husserl's phenomenology as merely a "logicized psychology" (or "a logicized version of pre-Lockean psychology" as Hook puts it).[19] Whereas psychology "deals with the actual nature of existent minds," Cairns points out that phenomenology "deals with the necessary nature of acts, quite apart from the reality or unreality of their exemplifications."[20] Hook reads Husserl's methodology as scientific, and in a naïve realist sense where this means, for Husserl, that the sciences presuppose "a universe of constituted transcendencies."[21] Such a reading is understandable if one assumes, as Hook does, following Cairns' Harvard mentors, that Husserl is to be placed among the new realists and that his philosophical project accepts the neorealists' call to develop a methodology with "a common technique, a common terminology, and so finally a common doctrine which will enjoy some measure of that authority which the natural sciences possess."[22]

To some extent Hook's reading is defensible. Husserl certainly understood transcendental phenomenology to be a "genuine science," but this is because the problem for phenomenology, as Cairns well knew, is not a matter of best developing a methodology and terminology to address "constituted transcendencies," but rather it is the problem of the *constitution* of these transcendencies themselves that is central to Husserl's project. Husserl thus sought to develop phenomenology as the "genuine science" that is presupposed by all the natural sciences, whereas Hook and the Harvard school saw it as continuous with them.

Hook, in other words, remained captive to what Husserl refers to as the naïveté of the natural attitude, when it is the task of phenomenology to detail the constitutive acts of consciousness, regardless of the reality or unreality of the objects being constituted. Returning now to the modernist narrative, and to Ladyman and Ross's placement of Hume at the head of its pantheon of heroes, it appears that it may be quite inappropriate to associate Hume with Husserl, as is indeed what I argue. Is not Hume, as the modernist narrative tells us, calling for an embrace of the natural attitude, and its attendant scientific realism, when the key move of phenomenology is to bracket the natural attitude altogether and thus not take into consideration the reality or unreality of the constituted objects but rather the constitutive processes themselves? In short, how could Humean empiricism, with its embrace of the natural attitude, be reconciled with the phenomenological bracketing of the natural attitude?

The problems just highlighted begin to vanish, however, when one looks at the historical narrative Husserl himself offered as part of the rationale behind the development of phenomenology. As Husserl understands it, an important part of phenomenology's impetus was its effort to grapple with a problem that Husserl claimed was discovered by Hume, and a problem that was central to Hume's own project. Husserl refers to this as the "universal concrete problem of transcendental philosophy," which is the "'constitutional' problem of accounting for how the transcendence of beliefs [in causal necessity, for instance] can be constituted solely on the basis of the givens immanent to the mind."[23] Thus, in Hume's *Treatise,* the problem was one of taking "the repetition of perfectly similar instances [that] can never alone give rise to an original idea," and then show how an original idea, such as the idea of causal necessity, came to be.[24]

For Husserl, however, Hume did not develop the full implications of the "constitutional" problem and did indeed remain captive to the naïveté of the natural attitude and its embrace of "naturalistic sensualism" when he failed to grasp the essential constitutive relationship between the data of sensualism and an intentional consciousness. According to Husserl, Kant did not make this mistake and went to great lengths to address the "concrete problem of transcendental philosophy" by showing how the very objects of experience presuppose certain pure concepts of the understanding. By recognizing the importance of such pure concepts, Husserl argues—unlike the empiricists such as Hume, who thought of formal logic "as mostly a worthless scholastic survival"—that Kant's approach rehabilitated the legitimacy of formal logic. And yet Kant, Husserl claims, "asked no transcendental questions about formal logic."[25] In short, what is needed, according to Husserl, is both a formal logic and a transcendental logic. Kant did the former but not the latter, whereas Husserl did both.

The last major piece of the historical puzzle that set the stage for Husserl's own project was Brentano's discovery of the intentionality of consciousness. Whatever the transcendent unities and objects of consciousness may be, whether formal or empirical, they are all related to the consciousness that is the consciousness of these unities, or consciousness simply is the consciousness of something. But even Brentano had not gone quite far enough, according to Husserl. Although Brentano discovered the importance of the intentionality of consciousness, there was "no unraveling of the intentionalities involved, no uncovering of the 'multiplicities' in which the 'unity' becomes constituted."[26] In other words, we are back to Hume's "constitutional" problem of accounting for the constitution of unities from amidst a multiplicity of intentionalities.

A case can indeed be made, then, that Husserl should be correctly linked with Hume, but not for the reasons Hook might have offered—namely, that both Husserl and Hume exemplify realist reactions to the anti- or nonscientific philosophical atmosphere of the day. As we have begun to see, what connects Hume and Husserl is the shared problematic, the constitutional problem, and not only does this problematic not fit snugly within the modernist narrative as told by Ladyman and Ross (among others), but it also problematizes key presuppositions of this narrative. To begin to see how this is so, I will turn now to a discussion of Whitehead, and then follow this up with a discussion of Deleuze. A consequence of these discussions will be a history of modern philosophy that is a viable alternative to the modernist story that is so widely accepted among those who accept the vision for philosophy that scientism proposes. In short, I will outline a tradition of Humean phenomenology that includes Husserl, Whitehead, and Deleuze (and given enough time, it could be shown to have roots in Spinoza).

Whitehead might initially seem to be even more strongly aligned with the early twentieth-century neorealists than Husserl. After all, Whitehead cowrote *Principia Mathematica* with Russell, a book that would be a profound influence upon the Vienna Circle and Carnap's *Aufbau* in particular.[27] Without venturing too far into the history of Whitehead's intellectual development, and the extent to which Whitehead departed from his early work with Russell, one can say that it is clear that by the time of the publication of *Process and Reality* (1929) Whitehead had developed a metaphysics that draws from Hume in a way that connects along important lines with the work of Husserl and Deleuze.

Stated baldly, the central problem of *Process and Reality* is the constitutional problem that preoccupied Husserl, and even with Whitehead, there appear a series of "critiques" of the historical tradition that mirror Husserl's. As Husserl criticized Hume, Kant, and Brentano for not fully embracing the constitutional problem, so too does Whitehead embrace the constitutional problem and see a crucial part of his metaphysical project as being the task of critique.[28] More precisely, Whitehead argues that unities are derivative of a constitutional process, and he criticizes philosophical positions that make the derivative *(unities)* primary and the primary *(process)* derivative. This is, for example, exactly Whitehead's critique of Hume. As Whitehead puts it,

> Our bodily experience is primarily an experience of the dependence of presentational immediacy upon causal efficacy. Hume's doctrine inverts this relationship by making the causal efficacy, as an experience, dependent upon presentational immediacy. (*PR*, 176)

Key to unpacking Whitehead's criticism of Hume is to understand how Whitehead sees "presentational immediacy" being derived from a "causal efficacy." The first thing to note is that Whitehead does not call for a scientific account of experience, one that accounts for the "presentational immediacy" of conscious experience in terms of determinate causal factors (biological, neurological, etc.). The crucial concept Whitehead develops *(creates)* to account for "presentational immediacy" is *prehension,* and Whitehead is quite forthright that this account is not one founded on firsthand experience (that is, in terms of presentational immediacy): "But prehensions in the mode of presentational immediacy are among those prehensions which we enjoy with the most vivid consciousness. These prehensions are late derivatives in the concrescence of an experient subject" (*PR,* 162). In other words, the prehensions of presentational immediacy, the evidence of firsthand experience, are derivative of more fundamental prehensions that allow for the possibility of the experient subject itself as well as this subject's determinate, identifiable experiences.

To understand the relationship between the prehensions that take on the "mode of presentational immediacy" and those prehensions from which they derive, it is important to see the manner in which Whitehead believes that his project involves "extending and rigidly applying Hume's principle, that ideas of reflections are derived from actual facts" (*PR,* 40). As Hume sets forth the difference between impressions and impressions of reflection early in his *Treatise,* he claims that the first "kind arises in the soul originally, from unknown causes . . . [and] the second is derived in a great measure from our ideas."[29] As an example, Hume offers that the "idea of pleasure or pain, when it returns upon the soul, produces the new impressions of desire and aversion, hope and fear, which may properly be called impressions of reflexion, because derived from it."[30] For Whitehead, however, the "actual facts" from which the impressions of reflection are ultimately derived are not facts as self-contained identities and existents. Whitehead repeatedly criticizes Hume for beginning with such self-completed identities, what he calls the "full Positivist doctrine of Hume," whereby "every impression of sensation is a distinct existence" (*AI,* 129, 125). This criticism follows naturally from Whitehead's working premise, which is that what is ultimate is "process" rather than "facts"; unfortunately, much of Western philosophy (though not Eastern, Whitehead notes) has put facts before process (*PR,* 7). For Whitehead, by contrast, the "ultimate facts of experience are actual entities, prehensions, and nexus. All else is, for our experience, derivative abstraction" (*PR,* 20).

To detail what Whitehead means by an "actual entity," and how it is to be contrasted with "facts," would take far too much space to cover in this essay, for it is one of the central tasks of *Process and Reality* as a whole to elaborate this distinction and to make the case that the ultimate is process or "creativity," while completed, distinct facts are abstractions. We can, however, by continuing to focus on Whitehead's reaction to and extension of Hume's project, gain an illuminating window on Whitehead's project and in turn prepare the way for a discussion of Deleuze. Whitehead does indeed reject aspects of Hume's approach, as we saw, but he argues that Hume will, almost despite himself, do much to prepare the way for the philosophy of organism that Whitehead pursues in *Process and Reality.* For example, while claiming that each impression has a "distinct existence," Whitehead argues that it is significant that Hume then goes on and "clothes each impression with force and liveliness," adding that it "must be distinctly understood that no prehension, even of bare sensa, can be divested of its affective tone, that is to say, of its character of a 'concern' in the Quaker sense. Concernedness is of the essence of perception" (*AI,* 180). The reference to the Quaker use of the term "concern" is telling. As Quakers use the term, a concern is an "urgent interest, implicitly God-given," to take on a particular action or service, and this is to be contrasted with a notion that does not prompt such a crusade or calling, or it is a concern that does not survive rigorous testing.[31] As a concern a prehension is thus an affective or subjective feeling that calls for a realization, for a bringing into being. What this affective feeling or prehension is bringing into being, however, is the subject of the feeling itself; or, as Whitehead makes clear, actual entities share with God the character of self-causation, which for Whitehead is simply another way of saying that "an actual entity feels as it does feel in order to be the actual entity which it is" (*PR,* 222).

This coming to be of an actual entity entails a process of prehending a substantive multiplicity of eternal objects as well as other actual entities. By "substantive multiplicity" what is meant is that eternal objects do not constitute a determinate and predetermining set of entities (neither a predetermining unity nor multiple).[32] "Eternal objects" is the term Whitehead uses instead of the traditional term "universal," and "actual entity" is what he uses instead of "particular."[33] The reason Whitehead departs from the use of the term "particular" is that a particular has generally (but falsely) come to be thought of "as being just its individual self with no necessary relevance to any other particular" (*PR,* 50). By contrast, for Whitehead, "if we allow for degrees of relevance, and for negligible relevance, we must say that every actual entity is present in every other actual entity" (*PR,* 50).[34] Whitehead similarly breaks with the traditional understanding of universals whereby they too are thought of in the manner of abstract particulars that are unrelated to other universals. On the one hand, Whitehead does continue to think that "each eternal object is an individual," and that this "particular individuality is the individual essence of the object, and cannot be described otherwise than as being itself," and therefore the "[eternal] object in all modes of ingression is just its identical self" (*SMW,* 159). On the other hand, Whitehead is quite clear in arguing that an "eternal object, considered as an abstract entity, cannot be divorced from its reference to other eternal objects" (*SMW,* 159). Eternal objects are thus related to one another, or each eternal object has what Whitehead calls a "relational essence," and the prehension of eternal objects as well as of other actual entities results in what Whitehead calls the "ingression" (or "participation" in deference to Plato) of the eternal objects into the processual nature of an actual entity (*SMW,* 160). With respect to any actual entity (or actual occasion, the terms being synonymous for Whitehead),[35] there is an indeterminate relationship between the eternal objects and actual entities. In other words, the eternal objects do not predetermine the manner in which they will be actualized (or ingressed) within an actual entity, but as prehended in the actualization of an actual entity, the eternal object constitutes the determinate, identifiable nature of an actual entity.[36] In other words, Whitehead's theory of the prehension of eternal objects is an attempt to account for the emergence of a new, identifiable entity without presupposing the identities that would determine this entity; that is, Whitehead is addressing the "constitutional" problem.

Whitehead's version of the constitutional process is not carried out by way of any "regulative principle," and thus Whitehead breaks with the Kantian approach of calling upon the pure concepts of the understanding to provide the rules for the synthesis of the manifold or multiplicity of data. Whitehead would also reject Husserl's claim that the constitutive processes are ultimately grounded in a pure, transcendental ego.[37] In the cases of Kant and Husserl, the Humean "constitutional" problem is abandoned because unity and identity are assumed in the very account of the constitution of unity and identity themselves. This is why the self-cause of actual entities is so important to Whitehead, for in this way we do indeed have process or creativity as the ultimate, and the unities and identities of facts are derivative. It is thus in the process of the prehension of eternal objects as indeterminate substantive multiplicity, and the resulting self-constitution of an actual entity, that a regulative rule comes into being in accordance with this self-constitution. As Whitehead puts it, "these data [namely, eternal objects and actual entities] in their own separate natures do not carry any regulative principle for their synthesis. The regulative principle is derived from the novel unity which is imposed on them by the novel creature in process of constitution" (*AI,* 255).

It appears then that Whitehead has fully embraced the Humean problematic—namely, to account for the emergence of order and identity without presupposing order and identity. Even God, Whitehead argues, "is not to be treated as an exception to all metaphysical principles, invoked to save their collapse. He is their chief exemplification" (*PR*, 343). In other words, God is to be understood according to the same metaphysics as are all other actual entities and are not taken by Whitehead to be a presupposed, already completed identity that forestalls the collapse of becoming into chaos. Nonetheless, God provides what you might call the formal impetus of all actual entities, and an impetus that ultimately does stave off the veering of process into chaos. "God," Whitehead argues, "is the principle of concretion; namely, he is that actual entity from which each temporal concrescence receives that initial aim from which its self-causation starts" (*PR*, 244). It is at this point where we find Whitehead wavering in his commitment to what has been identified as the Humean problematic. Towards the end of *Process and Reality*, Whitehead claims that the "universe includes a threefold creative act composed of (1) the one infinite conceptual realization, (2) the multiple solidarity of free physical realizations in the temporal world, (3) the ultimate unity of the multiplicity of actual fact with the primordial conceptual fact" (*PR*, 346). In fleshing out his claim that reality is the marriage of opposites, of God and World, eternal and temporal, Whitehead contends that actual entities occur in the middle realm between God and World—or stated more precisely, that actual entities are nothing less than the process that involves both the infinite conceptual realization of eternal objects and their physical realizations in the temporal world. But these realizations as process and creativity are "free"—they are not predetermined—and hence there is the potential for chaos, for a becoming that becomes cancerous and disorderly, or for one that becomes stifling and overly stratified. Coming to the rescue, however, according to Whitehead, is "the patience of God, tenderly saving the turmoil of the intermediate world by the completion of his own nature" (*PR*, 346). There are thus two related senses in which Whitehead's metaphysics does not fully embrace the Humean problematic. First, God is the exemplary actual entity that provides the "initial aim" from which the temporal concrescence of self-causing actual entities gets its start; and secondly the "completion of God's nature" assures an orderly world of actual entities.

Whitehead thus follows through on his claim to "construct a critique of pure feeling, in the philosophical position in which Kant put his critique of Pure Reason" (*PR*, 113). Whereas Kant, according to Whitehead, presupposes an "orderliness of feeling" in his account of how the impressions come to be synthesized by way of the transcendental aesthetic, Whitehead provides a critique that accounts for the constitution of the orderliness of feelings themselves. But a constitutive process inseparable from the self-constitution of actual entities, and a process guided by the feelings and concern of the prehensions of the actual entity, are nonetheless intimately connected to a guarantor of successful realization—namely, God. With this move, we see that despite a significant return to and use of Hume in the development of his metaphysics— and a metaphysics that gives a distinctive place to philosophy—Whitehead does not fully embrace the Humean project as it is sketched here in this essay. Turning now to Deleuze, we will find that he too was working within the Humean problematic, but in a way that is perfectly consistent with Whitehead's project.

It is generally recognized among Deleuze scholars that *Difference and Repetition* is probably Deleuze's most significant contribution to philosophy. It was, as Deleuze himself admits, the first time he sat down to do philosophy rather than comment on and think through other philosophers. Central to his philosophy are two key concepts: difference and repetition (unsurprisingly!). As for the concept of difference, Deleuze argues in the 1994 English edition preface that "All that I have done since, including what I wrote with Guattari," has consisted in attempting to avoid what "the majority of philosophers had done," which was to subordinate "difference to identity or to the same"; his task, instead, was to think difference in itself. This theme has been covered quite thoroughly in the literature.[38] The other concept, repetition, has not been discussed nearly as much.[39] For the purposes of this essay, however, this concept is crucial, for not only does Deleuze begin his chapter on repetition with an analysis of Hume, but Whitehead's most pressing criticism of Hume is that Hume failed to fully grasp the significance of repetition, despite relying on it implicitly. More importantly, Whitehead also went on to argue that "In the organic philosophy the notion of repetition is fundamental" (*PR*, 137).

With the very first sentence of the second chapter of *Difference and Repetition,* "Repetition for Itself," Deleuze begins with another Humean problematic, and with the "famous thesis" that was the result of Hume's efforts to address the problem. As Deleuze states the thesis, "Repetition changes nothing in the object repeated, but does change something in the mind which contemplates it"[40] As Deleuze goes on to lay out the problem, we are confronted with a repetitive series, AB, AB, AB, AB, and then when next confronted with A, the problem is one of accounting for why we come to expect B when there is nothing in the nature of A itself that would lead us to this expectation. As Hume famously presents the problem in the *Treatise,* after a series of repetitions of AB, we come to have the "idea of a cause and effect, of a necessary connexion of power, of force, of energy, and of efficacy,"[41] and it is this power that connects, in our minds, A and B. The question for Hume is why this happens, for, he argues

> The repetition of perfectly similar instances can never *alone* give rise to an original idea, different from what is to be found in any particular instance. . . . Since therefore the idea of power is a new original idea, not to be found in any one instance . . . it follows, that the repetition *alone* has not that effect, but must *discover* or *produce* something new, which is the source of that idea.[42]

The repetition of AB in itself does not produce a new original idea, but it does produce something in the mind. The repetition of "the shock of two billiard balls," for instance, involves distinct, separable instances of AB. Each break of the rack is a distinct, separable instance, and the repetition in itself of each break "can never," Hume claims, "produce any new quality in the object," and yet, he adds, "the observation of this resemblance produces a new impression in the mind."[43] And thus we come to Hume's famous thesis.

Although Whitehead accepts Hume's move toward placing the origin of a new idea within the mind rather than in the repeating elements themselves—or more precisely that this occurs within the subjective forms of prehension—Whitehead nonetheless finds Hume's account inconsistent and plagued with circular reasoning. As Whitehead understands Hume's project, Hume is concerned both with accounting for how a multiplicity of simple impressions and ideas become a unified complex idea—that is, the "constitutional" problem—and with seeking, as Whitehead puts it, "a standard of propriety by which to criticize the production of ideas" (*PR,* 133). And the sole standard of propriety Hume has at his disposal, Whitehead claims, is repetition: "the more often impressions are repeated, the more proper it is that ideas should copy them" (*PR,* 133). Thus when we come to the idea of "cause and effect," the propriety of this idea lies not in the power of the imagination to associate and connect A and B, but the repetitions of AB. Echoing Hume, Whitehead recognizes that "this manner of connection [between A and B] is not given in any impression. Thus the whole basis of the idea, its propriety, is to be traced to the repetition of impressions" (*PR,* 134). It is at this point that Whitehead charges Hume with circular reasoning:

> Hume's argument has become circular. In the beginning of his *Treatise,* he lays down the 'general proposition': "That all our simple ideas in their first appearance, are derived from simple impressions, . . ." He proves this by an empirical

> survey. But the proposition itself employs—covertly, so far as language is concerned—the notion of 'repetition,' which itself is not an 'impression.' (*PR*, 135)

By relying covertly on an idea that is not derived from a simple impression—namely, repetition—Hume's philosophy is ultimately inconsistent in its foundations, and then the reasoning becomes circular when the appeal to custom and habit presupposes this foundation. For as Whitehead concludes, "It is difficult to understand why Hume exempts 'habit' from the same criticisms that applied to the notion of 'cause.' We have no 'impression' of 'habit,' just as we have no 'impression' of 'cause.' Cause, repetition, habit are all in the same boat."[44] What Hume ought to have done instead was to make explicit the role of the continuity of the subjective forms of experience, forms that rely upon repetition. "Experience," Whitehead claims, "involves a becoming, that becoming means that something becomes, and that what becomes involves repetition transformed into novel immediacy" (*PR*, 136).

Deleuze believes Hume does thematize becoming in experience, and thus far from launching into a Whiteheadian critique of Hume, Deleuze makes Hume a central figure in the development of his concept of repetition. What is pivotal to Whitehead's critique of Hume is the assumption that repetition is simply the repetition of discrete, separable, individuated elements, A and B, of the sort that figure within the positivist, empirical sciences. For Deleuze, however, there is another repetition at play in Hume's thought, and a repetition closely aligned with Whitehead's own project. First, as Deleuze reads Hume on repetition, he notes that what happens when repetition changes "something in the mind which contemplates it"[45] is that the imagination "contracts cases, elements, agitations or homogenous instants and grounds these in an internal qualitative impression endowed with a certain weight [or what Hume called 'force and vivacity'] . . . a force corresponding to the qualitative impression of all the contracted ABs."[46] This contraction of elements that results in an "internal qualitative impression" is not, as Deleuze makes clear, a matter of memory, nor is it an operation of the understanding. In other words, it is not a matter of a repetition that begins only with the identification of the elements being repeated, remembered, or understood; rather, Deleuze argues that "Properly speaking, it [the contraction of elements] forms a synthesis of time."[47] The syntheses of memory and understanding, the syntheses Whitehead claims are foundational for Hume and which thus leave Hume susceptible to charges of inconsistency and circularity, are more properly to be understood as active syntheses made possible by the passive syntheses of time. Deleuze is clear on this point: "the active syntheses of memory and understanding are superimposed upon and supported by the passive synthesis of the imagination."[48]

To clarify further, Deleuze turns to Bergson's example of repetition, which differs from Hume's in one important respect. Whereas Hume's repetition is of two different elements, A and B, Bergson discusses the repetition of the same element, A. Bergson sets forth the example as follows:

> When the regular oscillations of the pendulum make us sleepy, is it the last sound heard, the last movement perceived, which produces this effect? No, undoubtedly not, for why then would not the first have done the same? Is it the recollection of the preceding sounds or movements, set in juxtaposition to the last one? But this same recollection, if it is later on set in juxtaposition to a single sound or movement, will remain without effect. Hence we must admit that the sounds combined with one another and acted, not by their quantity as quantity, but by their quality which their quantity exhibited, i.e., by the rhythmic organization of the whole.[49]

As Deleuze reads the examples from Hume and Bergson, what we have here is a difference between closed and open repetition. In the case of AB, there is the passive synthesis of elements that results in the qualitative impression, but there is also the containment of the difference between A and B within each particular case, AB, and it is the repetition of cases themselves that opens up to yet another passive synthesis, this time of cases. In Bergson's example, we have the open repetition of A's which involves passive synthesis as the repetition of sounds are combined, to cite Bergson again, "with one another and acted, not by their quantity as quantity, but by their quality which their quantity exhibited." In both Hume's and Bergson's examples, however, we have what Deleuze refers to as a "difference without concept." Whether this be the cases AB or elements A, there is no conceptual difference between them, such as there is between cats and dogs; nor is this a difference intrinsic to the concept such as the difference between springer spaniels and golden retrievers as different types of dogs.[50] But this is a difference between two or more elements that are "represented by the same concept." This is therefore an external difference, a difference understood in terms of the identity of the elements or cases that are repeated. But each repeated element, each repeated case, is the same, the same AB or A, that is differentiated by virtue, Deleuze claims, of the "indifference of space and time," or the passive synthesis of time and thus "the difference is internal to the Idea; it unfolds as pure movement, creative of a dynamic space and time which correspond to the Idea."[51] This is why, Deleuze argues, when addressing Leibniz's famous example of challenging the court women to see whether or not any two leaves of a given tree were identical—that is, whether or not they exemplify the same concept—we are bothered because "the problem is not properly defined so long as we look for the criterion of a principium individuationis in the facts . . . [for] a difference can be internal, yet not conceptual . . . internal differences which dramatize an Idea before representing an object."[52] In other words, the reason we are bothered by Leibniz's example is because we want to claim, contra Leibniz, that the leaves are the same, and yet there is a difference, what Deleuze calls an "internal difference."

At this point we come to one of the central innovations of Deleuze's philosophy of difference, for in his effort to think difference in-itself what emerges as pivotal is precisely the manner in which extensive, objective differences, such as between the leaves, and hence the repetition of these differences, "dramatize an Idea." For Deleuze, therefore, when it comes to repetition, it is important "to distinguish between these discrete elements, these repeated objects [e.g., AB and/or A], and a secret subject, the real subject of repetition, which repeats itself through them . . . the singularity within that which repeats."[53] And Deleuze will refer to this "secret subject," this "repeater" that repeats, as the Idea, and this is in both the Platonic and Kantian sense of the term. It is in the Platonic sense, perhaps surprisingly, if, as Deleuze argues in his "Method of Dramatization" talk,

> we think of the Plato from the later dialectic, where the Ideas are something like multiplicities that must be traversed by questions such as *how? how much? in which case?*, then yes, everything I've said has something Platonic about it. If you're thinking of the Plato who favors a simplicity of the essence or an ipseity of the Idea, then no.[54]

Likewise in the case of Kant, Ideas are understood in a manner similar to the notion of transcendental ideas whereby, for Kant, "although we cannot have any knowledge of the object which corresponds to an idea, we have yet a problematic concept of it."[55] Ideas are thus the problematic concepts without objective solutions, multiplicities that cannot be reduced to a clear and distinct Idea; rather, as Deleuze argues in reference to Leibniz's example of hearing the waves of the sea, what is primary are confused and obscure Ideas:

> Either we say that the apperception of the whole noise is clear but confused (not distinct) because the component little perceptions are themselves not clear but obscure; or we say that the little perceptions are themselves distinct and obscure (not clear): distinct because they grasp differential relations and

> singularities; obscure because they are not yet 'distinguished,' not yet differenciated. These singularities then condense to determine a threshold of consciousness in relation to our bodies, a threshold of differenciation on the basis of which the little perceptions are actualized, but actualized in an apperception which in turn is only clear and confused; clear because it is distinguished or differenciated, and confused because it is clear.[56]

In other words, an Idea as Deleuze understands it is the passive synthesis and fusion—con-fusion—of pre-individual singularities, or the component little perceptions, and the Idea is clear only on the condition of this confusion; and similarly an Idea is distinct only on the condition that the component little perceptions are obscured and filtered from the scene in order to become the distinct, extensive qualities and properties that become the basis for empirical, natural science.

In another variation upon Plato, Deleuze also refers to Ideas as "concrete universals."[57] In giving an example of an Idea as "concrete universal," he offers the Idea of color, which he claims "is like white light which perplicates in itself the genetic elements and relations of all the colours, but is actualized in the diverse colours with their respective spaces; or the Idea of sound, which is also like white noise."[58] What we are to make of this, put briefly, is that the Idea is not a predetermining identity or simplicity of essence that in effect preforms the determinate identities that come to instantiate the Idea (on the model-copy reading of Plato for instance); rather, Ideas as understood from a perspective of Deleuzian Platonism, are concrete universals—a substantive multiplicity—that we get as the intensive variations of colors come to be condensed into a passive synthesis of intensive variations, and a synthesis with a qualitative and intensive power or force. But to think of it this way is not quite right if we take the field of intensive variations to be the result of the condensation of different colors rather than the condition for differentiating among different colors in the first place. Deleuze makes this point quite clearly in an early essay on Bergson when discussing how white light is a concrete universal that we get when

> we send the colors through a convergent lens that concentrates them on the same point: what we have then is "pure white light," the very light that "makes the differences come out between the shades." So, the different colors are no longer objects *under* a concept, but nuances or degrees of the concept itself.[59]

The point is worth repeating: white light is what "makes the differences come out between the shades," and with this move we come to the core of Deleuze's project: an affirmation of the univocity of Being as Difference, or a full embrace of Hume's "constitutional" problematic in that with the Idea we have the difference that makes identifiable differences and unities possible. White light is thus not the combination of all the colors that fall under the abstract concept or Idea of color, with Idea understood as simplicity of essence, but rather the Idea as problematic concrete universal and substantive multiplicity is the very real and concrete condition for the differences between the identifiable colors themselves, and for the extensive spacing that results in the identification of their qualitative properties.

With all this in place, we can see now that the differences of the series AB and A do indeed entail a repetition of the Same, the same AB (including the encapsulated difference between A and B in the *case* AB) and A, but then there is a second difference, a difference that "includes itself in the alterity of the Idea,"[60] or that involves an "internal genesis [that] seems to [Deleuze] to consist of intensive quantity rather than schema, and to be related to Ideas rather than to concepts of the understanding."[61] "One," Deleuze claims, "is repetition in the effect, the other in the cause. One is extensive, the other intensive."[62] And finally, Deleuze claims, the "two repetitions are not independent. One is the singular subject, the interiority and the heart of the other, the depths of the other. The other is only the external envelope, the abstract effect."[63] And with this we return to Whitehead's claim that experience involves a becoming, and the something that "becomes involves repetition transformed into novel immediacy" (*PR*, 137). With Deleuze's extension and reading of Hume, we can see that this is precisely how Deleuze understands repetition. There is in Deleuze's reading of Hume a repetition as cause, as Idea and "internal genesis," and then there is the other repetition that is "only the external envelope, the abstract effect." Whitehead sees only the latter repetition in Hume, while Deleuze sees both.[64]

Returning now to the theme with which this essay began—namely, the modernist narrative as proposed by the proponents of scientism—we can see now that there is an alternative narrative of the philosophical tradition since Hume. This tradition takes as its task the development of concepts in response to what Husserl identified in Hume as the constitutional problem. Husserl, although initially thought to be solidly within the modernist tradition, was in fact integrally engaged with the Humean problematic. Moreover, this engagement led Husserl to develop important philosophical techniques and concepts—for example, the phenomenological method of bracketing the natural standpoint associated with the phenomenological *epoché*, and the concept of the *noema* as the immanent though transcendent correlate of the constitutive acts of consciousness that are the "realities" (or, better, the "phenomena") that constitute the proper field of study, regardless of whether these realities are objectively real or not. A consequence of Husserl's efforts to tackle the Humean problematic is that phenomenology, as Husserl understands it, becomes a philosophical approach quite distinct from the approaches that are to be found among the natural sciences. For example, among the noematic correlates of constitutive consciousness are those values that are irreducible to the objective realities that are the subject of the natural sciences. From a phenomenological perspective, such values are simply one of the examples of the types of noematic correlates to a constituting consciousness and are thus legitimate subjects of study for philosophy. The positivistic sciences, however, largely ignore such objectivities, or leave them to the study of "philosophical anthropology," and it is precisely this displacement of ethics and values by the objective natural sciences that puts science into crisis, which is a theme that would become a dominant concern of Husserl's late in his life.

Despite Husserl's moves in the direction of addressing the Humean problematic, Husserl continued to rely upon a basic unity, the pure transcendental ego, as the condition for the possibility of the constitutive acts of consciousness themselves. A thoroughgoing engagement with Hume's constitutional problem leaves one needing to account for this unity as well; in short, the problem is precisely one of accounting for the synthesis and emergence of identifiable unities without presupposing such an identifiable unity. As we have seen, Whitehead sees in Hume's philosophy a proponent of the "Positivist doctrine," and thus he would likely agree with Ladyman and Ross when they place Hume, along with Russell and Carnap, among the heroes of scientism within the modernist narrative. Hume was nonetheless indispensable for Whitehead because Whitehead found that Hume, despite his explicit positivist claims, was implicitly developing a theory of prehensions and actual entities that Whitehead would then make explicit in his own work. Because Hume did not recognize and develop the theory of prehensions implicit within his own philosophy, Hume was led, Whitehead concludes, into inconsistencies and circular reasoning.

Had Hume recognized the implicit theory of prehensions and actual entities in his own work he would, in short, have become a process philosopher; and a process philosopher is primarily concerned with Hume's constitutional problem. As Whitehead makes clear, the facts so dear to the positivists are simply abstractions that come at the end of processes whereby eternal objects become prehended by and individuated in (or "ingressed," to use Whitehead's term) actual entities. The "actual world," according to Whitehead, "is a process, and the process is the becoming of actual entities"; moreover, these actual entities, as we saw, are self-caused and nothing but the process of becoming themselves (*PR*, 22). Once an actual entity has become completely actualized, it is no more, for to be is to become for Whitehead. Whitehead is clear on this point: "an actual entity has 'perished' when it is complete" (*PR*, 81). As was discussed earlier, eternal objects and other actual entities become the "data" that is prehended by the self-caused becoming of an actual entity. This prehension is characterized by Whitehead as a "concern" in the Quaker sense of the term. In other words, the process of becoming an actual entity is infused with a value and concern that impel the process toward completion, as in a personal crusade (to draw from the Quaker understanding of the concept of *concern*). Moreover, the Quakers identify a concern with a motivating Spirit, a subjective feeling that then gets tested and challenged by other facts and actual entities. If the concern fails such tests, it becomes what the Quakers call a *notion*, or a thought that no longer impels one to complete it. At the heart of Whitehead's metaphysics, therefore—and this distinguishes it in his mind from the positivistic natural sciences, or from scientism as I have argued—is the presence of a qualitative value and concern that is inseparable from each and every actual entity.

Whitehead's response to the Humean problematic did not, however, completely embrace the problematic for it gave privileged status to God's "completed" nature in order to save the constitutional processes of the world from veering into chaos. Thus, despite arguing that God is an actual entity just like any other and subject to the same metaphysics of self-cause, the saving grace of God nonetheless serves as a unity—God's "completed" nature—that assures the successful becomings of the actual world. Deleuze, by contrast, accepts the Humean problematic full stop. As Deleuze himself recognized in the 1994 preface to the English language edition of *Difference and Repetition,* everything he had done since this book has been a continuation of his effort to think identity in terms of difference, or to account for the constitution and synthesis of determinate identities without presupposing identity. Integral to this effort was Deleuze's use of the notion of *Ideas,* understood as problematic or substantive multiplicities. Deleuze also refers to Ideas as concrete universals, and with the example of white light, we saw that white light as a concrete universal is not a determinate, identifiable color, but is rather the condition that makes it possible for one to identify the determinate differences between colors as colors become individuated. This is the sense in which for Deleuze "Ideas are actualized in species and parts, qualities and extensities which cover and develop these fields of individuation."[65] As discussed in the context of

Deleuze's extension of Hume's "famous thesis" regarding repetition, there were two repetitions, as we saw. There was the repetition as cause, as intensive genesis and passive synthesis, and there was repetition as abstract effect, as the bare repetition of abstract qualities and extensities. It is not, however, that there is a repetition holding itself in reserve, a remainder that is in some sense determinately other than the bare repetition of abstract qualities and extensities. To the contrary, and as Deleuze argues, the first repetition "is not hidden by something else but forms itself by disguising itself; it does not pre-exist its own disguises and, in forming itself, constitutes the bare repetition within which it becomes enveloped."[66] It is the latter repetition that becomes the subject of functional equations that map the relationships between determinate entities such that the determinate details of a state of affairs can be related to past and future states of affairs. As David Lewis puts this in discussing "Humean Supervenience," the laws of nature supervene upon a given distribution of determinate facts of the world at a given time, W_1, such that given the same laws and the same distribution of facts, we would have the same distribution of facts at all later times and at all possible worlds, $W_{2, 3, 4}$ . . .[67] For Deleuze, however, although Lewis is quite right with respect to how the sciences understand laws of nature, the scientific understanding of laws of nature relies upon the bare repetition of extensive qualities and properties of determinate facts. This bare repetition is for Deleuze the abstract effect of the intensive repetition, the repetition of Ideas as concrete universals. To the extent that philosophy addresses and draws attention to Ideas understood as concrete universals that are the condition for the possibility of the determinate facts that are the subject of the empirical sciences, or what Deleuze calls "simple empiricism," then philosophy is not reducible to being an empirical science but is rather what Deleuze refers to as "transcendental empiricism." With respect to laws of nature, Deleuze is forthright: "The domain of laws must be understood, but always on the basis of a Nature and a Spirit superior to their own laws, which weave their repetitions in the depths of the earth and of the heart, where laws do not yet exist."[68] It is philosophy, among other intellectual activities perhaps, that draws our attention to matters that science is ill-prepared to address—namely, to matters of the Spirit—and it is the task of attending to these matters, as Husserl and Whitehead also argued, that is the proper concern of philosophers. The modernist narrative of those such as Ladyman and Ross who see Hume as one of the heroes of scientism tells us only one story, and this story relies upon the most abstract and derivative of details; it is to philosophers like Hume, Whitehead, and Deleuze (though we could include many others such as Spinoza and

Nietzsche) where we turn to get the other side of the story, the side with Spirit, with the qualitative and intrinsic values that are inseparable from, and pose a potential problematizing challenge to, the truths the scientists give us.

Notes

1. Stephen Hawking, *The Grand Design* (New York: Bantam Books, 2012), 5.

2. Of the many essays by Russell that one could cite, his 1914 essay "On Scientific Method in Philosophy" offers the most succinct statement of his position. See Bertrand Russell, *Mysticism and Logic and Other Essays* (London: Longmans, Green and Co., 1919).

3. James Ladyman and Don Ross, *Every Thing Must Go* (Oxford: Oxford University Press, 2009), 5. The previous two quotes are also from this page.

4. See Michael Della Rocca, "The Taming of Philosophy," in *Philosophy and Its History,* edited by Mogens Lærke, Justin E. H. Smith, and Eric Schliesser (Oxford: Oxford University Press, 2013): 178–208; L. A. Paul, "The Context of Essence," *Australasian Journal of Philosophy* 82, no. 1 (2004): 170–84; and Eric Scliesser, "Newton's Challenge to Philosophy," *HOPOS: The Journal of the International Society for the History of Philosophy of Science* 1, no. 1 (Spring 2011): 101–28.

5. See my *Philosophy at the Edge of Chaos: Gilles Deleuze and the Philosophy of Difference* (Toronto: University of Toronto Press, 2006), where I argue for the importance of dynamic systems theory in understanding Deleuze's philosophical project. In Deleuze's hands, however, the insights, concepts, and researches of dynamic systems theory come to be used in the development of distinctively philosophical concepts that target distinctively philosophical problems. For more on the dynamic systems reading of Deleuze, see especially the work of John Protevi, Brian Massumi, and Manuel DeLanda.

6. Ladyman and Ross, *Every Thing Must Go,* 26.

7. Ibid.

8. Abraham Stone's "Heidegger and Carnap on the Overcoming of Metaphysics," in *Martin Heidegger,* ed. Stephen Mulhall (Farnham, U.K.: Ashgate, 2006), shows how this traditional story obfuscates the complex and serious engagement between the two thinkers, and the broad areas of agreement and overlap between them.

9. See Della Rocca, "The Taming of Philosophy."

10. See Stone, "Heidegger and Carnap."

11. Ibid., 7. As Stone shows, in important respects Carnap and Heidegger are methodologically and philosophically closer to one another than either is to Husserl, for while Carnap and Heidegger maintain the Kantian rejection of a supersensible being, Husserl, with his pure transcendental ego (as we will see further on in the chapter) does not.

12. Sidney Hook's account was published as "A Personal Impression of Contemporary German Philosophy," *Journal of Philosophy* 27, no. 6 (March 1930): 141–60. Cairn's critique is in "Mr. Hook's Impression of Phenomenology," *Journal of Philosophy* 27, no. 15 (July 1930): 393–96.

13. This manifesto was published in *Journal of Philosophy, Psychology and Scientific Methods* 7, no. 15 (July 1910): 393–401, and the other signatories included Edwin B. Holt, Walter T. Marvin, W. P. Montague, Walter B. Pitkin, and Edward Gleason Spaulding.

14. The Vienna Circle manifesto, *Wissenschaftliche Weltauffassung. Der Wiener Kreis (The Scientific Conception of the World. The Vienna Circle),* was published in 1929 and was dedicated to Moritz Schlick, who was chair of philosophy of the inductive sciences at the University of Vienna and the one who organized the meetings that brought together many of the central figures of the Vienna Circle, including Carnap, whom Schlick brought to Vienna in 1926. The manifesto can be found in Sahorta Sakar, *The Emergence of Logical Empiricism: From 1900 to the Vienna Circle* (New York: Routledge, 1996), 321–40.

15. Edwin B. Hold, et. al., "The Program and First Platform of Six Realists," *The Journal of Philosophy, Psychology and Scientific Methods,* 7, no. 15 (July 21, 1910), 7.

16. As Cairns puts it in his online autobiography, "My Autobiography" 1972 (at http://dorioncairns.net), "It was common in those days for people in the English speaking world to construe Husserl as a realist and in consequence of Russell's highly favorable remarks on Husserl for me to think that I would like to learn more about Husserl." It is unclear what "highly favorable remarks" Cairns is referring to. Cairns claims it was from a piece Russell wrote in the journal *Mind,* but of the pieces written for *Mind,* most notably "On Denoting" (1910) and a number of reviews (many thanks to Michael Kremer for alerting me to these reviews), the glowing praise Cairns alludes to regarding Husserl is lacking. A more likely scenario is that Cairns had heard through the grapevine, probably by way of Raphael Demos, of Russell's positive reaction to Husserl's *Logical Investigations,* which he read while in prison (for protesting World War I), and which he described in a 1920 letter to Husserl (his only known letter to Husserl) as a "monumental work." Cited by David Bell and Neil Cooper, *The Analytic Tradition: Meaning, Thought, and Knowledge* (London: Basil Blackwell, 1990). Original letter is in Husserl Archives, University of Louvain; copy in RA 710.056606-.056506. Location: CaOTV.

17. Hook, "A Personal Impression of Contemporary German Philosophy," 152.

18. Cairn, "Mr. Hook's Impression of Phenomenology," 394.

19. Hook, "A Personal Impression of Contemporary German Philosophy," 152.

20. Cairn, "Mr. Hook's Impression of Phenomenology," 396.

21. Edmund Husserl, *Formal and Transcendental Logic,* trans. Dorion Cairns (The Hague: Martinus Nijhoff, 1969), 251.

22. "Platform of Six Realists," 394.

23. Ibid., 256.

24. David Hume, *A Treatise of Human Nature,* ed. L. A. Selby-Bigge (Oxford: Clarendon Press, 1978), 163 (1.3.14).

25. Husserl, *Formal and Transcendental Logic,* 258.

26. Ibid., 262.

27. For influence of Whitehead on Carap, see Alan W. Richardson, *Carnap's Construction of the World: The Aufbau and the Emergence of Logical Empiricism* (Cambridge: Cambridge University Press, 1997), 7.

28. See Alfred North Whitehead, *Process and Reality:* "But Kant, following Hume, assumes the radical disconnection of impressions qua data; and therefore conceives his transcendental aesthetic to be the mere description of a subjective process appropriating the data by orderliness of feeling. The philosophy of organism aspires to construct a critique of pure feeling, in the philosophical position in which Kant put his Critique of Pure Reason" (113). In other words, what Whitehead seeks to do with his "critique of

pure feeling" is to account for the "orderliness of feeling" rather than presuppose it—in short, Whitehead is cognizant of the constitutional problem.

29. Hume, *A Treatise of Human Nature,* 7.

30. Ibid., 8.

31. For a list of Quaker terms, see http://quakerjane.com/spirit.friends/spirituality-glossary.html#concern.

32. As will be brought out in the text below, Deleuze uses the term "multiplicity," which he gets from Bergson, to contrast it with the one and the multiple (i.e., multiples of one).

33. See *Process and Reality*: "the philosophy of organism admits two ultimate classes of entities, mutually exclusive. One class consists of 'actual entities,' which in the philosophical tradition are mis-described as 'particulars'; and the other class consists of forms of definiteness, here named 'eternal objects,' . . . mis-described as 'universals'" (158).

34. I will discuss this further when examining Deleuze's claim that an Idea as problematic substantive multiplicity is to be thought of as a concrete universal. Deleuze gives the example of white light as one such concrete universal, and understood in this way, we can see that each color is indeed in every other color insofar as all colors are in the concrete universal that is white light.

35. See *Process and Reality:* "In the philosophy of organism 'the soul' . . . [is] replaced by the phrases 'the actual entity,' and the 'actual occasion,' these phrases being synonymous" (141). I shall use the phrase "actual entity" throughout this essay.

36. See *Science and the Modern World,* where *A* is an eternal object and *a* is an actual entity (or occasion): "Thus the general principle which expresses *A's* ingression in the particular actual occasion *a* is the indeterminateness which stands in the essence of *A* as to its ingression into *a,* and is the determinateness which stands in the essence of *a* as to the ingression of *A* into *a*" (160).

37. I am unaware of Whitehead's explicitly leveling this criticism against Husserl. Whitehead was certainly aware of Husserl's work. When Dorion Cairns returned to Harvard after studying for two years with Husserl, Whitehead had joined the faculty and no doubt heard from Cairns about Husserl.

38. See, among others, Bell, *Philosophy at the Edge of Chaos,* and Levi Bryant, *Difference and Givenness* (Evanston, Ill.: Northwestern University Press, 2008).

39. There are notable exceptions: See James Williams' *Gilles Deleuze's Difference and Repetition: A Critical Introduction and Guide* (Edinburgh: Edinburgh University Press, 2003), as well as his *Gilles Deleuze's Philosophy of Time: A Critical Introduction and Guide* (Edinburgh: Edinburgh University Press, 2011).

40. Gilles Deleuze, *Difference and Repetition,* trans. Paul Patton (New York: Columbia University Press, 1994), 70.

41. Hume, *A Treatise of Human Nature,* 162.

42. Ibid., 163.

43. Ibid., 165.

44. Ibid., 163.

45. Deleuze, *Difference and Repetition,* 70.

46. Ibid.

47. Ibid.

48. Ibid., 71.

49. Henri Bergson, *Time and Free Will: An Essay on the Immediate Data of Consciousness,* trans. F. L. Pogson (Mineola, N.Y.: Dover Publications, 2001), 105–106.

50. Deleuze refers to Kant's *Prolegomena to Any Future Metaphysics,* trans. L. W. Beck (New York: Macmillan, 1950). In particular, Deleuze focuses on Kant's discussion in Part One, §13 from the Prolegomena to highlight Kant's own efforts to grapple with the notion of an intrinsic difference.

51. Deleuze, *Difference and Repetition,* 23–24.

52. Ibid., 26. In this passage Deleuze also refers to Max Black's famous example concerning the principle of indiscernibles where he uses two identical spheres whereby there are internal differences without a conceptual difference. See Max Black, "The Identity of Indiscernibles," *Mind* 61 (1952): 153–64.

53. Ibid., 23.

54. Gilles Deleuze, "Method of Dramatization," in *Desert Islands and Other Texts,* trans. Michael Taormina (Los Angeles, Calif.: Semiotext(e), 2004), 116.

55. Immanuel Kant, *Critique of Pure Reason,* trans. Norman Kemp Smith (Boston: Bedford St. Martins, 1965), 327 (A339/B397 [traditional pagination]).

56. Deleuze, *Difference and Repetition,* 213.

57. See ibid., 176.

58. Ibid., 206.

59. Gilles Deleuze, "Bergson's Conception of Difference," in *Desert Islands,* 43.

60. Deleuze, *Difference and Repetition,* 24.

61. Ibid., 26.

62. Ibid.

63. Ibid., 24.

64. For more, see my book *Deleuze's Hume: Philosophy, Culture and the Scottish Enlightenment* (Edinburgh: Edinburgh University Press, 2009).

65. Deleuze, *Difference and Repetition,* 279.

66. Ibid., 24.

67. See David Lewis, *Philosophical Papers II* (Oxford: Oxford University Press, 1987), "Introduction."

68. Deleuze, *Difference and Repetition,* 25.

THREE

What Is the Style of Matters of Concern?

Bruno Latour

> We find ourselves in a buzzing world, amid a democracy of fellow creatures; whereas, under some disguise or other, orthodox philosophy can only introduce us to solitary substances, each enjoying an illusory experience.
> —Alfred North Whitehead, *Process and Reality*

Nature at the Crossroads: The Bifurcation of Nature and Its End

In "A Theological Treatise," Czesław Miłosz offers us a vivid image of what it is like to inhabit the "illusory experience" to which Whitehead says that orthodox philosophy introduces us. After linking the "notion of truth" with poetry, he presents the "behavior" of the latter as that of

> . . . a bird thrashing against the transparency
> Of a windowpane that testifies to the fact
> That we don't know how to live in a phantasmagoria.
> Let reality return to our speech.[1]

And yet we seem to know very well how to live in a phantasmagoria, and it seems more and more difficult to "let reality return to our speech." Why is this so? Probably because we have difficulty associating truth and poetry as Miłosz does. Is it not poetry itself that allows us to "escape" from the harsh truth conditions of referential language? What forces us to suspend belief and disbelief and enjoy the sheer beauty of language, independently, so the formalists say, of any acquaintance, any association with reality? And yet Miłosz asks us to follow the movement of a bird, a bird, he says, that has the strange behavior of "thrashing against the transparency of a windowpane."

This must have happened to you, surely: you hear the fluttering noise of a bird, which by some mistake, some strange conduit, has become a prisoner of the room where you are sitting; desperate to escape, it comes thrashing against the windowpane, which it takes, mistakenly, for the open sky, unaware as it is of the human invention of transparent glass. What do you do then? You try to open the window without frightening the bird.

Can we, too, open the window and follow the poet who directs us to carefully follow the behavior of the bird?

The difficulty of becoming, in effect, the ethology of such behavior, of such a bird, of such poetry, of such an escape toward reality, comes, as I will argue, from a strange philosophy invented somewhere in the seventeenth century, which has made it impossible to "let reality return to our speech."

The diagnosis of this philosophy has been discussed by Alfred North Whitehead under the name of the "bifurcation of nature." "What I am essentially *protesting* against," (emphasis added) he writes,

> is the bifurcation of nature into two systems of reality, which, in so far as they are real, are real in different senses. One reality would be the entities such as electrons which are the study of speculative physics. This would be the reality which is there for knowledge; although in this theory it is never known. For what is known is the other sort of reality, which is the byplay of the mind. Thus there would be two natures, one is the conjecture and the other is the dream. (*CN*, 30)

Now Whitehead was the quietest and the most urbane and polite of philosophers, so when he "protests" you should take that as a typically British understatement and hear instead an ear splitting scream of indignation! Why? Because the result is to make impossible the *truth* of poetry, as well as, as we will see later, the *realism* of science:

> Bodies are perceived as with qualities which in reality do not belong to them, qualities which in fact are purely the offspring of the mind. Thus nature gets credit which should in truth be reserved for ourselves; the rose for its scent; the nightingale for his song; and the sun for his radiance. The poets are entirely mistaken. They should address their lyrics to themselves, and should turn them into odes of self-congratulation on the excellence of the human mind. Nature is a dull affair, soundless, scentless, colorless; merely the hurrying of material, endlessly, meaninglessly. (*SMW*, 54)

In a nature so bifurcated, it is in vain that the nightingale sings: the singing is entirely in our mind, or even in our brain. If we could look directly at nature (I will come back to that way of looking further on), it would be soundless: the throat of the nightingale would simply agitate the air, the waves of which will strike our eardrums, triggering some electric effects in our neurons, and somewhere in the auditory folds of our cortex, a pure invention will emerge that has no correspondence whatsoever with anything of a similar tone in nature: the song of the soundless nightingale.

I do not know if Miłosz's bird, the bird to which he compared the obstinacy of poetry and its will to escape the prison of language, was a nightingale or not. But surely, if Whitehead's diagnosis is right, in the philosophy that has been developed around a bifurcated nature, the bird will come thrashing against a transparent windowpane, and there is not the slightest chance for reality "to return to our speech": the world is made of primary qualities for which there is no ordinary language but that of science—a language of pure thought that nobody in particular speaks and that utters law from nowhere; as to ordinary language, it deals with secondary qualities that have no reality. On the one hand, there is nature, which is real, but is a "dull and meaningless affair, the hurrying of material endlessly"; on the other hand, there is the lived world of colors, sounds, values, meaning, which is a phantasmagoria of our senses but with no other existence than in the circumvolution of our brain and the illusions of our mind.

In this philosophical world, how could we follow Miłosz's appeal if the poets, as Whitehead amusingly suggests, have to devise "odes to themselves"? Far from having the behavior of a bird thrashing against a windowpane, poetry should rather accept its limits and habituate us to "live in phantasmagoria." Instead of behaving as if they could grasp reality, poets should rather help us say things like: "O my temporal lobe how beautiful you are, and you my cochlear nucleus how clever you are to make me hear the nightingale, and you my olfactory bulbs how nice of you to invent the smell of the roses, and you my nicely moist striate cortex, how elegant of you to let me feel the splendor of a sunset when there is nothing more than the connections between my hypothalamus and my cerebellum." Exit the poets, enter the neuroscientists.

And yet Whitehead, even more forcefully than Miłosz, suggests that we had better believe the poets. Even though philosophers have, for three centuries now, tried to make us live in a phantasmagoria, we—I mean we the common-sense folk—have never believed them and have never abandoned the idea of "letting reality return to our speech." But for this obdurate reaction, for this obdurate attempt to escape from the prison of being registered in any way, we first have to redress the bifurcation of nature.

I know this is difficult, so difficult indeed that it might explain why the attempts of Whitehead have been so thoroughly abandoned by most philosophers after him. Actually, he was so well aware of this difficulty that in the preface of *The Concept of Nature* he warned his reader by saying: "It is, perhaps, as well to state explicitly that if the reader indulges in the facile *vice* of bifurcation not a word of what I have here written will be intelligible" (emphasis added *CN,* vii). I am afraid that this warning applies to my essay as well: the difficulties do not come only from what I am going to say—although I am ready to take my fair share of blame—but also because my readers might indulge in the "facile vice" of letting nature bifurcate. And I would say the more philosophically literate you are, the more this vice passes for a virtue, indeed for the greatest virtue of thinking like a philosopher—a modernist philosopher, that is—instead of simply clinging to common sense. (If you complain that you have never indulged in this vice, then think for a moment whether the reason might not be that you take the bifurcation so thoroughly for granted that you have accepted working on *one side* of it without ever realizing that you have abandoned half of what "is given into experience.")

Anyway, it is no exaggeration to say that since the time of Galileo and Locke—the inventors of the distinction between primary and secondary qualities—all the way up to contemporary so-called cognitive science, a large part of what it is to be a philosopher consists in deriding common sense because it believes naively that the nightingale sings, the rose has an odor, the sunset is red, and that reality has never left speech. "Poor folk," we seem to tell them with an amused and condescending smile, "you have forgotten that *no resemblance* exists between primary qualities, the dull and senseless stuff out of which nature is really made, and the secondary qualities with which you add a meaningless and arbitrary meaning to the senseless and meaningless hurrying of matter." Since the time of Locke, philosophers, in the name of what I call the "first empiricism," have forced upon common sense a rather stark choice between *two* types of meaninglessness: either the meaninglessness of senseless but real nature or the meaninglessness of meaningful but unreal values.

Forced to impose this amazing choice, this bifurcation, is it really surprising that philosophy, the bearer of such bad news, goes from crisis to crisis and triggers in ordinary people a sort of well-founded suspicion? "Who are those guys who give me no choice about the way to live except for throwing myself either into 'conjecture' or into 'dream'—that is, into meaninglessness one or meaninglessness two?" And the common folk keep insisting, "Why can't I say that I hear the nightingale, that I smell the rose, and that the sunset is red without, for that reason, losing the science of ethology, the chemistry of odors, and the spectral lines of solar physics?" Would it not be a poor philosopher who would retort to this brave and insistent appeal by saying, "Because you have to learn to live in a phantasmagoria, make the best of it, forget that speech can articulate truth; reality is one thing, meaning another; become adult at last; shut the window and be content to look at the desolate spectacle of the dull world as it is reflected through the fully opaque windowpane of your well-sealed prison."

And yet the bird keeps on having the behavior of thrashing against this windowpane, and the poets are proved right against the philosophers—or, rather, we have to follow those rare philosophers who accept that they must follow the poets in their relentless quest for reality.

How can we do this? Whitehead tells us: by not letting nature bifurcate—that is, by not letting the primary and secondary qualities go their separate ways. The reception of Whitehead's cosmology over the last century is proof enough that this is not an easy matter. So how can I do my little bit to help, with my feeble resources, to make it impossible for philosophy to deride common sense in the way I have just mockingly suggested?

I want to try this impossible feat by tackling the problem via its two opposite ends: the social first, and then the natural.

Imagine the following scene: you are trying to build a bridge over a rather tumultuous river. Let us say that one bank of this river is the "social" and the other, far away, inaccessible, separated by a violent current, by many eddies and dangerous rapids, is the "natural." Now suppose that, instead of trying to cross this river and build this bridge, you decide instead to go with the flow—that is, to get involved in a bit of canoeing, kayaking, or rafting. Then the absence of a bridge is not such a problem. What counts is your ability to equip yourself with the right paraphernalia so that you can go down the river without drowning. You might be scared to get into the turbulent river, you might regret leaving off the task of bridge-building, but you will probably agree that the two riverbanks are bound to look rather different once you apprehend both of them from the point of view of such a kayaking movement forward. This flowing lateral direction, turned at a ninety-degree angle from the obsessive question of bridge-building, is, if I am not mistaken, what William James called "pure experience."

What I invite you to participate in is a little bout of kayaking, or rafting—and also, I am afraid, a bit of drifting. My question is: what will happen if, instead of trying to bridge the distance between words and worlds, we were trying to move sideways along with the various elements that appear to go in the same direction? What would happen to the "senseless hurrying of matter" called nature if we were to go in the same direction? Would it be as senseless as before? What would happen to the so-called secondary qualities if they were viewed as being that which allows us to grasp the other entities with which we keep moving? Would they appear as "secondary," their meaning as devoid of any importance and reality as before? My intuition is rather that the two riverbanks would take on an entirely different meaning and that nature, having stopped bifurcating because of the way we have let it *pass* ("passage of nature" is another of Whitehead's expressions), will be now able to mingle with our speech and other behaviors in many more interesting ways. This is, at least, the way I would advertise the kayak trip before you embark on it—it is for you to tell me at the end if I have committed the sin of false publicity.

So I will here start from one bank, the "social" one, and, in the next section I will start from the other. The social sciences too have their Whitehead: his name is Gabriel Tarde. He lived at the end of the nineteenth century, was first a judge, then a criminologist, and then the most famous sociologist in France.[2] However, his overhaul of French sociology has been even more thoroughly buried than Whitehead's renovation of speculative philosophy. What is of interest for me here is that Tarde, an attentive reader of Darwin and Marx—among countless others—makes no attempt, at any point in his sociology, to distinguish human from natural *societies*—nor does he make, and this is of course important for me, any distinction between social sciences and philosophy, as is clear in his *Monadologie et sociologie* (1895), a book that has had a crucial influence on Gilles Deleuze. I quote:

> this means that every thing is a society and that all things are societies. And it is quite remarkable that science, by a logical sequence of its earlier movements, tends to strangely generalize the notion of society. It speaks of cellular societies, why not of atomic societies? Not to mention societies of stars, solar systems. All of the sciences seem fated to become branches of sociology.[3]

What is important for my purpose here is that Tarde is one of those philosophers *qua* scientists who goes with the flow, moves sideways, does not try to bridge some imaginary gap between a symbolic order—that of humans—and the material world out there. He is out there from the start, moving through the eddies and immersed in the stream of associations (it is not by accident that he was the predecessor of Bergson at the Collège de France since Bergsonian *durée* has obviously some—only some—of the characteristic of the flow I am trying to descend into here).

When Tarde begins with societies and extends the notion to every group of agencies, this does not mean that he is *naturalizing* human societies; he is too much of a reader of Darwin to indulge in any *social* Darwinism, and this for a reason that goes already to the heart of our question: social Darwinism is impossible because organisms are already societies and highly complex ones. Here we begin to see the advantage of *kayaking* over *bridging:* naturalization is what happens when you try to transport, to transfer the "senseless hurrying of matter" from the nature bank to the social or human side. That is when you treat the human with the strange notion of primary qualities handed down to you by an *already* bifurcated nature. It is because of this treatment that humanists of all hues and colors recoil in horror, and rightly so. They clearly see the imposture of treating humans as objects—but what they do not realize is that it is also an imposture to treat *objects* as objects—that is to reduce the maintaining in existence of organisms to the "dull hurrying of nature." What is important to remember is that bifurcation is unfair to *both* sides: to the human and social side as well as to the nonhuman or "natural" side—a point always missed by phenomenologists.

So for now the question is as follows: how do things look when you begin to move sideways and go with the flow? You quickly realize that all societies share some common features: they are never faced with the rather absurd choice of hurrying forward without any sense or of adding meaning without reality—only the bridge-makers are faced with this choice. No, they have another entirely different set of decisions to make: they have to repeat themselves in existence, to oppose one another in order to proceed forward, or to adapt to one another by differing from one another no matter how slightly. "Repetition," "opposition," and "adaptation" are the three "social laws" that are common, according to Tarde, to everything that moves forward in the same direction and that he calls "societies."

But remember that "society" is not a word specifying in advance the *type* of associations—as if human societies were different from plant, plankton, stellar, or atomic societies; instead, it means only that it is necessary to associate with others in order to remain in existence. Contrary to the classical *conatus,* which is the persistence of being through substance, Tarde defines *conatus* as persistence through *difference.* Any society has to "buy," if I may say that, its continuation in existence through the exploration of new types or new degrees of difference. "Exister c'est différer": such is Tarde's redefinition of *conatus.*

> To exist is to differ; difference, in one sense, is the substantial side of things, what they have most in common and what makes them most different. One has to start from this difference and to abstain from trying to explain it, especially by starting with identity, as so many persons wrongly do. Because identity is a minimum and, hence, a type of difference, and a very rare type at that, in the same way as rest is a type of movement and the circle a type of ellipse.[4]

To persist in being, you cannot count on a substance, a substrate behind your properties or qualities that would allow you to subsist indefinitely per *inertia* so to speak. Substance has become *subsistence* not substrate (cf. *SMW,* 108). On the contrary, you have to persist by having new properties in the renewed sense Tarde gives to this tired little word. In an amazing feat of sociological metaphysics, Tarde proposes replacing "being" by "having":

> So far, all of philosophy has been founded on the verb *To be,* whose definition seemed to have been the Rosetta's stone to be discovered. One may say that, if only philosophy had been founded on the verb *To have,* many sterile discussions, many slowdowns of the mind, would have been avoided. From this principle "I am," it is impossible to deduce any other existence than mine, in spite of all the subtleties of the world. But affirm first this postulate "I have" as the basic fact, and then the had as well as the having are given at the same time as inseparable.[5]

See the change of perspective? A philosopher can write *L'être et le néant, Being and Nothingness,* but there is no sense in writing *Having and Nothingness.*

So what does the front line of this current, this stream forward, look like now? It is made up of what could be called "betting organisms having differences among themselves," provided you accept the use of the word "organism" as a synonym of "society,"—that is, provided you extend the difficulty of being to all organisms, to the so-called material, biological ones as well as the so-called social ones. Those betting organisms have *trajectories* that define what they have been and what they might become *if* they manage to persist by exploring enough differences. Sociology (conceived by Tarde as a really general science) becomes the documentation of those trajectories, or those networks, to use my own expression, of what is transported, sent, carried over, enunciated, from one moment to the next, from one site to the next, from one actant to the next.[6]

I hope it is already clear that the relations of a nightingale, the potential mates of the nightingale, the poet, the common listener, and, let us add it now, the bird ethologist outfitted with recording equipment, will be rather different if they are all seen as moving forward, as so many betting organisms, each of them entering into relations in order to *have* enough differences to prolong their existence a bit longer. This shift in the orientation of philosophy, no matter how small, might offer a better chance for the bird to escape from the room inside which, since the beginning of this essay, it has been doing nothing, according to Miłosz, but "thrashing helplessly against the transparent windowpane."

It should also be clear that this type of relation, what Tarde calls "society," is impossible to detect for those who are carrying on the bridge-building engineering feat—and there is no question that it is a feat. This is the sort of change between incompatible viewpoints that relativity theory has rendered familiar to us with its little anecdotes of a falling body viewed from an embankment and the same falling body viewed from the inside of a train carriage. Except here the different accounts are irreconcilable: from the bridge nothing is seen except the passage of a violent stream, which has to be deflected by the building up of sturdy pillars. The only question for the bridge-engineers is to decide whether or not with a word one can reach a reference "out there," on the other bank, in the world. The grave question is to know if one can *escape* the constraints of one social and linguistic limitation in order to jump to the other bank through this *salto mortale*—to use James's mocking expression. This relation, the bridge one, is a zero-sum game: either you are on one bank or you are on the other; the more you remain close to language, the further away you are from reference; the further away you are from the "nature" bank, the freer you have become from the "limitations" of language. But along the flow, many other connections may become possible. This at least is what I am suggesting.

Before we consider some of those intriguing possibilities—the only way, in my view, to "let reality return to our speech"—we have to consider two more crucial inventions made by Tarde in his efforts to redefine sociology. The first is that there is, in fact, a difference between human and nonhuman societies. But it is not what you might think: it is a difference of *numbers* not of kinds; paradoxically, nonhuman societies are much *more* numerous than human societies. There are only nine billion humans, but the smallest stone, the tiniest brain, the humblest table has many orders of magnitude more atoms, neurons, or molecules than the largest human society. Because of their small numbers, we have a much more intimate knowledge of human societies than we have of other nonhuman societies viewed from the outside and so to speak in bulk, or statistically. I quote:

> It means that we experience the sensation of a sentient thing, the volition of a conating thing, and the belief in a believing thing,—the perception, in short, of a personality in which the perceiving personality is reflected, and which the latter cannot deny without denying itself.[7]

Everywhere else, we might believe that there is some superstructure holding things in place: a sort of Body Politik, or at least a whole that is more than the sum of its parts. But not for human societies, viewed from inside: we know for certain that, in this case, the sum is always *less* than the tiniest of its parts. To summarize Tarde's argument: when a society is seen from far away and in bulk, it seems to have structural features—that is, a set of characteristics that floats beyond, or beneath the multiplicity of its members. But when a society is seen from the inside, it is made up of *differences* and of *events* and all its structural features are provisional amplifications and simplifications of those linkages. Do not immediately rule out Tarde as a French madman—and do not rule me out as even madder for resuscitating such an odd way of considering the social sciences. (Tarde, for many years, directed a statistical institute and wished for nothing more than finding the right quantum for a science of the social.)[8]

To render his argument less strange, look at the consequences it has for social theory. Structures, social structure especially, are just the illusion one has to escape to establish a solid sociology:

> This conception is, in fact, almost the exact *opposite* of . . . Monsieur Durkheim's. Instead of explaining everything by the supposed supremacy of a law of evolution, which compels collective phenomena to reproduce and repeat themselves indefinitely in a certain order,—instead of thus explaining lesser facts by greater, and the part by the whole,—I explain collective resemblances of the whole by the massing together of minute elementary acts—the greater by the lesser and the whole by the part. This way of regarding phenomena is destined to work a *transformation* in sociology similar to that brought about in mathematics by the introduction of the *infinitesimal* calculus.[9]

Yes, I know, Tarde was not as lucky as Leibniz: his monadology did not transform sociology as much as the infinitesimal calculus transformed mathematics. But history is still young, and if nature stops bifurcating, Tarde's prediction might still come true.

The reason why it is so important for me to make structural features a local consequence of looking at societies in bulk and from the outside, is that this view is one of the main reasons why philosophy lets nature bifurcate: on the one hand, you have the pulverization of small elements—atoms, humans, situations, acts of language—and on the other hand, you have laws of transformation to which those small elements should conform but to which they contribute no part whatsoever. It is permissible to explain events by appealing to other sets of connections, not to provide the explanations through their own connections with one another and, so to speak, laterally. The case of social theory is only one place where the danger of structural explanation is seen by Tarde as a philosophical imposture:

> The evolutionists of his school [he has Spencer in mind], in thus formulating the laws of linguistic, religious, economic, political, moral, and aesthetic development, understand, at least implicitly, that these laws are capable of governing, not merely the single succession of peoples whose privilege it is to be called historic, but equally well all peoples that have existed or are to exist in the future. But still, in a multitude of forms, though on a smaller scale, the same error always comes to light, namely, the error of believing that, in order to see a gradual dawn of regularity, order, and logic in social phenomena, we must go outside of the details, which are essentially irregular, and rise high enough to obtain a panoramic view of the general effect; that the source and foundation of every social coordination is some general fact from which it descends gradually to particular facts, though always diminishing in strength; in short, that man acts, but a law of evolution guides him."[10]

What is the problem with structure? What does this *topos* or rather cliché of social theory—namely the micro/macro distinction—have to do with our question? Because the link between a structure and some event is what happens to the bridge-builders and not to the kayakers. For the bridge-builders, events are always lacking something—namely, the law of their development, which is always supposed to be *somewhere else*, and this somewhere is either a Platonic idea, or a thought, or a projection, or some law dictating its pronouncements from nowhere. In the same way that in perception, where the mind has to do the work of adding secondary qualities to meaningless primary qualities in order to obtain something that makes sense, so in social sciences—and in science generally—the structure is needed to make the elements have a connection that has been withdrawn first by the divide between agencies:

> This attempt to confine social facts within lines of development which *would compel them to repeat themselves* en masse *with merely insignificant variations,* has hitherto been the chief pitfall of sociology, whether under the more rigid form conceived by Hegel, consisting of successions of triads, or under the more exact and scientific form that it has since received at the hands of the modern evolutionists. . . . It remained to be discovered later that these supposed rules

> are honeycombed with exceptions, and that evolution, whether linguistic, legal, religious, political, economic, artistic, or moral, is not a single road, but a *network* of routes with many intersecting cross-ways. (Emphasis added.)[11]

You might be worried that by going into social theory with Tarde, I have been forgetting our imprisoned nightingale. I hope you understand that I have not left it for a single minute: in the primary/secondary qualities *scenography*—I will explain this term below—the only problem that the bridge-builders could solve was the one of knowing whether or not our sense perceptions were right or misleading or a little bit of both. But in the second scenography, the one I associate with the art of kayaking, rafting—and yes, drifting too—the situation is already entirely different: the nightingale is a society—a society of societies actually[12]—but so is the listener of its song—for instance the poet—and so is the potential mate of the nightingale; and so, as I said, is the ethologist recording the songs and trying to make sense of the present crisis nightingales are going through (more on this in a minute). The first scenography (on the bridge) forces us to be interested in the rather impossible question of the song *an sich;* in the second you might become aware of the relations of all those various societies or organisms *inter se,* to use Whitehead again. The shift from German to Latin is quite considerable. The nightingale bets that it can do something with his song, but so does the poet and so does the bird's mate—and *so does the ethologist.* Relations established between betting and risking organisms—repetition, opposition, and variation—are not the same as those between words (in the plural) and the world (in the singular). New connections are possible—*inter se*—that were impossible, absurd, or simply had no room, in the narrow path and along the only movement allowed on the bridge. To use one of my terms, the various organisms that all go forward may be *articulated* in ways infinitely more varied and surprising than what was available to them when a human mind was trying to look through the transparent windowpane—in the next section of this essay I will propose a genealogy for this pane, which I will extract in part from art history, and particularly from painting.

What are the advantages of going with the flow then?

"Because the first must be first," let us look at poetry. It is now perfectly possible that Miłosz could strike a correspondence with something of the nightingale through the clever use of his unmatched poetry. Do you begin to see the differences between the two scenographies, between the engineering feat of the bridge-builders and what the kayaking people see? For bridge-builders, poets either bridge the gap or else they just live in a phantasmagoria and their metaphor has no reference except in their imagination: what does not clearly lead toward the outside should be placed firmly inside the mind. Not so in the second scenography: the metaphor—and what is a metaphor if not an attempt to drift forward with the rest of the world and get entangled with it in surprising ways—might find itself enmeshed in some surprisingly *accurate* ways with the nightingale's life trajectory. In other words, the poet's metaphor could begin to *correspond* to the nightingale's own experience in betting on life. Yes, finally, a *correspondence theory of truth,* but where correspondence takes on an entirely different meaning from that which is acceptable to the bridge-builders: the poet's metaphorical drift and the nightingale's drift might *co-respond* to one another, that is, involve one another in some of the new differences necessary for them to persist in their being—or rather in their "having." Wouldn't that begin to bring some reality back to our speech?

All the more so, if we could do for science—for instance, bird ethology, the physiology of bird songs, and the acoustics of evolution—the same relocalization that I just did with the poet's metaphors. I told you at the beginning: let us follow the poets in their quest for reality; let us believe the poet who tells us that nature has not bifurcated, more than the first empiricist who tells us that, of course, it did. Is there a way to locate the power of the sciences in extracting new correspondences from the nightingale in a way that does not force us to generate the phantasmagoria of primary and secondary qualities? And here I want to stress the second of Tarde's innovations, which is very important for me as a science student: the sciences (in the plural) are adding differences of equipment and attention to the world; they are not what allows us to jump to the other side of the bank smack in the middle of the primary qualities—which "are real but unknown" if you remember the quotation from Whitehead.

For Tarde—and this is what sets him apart from all other social scientists—you should let the sciences go with the flow as well:

> As regards the structure of science, probably the most imposing of human edifices, there is no possible question. It was built in the full light of history, and we can follow its development almost from the very outset down to our own day. Our sciences began as a scattered and disconnected collection of small discoveries, which were afterward grouped into little theories (each group being itself a discovery); and the latter were welded, later, into broader theories, to be confirmed or amended by a host of other discoveries, and finally bound firmly together by the arches of hypotheses built over them by the spirit of unification: this manner of progress is indisputable. There is no law or scientific theory (any more than there is a system of philosophy) that does not bear its author's name still legibly written. Everything here originates in the *indi-*

> *vidual;* not only the materials, but the general design of the whole, and the detailed sketches as well; everything, including what is now diffused among all cultured minds, and taught even in the primary school, began as the secret of some single mind, whence a little flame, faint and flickering, sent forth its rays, at first only within a narrow compass, and even there encountering many obstructions, but growing brighter as it spread further, it at length became a brilliant illumination. (Emphasis added.)[13]

Science is *adding itself* to the world. For the bridge-builders this addition is impossible without having to be faced with the following choice: either you have to forget the networks of individuals, the welter of equipment, the pullulations of occasions that make science possible, or else you have to deny its truth value and turn it into an illusion, or at least a social construction, or, slightly better, a useful convention. No wonder: the only movement allowed on the bridge is toward the world or away from it. The only game is a zero-sum game. But if the sciences can be added to the flow of experience as yet another way to fold oneself inside it, to let organisms correspond to one another on, so to speak, another wavelength, then you could finally obviate the primary/secondary quality divide—you could, in other words, retain the reality of the scientific grasp without its fanciful epistemology: nature would have stopped bifurcating.

Isabelle Stengers, the Belgian philosopher of science and one of Whitehead's greatest commentators, has been trying to pinpoint the exact point of inflexion when the fabulous invention of the sciences, which are adding to what is given in experience, is suddenly turned into a way of disqualifying this experience. When do science studies turn into epistemology? When, in other words, does the nightingale ethologist who is recording the song as a wave, begin to claim that this wave allows him or her to deduct the song you hear from the total sum of experience?[14]

James defined radical empiricism, what I prefer to call *second* empiricism, as a way not to choose: we do not want more than what is given in experience, he said, but we certainly do not want less either. This is what the kayakers keep wondering about the bridge-builders: why is it that instead of giving us *more,* the sciences have been kidnapped into the rather dirty business of giving us *less?* Here is Whitehead's plea, again from *The Concept of Nature*:

> For natural philosophy everything perceived is in nature. We may not pick and choose. For us the red glow of the sunset should be as much part of nature as are the molecules and electric waves by which men of science would explain the phenomenon. . . . For example, the fire is burning and we see a red coal.

> This is explained in science by radiant energy from the coal entering our eyes. . . . The real question is, *When red is found in nature, what else is found there also?* Namely we are asking for an analysis of the *accompaniments in* nature of the discovery of red *in* nature." (*CN,* 29, 41, emphases added)

Notice Whitehead's repetition: "*in* nature of the discovery of red *in* nature." Not in our mind. No bridge-building here, no two banks, no *salto mortale,* no reconciliation, no dialectic, no clever intermediary solution: "So far as reality is concerned all our sense-perceptions are in the same boat, and must be treated on the same principle" (*CN,* 44). The attempt of science studies, of sociology—in Tarde's sense—is to look at those "accompaniments" in order to detect what "else is found also." How many other things are accompanying, flowing with the flow, when we try to be attentive to new features of what is *also* given in experience? Answering those questions would allow us to find an exit for Miłosz's bird and to respect the truth-telling of poetry and the verities of the sciences without, for this reason, confusing them with one another.

There is a third way in which connections can be made if we go with the flow, a way that is impossible if we stay on the bridge: the nightingale specialists—some of them like Marc Naguib and Valentin Amrhein have written hundreds of articles[15]—tell us that the songs of the males have been dramatically altered in recent times because of the noise of traffic—they have to raise their voices—and because of the fragmentation of their forest habitat—they have to sing at a higher and higher pitch and for longer and longer to be listened to and to find a mate. The result is that their voice becomes hoarse, and they exhaust themselves in singing, so much so that they might, in the end, be incapable of fulfilling their marital duty even if they have ended up finding a mate. Now, where would you lodge this type of relation, or rather interference, inside the scenography of the bridge-building? It would be at best interesting but immaterial to the knowledge activity, or at least on an entirely different plane from the word/world referential business. And yet, who could deny that those sorts of relations, of interferences, of intermingling have become so crucial in recent years that the very existence of one of the terms, namely the nightingale, could be interrupted? The nightmare of idealism was that when the mind was shut off, the world itself vanished. Idealism has now come true: human minds might be able to shut the nightingale song out of existence altogether. Surely you would agree that there should be a philosophy that allows ecological relations to be added to those of science creation and to the grasp of poetry.

I hope I have shown why we do not know how to live in the phantasmagoria of divided experience, having to choose between meaning without reality and reality without meaning. Organisms and societies, in other words, might not have the luxury of being disciples of Kant: they might have no time to add secondary qualities on top of primary ones in order to fumble for a synthesis, especially if such a synthesis is impossible. To the inevitable *an sich* they might prefer the connections *inter se*.

The Aesthetics of Matters of Concern

An active school of philosophy is quite as important for the locomotion of ideas, as an active school of railway engineers is for the locomotion of fuel.
—Alfred North Whitehead, *Science and the Modern World*

Adrian Walker is posing for the great photographer Jeff Wall.[16] A mummified limb is also posing, detached rather unwillingly from the rest of a body once alive, its shapes and shadows brightly contrasted on a greenish-blue tablecloth. The artist is pondering how to complete his drawing whose shape and shadows are clearly detached on the large, white, brightly lit drawing paper—the greenish-blue tablecloth and the white paper being of almost the same size. No doubt that the artist, Adrian Walker, is also pondering what it means to be a model for a fastidious photographer like Jeff Wall. After all, what he is attempting with the limb, Wall is trying to do to him—that is, to capture the whole site through the highly elaborated and carefully staged pellicle of his analogue photographic machinery, much as Walker himself has been trying for some time now to have the limb jump from out of the greenish-blue cloth to the white paper (and surely it takes as much time to draw so delicately as it does to take photographs in such a carefully staged manner).

Walker is absorbed in his task, so much so that the art historian Michael Fried, in commenting on this image, considers it as a very contemporary example of what he calls *absorption*—in opposition, to use the terms he borrows from Diderot, to "theatrical" art, and to art that is turned explicitly toward the spectator.[17] So while this scene has been staged, it is a picture of total, almost maddening absorption, both for Walker drawing his limb and for Jeff Wall photographing "his" Walker pondering over "his" limb. And I do not doubt that your response will be the same as Fried's or mine: total absorption in the total strangeness of this scene. What is happening here?

Figure 3.1. This image of Adrian Walker dramatizes the scenography of matters of fact. Adrian Walker, artist, drawing from a specimen in a laboratory in the Department of Anatomy at the University of British Columbia, Vancouver, 1992. Transparency in lightbox, 119 × 164 cm. Photograph by Jeff Wall. Courtesy of the artist.

You will surely have noticed the plastic containers and the white tiling, so white and so reflective that it is as if the northern light, so important for art history, had almost overexposed the whole print. We are not in an artist's studio; rather, the full title of the work clearly gives us *Adrian Walker, artist, drawing from a specimen in a laboratory in the Deptartment of Anatomy at the University of British Columbia, Vancouver, 1992.* This is an instance of Laboratory Life: the white light of the Enlightenment floods over the skills of the draughtsman in one of the rare remaining disciplines, namely anatomy, where drawing remains superior in scientific precision to photographs and the direct impressions produced by automated techniques. To this day, competent artists are still necessary to make a limb jump from the tablecloth to the paper. And this mysterious jump, or rather this abysmal gap between the model and its copy, might be what has suspended Adrian Walker's gaze and made him hold his chin in a posture just as absorbed as that of Rodin's *Thinker*. Indeed, for an artist as well as for a scientist—or for any combination of the two—what is more mysterious than this gap between a copy and a model? So mysterious that Jeff Wall, the second in line, has accepted running the risk that his whole canvas, I mean his print, is devoured by such an obsessively bright light.

And yet we, who are third in line in this chain of contaminating absorption, should resist this bright light, which is blinding us to the utter implausibility of such a staged situation. What is fascinating in this print is that a contemporary artist, Jeff Wall, gives us in one shot the history of three centuries of a very peculiar aesthetic, at the very moment when it has so thoroughly disappeared. Or this is, at least, how I wish to interpret this photograph.

I want to say that this print summarizes the whole *aesthetic of matters of fact* as it has emerged around the sixteenth century in a close and complex association of artists, scientists, theologians, and their various patrons. One could object at this point: how could matters of fact depend on any sort of aesthetic? Matters of fact are matters of fact and if there is something that escapes any staging, any artificial trick, any mediation it is exactly that: a goddammit solid matter of fact beyond any human intention: "It is there whether you like it or not!" (And here, we can imagine the point being punctuated with the banging of a fist.)[18] But the splendid beauty—not to say the subtle irony—of Jeff Wall's print tells the exact opposite story: there is nothing more amazingly artificial, more carefully staged, more historically coded than meeting a matter of fact *face to face*.

Look at the picture again: you can say everything you want to about this scene but *not* that it is a summary of common-sense experience! Where on earth would you meet a mummified limb on a tablecloth? Is this the way you recognize your own limb, or caress the arm of your lover, or indeed encounter the fist of the realist who is trying to punch you in the nose with hard facts much like Thomas Gradgrind in Dickens's *Hard Times?* Of course not. When is it the case that you find yourself seated, quietly facing such a matter of fact? Even cannibals, if there still are any, would not remain seated like that in front of such an appetizing delicacy. Most of our experience is not obtained that way: instead we run with a pack of simultaneous events running parallel to us. And tell me, if, by the most extraordinary contrivance, you were asked to be seated face to face with a piece of dead body, when would you be requested in addition, not to touch it, not to hold it with your own hand, not to vomit on it out of disgust much like Roquentin, but instead to *draw* it from a distance of about forty centimeters, as if you wanted, through a feat of an even more extravagant anatomy, to detach its drawable *shape* from its undrawable *material* composition?

Everything in this scene is implausible, contrived, in such a face-to-face situation of a human mind pondering over the yawning gap of an object that he or she wants nonetheless to transport by building an impossible bridge between the greenish-blue tablecloth and the white rectangular paper. No surprise that Adrian Walker has been asked by Jeff Wall to hold his chin in his hand and let his attention self-destruct in the most suspended, self-absorbed meditation, in the brightest, self-disappearing light. In the white space, it is the notion of matters of fact, indeed it is its whole aesthetic, that is being suspended and that is fading away.

Still, one could object and say that this scene, because it takes place in a laboratory, reveals the normal, mundane ways in which *objectivity* is produced. Although it might seem extravagant in terms of daily experience, because, apart from butchers and cannibals, no one meets detached limbs this way, there is nothing strange in having scientists face an object that they try to make jump from a three-dimensional material reality into a two-dimensional shape on a piece of paper. This is not what ordinary people do, but it is for sure what anatomists do.

I am sorry to say that this is far from the case, and here I have some experience in studying laboratory practice. In a laboratory, investigators do not take the pose of Rodin's *Thinker,* but rather the active pragmatic pose of the Tinkerer, actively engaging in pipetting, shaking reagents, taking notes, none of which could be accounted for in terms of a single *salto mortale* from "the world" to "the word." Instead, scientific practice establishes chains of reference that researchers anxiously follow through successive reincarnations.[19] If you had to follow objectivity-making practice, you would have to use a very long videotape in which many different actors would also appear. So, in no way, can the aesthetic of matters of fact pass for a *description* of what it is that scientists do.

Is it not extraordinary then that the primeval scene of matters of fact remains the total absorption of one mind *facing* a piece of dead material, when such a stage cannot pay justice even to the making of objects so dear to epistemologists, namely scientific facts? How can we explain that we take matters of fact to be the ahistorical ingredients of the world, when they are visible only in highly artificial sites, where you need a seated human—usually a middle-aged male—gazing (not touching, not hearing, not manipulating) at something that is of middle size, brightly lit, highly contrasted; something that, in addition, is situated at about average height (not much higher or lower than the horizon line); standing never much farther away than a distance of about a meter; a strange situation in which both the man and the object are engaged in the amazing feat of crossing the bridge, without any visible intermediaries, between *only two elements,* the *copy* and the *model,* which are themselves related *mimetically:* the copy has to *resemble* the model, and ideally to be super-imposable onto it? Nowhere, in any laboratory that we know, has any objective fact ever been produced that way, and yet this is the model for all our relations to matters of fact: the limb is on the blue tablecloth; the cat is on the mat; "The facts are there, goddammit, whether you like it or not."

In the previous section of this essay, I contrasted two ways of rendering what is given in experience. I used the metaphor of riverbanks, one of the sides being the word—or the social, or the mind—while on the other side lay the world—or the material, or the natural. One enterprise consisted in trying to bridge the river by achieving the feat of accurate reference. But there was another enterprise, as I showed, that consisted of going with the flow and considering what sort of grasp we have of experience when, drifting sideways, we practice a bit of what I called "kayaking." I proposed that we consider that the mystery of bridging the gap—this abyss that makes Adrian Walker ponder in such a self-absorbed way—is not as deep and revealing as the experience of going with the flow: this is what would happen for instance if Jeff Wall had tried to capture the movements, the duration in which those organisms are by necessity involved; for instance if he had followed the rotting flesh of the limb; or, if using Peter Sloterdijk's type of interest, we had become suddenly sensitive to the tiny bubble *inside which* this whole scene takes place: what sort of *envelopes*—Sloterdijk's expression—have to be in place for Walker to work in peace, without any noise, disturbance, agitation?[20] What is the strange *air-condition*—another of his concepts—needed for the very scene to unfold? If we had shifted our attention in any of those ways, no doubt suddenly, The Gigantic Gap between the World out There and the Mind in Here would have vanished because another entirely different topology of inside and outside would have appeared: this time the one between the Vancouver Department of Anatomy and the rest of the university: a tiny bubble of objects and subjects mixed up *within* a fragile foam of other tiny bubbles whose presence is deduced from the picture but who remain nonetheless wholly invisible.

No doubt that if we were practicing such a series of operations, we would consider Jeff Wall's print as a freeze frame of a highly mobile and quickly changing film presenting us with an entirely different story, much as Svetlana Alpers did when, in her masterpiece *The Art of Describing,* she forced the amateurs of still lives and Dutch paintings to replace their fascinated gaze over so-called objective and mimetic style by an inquiry into the whole Dutch Republic Empire.[21] No doubt, matters of fact are the result of a specific style; they do not stand for reason; they do not stand even for empiricism, if by this label we mean what is given in experience. And they certainly do not stand for the sciences, as if those had nothing else to do but to bridge the gap between words and world.

What I will argue here is that the other mystery to ponder, the one to make us seize our chin in our hand and imitate Rodin's pose for a very long time, is not how we can convince the world to jump into representation (or a human limb to somersault onto a piece of paper much like a lion through a circle of fire), but how come we have, for three centuries, *discounted* what is given to us through experience and *replaced* it instead with something *never* experienced that philosophers nonetheless have the nerve to call "empirical" and "matters of factual"? Now, this is quite a feat! As I said earlier, using Alfred North Whitehead's marvelous expression: how did we manage to behave as if Nature had "bifurcated" into primary qualities—which, if you remember, are real, material, without value and goals, and known only through totally unknown conduits—and secondary qualities—which are nothing but "psychic additions" projected by the human mind onto a meaningless world of pure matter and which have no external reality although they carry goals and values. How did we succeed in having the whole of philosophy reduced to a choice between two meaninglessnesses: the real but meaningless matter and the meaningful but unreal symbol?

This situation, which was fully developed in the seventeenth century, has been well summarized by the great historian of science E. J. Dijksterhuis:

> The distinction in question may be defined as an *objective* treatment of the primary qualities and a *subjective* treatment of the secondary qualities, i.e., the former are considered as objectively present, independent of the perceiving subject, in the physical body perceived, and the latter as only existing in the consciousness of the perceiving person. . . . The fact that the primary qualities (size, shape, motion) are, after all, presented to us only through sense perception, so that the very distinction is really futile, was realized very seldom. The feeling that in mathematics and mechanics it was possible to arrive, apparently without any recourse to sense-experience and yet with a sense of being supported by sufficient evidence, at an extensive knowledge of the geometrico-mechanical qualities, inevitably gave these sciences a place apart. (Emphasis added.)[22]

And then he adds:

> While for science the mechanistic conception was stimulating and productive, it confronted philosophy with the difficult problem of the real relation be-

> tween the world of our perceptions and feelings and the world of the mechanical process outside, which is so entirely different in character. The natural sciences were faced with the difficult *but promising* task of devising mechanical systems to account for physical facts; philosophy, on the other hand, had to solve *the hopeless problem* of deriving psychic from physical phenomena. It is not surprising that their ways began to *diverge*, that the natural sciences began to follow a course of their own without bothering too much about the philosophical legitimacy of what they were doing, and that philosophy proved less and less capable of fulfilling, with regard to the study of nature, the leading role it ought to have played in an ideal co-operation of the mental faculties. (Emphasis added.)[23]

So, no matter how "futile" this distinction has been, philosophy until now has been trying to solve "the hopeless problem" of bridging a nonexistent gap. The question before us now is to see whether or not we can exert the rights of reason all the way—that is, along the flow of experience—abandon this "hopeless" task, and lead our "mental faculties" along a more promising path. Can we end the bifurcation of nature and pay our respects to experience without having to discount it on behalf of a totally artificial and implausible feeling that passes for common sense? This is how Whitehead puts the problem in *Modes of Thought*, with the illustration of President Roosevelt's second inauguration in 1937:

> My aim in these lectures is briefly to point out how both Newton's contribution and Hume's contribution are, each in their way, gravely defective. *They are right as far as they go.* But they *omit* those aspects of the universe as *experienced*, and of our modes of experiencing, which jointly lead to the more penetrating ways of understanding. In the recent situations at Washington, DC, the Hume-Newton modes of thought can only discern a complex transition of sensa, and an entangled locomotion of molecules, while the deepest intuition of the whole world discerns the President of the United States inaugurating a new chapter in the history of mankind. In such ways the Hume-Newton interpretation omits our intuitive modes of understanding. (*MT*, 135–36, emphasis added)

Violence is committed to common sense when we are asked to "omit from our understanding" that an important event has been happening and we are requested to accept as "scientific" a gaze from nowhere: "you are mistaken, nothing has happened, only molecules in agitation." This is exactly the same violence, to use my previous example, as that which occurs when we are asked to consider that the nightingale sings only in our mind (or our brain) and not in the world out there, because hearing a song is not part of the list of primary qualities (a list that is, remember, established for the most "futile" and fleeting of historical reasons).

Let us be careful here: I am not saying that we have to "reconcile" the scientific with the poetic worldviews, to "bring together" science and art, because such an enterprise would produce only the most monstrous hybrid: two artifacts brought together just makes for a third artifact, not for a solution. What we have to do, if we want to be faithful to what William James called *radical empiricism*, is to deny the claims of the "bifurcates" in the first place to represent common sense and to speak in the name of science. We do not have, on the one hand, a harsh world made of indisputable matters of fact and, on the other, a rich mental world of human symbols, imaginations, and values. The harsh world of matters of fact is an amazingly narrow, specialized type of scenography using a highly coded type of narrative, gazing, lighting, distance, a very precise repertoire of attitude and attention, of which historians of science like Lorraine Daston, Horst Bredekamp, Steven Shapin, Simon Schaffer, and Peter Galison, to name a few, have made a careful inventory. While it seemed barely possible in the time of Whitehead to overcome the bifurcation of nature because of the total grasp the first empiricism had on European minds, it is much easier now that matters of fact appear for what they always were: a certain style as convoluted, as interesting, as historical, as artistic as Louis XIV's court etiquette, Leibniz's baroque monadology, Maurice of Nassau's invention of military drilling, or Immanuel Kant's interpretation of the Copernican Revolution. Indeed, it is, in my view, precisely *because* matters of fact have become so historical that Jeff Wall has been able to stage his meditation of a self-absorbed artist *qua* scientist: no scientist can pretend anymore to gaze at the world that way. The opportunity is there to be seized: science has been so thoroughly historicized that we can now ask in an entirely new light, what has happened to us under the name of (first) empiricism? How can it be that common sense has been forced to drift so far from what is seized on by experience? And even more important: what's next?

In order to code this huge sea change between two empiricisms—the first and the second—I have proposed using the contrast between matters of fact and *matters of concern*—a banal expression in English that I wish to render more technical.[24] A matter of concern is what happens to a matter of fact when you add to it its whole scenography, much as you would do by shifting your attention from the stage to the whole machinery of a theater. This is, for instance, what has happened to science when seized by the recent "science studies," what has happened to Dutch landscape painting in Svetlana Alpers's able hands, and what has happened to anatomical drawing when restaged by a contemporary artist like Jeff Wall. Instead of simply being there, matters of fact begin to look different, to render a different sound. They start to move in all directions, they overflow their boundaries, they include a complete set of new actors, they reveal the fragile envelopes in which they are housed. Instead of "being there whether you like it or not," they still have to be there, yes (this is one of the huge differences), but *they have to be liked,* appreciated, tasted, experimented upon, mounted, prepared, put to the test.

It is the same world, and yet everything looks different. Matters of fact were indisputable, obstinate, simply there. Matters of concern are disputable, and their obstinacy seems to be of an entirely different sort: they move, they carry you away, and, yes, they also *matter.* The amazing thing with matters of fact was that, although they were material, they did not matter a bit, even though they were immediately used to enter into some sort of polemic. How really strange they were.

Another extraordinary feature, as I have shown at length in *The Politics of Nature,* is that although they were mute, they were supposed to speak directly—"facts after all speak for themselves, don't they?"—and not only that but, through an amazing feat of spokesmanship, mute and yet speaking facts were able to shut the dissenters' voice down.[25] And those who have invented this amazing feat of "inanimism" are deriding the poor people who believe in *animism.*[26]

But before we bid farewell to this scenography, we need to fathom its extraordinary power, what Dijksterhuis considered to be its main technical source of efficacy. To do so, however, it would be insufficient to look only at worldviews, at ideas, at a "mechanization of the world picture," unless, that is, we take the world *picture* literally and not metaphorically as he does and as so many historians of the Scientific Revolution have done after him. More humble mediators have to be added to make clear the history of this odd divide between primary and secondary qualities: namely, the mediator of *drawing itself,* of the very nature of what it is to picture something. As is well known to historians of empiricism, John Locke was obsessed with metaphors from painting, camera obscura, wonderkammer, and stocks of various goods as is clear from *An Essay Concerning Human Understanding* (1690).

> All ideas come from sensation or reflection. Let us then suppose the mind to be, as we say, *white paper, void of all characters, without any ideas:*—How comes it to be furnished? Whence comes it by that *vast store* which the busy and boundless fancy of man has *painted* on it with an almost endless variety?

> Whence has it all the materials of reason and knowledge? To this I answer, in one word, from Experience. In that all our knowledge is founded; and from that it ultimately derives itself. . . . The senses at first let in particular ideas, and *furnish the yet empty cabinet,* and the mind by degrees growing familiar with some of them, they are lodged in the memory, and names got to them. Afterwards, the mind proceeding further, abstracts them, and by degrees learns the use of general names. In this manner the mind comes to be *furnished with ideas and language,* the materials about which to exercise its discursive faculty. And the use of reason becomes daily more visible, as these materials that give it employment increase. (Emphasis added.)[27]

You need some extraordinary situations, as Jeff Wall has shown us, to try to take knowledge as being what appears on a white piece of paper after the material qualities have been peeled away from their form. It is possible, as Jonathan Crary has argued, that Locke has imagined the mind to be one of those boxes where, once again, a silent mind meets the world as what can be projected flat onto a piece of paper.[28] What a strange box for Locke to lock his mind into! A camera box even more artificial than the one captured by Jeff Wall. And yet, it is the only practical situation where the divide between what is transportable on a piece of paper—and what is geometry—and what is not—sound, odor, agitation, duration—can be easily separated.

This is what Locke readily recognizes:

> When we set before our eyes a *round globe* of any uniform color, e.g., gold, alabaster, or jet, it is certain that the idea thereby imprinted on our mind is of a *flat circle,* variously shadowed, with several degrees of light and brightness coming to our eyes. But we having, by use, been accustomed to perceive what kind of appearance convex bodies are wont to make in us; what alterations are made in the reflections of light by the difference of the sensible figures of bodies;—the judgment presently, by an habitual custom, alters the appearances into their causes. So that from that which is truly a variety of shadow or color, collecting the figure, it makes it pass for a mark of a figure, and frames to itself the perception of a convex figure and a uniform color; when the idea we receive from thence *is only a plane variously colored,* as is *evident in painting.* (Emphasis added.)[29]

Without the experience of being tricked by painting in taking a "plane variously colored" for a "convex figure," philosophers would never have sustained for long the idea that the world itself could be made of primary streams of causalities that our mind transforms into nonexisting secondary qualities. Similarly, without the obsessive metaphor of painting, epistemologists would never have imagined that in science there are only *two* steps—a copy and a model—and that there is a mimetic relation between the two. To put it much too bluntly: the idea of a bridge between representation and the represented is an invention of visual art.

I hope you see the reason why it would be useless to try to "reconcile art and science," since what we take for science is nothing, most of the time, but a derivative epistemology, without any relation to the "visual effects" of science, and which is a scion of a highly specific moment in art history. I am sorry to say but epistemology is the fault of Dutch painters and merchants. The Dutch impressed visitors so much, and especially Descartes, that he ended up confusing the white piece of paper on which figures are drawn with its *res extensa!* Catastrophic consequences for philosophy: never did it recover from this confusion between ontology and visualization strategies.

No one has understood this better than the genial curator of prints William Ivins. There are, he argues, two very specific reasons why the white sheet of paper on which only shapes are drawn in a geometrical idiom was able to become such an enormously powerful tool. Before the Renaissance, he claims:

> There were two great reasons for this inefficiency; one, that no picture could be exactly *duplicated*, and the other, that there was no *rule* or grammatical scheme for securing either logical relations within the system of pictorial symbols or a *logical two-way,* or *reciprocal correspondence* between the pictorial representations of the shapes of objects and the locations of those objects in space.[30]

But after print and later perspective drawing were invented, followed half a century later by projective geometry, for the first time in the history of human codes, a two-way connection could be established between people about the things they meant, even though they remained thoroughly incapable of describing them in words. The Platonic power of geometry was at last incarnated into a practice: the Book of Nature was written in geometric characters, but we should not forget that it was a printed book made of many sheets of white drawing paper:

> The most marked characteristics of European pictorial representation since the fourteenth century have been on the one hand its steadily increasing naturalism and on the other its purely schematic and logical extensions. It is submitted that both are due in largest part to the development and pervasion of methods which have provided symbols, repeatable in invariant form, for

> representation of visual awareness, and a grammar of perspective which made it possible to establish logical relations not only within the system of symbols but between that system and the forms and locations of the objects that it symbolizes.[31]

You see that Dijksterhuis' the Mechanization of the World "Picture" is an apt title: it is indeed a picture allowing us to see things in a mechanical way because you can turn around and predict their deformations and projections. To use my terms, they are *immutable mobiles*: for the first time you can reconcile the mobility of information with the immutability of what is being transported: it is as if Parmenidian forms could be extracted out of Heraclitus's flow. No wonder every literate mind all over Europe became intoxicated with such a fabulously powerful aesthetic of reason. And yet, it remains an aesthetic, a way to draw things together.[32]

To enter into a debate over perspective, its history and its importance, would be of course impossible in the short space of this essay, but what Ivins has seen with unmatched clarity is the missing link in Whitehead's philosophical account of the bifurcation of nature—namely, the confusion by philosophers and scientists alike of what is given in experience with what Whitehead calls "the operations of the mind" required to transmit information from someone to someone else. I quote from *The Concept of Nature*:

> Thus what is a mere *procedure of mind* in the translation of sense-awareness into discursive knowledge has been *transmuted* into a *fundamental* character of nature. In this way matter has emerged as being the metaphysical substratum of its properties, and the course of nature is interpreted as the history of matter. (*CN*, 16, emphasis added)

And again:

> Thus matter represents the refusal to *think away* spatial and temporal characteristics and to arrive at the bare concept of an individual entity. It is this refusal which has caused the *muddle* of *importing* the *mere procedure of thought* into the fact of nature. The entity, *bared* of all characteristics except those of space and time, has acquired a physical status as the ultimate texture of nature; so that the course of nature is conceived as being merely the fortunes of matter in its adventure through space. (*CN*, 20, emphasis added)

Here Whitehead offers his own historical explanation, which has to do with the differential development of the scientific disciplines:

> This distinction is the product of an epoch in which physical science has got ahead of medical pathology and of physiology. Perceptions of push are just as much the outcome of transmission as are perceptions of color. When color is perceived the nerves of the body are excited in one way and transmit their message towards the brain, and when push is perceived other nerves of the body are excited in another way and transmit their message towards the brain. (*CN*, 44)

And yet "pushiness" has been attributed to primary qualities and color to secondary ones. See how "futile" this whole distinction is?

But the muddle remains unclear: how on earth could Descartes have made the amazing mistake of confusing *res extensa* with what happens when you begin to draw a form geometrically on a piece of white paper? What Ivins and more recent historians account for is the connection established between the recently emerging scientific community and this new geometrical idiom: a two-way connection can be established between savants because on the paper (plates, diagrams, figures, or the calculations they depend on) transformations can be accurately predicted. Once the operations of the mind are brought in, it is only a small step to confuse immutable mobiles as a solution for communications, with immutable mobiles being what the world itself is made of. Matters of fact shift from being a descriptive mode, a style of reasoning, to *what* is furnishing the world itself.

Here is Ivins again:

> From being an avenue of sensuous awareness for what people, lacking adequate symbols and adequate grammars and techniques for their use, regarded as *"secondary qualities,"* sight has today become the principal avenue of the sensuous awareness upon which systematic thought about nature is based. Science and technology have advanced in more than direct ratio to the ability of men to contrive methods by which phenomena which otherwise could be known only through the sense of touch, hearing, taste, and smell, have been brought within the range of *visual recognition and measurement* and thus become subject to that logical symbolization without which rational thought and analysis are impossible. The discovery of the early forms of these grammars and techniques constitutes that beginning of the rationalization of sight which, it is submitted, was the most important event of the Renaissance. (Emphasis added.)[33]

None of us, I suppose, will deny that Ivins is right: for proof, you simply have to look at your computer, the epitome of Renaissance space to which we should add the ideal Leibnizian library. Digitalization, as Simon Schaffer and Adam Lowe have shown, is not so much an innovation as the achievement of a three centuries' old dream. Leibniz's nickname is Google scholar.[34] Whether you are architects using CAD design, engineers, accountants, physicians pondering over patients' files, downloaders of some sort, videogame addicts, you live in the "Rationalization of Sight" (Ivins's title). And yet what is amazing is that this enormously developed and materialized aesthetic of matters of fact has been unable to evolve to absorb the new matters of concern. Inundated by innovations, we are living in a more and more archaic representation of our real state of affairs.

But before I reach this last question, I have to summarize our progress so far. If you remember the argument made in the previous section, you will notice that we now have a precise conduit for explaining the bifurcation of nature. The distinction between primary and secondary qualities is the professional hazard of watching mummified limbs for too long. Then the idea might come to you to separate what you can draw on the white paper—the form—from the matter—the limb *an sich*—and then, through another extraordinary move, to fuse the ability of Adrian Walker to transport the painted limb to some other place without this limb rotting or being in any way corrupted into the ways in which *the limb itself* transports its material components through time. Substance is a digital dance on paper. By complementing Whitehead with Ivins, we can now understand these enigmatic sentences of *The Concept of Nature:*

> Thus even if you admit that the adherents of substance can be allowed to conceive substance as matter, it is a fraud to slip substances into space on the plea that space expresses relations between substances. (*CN,* 21)

> My argument is that this dragging in of the mind as making additions of its own to the thing posited for knowledge by sense-awareness is merely a way of shirking the problem of natural philosophy. That problem is to discuss the relations inter se of things known, abstracted from the bare fact that they are known. . . . Natural philosophy should never ask, what is in the mind and what is in nature. (*CN,* 30)

The question before us is to see how can we suspend this "fraudulent export" of ways of knowing (in Ivins's rendering: drawing in perspective) into the relations *inter se* among betting organisms. But at least we now have a comprehensible historical path of intermediaries through which nature bifurcated and thus presented to the philosophical mind, from Hume all the way to contemporary neurophilosophers, the "hopeless task" of bridging a nonexistent gap. There is no gap to be bridged but there is a joint history of science, of art—and I will add, of politics—to be taken up. Now that we begin to see how the aesthetic of matters of fact works, it is a much less impossible undertaking to explore what would happen were we to modify the scenography through which experience tries to capture matters of concern.

I hope it is clear that there is no possible reconciliation between art and science, no aestheticization of beautiful results of science (fractals, galaxies, brain scans, etc.), but an immense building site where once again, just as in the sixteenth and seventeenth centuries, every intellectual skill from artists, scientists, politicians, statesmen, organizers of all kinds, merchants and patrons, are trying to reinvent an Art of Describing, or rather an Art of *Re*describing matters of fact to stop the "fraudulent export" and take up "what is given in experience."

I am afraid that it must also be terribly clear how unfit I am for the task that I have now laid before us. And yet, even though it is much more difficult to discern the future than to make a history of the past, I have to sketch at least what would happen if we possessed an aesthetic of matters of concern. The only way to do that in the space remaining is to briefly indicate what, in industry, is called the *specifications* of the tender—not the project itself but the conditions that you have to fulfill if you want to submit a proposal for the tender. Here are a few that this alternative scenography should be able to stage through whatever means you see fit. And I have no doubt that there are many people more competent that I to submit a proposal.

Specification one: matters of concern have to *matter*. Matters of fact were distorted by the totally implausible necessity of being pure stuff of no interest whatsoever—just sitting there like a mummified limb—while at the same time being able to "make a point," humiliate human subjectivity, speak directly without speech apparatus and quiet dissenting voices. Now, this is a bit too much to do at once for some "middle-sized dry goods." Can we do better and distinguish those various and confused layers to make sure that our scenography registers that they matter for some people who have to be specified, and for whom they are the source of an intense interest and a redirected attention? The matter of materialists was a fraudulent mixture of politics, art, and science; by contrast, let matters of concern distinguish clearly the population of those for whom they matter. The mummified limb does not tell the story of why Adrian Walker has taken the pains to draw it so carefully; but if the nightingale song has drawn the attention of bird watchers, let this conduit for attention be now visible, instead of playing this strange dance of inanimism through which pure disinterested objectivity interests no one and yet seems of great import in our quarrels.

Specification two: matters of concern have to be *liked.* The great Act I, scene 1, of table-thumping realists was that matters of fact were there "whether you like it or not." Except that this indisputable presence was at once turned into a way of *stopping* the dispute. Now we have to choose: if matters of concern have to be closed, then a dispute has to be put to an end, and not by thumping on the table and saying, "the dispute has ended because the facts are there." The matters of facts are there, and the dispute has to go on until closure is obtained. It is fair to say that the whole first wave of empiricism had an odd way of conceiving democracy and was rather a clever way of escaping controversies by putting a premature end to them. Since discussions are what are in question with matter, then for God's sake, carry them on instead of stopping them abruptly and falling back, in the end, on brute force. Are you not tired of this odd succession whereby an appeal to undisputable facts is followed by pure violence? Here again, can we not do better? How can one be polite and still use matters of fact?

Specification three: matters of concern have to be *populated.* To use an expression I have somewhat overused, they have to become something that is to be explicitly recognized as a gathering, as *Ding* and not as *Gegenstand.* The best measure of the incredible archaism of our present modes of representation is that we are still portraying objectivity as if we were in the time of Locke, whereas every bit of science and technology has now become a convoluted, controversial *affair,* a *cause,* yes, a *res.* Objects have become things, and yet we have no way to represent them except in the bifurcated manner of "pure objects," on the one hand and human organizations on the other. Even though the space shuttle *Columbia,* to use this dramatic example, makes no sense as an object except *inside* the troublesome NASA, as was made clear during the inquiry launched after the disaster, we still have no way to describe technical entities other than Gaspard Monge's *assembly drawings*—strange drawings indeed that are incapable of showing the genuine assemblies necessary for the smallest object to come into being.[35] How can we still be stuck in modes of togetherness that our daily experience, our daily press, our daily encounters with artifacts contradict? How can a whole industry of visualization be wallowing in hype when we cannot even solve this simplest of all riddles: show me the people necessary to activate what you have drawn on CAD software. Soft indeed! Where are the artists, the designers, the programmers, who could finally extract us from the seventeenth century and bring us eventually to the twenty-first century?

Specification four: matters of concern have to be *durable.* Oddly enough, this is what was more widely vaunted about matters of fact: they remained there while the fickle history of our representations passed away. Except we now know that this was a "fraudulent export" of our ways of representing them in the passage of nature. If there is one thing that the Jeff Wall print does not account for it is the means, vehicles, and subsistence through which the print maintains itself in existence. Freeze framing is a pretty bad way of accounting for duration.[36] How do you keep a limb from rotting? Who is keeping up the whole Vancouver Department of Anatomy? What is allowing Adrian Walker to remain in his Rodin's pose forever? Facts are not the ahistorical, uninterpreted, and asocial *beginning* of a course of action, but the extraordinary fragile and transient provisional *terminus* of a whole flow of betting organisms whose reproductive means have to be made clear and paid to the last cent in hard currency. Endurance is what has to be *obtained,* not what is already given by some substrate, or some substance. Let us remember Whitehead here again:

> Then physical endurance is the process of continuously inheriting a certain identity of character transmitted through a historical route of events. This character belongs to the whole route, and to every event of the route. This is the exact property of material. . . . Only if you take material to be fundamental, this property of endurance is an arbitrary fact at the base of the order of nature; but if you take organism to be fundamental, this property is the result of evolution. (*SMW,* 108)

This is what Ludwig Fleck had so beautifully shown: all the drama of table-thumping realists will not allow a fact to remain in existence for one minute. Matters of concern, on the other hand, have to be kept up, cared for, accompanied, restored, duplicated, saved, yes, *saved*—we know that for our hard disks' content, and yet we still act as if facts could be *hard* forever, at no cost, without making any backup.[37] Once again, we represent our experience in a way that is appropriate for a century long past and for a scenography we have long deserted. We live in the ruins of modernism, and we seem to be content with them.

Many more specifications could be listed, but I have said enough to indicate the drift of this second empiricism. Let me conclude by offering a counter case. When Otto Neurath devised his isotypes, he was trying to do something that was the equivalent of what had been attempted during the Renaissance—namely, to link together in a powerful synthesis a certain conception of science (logical positivism), a certain political aspiration (the socialism of Red Vienna), with a certain artistic style (Bauhaus modernism).[38] When he created his Museum of Statistics, it was to render visible again the facts of the matter of economics to those mainly concerned by their scandalous destruction, namely the workers who were in the grips of the Great Depression.[39] When we look at his enterprise from the point of view I have presented, it is clear that nothing much remains of logical positivism, of socialism, and of modernist aesthetics. And yet, we are forced to say that at least he had respected the rights of reason by inventing for matters of fact a full scenography of great beauty and great relevance. We live in a different world. But at least Neurath gives us the exact magnitude of the task to be completed. If we have to redo every plank of his proverbial boat, which has to be refitted without ever reaching a dry dock, nothing less will do. I believe it is the responsibility of contemporary thinkers to refuse to live in the ruins of the modernist scenography and to have the courage, once again, to put their skills to work in devising for matters of concern a style that does justice to what is given in experience.

Notes

1. Czesław Miłosz, "A Theological Treatise," *Spiritus: A Journal of Christian Spirituality* 2, no. 2 (Fall 2002): 123–204.

2. Bruno Latour, "Gabriel Tarde and the End of the Social," in *The Social in Question: New Bearings in History and the Social Sciences*, ed. Patrick Joyce (London: Routledge, 2002).

3. Gabriel Tarde, *Monadologie et sociologie* (Paris: Les Empêcheurs de penser en rond, 1999), 58.

4. Ibid., 73.

5. This is at the heart of what I call "être en tant qu'autre" (being qua other) and not "être en tant qu'être (being qua being). Cf. Tarde: "The point is that the enduring organisms are now the outcome of evolution; and that, beyond these organisms, there is nothing else that endures. On the materialistic theory, there is material—such as matter or electricity—which endures. On the organic theory, the only endurances are structures of activity, and the structures are evolved" (*SMW*, 108).

6. Tarde is still known, at least in the United States, for having studied one of these trajectories quite thoroughly: imitation. But I won't deal with this here.

7. Tarde, *Monadologie et sociologie*, 19–20.

8. Bruno Latour, *Reassembling the Social: An Introduction to Actor-Network Theory* (Oxford: Oxford University Press, 2005).

9. Gabriel Tarde, *Social Laws: An Outline of Sociology*, trans. by Howard C. Warren (Kitchener, Ont.: Batoche Books, 2000), 35.

10. Ibid., 75.

11. Ibid., 18.

12. Didier Debaise, *Un empirisme speculative: Lecture de Procès et Réalité* (Paris: Vrin, 2006).

13. Tarde, *Social Laws,* 85–86.

14. Isabelle Stengers, *L'effet Whitehead* (Paris: Vrin, 2000); Stengers, *The Invention of Modern Science,* trans. Daniel W. Smith (Minneapolis: University of Minnesota Press, 2002); Stengers, *Thinking with Whitehead: A Free and Wild Creation of Concepts,* trans. Michael Chase (Cambridge, Mass.: Harvard University Press, 2011). Cf. Bruno Latour, "What Is Given in Experience? A Review of Isabelle Stengers's *Penser avec Whitehead,*" *boundary 2* 32, no. 1 (Spring 2005): 222–37.

15. http://www.uni-bielefeld.de/biologie/vhf/NG/Naguib_Publications.htm. Please see Marc Naguib's website https://www.nioo.knaw.nl/en/users/mnaguib.

16. Theodora Vishner and Heidi Naef, "Jeff Wall: Catalogue raisonné, 1978–2004" (Bâle: Schaulager, 2005).

17. Michael Fried, *Absorption and Theatricality: Painting and Beholder in the Age of Diderot* (Chicago, Ill.: University of Chicago Press, 1988).

18. Malcolm Ashmore, Derek Edwards, and Jonathan Potter, "The Bottom Line: The Rhetoric of Reality Demonstrations," *Configurations* 2, no. 1 (1994): 1–14.

19. Bruno Latour and Steve Woolgar, *Laboratory Life: The Construction of Scientific Fact,* 2nd ed. with new afterword (Princeton, N.J.: Princeton University Press, 1986).

20. Peter Sloterdijk, "Forward to the Theory of Spheres," in *Cosmograms,* ed. Melik Ohanian and Jean Christophe Royoux (New York: Lukas and Sternberg, 2005).

21. Svetlana Alpers, *The Art of Describing* (Chicago, Ill.: University of Chicago Press, 1983).

22. E. J. Dijksterhuis, *The Mechanization of the World Picture: Pythagoras to Newton* (Princeton, N.J.: Princeton University Press, 1961), 241.

23. Ibid.

24. Bruno Latour, "Why Has Critique Run Out of Steam? From Matters of Fact to Matters of Concern," *Critical Inquiry* 20 (Winter 2004): 25–48.

25. Bruno Latour, *The Politics of Nature: How to Bring the Sciences into Democracy,* trans. Catherine Porter (Cambridge, Mass.: Harvard University Press, 2004).

26. Philippe Descola, *Par delà nature et culture* (Paris: Gallimard, 2005).

27. John Locke, *An Essay Concerning Human Understanding* (London: Thomas Tegg, 1860), bk. 2, ch. 1, 51.

28. Jonathan Crary, *Techniques of the Observer: On Vision and Modernity in the Nineteenth Century* (Cambridge, Mass.: MIT Press, 1990).

29. Locke, *An Essay Concerning Human Understanding,* bk. 2, ch. 9, 81.

30. William M. Ivins Jr., *On the Rationalization of Sight: With an Examination of Three Renaissance Texts on Perspective* (New York: De Capo Press, 1973), 8–9.

31. Ibid., 12–13.

32. Bruno Latour, "Drawing Things Together," in *Representations in Scientific Practice,* ed. Mike Lynch and Steve Woolgar (Cambridge, Mass.: MIT Press, 1990).

33. Ivins, *On the Rationalization of Sight,* 13.

34. Adam Lowe and Simon Schaffer, "N01se, 1999," an exhibition held simultaneously at Kettle's Yard (Cambridge, 1999); the Whipple Museum of the History of Science,

Cambridge; the Museum of Archeology and Anthropology, Cambridge; and the Wellcome Institute, London.

35. Bruno Latour, "From Realpolitik to Dingpolitik; or, How to Make Things Public," in *Making Things Public: Atmospheres of Democracy,* ed. Bruno Latour and Peter Weibel (Cambridge, Mass.: MIT Press, 2005).

36. Bruno Latour and Peter Weibel, eds. *Iconoclash: Beyond the Image Wars in Science, Religion, and Art* (Cambridge, Mass.: MIT Press, 2002).

37. Ludwig Fleck, *Genesis and Development of a Scientific Fact* (Chicago, Ill: University of Chicago Press, 1981).

38. Thomas E. Uebel, Nancy Cartwright, and L. Fleck, *Otto Neurath: Philosophy between Science and Politics* (Cambridge: Cambridge University Press, 1996).

39. Frank Hartmann, "Humanization of Knowledge through the Eye," in *Making Things Public,* 698–707.

FOUR

The Technics of Prehension

On the Photography of Nicolas Baier

Nathan Brown

The true philosophic question is, How can concrete fact exhibit entities abstract from itself and yet participated in by its own nature?
—Alfred North Whitehead, *Process and Reality*

Nicolas Baier is a photographer, by which I mean: he digitizes the surfaces of antique mirrors and arrays lush black ink-jet prints of their distressed opacities over thirty feet of gallery space. Through a microscope, he meticulously photographs a postage-stamp-sized slice of meteorite over four thousand times and then assembles these thousands of photographs into a glossy six-by-eight-foot enlargement of impeccably precise resolution and immersive depth. When a computer crash saturates his monitor with a color field of densely pixilated red lines, receding toward an apparently distant horizon over a crimson sea beneath an incarnadine sky, he renders this image as a chromogenic transparency and displays it in a light box under the title *Failed.* When he travels to the south of France to view prehistoric cave paintings, Baier photographs the bare stone wall *beside* these inaugural images, recording the nonrepresentational traces, contours, and fractures of the rock. And at Parc des Buttes-Chaumont in Paris, he photographs a stream of light pouring through to the interior of a manmade cave built at the order of Napoleon III.

The resulting composition, *Photons (The World of Ideas),* is a digital allegory of the cave in twenty-five carefully arranged ink-jet prints. If we look at the composition closely, we can see from the angle of the light that Baier has inverted the image, so that light seems to fall *up* at a diagonal to stalagmites rather than down through hanging stalactites. The image of an inverted Platonism: a materialism of the Idea wherein it is the lens rather than the eye that turns away from Simulacra toward the Eidos, if only to render a simulacral image of that turning as a portrait of the medium. Digital

Figure 4.1. Nicolas Baier, *Vanitas 01,* 2007–2008. Ink-jet prints, installation view, 345 × 900 cm. Composed of digital scans of forty antique mirrors, *Vanitas 01* replaces a reflection of the viewer with the distressed topography of a material surface.

Figure 4.2. Nicolas Baier, *Meteorite 01,* 2008. Chromogenic print, 183 × 254 cm. *Meteorite 01* is a composite of more than four thousand photographs, taken through a microscope, of a postage-stamp-sized slice of meteorite.

photography, here, might be taken as the state of an art of exteriorization, of mimesis, that took its course on the walls of caves millennia ago and that now returns to render the materialist truth of those simulacral exteriorizations: that the world of ideas is particulate, that light is itself a *medium.*

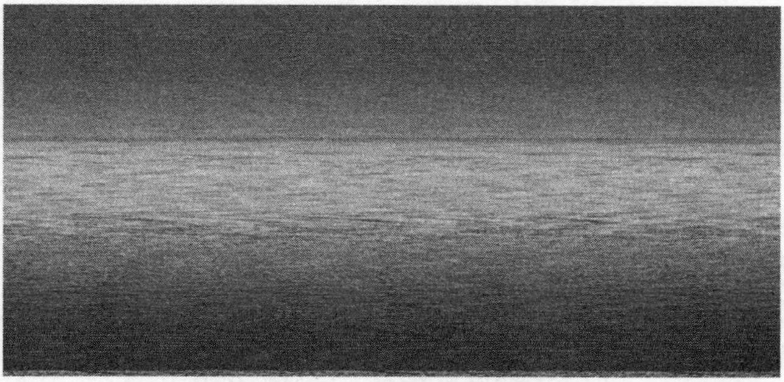

Figure 4.3. Nicolas Baier, *Failed,* 2008. Chromogenic transparency in LED light box, 122 × 244 cm. The image derives from a computer crash that saturated Baier's monitor with a color field resembling a red sea receding toward a distant horizon.

Figure 4.4. Nicolas Baier, *Canvas,* 2010. Ink-jet print, 295 × 445 cm. Rather than recording images of cave paintings in southern France, Baier photographs the stone wall beside these inaugural representations, presenting the bare "canvas" of the stone.

Across the gallery from *Photons,* poised on the facing wall behind an eight-foot square pane of plexiglass, hovers a glass replica of Baier's left eye ball. It is an eye that does not see, but that presides over the scene as we look at its blind unlooking. Like Lacan's sardine can glinting in the sea, it draws our gaze. And insofar as we turn our back upon it, toward *Photons,*

Figure 4.5. Nicolas Baier, *Photons (The World of Ideas)*, 2010. Ink-jet print, 152 × 183 cm. Light pours into an artificial cave in the Parc des Buttes-Chaumant, Paris. The image is inverted, disturbing the viewer's sense of spatial orientation and suggesting the materialist reversal performed by the title.

we can feel ourselves prehended by the Gaze itself, occupying a specific position within the field of vision of which the photographic apparatus functions as prosthesis. In Baier's installation, *The World of Ideas* is both a visual image upon which we look and a relation, which has to be thought, to an eye that does not see, to in-visibility. The field of the Gaze is this mediated relation of the sensible and the intelligible, a field in which we come to *feel* the factical presence of our body situated not only between looking and being somehow blindly looked at, but also between eye and mind, photons and Ideas. Two mediations then: the *corporeal presence* of a body and the *technical reproduction* of an image and an eyeball. In *Photons (The World of Ideas)* the light of the intelligible is cast as material photons into the cave, and it is the sensible experience of our embodied relation to this image that solicits thinking.

If *Photons* emphasizes the illumination of an obdurate stone surface, in *Vanitas,* Baier's monumental assemblage of scanned mirrors, this relation of light to surface to sight to the technics of photography is reversed. Here, the reflective surface of the mirror is not transmitted as an image; rather, its surface is rendered opaque by a process of digital recording that devours whatever light the mirror reflects back to the sensor of the scanner. "The scanner captures only the marks or the missing parts," notes Baier.

Figure 4.6. Nicolas Baier, *Photons* (left) and *Untitled,* 2010 (right). Installation view. When looking toward a cracked mirror at the end of the room, the viewer's body is situated between an image of light and thought, on the left, and a reproduction of the artist's eyeball, on the right.

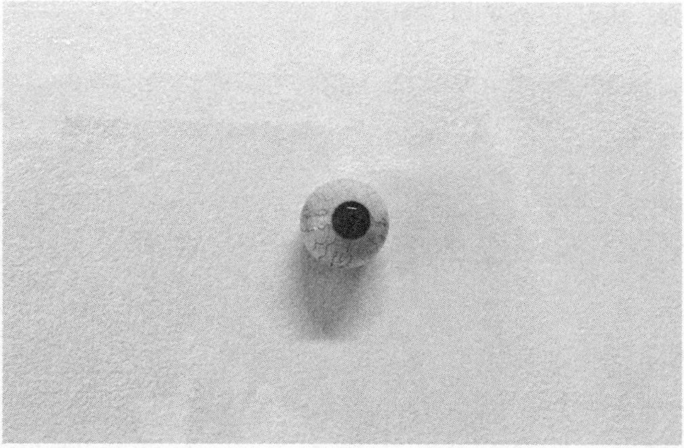

Figure 4.7. Nicolas Baier, *Untitled,* 2010. Eyepiece prosthesis, glass, 3 × 3 cm. The viewer is overseen or overlooked by the blind looking of the artist's eye, reproduced in glass. The eyepiece suggests a contextual detachment of the gaze, even as it generates the context in which an artwork on the opposite wall is seen.

"In closed circuit, the reflective plane does not receive information (the mirror facing itself). Once digitized, the avatar is revealed: a somber deep black span."[1] Reflection is subtracted from the surface by an absorptive recording of the light that it reflects, such that "in these images the surface does not reflect the viewers' likenesses back to them."[2] The viewer's likeness—my own image, which I *would have* seen—is subtracted along with the reflective surface: erased. In its place we are confronted with a "somber deep black span" of "marks or missing parts." It is as if the tain of the mirror, its obverse, had bled through to its hither side. As if these marks and missing parts, seen in lieu of ourselves, were the uncanny residue of this reversal. As if it had become the vocation of photography to *transmit the reversal of the obverse of the image.*

As if—but this is not what happens. What we see is not a reversal (itself a function of a mirror), but rather the remorseless exposure of a surface shorn of reflection: facticity rather than phantasm. It is the function of the mirror phase, in Lacan's account, to give way onto an "inexhaustible squaring of the ego's audits," torn as the *I* is, at the moment of its emergence as imago, by its splitting between identity and alienation, insufficiency and anticipation. And it is the mediation of the image—as *exteriorization*—that casts the specular "lure of spatial identification" which thus captivates the subject and "turns out fantasies."[3]

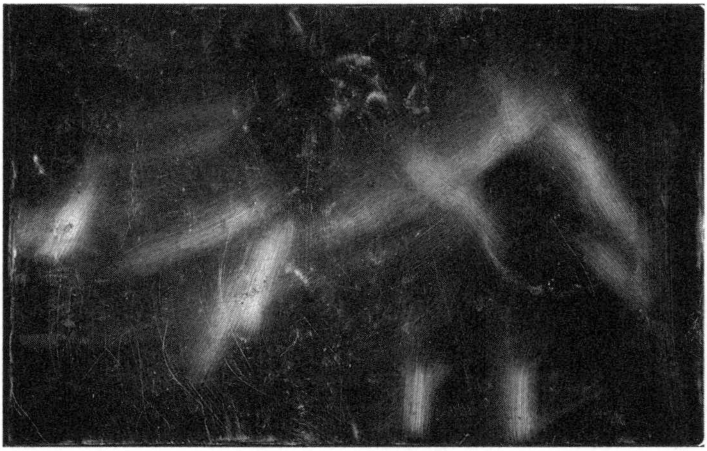

Figure 4.8. Nicolas Baier, *Vanitas 01,* 2007–2008 (detail). Ink-jet print, 62 × 96 cm. The image as *subtraction* of reflection and *reversal* of the mirror, as if obverse, the tain, had bled through onto its hither side. The scanner draws "a somber deep black span" from a surface.

The effect of Baier's *Vanitas* is more on the order of the scene from Lowry's *Under the Volcano* analyzed by Clement Rosset in *Le réel: Traité de l'idiotie.* "Why was he here," the Consul in Lowry's novel asks himself: "why was he always more or less, here?" "He would have been glad of a mirror," Lowry writes, "to ask himself that question. But there was no mirror. Nothing but stone."[4] For Rosset, the substitution of stone for mirror is emblematic of the *idiocy* of the real by which the Consul is confronted. The problem is not, as for Lacan, that of a spatial capture precipitated by the doubling of the real as an image, but rather the recondite and stupid sufficiency of the real to itself, over and against one's desire for reflection. Rosset reads Lowry's passage as follows:

> To know oneself, to know who one is and why one is there, one must have a *mirror;* but the world around him offers nothing other than *stone.* . . . There are, in effect, two great possibilities of contact with the real: rough contact, which runs up against things and draws from them nothing other than the feeling of their silent presence; and smooth contact, polished, in a mirror, which replaces the presence of things with their apparition in images. Rough contact is a contact without double; smooth contact does not exist without the help of the double.[5]

Whereas Medusa turns to stone when confronted by the mirrored doubling of her own gaze, Baier's *Vanitas* draws us into the idiocy of the real by turning the mirror itself to stone, subtracting its doubling function, as a specular apparatus, through the photographic representation of the opacity beneath its surface. To confront *Vanitas* is to confront a technical doubling of the real put under erasure, canceled out, as double, by the transmission of an obdurate *absorption.* In place of a reflection, we see a "somber deep black span" that one cannot see through or into. And again: it is the mediation of technics that performs this subtraction of the specular double. It is the mediation of a device (the digital scanner) that traces nothing other than the residue or remainder of a reflective mirage.

Mirror and stone. Cave painting and digital scanner. The rock wall beside the primordial inscription of an image and the somber deep black span beneath the surface of a specular double. These are not only the preoccupations of Baier's work as a photographer but also of Bernard Stiegler's work as a philosopher of technology. In the first volume of *Technics and Time,* Stiegler broods upon what he calls "the de-fault of origin" ungrounding the emergence of both the technical object and the human species. He investigates the coevolutionary process of "the technical inventing the human, the human inventing the technical" a process occurring through the slow course of a "genetic drift" whereby the development of the *who* and the *what*, of the cortex and the tool, take place together.[6] Stiegler's important revision of Heidegger's existential analytic consists in establishing that both historicality (the already-there) and projective anticipation (the not-yet)—as well as the ruptural temporalizing of their noncoincidence—depend in the first instance upon technics: upon the exteriorization of retention through the tool, the trace, the inscription, the organization of inorganic matter as *recording*.

For Stiegler, the coevolution of technics and the human occurs through a process of "embryonic fabrication" that cannot be localized on either side of the apparent divide between animal and man, inorganic and organic matter, technical object and living being. And this coevolution is initially effected in stone, through the carving of inscriptions with flint. What Stiegler calls "a mirror proto-stage" is this production of a psychic interior through exteriorization, a meeting of "grey matter and mineral matter" whereby the cortex "reflects itself . . . like a mirrored psyche, an archaeo- or paleonotological mode of reflexivity, somber, buried, freeing itself slowly from the shadows like a statue out of a block of marble."[7] Rendered by digital technology, the distressed opacity of Baier's mirrors returns us to this primal scene: an opaque *mise-en-abyme* wherein the difference between mirror and stone collapses. *Facticity rather than phantasm,* I said, by way of opposing Rosset's stone to Lacan's mirror. But with Stiegler in mind, we might say that it is the coevolution of facticity and phantasm that is legible in Baier's work. The "somber deep black span" of *Vanitas* is what Stiegler calls an "archaeo- or paleontological mode of reflexivity, somber, buried": one that has to be located at the surface of contact between gray matter and mineral matter.

It is the *feeling* of such contact that we can call, by way of reference to Alfred North Whitehead, a *prehension.* This modality of feeling cannot be grasped through the opposition of stone and mirror. A prehension entails neither brute contact with the sheer idiocy of the real, which draws from things "nothing other than the feeling of their silent presence." Nor does it involve the specular lure of the mirror, "which replaces the presence of things with their apparition in images." A prehension is a *determinate bond,* insofar as it either excludes or includes another item in the real internal constitution of what Whitehead calls an actual entity or an actual occasion. "Prehension" is a term equally applicable to the inscription by flint and cortex of a "somber, buried" mode of reflexivity, emerging over evolutionary time, or to the movement of a scanner's sensor over the surface of a mirror, its absorption of a reflected light that will not be reflected back to

Figure 4.9. Nicolas Baier, *Project Star (black)*, 2010. Installation view. An enlarged 3D reproduction of a piece of meteorite from Diablo Canyon is surrounded by what seem to be traces of the object's existence or effects.

Figure 4.10. Nicholas Baier, *Vanitas (2010)*. Mirror, aluminum, 114 × 81cm. Baier has reproduced a mirror, broken with his fist, through a painstaking mimetic process. The pieces of the mirror were individually scanned; then corresponding pieces were cut by hand from other mirrors and assembled into a jigsaw replica of the original.

the viewer's gaze. Between *Photons (The World of Ideas)* and *Vanitas,* it is *the technics of prehension* that is at stake for Baier: the manner in which contact, recording, exteriorization grasp, mediate, and transmit any relation to the real.

Figure 4.11. Nicolas Baier, *Impact,* 2010. Ink-jet print, 56×43 cm. *Impact* is a photographic reproduction of a hole in the wall of Baier's studio, made with his fist: his fist "acting like a meteorite," he says.

Baier's latest work—*Project Star (black),* an installation exhibited in the fall of 2010 as part of the exhibition *Transformations*—is a stunning demonstration of his commitment to thinking through the capacity of new media art to experiment with the technics of prehension. If we turn away from *Photons (The World of Ideas)*—from our eerie position between a digital allegory of the cave and an unseeing eyeball—and if we look toward the back wall of the gallery housing Baier's exhibition, we find our image reflected in a broken mirror, its fractures spiraling outward like a spider's web from a singular point of impact. Its title is a repetition: *Vanitas (2010).* Arrayed on the walls surrounding this fractured repetition of Baier's earlier work are several mysterious objects. Immediately to the right, a white ink-jet print stretched around a deep frame depicts a caved in-hole at its center.

Titled *Impact,* the piece seems to be a nonreflective double of *Vanitas.* It appears to be collapsed inward by a collision that the adjacent mirror projects and distributes outward, but in fact it is the image of such a collapse—a somewhat eerily two-dimensional photograph of an unspecified impact sustained by the wall of Baier's studio. To the right of *Impact* are photographs of two circular aluminum paint trays titled *Satellite 01* and *Satellite 02,* both of which bear traces of a grainy black substance. Across the room from these photographs is an oval canvas densely covered with what ap-

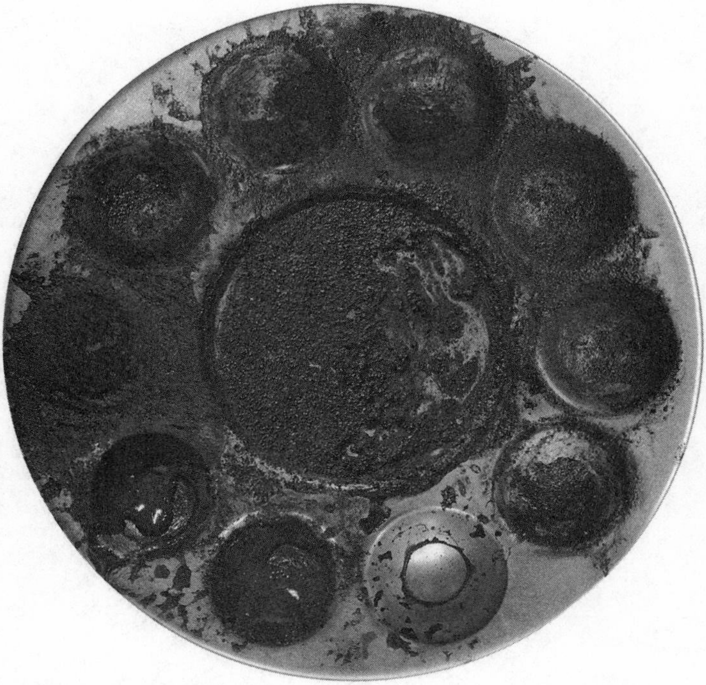

Figure 4.12. Nicolas Baier, *Satellite 01,* 2010. Ink-jet print, 25 × 4 cm.

pears to be the same dark substance with which the trays are stained. The trays activate a strange sense of the painting they confront across the room as the residue of its own composition.

The painting's black surface seems to draw in all the light of the gallery's white walls into its own opacity, stabilizing the play of reflections and repetitions by which it is surrounded. The piece is titled *Monochrome (black).* At the center of the installation I have been describing, functioning as a point around which it pivots, is a large acrylic, graphite, and steel sculpture titled *Star (black).* It appears to be a massive hunk of silver ore extracted from the earth, polished, and displayed on a rectangular stone plinth resembling Kubrick's black monolith. But in fact, what we are looking at is a replica of another object that is nowhere present, though its traces surround us in one form or another. *Star (black)* is a vastly enlarged reproduction of a palm-sized nugget of graphite

Figure 4.13. Nicolas Baier, *Satellite 02,* 2010. Ink-jet print, 25 × 4 cm.

meteorite acquired from Diablo Canyon, Arizona. Having held this piece of meteorite in my hand while visiting Baier's studio in November 2009, having written my name with it on a sheet of paper, having watched its owner toss it in his hand like a magician with something up his sleeve, for me, a simple question concerning this small but curiously heavy object comes to mind when confronted with Baier's installation: where is it?

In 2009, I hold this object in my hand; I prehend it. It is compact, heavy, uneven but smooth, scored with narrow crevices traversing its surface, dull black speckled with rust-colored patches in its indentations. In September 2010, I see a pitch black material evenly spread across an oval canvas on the wall of a gallery, fading in places toward an opaque grey, broodingly matte but with glinting speckles distributed across its roughly pebbled surface. And in between this art object and the residue of its production is a mas-

Figure 4.14. Nicolas Baier, *Monochrome (black)*, 2010. Meteorite graphite, acrylic medium on canvas, aluminum. 31 × 41 × 4 cm. Divided from its form, the matter of the meteorite, and images of its traces, are distributed around the central sculptural object.

Figure 4.15. Nicolas Baier, *Star (black)*, 2010. Acrylic, graphite, steel, 50 × 40 × 91 cm. Baier used 3D scanning and stereolithography to make an enlarged reproduction of a palm-sized nugget of meteorite from Diablo Canyon, Arizona.

Figure 4.16. Nicolas Baier, *Project: photo 01, Star (black),* 2010. Ink-jet print, 43 × 56 cm. A photograph of the "original" piece of meteorite. Scanned, printed, powdered, what remains of the object are reproductions of its form, residues of its matter, traces of its transformations.

Figure 4.17. Nicholas Baier, *Project: splitting, Star (black),* 2010. The process of reproducing the meteorite involved dividing a digital model of the scanned object into twenty discrete sections which could then be printed using stereolithography and reassembled as an enlarged replica.

Figure 4.18. Nicolas Baier, *Project: 9 stages, Star (black),* 2010. Like many of Baier's pieces, the reconstruction of the scanned and printed meteorite requires both sophisticated digital technologies and meticulous manual craft.

sive reproduction of the object I once held, at once entirely transformed and uncannily faithful to "the original."

The year before Baier told me what he planned to do with the meteorite I held in my hand. He would digitize its contours using a 3-D scanner, dividing the surface of the object into twenty discrete sections, each functioning as the digital map of a determinate surface area of the object. He would then "print" enlarged three-dimensional models of these discrete units using a stereolithography machine, before assembling them into a compound sculptural replica. Having produced this replica, he would then powder the meteorite and liquefy the graphite of which it is composed, using it to paint an oval canvas whose shape is intended to suggest images of anistropies in cosmic microwave background radiation.

Along with these works, he would exhibit the reproduction of a cracked mirror and of a ruptured gypsum wall, both of which he broke with his fist. His fist, he says, was "acting like a meteorite."[8] All of these pieces are what Baier calls "transformations," and their production is mediated not only by labor and technique—Baier's manual skill as an artist and the conceptual itinerary of his project—but also by sophisticated digital instruments, by technics.

Why speak of these transformations in terms of *the technics of prehension?* The process of transformation is *technical* not only because it involves the mediation of 3D scanners and stereolithography but more fundamentally, from the perspective of Stiegler's analytic of technics and time, because it involves *recording* and *transcription*. It is a process of *prehension* for much the same reason. For Whitehead a prehension is not only "the activity whereby an actual entity effects its own concretion of other things" ("actual entities involve one another by reason of their prehensions of each other"); it is also the activity by which an actual occasion *reproduces* the "perpetual perishing" of the past and the present. Whitehead specifies two kinds of process or "fluency," both of which depend upon the function of prehension. First, *concrescence* is "the process in which the universe of many things acquires an individual unity in a determinate relegation of each item of the 'many' to its subordination in the constitution of the novel 'one'" (*PR*, 211). Concrescence is the processual composition of one actual entity among others. Second, there is the fluency of *transition* from particular existent to particular existent. "Transition" (and we might consider Whitehead's term as analogous to Baier's title, *Transformations*) entails a perishing of the process of an actual entity whereby its particular existence is constituted as "an original element in the constitutions of other particular existents elicited by repetitions of process" (*PR*, 210). These two kinds of fluency have a precise relation: *transition* is the process whereby any actual entity becomes the datum for a new *concrescence*.

To speak of "the technics of prehension" is to specify the mutual pertinence of Stiegler's and Whitehead's conceptual itineraries as follows. What Stiegler calls the coevolution of technics and the human, a coevolutionary process that emerges from the mutual prehension of hand and flint, depends upon a particular relation of transition and concrescence. The technical exteriorization of memory as *recording*—what Stiegler calls the *tertiary memory* of technical retention—constructs the already-there of a contextual historicality from which further technical invention (involving projection, anticipation, planning) can emerge. "It is the process of anticipation itself that becomes refined and complicated with technics," writes Stiegler. Technics is "the mirror of anticipation, the place of its recording and of its inscription as well as the surface of its reflection, of the reflection that time is, as if the human were reading and linking his future to the technical."[9] *Epiphylogenesis* is Stiegler's term for the tracing of time as a process of technical retention and transmission, split between facticity and anticipation: a history of traces in which what *develops* (process, *genesis*) is *conserved* (concrescence, *epigenesis*) and *passed on* (transition, *epiphylo-*

genesis) through the coevolution of the human and the technical. To think *this particular* coevolution is not to formulate a theory of prehensions in general, but rather to think the *specificity* of the sort of prehensions made possible by the historicity of technics. If "flint is the first reflective memory, the first mirror,"[10] and if this is the coupling from which the coevolutionary history of technics unfolds, what sort of prehensions evolve as epiphylogenesis passes over into technical syntheses of memory made possible by digital technologies—that is to say, so-called new media?

While the destabilization by digital technologies of the indexical function of photographic recording and of the reliability of the photographic frame has often been emphasized by theorists of new media, it is evidently the indexical *exactitude* of digital recording that comes to the fore in Baier's installation. The capacity to precisely record and reproduce subtle contours of an object's surface—to *formalize* its surface in three dimensions, to *retain* that form in a digital medium, and to *characterize* a precise three-dimensional replica at a larger scale through stereolithography: this is made possible by the superior indexical exactitude of digital technologies. It is made possible by a superior capacity to *retain* and *transmit* complex traces of an existent object. Baier's *Project Star (black)* plays with different instantiations of the index as trace, but all of these foreground what Stiegler calls the "orthothetic" precision of digital images.[11]

Vanitas (2010) is perhaps the clearest emblem of this obsession. The piece that we see in the gallery is not simply the presentation of a cracked mirror; rather, it is an elaborate reproduction of that object. Baier reports that he scanned each of the pieces of a broken mirror, generating a vector document for each of the shards. He then laboriously chiseled out replicas of these fragments from other mirrors, assembling these into a painstaking reproduction of the broken surface.[12] This process, which took over three hundred hours, constitutes a glacial homage not only to the fraction of an instant during which fault lines initially spread from the point of contact across the mirror's surface, but also to the indexical exactitude of *scanning* the broken pieces and then *transferring* this digital record into the vector space serving as sculptural model. Baier's manual "craft" as an artist tests itself against the precision of these digital indices. The "reflective memory" first enabled by the coupling of cortex and flint now mirrors itself in carving of traces, inscribing the time of the work into the materials of its production through a complex coordination of object, thought, eye, hand, tool, and mnemotechnics.

Formalization, retention, characterization. The articulated, transversal process of recording and reproduction that we find in Baier's work—one that Whitehead and Stiegler allow us to describe as a process of concrescence and transition, of epiphylogenesis mediated by tertiary memory—pushes us to reframe debates between important positions in contemporary media theory. What is at issue in Baier's work is not primarily the affective "framing" of digital mediation by a human body (as for Mark Hansen),[13] nor primarily an excision of such a frame by the inhuman transmission of coded information by computational systems (as for Friedrich Kittler),[14] nor the middle road of "intermediation" emphasizing emergent processes operative through dynamic feedback loops between humans and computers (as for N. Katherine Hayles).[15] What each of these models relies upon is an initial distinction between human bodies and computational systems, however deconstructed or intermediated this distinction becomes. Reference to the technics of prehension, on the other hand, allows us to shed this provisional distinction and to begin, rather, with the flat ontology of actual entities/actual occasions, relationally constituted by prehensions. Moreover, beginning with Whitehead also enables us to shed the rhetorical entanglements encountered by Stiegler due to his use of the term "the human" to designate the conceptually deconstructed (yet terminologically retained) site of a structural coupling with technics. From this perspective, we can see that it is not the phenomenological nor "emergent" encounter of a "human" and a "tool" that is of interest in Baier's work (nor the "inhuman" processing and transmission of digital code), but rather the manner in which the pertinence of those categories is displaced by the specific particularity of reticulated prehensions instantiated in differential media, constituting and traversing processes of concresence and transition. It is from such a perspective, and through such a terminology, that we can grasp and come to terms with what Stiegler refers to as the "default of origin." It is *within* this default (neither "before" nor "after") that such categories as "human" and "tool" come to make sense in the first place. But this is as much as to say that they can neither *begin* nor *end* making sense because they have no origin and no telos. It is not that these categories have to be abandoned because they have been superseded but rather that they have always already been abandoned to the technics of prehension, to the constitution of the *already there* as tertiary memory that Stiegler unearths within Heidegger's existential analytic.

This terminological precision, however, does not mitigate the enigmatic *situation* of the object in Baier's installation. Let us return to our earlier question: *Where* is the meteorite that we seem to find everywhere displaced in *Project Star (black)*? What counts as the trace of such an object, and where can we find one? The object is nowhere present, but nevertheless larger than ever and *right in the middle of the room*. It has become the coherence of its technical construction, and the coherence of this construction thus circulates throughout the becoming of its traces. The object, existing neither here nor there as a simple location—but rather modulated in and through a series of *particular* transformations—has become the transversal resonance of their differential remainders. It inheres as much within the series of retentional, transcriptive traces as it does within any one term.

Discussing the morphological resemblance of the oval canvas of *Monochrome (black)* to the shape of a cosmic microwave anistrophe, Baier describes the piece as "an attempt to paint the universe with some star dust."[16] So, in the terms of C. S. Peirce's semiotic theory, is *Monochrome (black)* the *icon* of an anisotropy, a *symbol* of "the universe," or an *index* of the object with the powdered residue of which its black surface is composed? Perhaps this question would be no more pressing than asking if the *Mona Lisa* is an icon of the woman it depicts or an index of the flax plant from which the linseed oil of its paints was pressed—were it not for the presence in Baier's installation of an enlarged replica of the very powdered object with which *Monochrome* was painted. Situated precisely where a viewer might stand in order to apprehend the surface of the painting, the presence of the replica suggests that the interrogation of these questions has *already* been undertaken by the composition of the installation in which the painting is included. A mimetic reproduction of the object in question already occupies the place of the questioner—in front of a broken mirror, between a universe painted with star dust and the mundane satellites deployed in the process of the painting's production.

If, as Baier says, both *Vanitas (2010)* and *Impact* record the impact of his fist "acting like a meteorite," rather than the impact of the meteorite itself, then they record *an idea* evoked by an *object* enacted by a *body* recorded in a *substrate*. But given that the pieces of the broken mirror are scanned and recut rather than directly exhibited, and given that *Impact* is an ink-jet print of a digital photograph rather than a punctured slab of gypsum, what these pieces have in common is not their immediate presentation of an index but rather the technical mediation of indexical traces shifting through a network of prehensions. If there is a destabilization of the indexical function of technical retention in Baier's work, it is not due to the malleability of digital media (since, again, it is the retentional exactitude of the latter that is foregrounded). Rather, it is due to the radical *expansion* of the category of the index to include *any and all traces:* conceptual, affective, mnemonic, corporeal, technical.

We can approach this radicalization of the index in Baier's work by reading Peirce according to Whitehead's principle of relativity, which asserts that "every item in its universe is involved in each concrescence" (*PR*, 22). According to the principle of relativity, "an actual entity *is* present in other actual entities," and "in fact if we allow for degrees of relevance, and for negligible relevance, we must say that every actual entity is present in every other actual entity" (*PR*, 148). To decide, then, that a sign functions as an icon or a symbol rather than an index is to account for what Whitehead calls "degrees of relevance." Nevertheless, Whitehead's principle of relativity entails a recognition of the sense in which every actual entity *to some degree* functions as an index of every other. Each concrescence, that is, has a *real relation*, a determinate relation, to every item in its universe, and the actual entity it composes might be taken as a "sign" of such relation. If an index, for Peirce, is "a sign determined by its dynamic object by virtue of being in a real relation to it,"[17] then a *prehension* is the vector of that determination, the real relation of an actual entity to an object that it includes within its own constitution as datum, cause, condition.

Thus, given this radicalization of the index, what is crucial to Baier's work as a photographer and conceptual artist is not only to seize but to *delimit* the play of such indexical traces, to make manifest *specific* or *determinate* transformations. He does so by exploring the *technical conditions* of their recording and transmission. The problem of the relation between object, sign, and interpretant in Baier's *Project* is to specify what the installation *includes*, and this is largely what it means to ask "where" the object apparently motivating its transformations might be. That is, how are we to specify or to think the constitution of *that* which traverses *this* series of transformations?

The problem is proximate to the basic question of Descartes's wax experiment: *Where* is the wax, as all of its sensible properties undergo transformations in time when held up to the heat of the fire, and *what* then is the essence of this body—what does it essentially *include?* According to Descartes, there are *too many* modifications of the object for the imagination to follow their unfolding, "an immeasurable number of changes" he says.[18] We have to abstract from the mutability of secondary qualities, from any particular instantiation of the wax as this or that collection of sensible data, and thus, for Descartes, it is the mind alone that is capable of perceiving the intelligible object as extended, flexible, changeable. It is the mind alone that is capable of grasping the primary qualities of the wax as irreducible to the particularity of sensible concrescence.

We can situate Baier's exploration of the technics of prehension by considering his approach to this Cartesian problem in relation to two responses to Cartesian epistemology: that of Whitehead and that of Gaston Bachelard. For Whitehead, the conclusions Descartes draws from the wax experiment would be exemplary of the "bifurcation of nature" endemic to modern philosophy and encapsulated by the distinction between primary and secondary qualities. In *The Concept of Nature,* Whitehead rejects any division of knowledge into qualities that are apprehended (secondary qualities) and qualities that are the cause of apprehension (primary qualities) (*CN,* 27). He thus rejects what we could call, following Wilfred Sellers, the distinction between the manifest image and the scientific image.[19] Whitehead subverts the bifurcation of nature by reframing the distinction between "causal" and "apparent" components of an object in terms of the general framework of his theory of prehensions. But Whitehead does not account, in any detail, for the specificity of the *technics* of prehension in the constitution of scientific knowledge. Doing so will help us to grasp the specificity not only of scientific practice but also, in a different but related register, of an art practice like Baier's.

The conclusions drawn by Gaston Bachelard concerning the epistemological implications of non-Euclidean geometry and postclassical physics might seem starkly opposed to those of Whitehead, since Bachelard seems to affirm a distinction between the manifest and the scientific image. For instance, Bachelard asserts that "the world in which we think is not the world in which we live,"[20] where the world in which we think is that of scientific representation and the world in which we live is that of "everyday" sensory perception or intuition. What Bachelard calls "the philosophy of no" *(la philosophie du non)* is charged with the strict monitoring of this distinction. "The *philosophy of no,*" he writes, "would become a general doctrine if it could coordinate all the examples where thought breaks with the obligations of life."[21] "The philosophy of no" is Bachelard's term for a scientific epistemology capable of making the distinction between *intuition* and *scientific knowledge* and clearing away the epistemological obstacles of the former as impediments to the latter. "Intuitions are very useful," he states; "they serve to be destroyed."

For both Whitehead and Bachelard, however, contemporary physics requires us to reject the conditions for the determination of objects laid out by Kant in the *Critique of Pure Reason.* It turns out, both argue, that these conditions obtain only for a *particular class* of objects, which is relatively restricted (for example, it cannot account for the objects of non-Euclidean geometry or postclassical physics). And, with Whitehead, Bachelard rejects the vulgar materialist principle that you can determine an object as a simple location: that "you can adequately state the relation of a particular material body to space-time by saying that it is just there, in that place" (*SMW,* 49). Whitehead calls this the fallacy of misplaced concreteness. Against this fallacy, both he and Bachelard demand that we account for the dispersed, relational, and processual constitution of objects.

At the core of Bachelard's theory of scientific knowledge is an effort to reconcile the opposing claims of rationalist and empiricist epistemologies. He recognizes that *if* one rejects the Kantian effort to displace the opposition of rationalism and empiricism through transcendental philosophy, then the relation between them will have to be rethought. And this problem will help us to conceptualize the form of mediation that is at stake in Baier's work. "The philosophy of science," Bachelard argues,

> remains corralled in the two extremes of knowledge: in the study by philosophers of principles which are too general and in the study by scientists of results which are too particular. It exhausts itself against these two epistemological obstacles which restrict all thought: the general and the immediate. It stresses first the *a priori* then the *a posteriori,* and fails to recognize the transmutation of epistemological values which contemporary scientific thought constantly executes between *a priori* and *a posteriori,* between experimental and rational values.[22]

This "transmutation of epistemological values"—a toggling between the *a priori* and the *a posteriori,* the rational and the empirical—requires us to understand that "empiricism and rationalism in scientific thought are bound together by a strange bond, as strong as the bond which joins pleasure and pain." "Indeed," Bachelard states, "the *one triumphs by assenting to the other:* empiricism needs to be understood; rationalism needs to be applied." "The one completes the other," such that to think scientifically is "to place oneself in the epistemological terrain which mediates between theory and practice, between mathematics and experiment. To know a natural law scientifically is to know it as a phenomenon and a noumenon at one and the same time."[23] For Bachelard, science conjoins experiment and reason by constantly exposing each to the imperatives of the other. This is what Descartes misses in his analysis of the wax experiment. For Descartes, the empirical is *displaced* by the rational, rather than each assenting to the other. To deploy a term used in passing by Althusser, we could characterize Bachelard's epistemology as a *rationalist empiricism.*[24]

EMPIRICISM → TECHNICS ←——————→ FORMALIZATION ← RATIONALISM
(INSCRIPTION)

Figure 4.19. Rationalism and empiricism are conjoined through retentional traces (inscriptions) of technically processed phenomena (technics) and relations among mathematical signs (formalization).

More directly than Whitehead, Bachelard attends to the particular *mediation* of the relation between rationalism and empiricism, theory and practice, which constitutes the "epistemological terrain" of science.[25] And this will bring us back to Baier. What we find in this terrain, mediating between empiricism and rationalism, is the conjunction of *technics* (technique, technology) and *formalization* (proofs, formulae, inscribed chains of logical entailment). "In order to establish a determinate scientific fact, it is necessary to put a coherent technique to work," states Bachelard.[26] A *coherent technique* conjoins technics and formalization: an empirical rigor enabled by the disciplined application of procedures and instruments (technics), a rational coherence attested by legible demonstrations (formalization). Extrapolating from Bachelard, we might say that what mediates between technics and formalization are *inscriptions*. Rationalism and empiricism are conjoined, in their complex complementarity, through retentional traces of technically processed phenomena and relations among mathematical signs. This conjunction could be graphed as in Figure 4.19.

It is no paradox for either Whitehead or Bachelard to hold that scientific knowledge is both *objective* and *constructed*. If "the philosophy of no" is the general doctrine that would "coordinate all the examples where thought breaks with the obligations of life," the term "thought" does not refer us only to "mind" or "reason," but to the practical, a-subjective mediation of *technics* and *formalization*, which is the organon of this coordination. The epistemological terrain of science is that of the *technics* of prehension: of the transformation of technical retentions into formally coordinated chains of signifiers whose relations are subject to correction.

Perhaps we begin to see how this encounter with the technics of prehension and its bond with formalization—through the detour of scientific epistemology—might inform our understanding of Baier's photography. A photograph from Baier's 2006 exhibition, *Traces*, provides a simple demonstration, an argument as it were. The photograph is titled *Prehension*. In another photograph, the invitation card for the exhibition, we see a "realistic" representation of the boundary of a cemetery in winter, marked in particular by the leafless branches of somber trees extending and twisting

Figure 4.20. Nicolas Baier, *Prehension,* 2006. Ink-jet print, 109 × 127 cm. An inverted digital photograph of a tree at the Mont Royal Cemetery, Montréal. Baier felt that "the magnificently emaciated tree . . . seemed as though it was trying as hard as it could, sick and deformed as it was, to hug the space around it close to itself."

across a pale grey sky illuminated by a muted sun. In *Prehension,* we find the particularly contorted tree on the card inverted, as though growing upside down from the top of the frame. A text at the exhibition explains:

> A friend and I were sketching out the premise of a video at the Mont Royal cemetery. While he was struggling to film a few rushes, I spotted this magnificently emaciated tree. It seemed as though it was trying as hard as it could, sick and deformed as it was, to hug the space around it close to itself.

The tree *prehends* the space around it, "hugs" it: this is how Baier's prehends the tree. It *seems* to him as though the tree were doing so. In the photograph, the frame has been cropped, and the contrast and color have been adjusted (the sky from grey to a pale white background, the snow standing out more clearly against a rich brown trunk than it might otherwise). But the main gesture of the photograph is a simple one: the spatial inversion of the image in relation to the frame disorients the viewer, more thoroughly involv-

Figure 4.21. Nicolas Baier, Invitation Card, Traces Exhibition, 2006. The tree reproduced and inverted in *Prehension* is visible on the left side of the photograph.

ing us with the manner in which the tree is involved with the space around it, as we try to get a grip on the image in the absence of a gravitational foothold. In this case the process of technical mediation performs a reversal. The technical processing of *Prehension,* the photograph, entails a subtle mimesis of Baier's prehension of the tree: of its deformity and its groping after space. Considered through its title, this relatively minor transformation of the digital image might be taken to reflexively encode the manner in which an object becomes a technical object (and an "art" object) through the relation of perception, affect, concept, and technical mediation. The image is a concrescence of prehensions, which stresses the capacity of photography to *transform* an object. But it does so in a manner that draws us eerily close to the object in question, precisely recording its morphology. It transforms an object through an exact inscription of those objective qualities that render its transformation possible. The image is at once objective and constructed, and it is the exactitude of technical formalization that renders this dialectic operative as what Bachelard would call "a coherent technique."

A cave painting, a meteorite, an opaque mirror, an unseeing eyeball. The subjects of Baier's photography are primordial inscriptions, extraterrestrial objects, abyssal surfaces, canceled sensations. His work foregrounds the capacity of technical formalization to transform objects through the retentional exactitude of digital inscriptions, and thereby to render *evident*, though nowhere *apparent*, traces of their primary qualities. Quentin Meillassoux has argued that

> *all those aspects of the object that can be formulated in mathematical terms can be meaningfully conceived as properties of the object in itself.* All those aspects that can give rise to mathematical thought (to a formula or to digitization) rather than to a perception or sensation can be meaningfully turned into properties of the thing not only as it is with me, but also as it is without me.[27]

The constructive power of *formalization*—"a formula or a digitization"—renders the properties of an object irreducible to the correlate of a subject, through the complicity of technology with reason. Thinking this complicity of reason and technics (which is also to think the complicity of rationalism and empiricism) allows us to think the manner in which technics and formalization function as the filter not only of phenomenal immediacy, but also of the categorical restrictions upon the constitution of objects for which Whitehead and Bachelard reproach Kant's critical philosophy. We could say that *technical formalization is the sieve of the transcendental subject:* the means by which the forms of intuition and the categorical constitution of objects are *filtered out of* retentional traces. This, I think, is what Bachelard means by "the philosophy of no."

The technics of prehension situates thought outside itself because, according to Stiegler, thinking *already* bears its own outside within the default of its origin, due to its constitutive relation to technics. This *technicity* of thinking, which throws thought outside itself before it comes into its own, is one among the traces that Nicolas Baier photographs. Perhaps it is the real subject of his work, the non-site of his investigations. When we find ourselves surrounded by the remains of a vanished object, its traces mediated by technical retentions enabling the reproduction of its contours, we find ourselves forced to think beyond the simple location of objects, and beyond their constitution by our consciousness. The impetus to such thinking is what Bachelard calls "a coherent technique" that holds the object together, in its vanished tracing, through the technics of prehension. To encounter such an absent object, at once nowhere and everywhere present, is to recognize it as both *objective* and *constructed:* as the mediation of a real existence irreducible to a subjective correlate.

For Whitehead, to split the real into two different realities, one of speculative physics and the other of intuition, is to construct "two natures," where "one is conjecture and the other is dream." Whitehead rejects this schism, while Meillassoux affirms it. But both fail to adequately theorize the manner in which it is the technics of prehension that mediates the relation of these "natures," these two sides of the split real thought by modernity. With Stiegler, we can say that the technics of prehension at once institutes and ungrounds speculative thinking in the first instance. With Bachelard, we can say that the technics of prehension mediates a dialectic of the rational and the empirical that constitutes and constructs the object as in-itself rather than for-us. With and against Whitehead, we can say that the technics of prehension operates *between* speculative thinking and intuition, between conjecture and dream.

The technics of prehension, projecting thought outside itself from the somber mirror protostage of mineral inscription to the monochrome opacity of a black star, is the ek-stasis of conjecture and dream, the tracing of their *différance* by an inhuman mediation of rationalism and empiricism. To arrive at such a formulation is not only to think with Whitehead and Bachelard and Stiegler, but also to think through the photography of Nicolas Baier.

Notes

1. Nicolas Baier, "Vanitas," in *Paréidolies/Pareidolias* (Rimouski, Que.: Musée regional de Rimouski, 2009), 29.
2. Ibid.
3. Jacques Lacan, "The Mirror Stage as Formative of the *I* Function," in *Écrits*, trans. Bruce Fink (New York: Norton, 2006), 78.
4. Malcolm Lowry, *Under the Volcano* (New York: HarperCollins, 2000), 306; quoted in Clément Rosset, *Le réel: Traité de l'idiotie* (Paris: Minuit, 1997), 43.
5. Rosset, *Le réel*, 43 (my translation).
6. Bernard Stiegler, *Technics and Time, 1: The Fault of Epimetheus*, trans. Richard Beardsworth and George Collins (Stanford, Calif.: Stanford University Press, 1998), 137.
7. Ibid., 141.
8. Email communication with Nicolas Baier, November 3, 2010.
9. Stiegler, *Technics and Time, 1*, 153.
10. Ibid., 142.
11. On "orthotheticity"—the retentional exactitude of inscriptions—and for an investigation of the situation of contemporary techics within the theoretical framework developed by Stiegler in *Technics and Time, 1*, see Bernard Stiegler, *Technics and Time, 2: Disorientation*, trans. Stephen Barker (Stanford, Calif.: Stanford University Press, 2009).
12. Email communication with Nicolas Baier, November 3, 2010.
13. See Mark B. N. Hansen, *New Philosophy for New Media* (Cambridge, Mass.: MIT Press, 2004).

14. See Friedrich Kittler, *Gramophone, Film, Typewriter*, trans. Geoffrey Winthrop Young and Michael Wutz (Stanford, Calif.: Stanford University Press, 1999).

15. See N. Katherine Hayles, *My Mother Was a Computer: Digital Subjects and Literary Texts* (Chicago: Chicago University Press, 2005).

16. Email communication with Nicolas Baier, November 3, 2010.

17. C. S. Peirce, *Semiotic and Significs: The Correspondence Between Charles S. Peirce and Victoria Lady Welby*, ed. Charles S. Hardwick and J. Cook (Bloomington: Indiana University Press, 1977), 33.

18. René Descartes, *Meditations on First Philosophy*, in *The Philosophical Writings of Descartes*, trans. John Cottingham, Robert Stoothoff, and Dugald Murdoch, vol. 2 (Cambridge: Cambridge University Press, 1984), 21.

19. Wilfred Sellers, *Empiricism and the Philosophy of Mind*, ed. Robert Brandom (Cambridge, Mass.: Harvard University Press, 1997).

20. Gaston Bachelard, *The Philosophy of No: A Philosophy of the New Scientific Mind*, trans. G. C. Waterston (New York: Orion, 1968), 95.

21. Ibid.

22. Ibid., 5.

23. Ibid., 6.

24. Louis Althusser, "The Philosophical Conjuncture and Marxist Theoretical Research," in *The Humanist Controversy and Other Writings*, ed. François Matheron, trans. G. M. Goshgarian (London: Verso, 2003), 4.

25. See, however, chapter 9 of *Adventures of Ideas*, on "Science and Philosophy." Here Whitehead offers an account of how "science and philosophy mutually criticize each other" through the reciprocal relation of concrete fact and conceptual abstraction. His model of this dialectic is the relation between Aristotelian empiricism (observation, classification) and Platonic rationalism (the primacy of mathematics). Bachelard's epistemology is thus compatible with Whitehead's account of the relation between science and philosophy, though Bachelard attends in more detail to the relation between rationalism and empiricism *within* science and devotes considerably more attention to this problem over the course of his epistemological writings.

26. Gaston Bachelard, *The New Spirit of Science*, trans. Arthur Goldhammer (Boston: Beacon, 1985).

27. Quentin Meillassoux, *After Finitude: An Essay on the Necessity of Contingency*, trans. Ray Brassier (London: Continuum, 2008), 3.

Part II

THE METAPHYSICS OF CREATIVITY

FIVE

Whitehead's Involution of an Outside Chance

Peter Canning

Perhaps nothing more sublime has ever been said . . . than in that inscription above the temple of *Isis* (Mother Nature): "I am all that is, that was, and that will be, and no mortal has lifted my veil."

—Immanuel Kant, *Critique of Judgment*

The status of life in nature . . . is the modern problem of philosophy and of science. . . . The very meaning of life is in doubt.

—Alfred North Whitehead, *Modes of Thought*

Whitehead's challenge to the age of science is, at its deepest stratum, where "it hath no bottom," more clinical than critical. The claim to reduce the characteristic powers of life to an accidental result of the physical laws governing its elements is not simply an error; it is a symptom of the *mental* illness that affects human nature generally, but is florid in modernity with its "murder" of God. For God too is a symptom, but that symptom served to tie the knot whose unraveling exposes the brain to mental chaos and delirium when it tries to figure out what is going on with this life and how it got here. The delusion of scientism goes by the name of "mechanism," and is grounded in the notion of "universal law."

The challenge begins with what Whitehead calls "the Romantic protest"—essentially what is known and caricatured under the caustic rubric of "vitalism." The force of Romanticism, however, was to affirm the *reality* of life and mind and defend it against the bizarre temptation to reduce their powers to "epiphenomenal" manifestations of "fundamental laws and initial conditions." The Romantics were well aware that the real thing was being methodically overlooked and denied. They wondered what demon possessed the scientific mind to claim that life was a machine. They mounted a "hysterical" protest. But with that hysteria a new configuration was emerging and shaping itself: the Subject in the Act.

When science joined with history in the age of Darwin, their combined capacity to explain the evolution of the universe grew into what is now the standard "universal history." We have learned that earth is made of elements created in supernovae and exploded into space, which then gravitated into a ball. Life apparently invented or discovered itself here on this planet. It is a question, then, of how a group of molecules got together—or found themselves "associated"—and began to work together to transform this planet into the living Earth.[1] If it is true that "the power of self-assembly, of producing structures of growing complexity, even of reproducing, belongs to the elements that compose matter,"[2] then what does this imply about the nature of matter, its capabilities, its affects? It is true that only some of these elements—mainly the so-called SPONCH—participate in the biosphere, the part of Earth that is "actually" alive. But this actuality is supported by a vast and unfathomable virtual or nomadic prehistory (the Big Bang, the "phase transitions" to different elements and forces, the mysterious complexity of supernovae, and so on), which created new possibilities for "concrescence" and prepared the way for organic chemistry to find out what it can do on Earth (or anywhere else). This universal evolution is so impressive that a distinguished chemist exclaims, "The universe *is* life."[3]

Despite occasional outbursts of enthusiasm, however, the question of what life really is remains largely and deeply unanswered. At least some scientists are able to affirm that life is real and *irreducible* to whatever its elements are doing when they are not composing living molecular communities. Others still claim, obsoletely, that it can be reduced to the mechanics of its constituents. Of course, since those mechanical laws fail to explain what life does, how it emerged to sustain itself and create its future, it becomes necessary to invoke chance or "accident." "Nature . . . seems to be so designed that the *most important things in the real world* appear to be a kind of complicated accidental result of a lot of laws" (emphasis added).[4] In other words, precisely because the *power to live and think* ("the most important things") is inexplicable under mechanistic assumptions, the scientist finds himself compelled to leave everything to chance, while at the same time insisting that the power must be "the result of a lot of laws."

In the effort to explain, the scientific-historical method sees the present event as the result of a cause in the past—while the physical laws themselves are not oriented with respect to time direction. But life is oriented both to the past it remembers and to the future it anticipates, as its "present receives the past and builds the future" (*MT,* 31). Furthermore, what it builds is not predictable nor, therefore, reducible. So the procedure of analytic reduction *undoes* the very thing we are trying to understand, that power of creative construction. Richard Feynman used to warn that if you think you understand quantum physics, you don't know much about quantum physics. Is this not all the more true of life, which by its very process creates a future no one can predict, much less "understand"?

Today it is fashionable to invoke algorithms and programming—the universe, and life, are likened to a computer. In each epoch the technologies science finds most fascinating come to represent the powers of life: in the eighteenth century it was the dynamic automaton and clock designed, built, and wound up by God; in the nineteenth, the thermodynamic motor; and today it is the "thinking machine" with the added mystery that it "constructs itself"—accidentally. But each of these mechanisms is a poor simulation—not to mention that every one was designed by human minds and built by human hands. It is as though in each era the most stunning technology takes over the brain, which "becomes what it beholds" and, benumbed, disavows its own living consciousness and creativity.

What calls for thinking is not the program or mechanism or algorithm; it is the power of the *act* that *creates* the algorithm. Gödel and Tarski long ago punctured the logical fantasy that *affirming* "this is true" could be reduced to an axiomatic procedure or included in a complete "formalized language"; yet the wish for a total theory keeps returning in ever new versions. Is it the compulsion to know it all that tempts the theorist to foreclose the act of theorizing from his theory? While the technologist tries to endow an object with life and mind, the mechanist is denying the reality of that life and mind. But it is really the same pretension operating in both cases; for the "artificial life" the technologist designs into the machine is an inept simulation of a misunderstood "original" which the scientist models with his theory, itself just adequate to motivate that algorithmic simulation.

A true science of life must be able to distinguish between *being* a machine and *building* a machine, between *being controlled by* a program and *designing* a program. And if life emerged by accident, a true theory will affirm the power concealed in that radical chance. For living minds have thought up the machines and programs with which they hypnotize themselves; and they *use* the accidents and *take* the chances that come their way. Instead of dazzling themselves with admiration of technology, as though staring at the mirror image or double of their fantasy, future scientists will see the "machine that constructs itself" as a universal singularity *connecting* the present act to the genesis of the universe.

Is there something about the way science came to exist that causes it to disavow its own activity? The most likely place to begin to look for an explanation is in the rivalry between science and religion. Science eliminated God and replaced divinity with mechanics. But because it was not able to explain the main thing mechanically, it appealed to chance and accident. The creative power of God was relocated in "random dynamics," where the power itself was hidden from view. So today, the powers of life—in the sense of its *ability* to transform energy and materials and use them to build and sustain its body, to repair itself when damaged, to reproduce, and so on—are wrapped and obscured in the mystery of chance, as rationalized by the theory of probability. But probabilities can only be calculated once the initial set of all possible events is given in advance. As Bergson complained, the metaphysics of science gives itself all the possibilities and powers to be explained. It is a kind of Oedipal fantasy: to take the place of God; to reduce God to "chance" or "accident" or "possibility"; finally, to box that possibility into a complete totality, which the scientist imagines "observing" or contemplating from outside somehow. This is the main thrust of modern scientistic nihilism: in the first place, to replace God with mechanism, then when that fails to explain "the most important things," appeal to accident and the calculus of probabilities. And in the end, our own life is "nothing but" a series of accidents.

A careful interpretation of the second law of thermodynamics suggests that the accidents predicted statistically to disorganize organized systems cannot explain how a swarm of molecules can "catalyze" each other's power to *resist* that decomposition. (Hence Schrödinger speculated that the laws of dynamics might be *incomplete.*) What breaks down the machine cannot be the same *dynamic* that builds and repairs and reproduces it. Furthermore, during the history of life on Earth, the quality and number of these powers has been *increasing over time,* evolving and diversifying precisely *counter* to the "universal law" of increasing entropy or "probable disorder" rendering all matter-energy inert and disabled, erasing every difference. (The entropy is "exported to the environment.") Since life and its evolution *actively resist* that dissolution, counteracting the second law, repairing the damages due to accident, the reductionist, at a loss to explain this anomaly, dismisses it as an improbable blip that will eventually be canceled out and silenced. The struggle against entropy is nothing but a senseless random fluctuation. And the activity of life remains unexplained and disavowed.

It is with this turn of the screw of nihilism, however, that the countermovement too mutates, and invents a new strategy: what is relevant to the *meaning* of life is to *take the point of view of life itself.* Here Whitehead is unsurpassable. Consider, for example, what he says of Leibniz. Leibniz asked himself "what it must be like to be an atom." Instead of asking how an atom looks to someone observing it, weighing and measuring it and plotting the movements it makes, he "tells us how an atom is feeling about itself" (*AI*, 132) and the world around it. This is a radical change of perspective. Extrinsically considered, the molecules of the living cell can be observed to obey (or at least not violate) the physical laws as they move about—although the things they do to contribute to the life of the cell, their function, and how they ever managed to *begin* to do those things, are not *explained* by the laws currently known. They are the special transformations and movements attributed to the historical accident of biogenesis. At their best, however, scientists are not fooled by their official commitment to mechanistic ideology: "to recognize the purposiveness *[finalité]* of living systems is to say that one can no longer do biology without referring constantly to the 'project' of organisms, to the 'sense' that their very existence gives to their structures and functions."[5] Consider the neurons of the brain—cells performing acrobatics so strange and inexplicable from the perspective of automatic legal behavior. They are not just obeying laws and rules, but inventing them. As they work in concert to predict the future and to direct the organism toward goals set in the future, their own moves are unpredictable. How the future is involved in the workings of the brain is a perplexing question—the question of life itself. For every living being has to ask itself, Where am I going? What am I about? As the brain organizes images predictive of possible futures and chooses a path among them, deciding what to do, where to go, how to act, what it cannot see or predict are *its own moves*. Considered *intrinsically*, therefore, from the point of view of the living brain itself, we find ourselves *inventing* a future we can foresee only by becoming unpredictable ourselves. Thinking ahead, we play out possible futures in imagination and try to outwit our rivals and form alliances with coevolving organisms and machines, increasing our chances and options. None of this fundamental activity is predicted by any law, much less the law of increasing entropy, which the living strives to *controvert* with its search for energy, aiming to turn around the very order of predictable time.

Our "symbolic" culture intensifies this invention of procedures countervailing the "universal law"—in fact the brain has evolved such a degree of "plasticity" that the human subject has to be constrained by a new kind of rule which we properly call laws. It is telling that we feel compelled to retroject this "rule of law" back into inert physical mechanism! The organization of living cells together with our urges and "conceptual feelings" are so poorly represented by the notion of law, and the theories, models, and simulations based on it, that Whitehead discerns in "scientific realism, based on mechanism" a "radical inconsistency at the basis of modern thought," which "distracts thought" and "enfeebles it" (*SMW*, 76). To take the *perspective of life itself* is to counteract this mental entropy by affirming and channeling the thinking, feeling, planning, dreaming mind—like the one you are reading with now. From outside, "nothing but" the meaningless (if inexplicable) movement of mechanized molecules. When Descartes observed animals, he thought he might be looking at cleverly designed machines.

This bizarre infatuation with nature's law has been strongly (if marginally) challenged since at least the nineteenth century, by Nietzsche and Peirce, for example, who saw "habits" and "tendencies" and regularities in nature, but no laws or obedience. Spontaneities, rather, *chances*—and forms of spontaneous self-ordering. Peirce speculated that the "universal laws" themselves change and evolve—thus allowing for the emergence of new regularities as well as freedoms. The notion of a law of nature is an anthropomorphism piously and compulsively transferred from social legislation—meanwhile forgetting to distinguish creative legislating from obedience—and derived from ancient despotic cosmologies and ideologies, habits of mind apparently retained from our primate ancestry and organization in troops obedient to "alphas." Somehow it has veiled the spontaneity of emergent power—unless the observer is capable of "identifying with" the molecules and cells under observation. (Or as Deleuze would say, "becoming-molecule" with Leibniz.) What is each living being seeking, from its own point of view, if not to improve its lot and increase its powers? Again, power here does not primarily mean despotic privilege to command and be obeyed. It means the ability to move and think, to act, to perceive, to feel, to affect and be affected. All the living beings evolving together on Earth have consistently codirected their concerted energies toward increasing and diversifying their abilities. Sometimes at each other's expense, then again by forming communities of allied molecules in "mutual catalysis." In their individual and collective striving, their conatus, they *work against* the "universal law." For "creation is illegality itself."[6] And if it is "the increase of disorder or entropy with time . . . that distinguishes the past from the future, giving a direction to time,"[7] then the effort of life is to *reverse* that order of time. More precisely, it changes the *sense* of time by making use of the materials it encounters to transform the present and remake the future. It does not *actually* violate the "universal law," because the Earth is "far from equilibrium" and takes its cut of energy flowing from the sun to drive its life process. But this *tendency* to organize is a *virtuality* nowhere represented in physical law. And the tendency to reduce living processes to the mechanical dynamics science is able to recognize and claims to "understand" amounts to a foreclosure of the *new kind of future life has invented,* and toward which it directs its energies.

To turn toward the future is an intension intrinsic to "anticipatory systems":[8] looking out ahead, but also *feeling* our way "forward"—since we cannot actually *see* into time. This odd predicament—that we move not only in space but into an unknown configuration forming itself at the crest of time's becoming—challenges us to anticipate the unforeseeable. Even more strange is that this unknowable is nonetheless creatable *and* arrives somewhat by chance. An occasion for improvisation and *bricolage.*[9]

Seeing ahead in space but not in time—beyond what we can predict and imagine—means continually preparing for the unexpected, getting "ready for anything," almost anything but death. Evolution seems to have designed our cognition to recognize and predict habitual behavior, even as we ourselves generate unpredictable behavior. We guess the future moves of various kinds of bodies and act to intercept or avoid them; some of them, altering their own movements in response to ours, engage us in a kind of dance or displaced mimicry, escaping as we arrive, rejoining us when we try to get away. It is this complex orientation—guessing the future by generalizing from the past, but also creating a future the other cannot predict—that begins to set forth "the *necessary* and somewhat paradoxical role that chance and disarray play in the persistence of complex systems, because, without them, a system lacks the flexibility necessary to adapt and becomes defenseless in the face of novel perturbation."[10] This "chance and disarray" means not only getting used to surprise but causing it, by *becoming unpredictable in our response* and *counting that into* the economy of our pragmatism. What Nietzsche said of "men of knowledge," that "we are unknown to ourselves . . . and with good reason," holds true of life itself.

A concise example of internalized unpredictability as survival strategy of "higher" organisms is presented by the simple life-and-death two-step of the lynx and the hare, in which the hare changes direction *incerto tempore, incertis locis* (as Lucretius would say),[11] to throw off its pursuer, almost as if it had an inbuilt "mechanism" to generate semi-aleatory movement. Perhaps the lynx has not developed a similar random algorithm of pursuit because, on the contrary, it has to stay focused on its goal and aim. Is this aesthetic tension between goal and goal-lessness the "essence" of life? Does "effective complexity" require a sustained practice of the unknowable non-algorithmizable precisely because that outside future must be relocated mysteriously inside our mental guidance systems?

Dealing with other living bodies means reading their habits, deciphering their intentions, capturing prey, avoiding predators, gesturing, signaling, faking, suspecting, trusting, emitting signs and interpreting signs, planning and changing plans, taking aim and adjusting aim, forming purposes—appetition seeking satisfaction . . . all aspects of what Whitehead calls *importance* (*MT,* ch. 1). Only the living *feels* that living and the future are important. Otherwise, regarding this feeling as epiphenomenal, reductionist he sees the world as a grandiose machine that they fancy to be "comprehensible" and therefore "pointless."[12] Of course life is pointless and boring when one's own future seems either predictable or accidental. Only a lifeless mechanism—with its inevitable accidental breakdown—is predictable.

Putting feelers out into a spatially extended milieu means reaching blindly but purposively into time, screening the influx of elements to detect and select what feels important and relevant, to ignore and neglect what is insignificant. This act of filtering, a kind of primordial reading of "data" by every cell, descends from the emergence of a universe feeling its way out of chaos, and has evolved from particle systems to molecular structures and from cell membranes and internal somatic processors—already inexplicable—to the sensorium and the hundred billion neurons of the brain, whose possible ways of connecting are uncountable and ever growing. Such sorting and processing systems, together with our neurochemical imagination (combinatory memory and synthesizers), compose an evolving Crible *(cribrum)* or winnowing sieve.[13] Even the one-celled bacterium "knows its world."[14] We are the universe's very own perceptual apparatus, and our "emergence" from chaos through phase transitions seems due to a kind of auto-sifting, self-selecting urge the world must have had to be born. As the chaotic disappearing apparitions began to sense each other's presence in cosmogenetic sympathy, they took shape in mutual consistency, harmonic resonance. Attracted to each other, they gravitate and "feel the force." ("Every particle feels the force of gravity, according to its mass or energy.")[15] Philosophy shares with primitive cosmologies this sense of a world alive with affect everywhere—yet also shares with science the non-sense that the living God appears to be an accident. Whitehead himself defines God as the "primordial, non-temporal accident" of creativity (*PR,* 7). But accident means chance, and chance conceals the power to form, counteracting the "universal tendency" to dissipate.

By its power of reproduction, life "amplifies" those "fluctuations" or variations that are able to survive and reproduce. It never occurred to Darwin to reduce that power to the random mutation and "law" of natural selection it conditions. Today one appeals beyond law to "initial conditions" or the "quantum chaos" of "all possible universes" from which ours is selected somehow to emerge with the possibility of evolving living beings. But the metaphysical logic of representation is unchanged; as Hermann Weyl (who developed mathematical techniques for both relativity and quantum theory) remarked in 1948, "The dual nature of reality accounts for the fact that we cannot design a theoretical image of *being* except upon the background of the *possible*."[16] This metaphysics of possibility is deeply rooted in the nature of human thinking, and leads it into self-contradiction and "antinomies." In his *Critique of Pure Reason,* Kant drew a distinction that brought the era of classical metaphysics to a close and opened new directions for modern thought. Simply stated, he showed that while the possible is possible, the *act is real;* the possible and the actual differ in "modality." Since the God of metaphysics had been defined by that possibility together with the act of selective realization, this stark division of being indicates a division of God himself or a rift in the nature of reality. This *splitting of the divine subject* in *distinguishing the act from its possibility* was already latent in Leibniz's construction of God as the reader of possibilities who actively chooses a possible world for realization from among all those contained in the divine understanding (Deus Lector). And those possibilities descend from the Ideas of Plato, which are said to "participate" in actuality. So when Kant drew that line of ontological difference, his act began the deconstruction of transcendental metaphysics. Existence *differs* from possibility, and the act that causes something to exist is irreducible. Today we would say it *emerges* from its conditions of possibility. But was the actuality itself already possible before it emerged? If so then why did it not happen sooner? Why do conditions of realization need to develop? What does it mean for something to *become* possible? Where does possibility come from?

It is at this pass that Whitehead's own metaphysical commitment becomes somewhat obscure and seems ambiguous. A semantic analysis yields "two meanings of potentiality: (a) the 'general' potentiality, which is the bundle of possibilities, mutually consistent or alternative, provided by the multiplicity of eternal objects, and (b) the 'real' potentiality, which is conditioned by the data provided by the actual world. General potentiality is absolute, and real potentiality is relative to some actual entity, taken as a standpoint" (*PR,* 65). In the absolute, Possibility cannot be created (or destroyed)—"there are no novel eternal objects" (*PR,* 22)—and God, the "accidental" actuality of Creativity, nonetheless "does not create eternal objects; for his nature requires them as they require him" (*PR,* 257). It seems that

Whitehead considers *all* possibility to be a complete and given uncreated object; thus he adheres to the metaphysical ground of existential logic. However, that "eternal" absolute is not locatable in time, and so God's "unlimited conceptual realization of the absolute wealth of potentiality . . . is not *before* all creation, but *with* all creation" (*PR*, 343).

With his equivocal division of "potentiality," and of God into "primordial" and "consequent" natures, it seems that Whitehead is unable to assign a definite ontological status to pure possibility or, therefore, to God, who is required for its "ingression" into actuality. "The primordial nature is conceptual, the consequent nature is the weaving of God's physical feelings upon his primordial concepts" (*PR*, 345). Thus "any instance of experience" is said to be "dipolar"—mental and physical. "The origination of God is from the mental pole, the origination of an actual occasion is from the physical pole" (*PR*, 36), but that physical actuality "has its reception into God's [consequent] nature" (*PR*, 350).

Duality: The Identity of the Same

There is a way to begin to cut through the problem of possibility by going back to the ground of metaphysics. In fact, this is what Spinoza has already done for us. With his divine simplicity, he states that "the mind and the body are one and the same,"[17] so that "a mode of extension and the idea of that mode are one and the same thing, but expressed in two ways."[18] This radical *duality* (not dualism!) of the thing as *its own idea*, the material idea, affords a new way to grasp the notion of Form, and prepares a solution to the problem of possibility.

Spinoza's idea exists materially (energetically) "in extension" and has no need of actualization or realization; it is not an abstract possibility to be conceived or selected and realized. This does not at all mean that the idea-thing does not itself emerge or that it cannot be the object of an act of creation (although Spinoza did not see it that way); but however it comes to exist as idea, it simultaneously *(simul)* exists as thing.

It is as though Spinoza, like Plato, took his cue from language, the "structure" of the sign. But in Spinoza's semiotic, the signifier and its signified concept are the same, the signifying "body" is its own idea; also Plato's Idea seems to be the projection of an ideal meaning as Form. But in Plato's version, the signified form is *separated* from its signifying vehicle, which it "transcends"; whereas Spinoza's idea is real in every sense—it is material and immanent. Who could possibly entertain such a perfect idea if not God himself? The point to be taken, however, is that Spinoza has initiated a new way to investigate the nature of reality. The Form or Idea is no longer separated from its actuality. It is already physically real. And yet, "after Darwin," we can also affirm that it "emerges" and evolves—that it does not reside "all ready" in eternity—and wherever it is possible it is real, so this possibility too comes to exist in time. (This is where Whitehead hesitates.) Forced to choose between eternal Possibility and the pragmatics of its Becoming, the creation of new possibilities, we can say with Mallarmé that possibility is the "chance that accomplishes its own Idea."[19]

The most striking confirmation of Spinozist duality is that it resolves "mind-brain dualism" in precisely the manner required today in the age of neurochemistry. If every feeling or idea is a brain event, a movement of molecules, conversely those neurochemical formations are themselves ideas and feelings. There is no "parallelism" because the neurological event is its own idea and every affect is dual, every feeling a molecular idea. However, the thinking, feeling brain as it has emerged and evolved over more than a half-billion years, has developed a consciousness that does not itself possess or "have" those ideas—at least not "adequately." In fact, our ideas of our own feelings are notoriously misplaced or confused. Many of our instincts and impulses remain unconscious, and some operate very well that way. And when they do emerge into consciousness, they often present themselves in disguised or displaced or distorted form (which is the starting point of Freudian psychoanalysis). Nevertheless, those feelings and emotions or affects are themselves their own ideas, different from the ideas we have of them (which are again dual, mental-physical), and the mind and the brain are "one and the same thing, expressed in two ways."

The Form of any thing is just the thing itself in its idea (*eidos* or essential form), and whatever is formed is ideated *as* that form—though it does not "know itself" and no one (but God) has it adequately in mind. (The idea *of* an affect is not the affect/idea itself.) However, there is a glimmer of thought or mind in the most elementary particle of matter. That mind emerges as the form the matter takes, and evolves with its relations, its power to combine with other elements, to internalize its external relations in a living community of molecules, eventually to develop a proper brain or mind. The entire universe is a communal "organism" in which every element feels every other, and *consists* in its powers of interaction, its relational "plane of consistency": thus "a set of elementary particles could be treated as if composed in a self-consistent manner of combinations of those same particles."[20]

The universe emerges as its own idea, material expression which can be re-expressed (represented) by a set of equations or theory whose meaning is an idea *of* that idea; if the matter-idea mutates and evolves, then the equations (with the idea they express) too must change and evolve. The physicist's question, "What is it that breathes fire into the equations and makes a universe for them to describe?"[21] has already been answered by Spinoza's principle of duality. The equations are strings of symbols that express (signify) an idea of the Idea that *is* the Thing. This Idea does not *represent* the Thing it is; it is its formal Dual. It is represented (modeled) indirectly by the symbolic language of mathematics. Hawking appears to believe that, even if what the equations express is true, they must be *realized.* But if they are true, then their idea is real and *it is* the "fire" of matter-energy, fire *in the form* of the expressed idea. Possibility, on the other hand, as classically conceived (and Whitehead follows that metaphysical tradition), requires an *act* of realization, which is performed by God or the Power. In other words, the classical idea of possibility is like an idea that is formed first in our mind, or conceived in God's mind, and then realized (or not). The Spinozist idea is already real and material. It *is* the power. Pure or abstract possibility, Platonic Form, is ontologically insufficient, an unrealized idea, whereas Spinoza is able to dismiss the notion of possibility altogether.

Yet the classical notion does have a place, just not the place it was classically assigned. Its true place is in the *mind of the subject* who would have to act to make it real. Even there it is already real, but mental (a brain event), and must be powered by an *urge* in order to venture out from the animal brain into the world. The God of metaphysics—its possibilities, its understanding, and its act—is the projection of an idealized, infinitized human subject.

The subject is able to separate the idea from the act. But it thereby falls prey to a potentially delusional *disconnection* of its mind from its body and movement. This disconnect is further amplified by the philosophical ideal of theoretical "contemplation" and the scientific method of objective reference, neglecting to count the subject into the "universe of discourse" framing its representations. This enframement and omission may be endemic to verbal abstraction, or even rooted in sense perception, "the triumph of abstraction in animal experience." That "neglect of essential connections" affects "scientific practice" with "the same characteristic of omission" that is found in the metaphysical logic of substance and accident (*MT,* 73–74). Does this exclusive focus on reference also begin to explain the neglect of *preference* and futuring intrinsic to the living urge and available to intuition only through the practice of identification we call becoming (or "involution," below)? Doesn't life demand attention to its *relations* with the *outside,* eventually the whole universe, its *connections* outward to its milieu, ahead to the future it is designing, and inward through memory back to the very origin of things whence it derives?

This catastrophic disconnection, going back to Plato and amplified by Descartes, has provoked the ludicrous dismissal of the mind and its ideas as epiphenomenal. Bergson's question posed to neurobiologists in 1896, "can the nervous system be conceived living without the organism that nourishes it, without the atmosphere in which the organism breathes, without the earth bathing in this atmosphere, without the sun . . . ?"[22] is not merely rhetorical and resounds ever more urgently now that Gaia theory has established that life is a planetary phenomenon. "It takes a planet," and ours is alive, though not feeling so well just now. Somehow Bergson and James had the intuition of a living world misrecognized by a mind disconnected from it—and from itself. They ask us, in effect, where do you place yourself, your mind, your act in the world you describe? William James's 1908 manifesto of pragmatic "pluralism" stated our contemporary predicament perfectly: "Either what the philosopher tells us is extraneous to the universe he is accounting for . . . ; or the fact of his philosophizing is itself one of the things taken account of in the philosophy, and self-included in the description. In the former case the philosopher means by the universe everything *except* what his own presence brings; in the latter case his philosophy is itself an intimate part of the universe, and may be a part momentous enough to give a different turn to what the other parts signify."[23] The same question, more ethical (and clinical) than epistemological, must be posed to the scientist: How are you *involved* and *engaged* in the world you observe? How do you include your act into your theory? There is a call to practice of environ-*mentality.*

Today it is an ethical imperative to *include the subject in the theory.* As the future is somewhat predictable we must include the power and act of prediction; as it is somewhat imaginable, we must include imagination; since it is now being created by all the living acting in concert, coevolving, taking chances, we reject the notion that "the most important things" can be the *object* of any science.[24] If science is based on observation of "that entity exemplifying this quality, apart from any reference to things beyond . . . dismissing from consciousness all irrelevant modes of experience" (*MT,* 74), and if the urge "to things beyond" is the very essence of life and the future it involves, the world it is dreaming of, then "the whole of science is based upon neglected modes of relevance" (*MT,* 74).

Spinoza's material ideas do not evolve. Whitehead's "creativity" does evolve, but not the "eternal objects" (his version of Platonic Forms or Ideas, *PR,* 46), which, as uncreated and complete totality, seem to provide "metaphysical stability" (*PR*, 40) for Whitehead's philosophical practice. As in some versions of quantum cosmology, in which all "possibilities for histories" are given in the eternal chaotic quantum foam; as with the metaphysical fiction of "all possible worlds," which enabled Leibniz to complete a system of metaphysics; so Whitehead and his God need those eternal objects. God, who conceives and evaluates those possibilities for realization, has to comprehend everything (yet curiously God is "unconscious" in his primordial conceptual nature, *PR*, 345). But how does this assumption of complete totality accord with Whitehead's commitment to creativity, "the ultimate behind all forms, inexplicable by forms, and conditioned by its creatures" (*PR*, 20)? In one rather difficult passage to construe, creativity and possibility become obliquely synonymous: "The 'boundless, abstract possibility' means the creativity considered solely in reference to the possibilities of the intervention ["ingression"] of eternal objects" (*PR*, 220). Kant's reform of ontology taught us to distinguish between possibility and actuality; but if real possibility is Spinoza's material idea—Whitehead's "real potentiality"—then to say it evolves by chance is to say it is the creatable or discoverable power of immanent mind.

Theoretical biology has never been comfortable with the metaphysics of possibility as representational presupposition—the duplication of reality—and has finally begun to affirm a *radical creation of real possibility.* Perhaps Bergson was the first to affirm categorically "that in duration, considered as a creative evolution, there is a perpetual creation of possibility and not only of reality." Furthermore, he likens this power of creation to aesthetic procedure: "the artist in executing his work is creating the possible as well as the real."[25] This intuition of continual creation, confirmed by examination of the geological record, has been echoed by the theory of "emergent vitalism" expounded by Simpson in 1949: "There is not only an increase of life within the possibilities existing for it but also an increase of those possibilities"; "The sphere of life for terrestrial animals . . . was created only as plants slowly emerged from the waters and clothed the land. As animals followed, living on these early land plants, their emergence created spheres of life for other animals to prey on these . . . with each step creating still other possibilities."[26] Recently Robert Ulanowicz has broken the law barrier, affirming "that physical laws are incapable of *determining* what we see in the living realm—that the combinatorics of complexity simply create so many possibilities, or degrees of freedom, that any physical laws can be satisfied in a vast multiplicity of ways."[27] The picture emerges of a nature so exuberant, its variations so abundant, that the observer, overwhelmed, is forced to attribute it to chance or "miracle." Behind chance we intuit a real of unfathomable depth and power, unless our anxiety to "understand" (and control) compels us to assign all indeterminacy to quantum clouds and superstrings (as though these were understandable). Is that insistence on prepositing all possibilities, all histories, all universes, just a desperate clinging to the theocratic presuppositions of an obsolete metaphysics in the face of the unknowable? "If an event is unique for all time, it evades treatment by probability theory"; "Up to now, we have regarded chance as an exception, but now we realize it predominates in a complex world."[28] The *singularity* of chance is "generic"! It is the algorithmic generalities that are special cases.[29]

Another theoretical biologist who has seen the need to depart from the readymade presumption of all-possibility is Stuart Kauffman, who notes that Darwin already proposed a theory of "preadaptations" whereby "a feature of an organism of no use in the current selective environment might become of use in a different environment [and] so be selected, typically for a novel functionality."[30] Kauffman again affirms that "we cannot prestate the configuration space of a biosphere, hence cannot prestate the adaptations that may come to exist in an evolving biosphere . . . If so, then the algorithmic freedom of a biosphere is deeply important, for the science of Newton, Einstein, and Bohr all suppose prediction by algorithmic calculation."[31] The principle of universal law, long in crisis, is in disarray now that its metaphysics is collapsing as a "post-scientistic" age begins.

The mathematical logic implicit in naïve set theory, preconditioning the calculus of probability, entered its period of crisis when Cantor assumed the existence of the "set of all sets," until he realized it was inconsistent by showing that the set of its subsets had to be much larger. So even in pure mathematics there can be no closed set of "all"—the whole is *open* by the thread of time and its act (such as "forming the subset"), its process of becoming (Brouwer had this intuition). The epistemology of probability presupposes the representational metaphysics conditioned by "the sum-total of all possibility . . . of all possible predicates . . . completely determined through the mere idea" and hypostatized as "an individual being."[32] Does quantum cosmology, as well, surreptitiously hypostatize all possible universes as a given and complete *preexisting* set, in order to calculate probabilities, so that "a field of possibilities open into infinity has been mistaken for a closed realm of things existing in themselves"?[33] That opening to infinite alternatives is the real of time. Does the logic of science merely replicate the metaphysics of the divinity it supplanted—while forgetting to include the act of genesis?

Absolute Possibility is the metaphysical double that comforts our understanding confronted with the mystery of creation, but the "adventure" is to affirm the Absolute Creativity inside and outside our living bodies. Perhaps it is a matter of taste whether we choose to affirm the one or the other; but it is also a matter of topology and experiment. We can look at life—and the universe it organizes and that informs it—"from outside" and fancy ourselves its observer, declaiming the "final theory" in a grandiose metalanguage. Or we can take the risk of going outside our understanding to find life again inside the outside. The antinomy presented to our reason, of the absolute Possibility of creation and the absolute Creation of possibility, opens our minds to a chiasmus that turns out to have significant practical as well as theoretical consequences. For Life itself is the creator of possibility—including its own.

The problem of "final causality" is a major source of logical confusion. That living beings are oriented to the future is their defining character with respect to the order of time. All of our intending, predicting, anticipating, imagining, willing, hoping, fearing, dreaming is aimed at *making a difference* and thus reversing or resisting the tide of entropy. But there is no violation of the "order of time." It is not that the future somehow causes its past; it is that life creates an *image* or model of a *possible* future and a *plan* for its effectuation—that plan or "project" which structures its basic procedures for capturing and metabolizing energy and body-building materials—and puts its plan into action by, for example, "coding for" functional proteins. Already the bacteria swimming up the sugar gradient and down the toxin gradient are exercising their urge toward the future, for "Escherichia coli knows its world"[34] and which way to turn. For the future to be able to cause the past it would have to preexist itself—which is absurd, but is it not exactly what the metaphysics of science presupposes with its "set of all possible universes"?

Life's power does not preexist its own emergence; its temporal paradox is that it both is and is not possible before it acts—which is true of every free invention or improvisation. It is "eternally" possible only in absolute representation. Our very language conspires to make us believe in that timeless world of signified Ideas; but "as imagination bodies forth / the forms of things unknown," "such shaping fantasies, that apprehend / More than cool reason ever comprehends"—it is shaping the world to come. Desire, Eros, is the *real of time* that *opens possibility.* It is the replicating genome opening itself to unforeseeable mutation; neurons reshaping their synaptic networks as a child learns to catch a ball, or sings to itself. The absolute outside is death (unless that too is a beginning).

The swarm of "boundless abstract possibility" (*PR*, 220), whether creatable or eternal (or both), can be figured as a kind of psychic chaos, of which Nietzsche had the introspective intuition: "At every instant Chaos still pursues its work inside our mind: concepts, images, feelings are juxtaposed fortuitously . . . Here is the last little fragment of world where something new will compose itself . . . a new chemical combination which has never seen its like in the becoming of the world."[35] In this "transcendental chemistry of combinations,"[36] God himself might figure as primordial protoworld-brain taunted with the chaosmic phantasmagoria of "a void that is not a nothingness, but a virtual, containing all possible particles and drawing all possible forms which come forth only to disappear at once, without consistency or reference, without consequence."[37] With his attunement to the ambiguities of quantum physics, Whitehead seems to have constructed the act of God as "limitation" and "restriction" (*SMW*, 178)—or choice among possibilities—to reflect various interpretations of the "collapse of the wave function" selecting "a" world from the quantum delirium of alternatives. Quantum cosmology extends the ambiguity to the origin of "this" universe, where the values of universal constants are "chosen" either by God or at random: "No reason can be given for the nature of God, because that nature is the ground of rationality" (*SMW*, 178). But it is the *power* to emerge from chaos with the Form of "a world" *able* to evolve and create elements that "catalyze each other's reproduction" and come alive as molecular community: this is the irreducible, incalculable "being" hidden in chance and possibility. This power is self-reflecting in that a universe capable of evolving life and self-awareness (the universe's own self-consciousness) presupposes its own conditions of possibility—unless it is able to affirm the unknowable; it "posits its own presuppositions" as Hegel would say. (This is the current "anthropic"—biomorphic—procedure conditioning the determination of cosmological equations otherwise suspended in a cloud of unanchored improbabilities.)[38]

To register the distinction of real possibility (power) from its representational simulacrum, consider the perfect hand in bridge, or a royal flush in poker. What are the odds? Well, they are exactly the same as the odds for every other hand. The question of odds, probability, is a secondary distraction. The real question is, What is the Power? How did the rules of the game emerge? Even the staunch reductionist has to ask himself, around midnight, What does it mean that I live in a universe *able* to form living thinking acting bodies? And anyway how is it there is any Form at all and not just shapeless dust and randomness—or nothing at all? "Why does the universe go to all the bother of existing?"[39] Every theory presupposes not only the ability to formulate itself—a universe able to ask about itself—but the *desire* to do anything at all. In the cosmology of the future, the *act of the scientist* will be counted into the "final theory" as its internal outside. In other words, what is *outside* the "universe of discourse"—its enunciation—will be included inside it as what is *missing* there, missing from "everything" *necessarily* and *affecting "all" with its becoming—not-all*—as the future opens in the real of time. Then science will begin to diagram the topology of its own impossible metalanguage, in "that what cannot be—yet is" (*PR*, 350).

It appears that the metaphysics of scientism, far from having done away with the need for philosophy, has merely reproduced the fallacies Kant thought he destroyed more than two centuries ago. So the metabiologist imagines the set of all possible genomes from which ours are selected; the metalinguist fancies "all possible sentences" preexisting in the "Universal Library," forgetting that every act of enunciation opens language to its unknown outside future. The simple fact of our generic singularity is that every living gesture is unique and inexplicable, and creates its possibility.

The theory of probability is haunted by an allegory of algorithmic imbecility we may call the Shakespeare Monkey. It is hypothesized that enough monkeys banging on typewriters for a long enough time will eventually produce *Hamlet* (or any other text in the "Universal Library"). We have an algorithm (a rule of procedure), agents or hardware to run it on (monkeys with typewriters), and infinite time and patience, and voilà, the outcome is assured. Fair enough, only something has been left out of this sophomoronic fable, and that is the Shakespeare Reader—the Crible or sifter of signs—that other sort of agency that punctuates and referees the game by snatching up an aping typescript or mimeograph just at the very instant *Hamlet* is *recognized* as "finished," before another key is struck and not a moment too soon or too late. What is given in advance, in other words, in memory, is just *Hamlet* itself, in the mode of an editor or reader who knows what to look for and can act in time. The researcher forgets to count him- or herself and his or her act into the experiment as its framer and arbitrator. Scansion, the rhythm and timing of a punctuation, in actuality—undecidable, is "given" only so the scientist can forget himself. At their best, scientists see better than this: "Effective complexity is then related to the description of the regularities of a system by a complex adaptive system [cf. "organism"] that is observing ["prehending"] it."[40] In fact, it is not just a question of describing the system but of interacting with it by the very fact of arranging an experiment, setting parameters and constraints, sorting and "pruning" possibilities, *criblage*.[41] Establishing a frame of reference or universe of discourse means acting from outside that frame, from the real.

The power of decision, of rhythmic scansion, of making sense, of formation, can no more be taken for granted than aboriginal Possibility can. It comes from the future it creates, and the act of throwing the dice or "elements," letters or traits, and the response of interpreting them (selection and rearrangement) are indissoluble. The mind reads what the hand throws and riddles enigmatic combinations as they fall, onto a table, plane or screen, selecting elements to recombine into a "product," proteins or poetry, then rereads and edits that, keeping ("internalizing") some parts and discarding the rest, pruning away statistical noise and holding on to the harmonies and dissonant but agreeable contrasts that arise.

To propose that any formation is "random" is to confuse the way we come to know a thing with "how it is," its existence. Randomness is an epiphenomenal disguise of the power hidden in chance. No composition is ever random; its formation presupposes both component elements and their relations—the immanent "reader" that selects and arranges in a "second time." This is why Deus Lector cannot be dispensed with but keeps rearising in ever new disguises. There is mind "all the way down" and thinking is constitutive of formal reality. This is what Spinoza taught both Leibniz and Whitehead.

Projective Involution as Effective Practice

With Leibniz, Whitehead proposes to take the point of view of the molecule, a leap into the other and back and forth inside the outside: an *aperiodic* involution that is intrinsically incompletable, or what Deleuze would come to call "becoming-molecule" (or -animal, "Or any other wondrous thing / A man may be 'twixt ape and Plato"); and Spinoza's intuition discovered in each "mode" ("modes [are] the sheer actualities" [*PR*, 7]) a "substantial" power to affect and be affected—and to combine with other elements.[42] What kinds of interactions this involves we molecules do not know in advance of trying out our powers of movement and relation: "no one knows what a body can do" is Spinoza's modal battle cry relaunched by Deleuze. Experimentation, improvisation, "empiricism"—practically speaking, no one knows what we are capable of doing or becoming by "involving." And the poet "with a bird / Wren or Eagle, finds his way / To all its instincts."

Whitehead's intuition builds on the "physiological attitude" that "put[s] mind back into nature" by "projective reference beyond the body" so that "mental cognition is seen as the reflective experience of a totality . . . the prehension into unity of the patterned aspects of the universe of events" (*SMW,* 148). By this practice of projective intuition, "the private psychological field [becomes] the event considered from *its own* standpoint" (*SMW,* 150; emphasis added). "Its own" is ambiguous—but involution "goes both ways." In the language of projective geometry of which Spinoza and Leibniz were the first philosophers, the finite "monad-mode" is the "pole" to which its infinite environment is "polar"; but the event involves both in dipolarity, of which projective involution is the back-and-forth movement from unity to multiplicity. Finitude is the condition of actual form (spatio-temporal location), only if it "involves" the infinite universe by which everything is virtually everywhere. Practicing involution means getting involved with the world "outside." The infinite mind (life) incarnates immanently, nomadically here and there under conditions of finitude, as fractal process, the "infinitely self-referential . . . mind's ability to bloom."[43] We put mind into nature and life into mind and God (creativity) into Life. To read the Baroque ignoring this projective procedure is to leave out the power (affect) that enabled Spinoza and Leibniz to become-god becoming-molecule.

So the first step of our pragmatic involution is that "projective reference" that throws a mental lasso out to the other, whence it returns, as I "introject" the other's lasso of me—myself as the other's projection, the other relaying to still other others, and so on. Exactly what social animals do, only we extend this interactive projectivity all the way up to God and down to the infinitessimal. The "projective reference beyond the body" is not without *connection* to the other body (across the "fields" through which we *feel* each other). "External relations" are continually reinvented, readjusted, and reharmonized, composed by improvisation (also known as "living"), experimenting with due caution. Nonetheless, it can involve us in a sort of delirium, as we begin to feel the universe outside inside; we intuit and feel each other's feelings and ideas, sympathize, and wonder which of our imaginings are real or possible. Intuition must be checked by symbolic confirmation. It is best to draw a preliminary diagram purified of "empathic" presumptions about what the other is or should be feeling; here physics is extremely useful in finding out what the local elements are up to, doing and sensing; as the physicist hymns sympathetically, "every particle feels the force." Relations are external in the future of invention, internal to living memory. The procedure opens a vast universe in which "I [becomes] an Other" as the other involves me and other others; in fact, no one knows who anybody is or what they can do (together). Rimbaud's formula (relayed by Deleuze) revives and deepens Kant's theory of time: self-affection of the living subject means affection of the self by its outside—future—other. That loop outside-and-in is the vector of an *involution of the outside*. It is the "infinite movement . . . [of] a coming and going, because it does not go toward a destination without turning back on itself."[44] So it is also an e-volution of the inside. Going out it discovers and invents, coming back it internalizes its discoveries as some moves change the rules of the game, universal *bricolage*, recombining parts of "one's" extended self. "The infinite movement is double, and there is only a fold from the one to the other . . . image of thought [as] matter of being." It is this power of affective involution and rule-creating moves that presents itself in the dual form of Whitehead's "dipolar" mental-physical, Spinoza's "attributes," and Leibniz's Identicals "indefinable in themselves," with their mysterious formal distinction.[45]

The "ingression" of ideas (eternal objects) into actuality, requiring the arbitrary "intervention of God" without which "there would be nothing new in the world, and no order" (*PR*, 247), is a notorious stumbling block for Whitehead interpretation. Spinoza's intuition of duality (the idea is already real and material, it is the Form of Matter) solves that problem—there is no "ingression" of transcendence. The dipolarity is absolutely immanent. Every element is a mind/body (monad), the mind is the power (or affect) of the material idea to compose and combine. But mind thereby evolves through time by combining with other minds (bodies) to find out what they can do together (unless they exclude each other, or pass by indifferently). Atoms and particles "think-together" (com-pute) their relations: "systems at phase transition are caught up in *complex computations to determine their own physical state*" (emphasis added).[46] Ordering chaos is the universe's way of coming out, thinking materially, evolving thoughtfully.

Our projective intuition "evolutes" with matter through time, and involutes back into a single cell. The God of Whitehead is this material idea, body/mind, evolving and involving—though residual Platonism, restraining our Spinozist-Mallarmean Darwinism, prevents us from seeing that "chance its own idea" (possibility) itself evolves and emerges.

The animal mind (brain) contains its own ideas *of* the outer world-ideas. So in animals the mental (inner idea of outer material form) leads the physical pole: "The world dreams of things to come, and then in due season arouses itself to their realization. Indeed all physical adventure which is entered upon of set purpose involves an adventure of thought regarding things as yet unrealized" (*AI*, 279). These dreams may create real possibilities—that is, forms of thought realizable outside the mind—if, as

Leibniz said, they are *compossible* with other realities—that is, possible together in the same world. Otherwise some are excluded from realization—although they remain materially real in themselves, living on in the mind as desires, urges, awaiting their time, perhaps.

We see at once that there is not just one real world—as it includes that futuring mind (brain) desiring, creating, selecting, and realizing (or failing to realize) possibilities. "History can only be understood by seeing it as the theatre of diverse groups of idealists respectively urging ideals incompatible for conjoint realization." As "whatever is realized in any one occasion of experience necessarily excludes the unbounded welter of contrary possibilities" (*AI,* 276–77), a struggle ensues, nations go to war, rivals duel, "races" exterminate each other. Yet Whitehead also shows us, optimistically, his "intuition of the universe as everlasting process, unfading in its deistic unity of ideals" (*MT,* 103).

The problem is that actual minds in animal brains are not unified or harmonized unless by a Leibnizian Selector. They are Darwinian strugglers, sometimes joining together, otherwise killing or ignoring each other. Their "ideals"—fantasies as lures for action—become incompossible. And since desire is the real and active driving force of world-history, that real divergence and clash of aims means that living beings do not at all live and strive in one and the same world, and the real event is not one *in its becoming.* Despite his deistic optimism, this is what Whitehead more clearly sees: "there is an ideal peculiar to each particular actual entity"; "The notion of one ideal [for all] arises from the disastrous overmoralization of thought under the influence of fanaticism, or pedantry" (*PR,* 84). *When we include the mind or brain with its urges and ideals within the world,* we see the future diverging and multiplying into incompossible alternatives that "live" convoluted in our brains. Already the lynx with its predatory focus and the hare with its quasi-aleatory turns showed us a world forking into alternative pathways. In the hare's future-world, escape is followed by relief and rest in comfort; in the lynx's, capture is followed by raw meat and a digestive sleep. And living memory too is incompossible, with its conflicting versions, tales, reports, histories, interpretations. Only the actual present is "one"—the moment we include its real becoming, its life, it multiplies into labyrinthine possibilities, images inducing loops of mutual incitement and inhibition of each other's acts and sensations, as we anticipate each other's response to our responses. Plant or animal, *autrui* (other-life) affects my mind not only as projected possible scenario but as actualization making my world diverge from its course, and these alterities become internalized as new dimensions of our being (the self as other of *any* other).

It is inherent in the notion of *affect* (or affectability) that each "creature" prehends and enacts its world, with its own manner of expression (see *MT*, ch. 2). So the tick perceives and lives and makes one world, and the warm-blooded beast brushing by experiences another, and these "inner" worlds expressed and projected out into the future are strictly incompossible—the mammal does not plan to be sucked by a tick, and the tick does not project being picked off and crushed. Their mutually exclusive projects mean that each is "for its world" and these worlds are diverging, yet both futures are real and effective now in living efforts. Even the one-celled bacterium "knows its world" and strives for its future. Every living being is continually rebuilding its inner and outer milieus both physically through its activity, and mentally (even if it does not yet have a proper mind), imagining alternative possible futures, remembering variant pasts, sensing presences with its feelers, extending prehensile pincers or paws or hands to reshape the world, turning colors, dancing and howling, expressing itself.

There are at least three levels or dimensions of the incompossible:

1. Each organism has its basic "plan" encoded into its genome (proto-brain) and instincts; following that program, it attempts to shape the world in the image of its proper habitat, favorable for the development of itself and its kind. In their coevolution, all the organisms together compose a biosphere of converging and diverging projects. During replication, each gets a chance to rewrite its program and outwit its rivals in the next generation.
2. With the invention of the neuron and evolution of the brain, the organism becomes able to move (muscle) and act. The brain synthesizes a picture of that version of reality it is *able* to perceive, and imagines and projects its future, acting to reshape its environment in the image of its urges, to construct a provisionally secure home-niche, perhaps, all the while coevolving and interacting with terrestrial materials and other organisms. The animal dreams its world and enacts its dream, self-assembling its "sensory-motor schema."
3. The symbolic animal is the subject-agent of a new and explosive proliferation of the incompossible, the dimension (dit-mention) of triadic language, coevolving with our brains[47] and bonding societies together in symbolic acts and discourses. Producing mythic fabulations to support the rituals unique to its culture, each society consists in the multiple and varying psychic and material realizations of its projective ground-plan, the psychophysical construction of its symbolic structures and ideas. Each triadic order is strictly incompossible with every other—literally, materially distinct and diverging from its neighbors' *in their becoming.* (The

impossibility of translating poetry is an ancient sign of this symbolic diversity.) Not only every culture but each individual subject dreams and plans its futures in multimodal fabulations, and acts to realize some of those futures—often conflicting with each other. Within each brain or mind are diverse alternatives developing, and no one, not even the merest simpleton, is expressing and living in just one world. Societies and individuals are incompossible *in their anticipatory systems,* where the *real* event is going on, as each cooperates in sympathy or struggles in rivalry with other individuals, species, and societies, enacting the world it projects according to its idea(l)s, ruling out the future existence of countless other monad-worlds. It is thus not only in our brains (minds) that our realities are incompossible, but in our symbolic acts and the event of our becoming. To ignore this psychic reality is to miss what it means to be alive.

These cultural practices are human creations that are neither true nor false but expressive of affective possibilities. Failing to see the gruesome irony of its self-dismissal, the subject of contemporary neuroscientism abjectly submits to chemical normalization designed to suppress and inhibit those very thoughts and affects and "behaviors" that resist the mechanization of our lives. Psychiatric control treats any sign of vitality like a symptom of disease and the living brain like a machine to be serviced and repaired. The real of desire is leveled down to the mechanics of molecules. Our education system dumbs its subjects down to see the living world and themselves as programmed mechanism, and trains them to function as parts integrated in planetary megamachines. Thus our scientistic ideology, proclaiming the one referential reality, ignoring its becoming and foreclosing its own act, implicitly justifies the eradication of "primitive" cultures with their strange preferences and ritual practices and myths of a living Earth. How could it consistently respond to or resist that destruction, when it teaches that the techno-scientific monoculture processing the earth is the one based in reality? While the culture industry produces alternative fantasy worlds to divert and disconnect its subjects from the horror of their environment poisoned by machine waste, the advancing civilization is bulldozing and exterminating multiple living worlds, flattening and grinding them into data to feed the universal algorithm of homogeneous exchange. How can the scientist resist if he believes human aspirations are the illusions of programmed automatons? Yet all he would have to do is *look within* to see where the "many-worlds hypothesis" is verified. In the coming time of our environ-mentality, our response-ability, what must now be counted in are the creative and symbolic acts that determine how we live and *what we are living for,* what worlds we are projecting and already making possible and real. Philosophy is the thinking of this event, which it does not take for granted. In fact nothing is "given" to philosophy; everything must be constructed; there are no "data" yet "philosophy can exclude nothing" (*MT,* 2). That is its paradox: nothing is given and nothing is excluded. Even God cannot take himself for granted. He has to ask himself, *How?* How do I do it? Perhaps a clue is to be found in music, "prototype of the concert of natural forces."[48]

God is the Libido of self-realizing Possibility consisting in all the living thinking and acting together to "dramatize the idea" and realize the futures each is urging toward, "the world is an egg but the egg itself is a theatre,"[49] and it so happens that our theater lacks a director but not ideas, so long as we are able to assemble them, as the god of many affects (Dionysus) improvises and breaks up into so many converging and diverging lines into the futures we are aiming for. Each monad-mode is acting in the drama of its own imagining, a play without author or director and whose plot is continually under revision, incomplete, as the monads encounter each other blind to what is happening inside the other's world, make signs to each other, and read the other's gesture and attitude, relinking to some, passing on others, never knowing in advance what world-play the other players are acting and imagining, so many versions of "the ultimate," as we all intuitively channel and project each other's possibilities and take our chances, redoing rules, composing and executing this sublime schizophrenic melody and *concordia discors.*[50] And that, "chance its own Idea," is pragmatic activism as a radical pluralist empiricism.

Kant led philosophy out of the fog of metaphysics, forged ahead and broke a path into a new pragmatics, by inventing a new relation between reason and action. For the significance of "practical reason" is not that it can purify morality or desire, nor even that it teaches us to act "as if" God or the fictitious Ideal were real; it is that by orienting the subject to a *future of its own making,* to living and acting guided by an image of desire, ethical procedure *realizes* a radical creativity that inherits the "life-force" it modulates, and becomes *effective through ideas* as it works through *preference beyond reference.* The Ideal is a fiction, but this fiction is a true creation (already real in mind) and has practical consequences according to what we make of it. Every society on Earth creates an image of its future and acts to realize that image. Perhaps God is the future, and the task life has assigned itself in the symbolic animal is to create God, to *realize* that Idea, that Spirit.

Our current world crisis is not just a matter of pollution, overpopulation, and climate change. It is not just that machine exhaust and waste are poisoning our soil, water, and air and cancering our genes. Nor even that the breeding and mutation of the machine have turned so rapid that living organisms are in shock—as they surely are. The true depth of this crisis is metaphysical, and our illness is mental. If we continue to believe that we, together with other living beings, are somehow just more complicated versions of the robots we are cultivating, then we will be content to treat each other and ourselves like robots, behaving and reacting automatically, and will eventually decide that computers can think better than we can and should decide our future for us. That will be the point of no return, of which current "transhumanist" fantasies are a precursor and the frantic search for energy to fuel machines is a manic symptom. On behalf of the mechanisms on our minds, we betray the living and side with "artificial life." But until the machine completes its takeover of the human brain, many of us will continue to coevolve with the living and try to restore our mutual environment by cultivating ecosystems. However, the human obsession with morbidity has made us vulnerable to the fantasy of controlling the genetics of organisms and eventually replacing ourselves with immortal mechanisms (thus ending that phase of evolution which requires individual mortality to make way for new organisms), so that the practice of becoming-Earth is being eclipsed as "individuals" unable to face death alone degenerate into panicked "cyborgs."

Science is the most powerful method of prediction ever devised. But it has inherited from religion the delusion of a world that is predictable in principle if only we knew the "mind of God." This presumption has obscured the unconscious unknowable involving radical chance and the real future forming on the outer edge of time bordering on ever-looming death and entropy. No science can predict its own moves and aims, desires, theories, changing games and rules, brewing diagrams and projecting futures—the most important thing, Life Itself. On the day it begins to include its own activity in its theory, a new science will be born. Or perhaps it will no longer be science, but will join art and philosophy in including its enunciation in its statement, the producer in its product, as what is missing there necessarily insofar as that act is creating something new on Earth, and needs real time to become what it will be. That becoming is our inside-outside, futuring. One day science will affirm itself as a living language, a living artifact of creatable incompleteness, and will rejoin the becoming Earth. With this self-inclusion its topology will mutate: no longer captured by the illusion of spherical closure, it will theorize its real practice: the involution of its outside chance.

Notes

1. See James Lovelock, *Gaia* (Oxford: Oxford University Press, 1979); Lovelock, *The Ages of Gaia* (New York: Norton, 1987); both well summarized by John Gribbin, *In the Beginning* (Boston: Little, Brown, 1993), and Lee Smolin, *The Life of the Cosmos* (Oxford: Oxford University Press, 1997), both of whom connect the Earth-life with its prehistory.

2. François Jacob, *La Logique du vivant* (Paris: Gallimard, 1970), 327.

3. Christian de Duve, *Vital Dust: The Origin and Evolution of Life on Earth* (New York: Basic Books, 1995), 293; "life is an obligatory manifestation of the combinatory properties of matter" (xiv).

4. Richard Feynman, *The Character of Physical Law* (Cambridge, Mass.: MIT Press, 1965), 122.

5. Jacob, *La logique du vivant,* 321. ("Sens" also means "direction.") Jacob refuses to assimilate the new molecular biology, which he codeveloped, to "the reductionism that has long prevailed."

6. Adapted from Ilya Prigogine and Isabelle Stengers postface to Michel Serres, *Hermes* (Baltimore, Md.: Johns Hopkins University Press, 1982), 153: "Creative chaos is illegality itself."

7. Stephen Hawking, *A Brief History of Time* (New York: Bantam, 1988), 145. Hawking also mentions a "psychological arrow" but derives it from the thermodynamic.

8. Robert Rosen, *Anticipatory Systems: Philosophical, Mathematical and Methodological Foundations* (Oxford: Pergamon Press, 1985). Rosen is one of a growing number of scientists (including Elsasser, Morowitz, Kauffman, Ulanowicz, Deacon, and others) who have realized that the "machine metaphor" or mechanical model of living systems is misguided.

9. See François Jacob, *The Possible and the Actual* (New York: Pantheon, 1982). *Bricolage,* or "tinkering" is Lévi-Strauss's term for making do with materials at hand, as opposed to planning and engineering.

10. Robert Ulanowicz, *A Third Window: Natural Life beyond Newton and Darwin* (West Conshohocken, Penn.: Templeton Foundation Press, 2009), 7–8. "Our inclination under the monist approach is to drive the aleatoric to extinction, but to do so beyond a certain point is to *guarantee* disaster."

11. See Michel Serres, *La naissance de la physique dans le texte de Lucrèce* (Paris: Éditions de Minuit, 1977). The Latin phrase means "at uncertain time and place."

12. See Steven Weinberg, *The First Three Minutes: A Modern View of the Origin of the Universe* (New York: Basic Books, 1977), 154: "The more the universe seems comprehensible, the more it (also) seems pointless."

13. This figure is constant from Plato to Whitehead and Deleuze, and derives from early cosmogonies.

14. Stuart Kauffman, *The Origins of Order: Self-Organization and Selection in Evolution* (Oxford: Oxford University Press, 1993).

15. Hawking, *A Brief History of Time*, 70.

16. Hermann Weyl, *Philosophy of Mathematics and Natural Science* (Princeton, N.J.: Princeton University Press, 1949), 131.

17. Benedict de Spinoza, *Ethics* III, prop. 2, Schol., in *A Spinoza Reader: The Ethics and Other Works*, ed. and trans. Edwin Curley (Princeton, N.J.: Princeton University Press, 1994), 155.

18. Ibid., II, prop. 7, Schol., 119.

19. Stéphane Mallarmé, *Igitur*, in Oeuvres complètes, (Paris: Bibliothèque de la Pléiade, 1945), 441.

20. Murray Gell-Mann, *The Quark and the Jaguar: Adventures in the Simple and the Complex* (New York: Henry Holt and Company, 1994), 128, sketching the "bootstrap principle" of string theory: "Such a particle system, if it exists, gives rise to itself" and begins to evolve as its symmetry breaks.

21. Hawking, *A Brief History of Time*, 174.

22. Henri Bergson, *Matière et mémoire*, (Paris: Presses Universitaires de France, 1939), 19–20.

23. William James, *A Pluralistic Universe* (New York: Longmans, Green, and Co., 1909), 35–36. Counting one's own act and "haste to conclude" into the situation one is trying to "comprehend" is the basis of Lacan's practice of *logical time* in psychoanalysis. Cf. Jacque Lacan, *Ecrits*, trans. Héloïse Fink and Russell Grigg (New York: W. W. Norton and Company, 2002), 161–75.

24. Jacob acknowledged in 1970 that scientists "no longer interrogate life in the laboratories"; instead they "analyze living systems, their structure, their function, their history" (*La logique du vivant*, 320–21).

25. Henri Bergson, *The Creative Mind: An Introduction to Metaphysics*, trans. Mabelle L. Andison (New York: Philosophical Library, 1946), 21, 103.

26. G. G. Simpson, *The Meaning of Evolution* (New Haven, Conn.: Yale University Press, 1949), 115.

27. Ulanowicz, *A Third Window*, 48.

28. Ibid., 46–47.

29. See Robert Rosen, *Essays on Life Itself* (New York: Columbia University Press, 1999).

30. Stuart Kauffman, foreword to Ulanowicz, *A Third Window*, xiii.

31. Stuart Kauffman, *Investigations* (Oxford: Oxford University Press, 2000), 125. "An ecology of autocatalytic systems interacting with one another, coevolving, would explore an increasing domain of molecular possibilities, creating a biosphere of expanding molecular diversity." Kauffman, *At Home in the Universe: The Search for the Laws of Self-Organization and Complexity* (Oxford: Oxford University Press, 1995), 275.

32. Immanuel Kant, *Critique of Pure Reason*, trans. Norman Kemp Smith (New York: St. Martin's Press, 1965), 489–90. Cf. Gilles Deleuze, *Logique du sens* (Paris: Les Editions de Minuit), 129, 163, 342–44.

33. Weyl, *Philosophy of Mathematics and Natural Science*, 234.

34. Kauffman, *The Origins of Order*, 233.

35. Friedrich Nietzsche, quoted (from notebooks) by Pierre Klossowski, *Nietzsche et le cercle vicieux* (Paris: Mercure de France, 1969), 13.

36. Jean-François Lyotard, "Sensus communis," in *Après le sujet QUI VIENT? Cahiers Confrontation* 20, (Paris: Aubier, 1989), 161–79. It is in the Third Critique that Kant began to radicalize the idea of living community as the attunement of cosmic feelings.

37. Gilles Deleuze and Félix Guattari, *Qu'est-ce que la philosophie?* (Paris: Les Editions de Minuit), 111.

38. This "logic loop" is called the Anthropic Cosmological Principle. See John D. Barrow and Frank J. Tipler, *The Anthropic Cosmological Principle* (Oxford: Oxford University Press, 1986), and the recent controversy over the use of anthropic reasoning to determine physical values for string theory, which cannot be tested experimentally. Lee Smolin, *The Trouble with Physics: The Rise and Fall of String Theory, the Fall of a Science, and What Comes Next* (New York: First Mariner Books, 2006), and the web debate between Smolin and Susskind, http://edge.org/3rd_culture/smolin_susskind04/smolin_susskind.html; cf. also Steven Weinberg, "Living in the Multiverse," in *Universe or Multiverse?*, ed. Bernard Carr (Oxford: Oxford University Press, 2007). Black holes present the limit case of an "event horizon" beyond which everything is sucked into the absolute. Elsewhere in which Law is undone and "anything's possible" (is that where baby universes come from?)—but with which there appears to be no possibility of communication. Cf. various popular presentations by cosmologists and particle physicists such as Alan Guth, Andrei Linde, Martin Rees, and Lee Smolin.

39. Hawking, *A Brief History of Time,* 174. Hawking implies the universe must have an urge, a desire to exist.

40. Gell-Mann, *The Quark and the Jaguar,* 50.

41. On "pruning rules," see Eugene Holland, *Emergence* (Cambridge: Basic Books, 1999) and Harold Morowitz, *The Emergence of Everything* (New York: Oxford University Press, 2002). Gell-Mann discusses "possibilities for histories" but not the invention of selection algorithms, in *The Quark and the Jaguar.*

42. The operation of involution (a function that is its own inverse) normally generates a loop of "period 2" by which repetition (like double negation) returns identity. It presupposes a "universe" in which its "category" is satisfied. See William Lawvere and Stephen Schanuel, *Conceptual Mathematics* (Cambridge: Cambridge University Press, 1997). So what would it mean to involute and "involve" the Outside of all categories and universes, to "prehend" the future? Is this not what living is about? On the inclusion of the Outside, see James, *A Pluralistic Universe.*

43. James Gleick, *Chaos: Making a New Science* (New York: Penguin, 1987), 299.

44. Deleuze and Guattari, *Qu'est-ce que la philosophie?* 40–41 (for this quote and the next).

45. See Gilles Deleuze, *Le pli: Leibniz et la Baroque* (Paris: Editions de Minuit, 1988), ch. 4.

46. Christopher G. Langton, "A Dynamical Pattern," in *The Third Culture: Beyond the Scientific Revolution,* ed. John Brockman (New York: Touchstone, 1995), 352.

47. Cf. Terrence Deacon, *The Symbolic Species: The Co-Evolution of Language and the Brain* (New York: W. W. Norton and Company, 1997). Charles Sanders Peirce first articulated the irreducibly triadic structure of the sign, forcing the indirect transmission of symbolic value.

48. Marius Schneider, "Le rôle de la musique dans la mythologie et les rites des civilisations non européennes," in *Histoire de la musique sous la direction de Roland-Manuel* (Paris: Encyclopédie de la Pléiade, 1960), 1: 131–214, 139.

49. Deleuze, *Différence et répétition*, (Paris: Presses Universitaires de France, 1968), 279.

50. Deleuze elaborates on this baroque-mannerist "psychosis" or "properly schizophrenic reconstruction" (in which Whitehead fully participates in his expressive manner), in *Le pli*, 93 and 93n, and indicates its source in Freud.

SIX

Multiplicity and Mysticism

Toward a New Mystagogy of Becoming

Roland Faber

Alfred N. Whitehead's work exists, it seems, always anew, only in the form of its rediscovery. In fact, it is self-situated in between philosophy, science, and religion in such a form that it always arises in their interstices, today especially (as odd as it might seem) in the context of both poststructuralist philosophy and theology.[1] What at first glance looks dangerously inoperable and mutually exclusive has led me to think intensively about the rhizomatic connections between Whitehead and Deleuze, on the one hand, and points of contact "at the interstices" of poststructuralism and theology, on the other.[2]

Given that these relations of renewal have recently gained some excellent attention,[3] addressing the strange mutual attraction between French philosophies and matters of metaphysics and theology,[4] the Deleuzian potential of Whitehead,[5] the subversive poststructuralist strand in Whitehead's work,[6] and a poststructuralist sensibility for the (ancient) theological dimensions of philosophy,[7] I want to explore further whether, and if so, in what sense, the work of Whitehead and Deleuze resonate in this mutually reactive multiplicity. It will by my thesis that a mutually attractive trace of mystical language remains vital in both Whitehead and Deleuze and that it must not be viewed as a contamination of their thought by dogmatics, but as a genuine expression of their respective philosophies.[8] I will further explore whether the *theoria* of their philosophies of becoming also indicates a new experiential and experimental praxis (a philosophical life)—in the sense of a mystagogy of becoming.

The Platonic Trilemma

The first thing to recognize about the strange triangle of connections indicated before, in which to situate the resonance of Whitehead and Deleuze and to detect the novelty of Whitehead's philosophical reception today, is that it is not a new turn of things at all. It rather indicates the very story of the birth of (Greek) philosophy as such. Since Plato's differentiation of two discourses from philosophy proper—namely theology and sophism—this birthplace must be considered a constitutive, although strained triangular relationship. While Plato considered poetry (with theology), the articulation of the divine (from myths of the old ages), as precisely that which philosophy has to tame and overcome,[9] he fought sophism as a powerful opponent of philosophy.[10] Ironically, both have survived and remained unloved sisters of philosophy ever since. While, at one point, theology not only married itself to philosophy but also made it an instrument of dogmatics,[11] sophism has reappeared as philosophy precisely in the form of the relativism and pluralism of certain postmodern modes of thought.[12]

In this triangle, the watershed between Whitehead and Deleuze appears to be Whitehead's stubborn clinging to the poetic moment of transcendence (and the divine as its expression) as a vital element of philosophy,[13] while Deleuze became profoundly convinced that theological language has to be eradicated because it negates precisely what defines philosophy—namely, immanence itself.[14] On the other hand, Deleuze seems to embrace the relativism of the sophistic attitude towards truth that Plato despised,[15] hence shifting the epicenter of the force field again.

Nevertheless, things are far from being that obvious. Doesn't Deleuze curiously engage philosophers who were far from abandoning divinity? Hasn't he studied medieval philosophy and learned to value mysticism through his teacher Maurice de Gandillac?[16] And isn't his invocation of, for instance, Spinoza and John Duns Scotus indicating a kind of theological discourse in its own right?[17] Conversely, hasn't Whitehead studied theology over many years and then left it disappointed because of its dogmatic presuppositions?[18] Doesn't Whitehead always warn us against introducing God only to justify our little metaphysical systems (see *RM,* 148–49)? And isn't Whitehead always suspicious of transcendence in light of his emphasis on immanence (see *AI,* 236)?

In fact, on second thought, Whitehead and Deleuze form a strange alliance in how they articulate the Platonic trilemma of philosophy, theology, and sophism by giving up neither, rather affirming all of their spheres:

thought (the creation of concepts), mystery (the ineffable), and multiplicity (the khoric space). While Whitehead is still widely conceived as a rationalist with inclinations toward theology, he is, in fact, a profound pluralist for whom there is no ultimate order preforming becoming, but ultimate fluency that, hence, expresses a deep mystery that can never be rationalized.[19] Deleuze, on the other hand, although conceived as a poststructuralist pluralist, in his turn never gave up interest in systematic thought[20] and never feared to engage theologians and mystical thinkers like Duns Scotus, Nicolas of Cusa, and the like.[21] Things are complicated, indeed!

Finally, in direct reception, Deleuze always exhibits a deep appreciation of Whitehead's empiricism and pluralism,[22] Whitehead's categoreal scheme with its creative relativism,[23] the strange "vitalism" that connects both philosophies (*PR*, 102),[24] and even Whitehead's profoundly processual divinity in a processual world.[25] Whitehead was, in a new form, embracing the whole force field, and Deleuze did not deny the creativity of this move but instead mapped out its complexity and great importance for the formulation of his own work.[26]

The Ultimacy of Becoming

If there is a focus revealing the synchronicity of their philosophies, it probably is their claim of the ultimacy of becoming over against all metaphysical principles, cosmological orders, or epistemological categories.[27] Whitehead articulates this ultimacy of becoming with his concept of "creativity"—as "the ultimate behind all forms" (*PR*, 20) that "makes process ultimate" (*PR*, 7). Deleuze again engages the concept of "difference" for that which cannot be repeated as order and, at the same time, is what alone repeats as difference itself.[28]

Insofar as their respective philosophies of becoming integrate the Platonic trilemma of philosophy, mysticism, and pluralism, they profoundly transform its meaning to express a resistance against three of its original characteristics: unquestionable givenness of presuppositions; preordained order; and determined teleology. Instead, "becoming" gears toward three alternatives: infinite process (never beginning, never ending, never settling); chaos (movement "beyond" all organization); and immanence (without transcendently controlled aims).[29]

If we ask, "Why becoming?" the answer is as simple as it is surprising. "Becoming" is not primarily set against "being" as stabilization of power, logocentric order, the illusion of ultimate structures, or the preformation of reality. Although these reasons are prominent in poststructuralist discourse, both Whitehead and Deleuze have a different agenda. Their motivation is a metaphysical one—the conceptualization of novelty.[30]

While Whitehead's "creativity" *is* the "principle of novelty" (*PR*, 21), Deleuze redefines the whole philosophic project by reversing its quest from "attain[ing] eternity"—which remained its very motivation despite the Platonic expulsion of poetry/theology—to its radical reversal: "the production of novelty." Despite the different reorganization of the classical Platonic triangle, it is essential for both philosophers that the "best of all worlds is not the one that reproduces the eternal, but the one in which new creations are produced, the one endowed with the capacity for . . . creativity." Deleuze understands this shift as nothing less than "a teleological conversion of philosophy."[31]

The Shakespearian Question

Since "philosophy of becoming" not only expels the theological from the philosophical, but also the theological quest—the search for Truth—from the philosophical by becoming more akin to sophistic relativism, the grounding power of "transcendence" and "vertical Being"[32] must fade, and philosophy of becoming must find consolation in Nietzsche's divination of "becoming" itself against the forces of "being." After this conversion, we can never go back behind Nietzsche's "Death of God."[33] How could we ever again want to reestablish any (language of a) "divinity" expressing givenness, order, and teleology instead of becoming, novelty, and creativity? Eternity versus novelty—this is the Shakespearian philosophical question. This alternative most certainly forces us to side with either affirming or excluding novelty or eternity and hence to affirm "divinity" in, or to expel it from, the philosophical endeavor. This seems, again, after Plato, to become a question of self-identity of the philosophical project.

Yet while Deleuze, on first glance, seems to draw this conclusion, Whitehead obviously ignores the whole framework of mutually exclusive alternatives and—ironically—in a Deleuzian-empiricist manner says "Yes, AND."[34] In fact, Whitehead avoids the alternative by understanding divinity as the very expression of creativity whereby it becomes a moment of the metaphysical situation of the production of novelty—not its enemy.[35] Whitehead had a price to pay: not only did it ruin his reputation among philosophers; against all theological dogmatics, it also radically altered his understanding of divinity—from a transcendent substance to an event of immanence, from an eternal being to a process of becoming, from a *logos* of compatible order to an *eros* "affirm[ing] incompossibilities."[36]

Although Whitehead and Deleuze may differ on how to evaluate novelty in relation to the very possibility of any affirmative language regarding divinity, in viewing novelty as the signature of a world of infinite becoming they *remain aware of the "place" where divinity has left the stage* and in its disappearance (or its "disfiguration" from the standpoint of classical theology and theistic philosophy) left a trace that still must be addressed. It is crucial to note that this "place" is important for Whitehead and Deleuze *not* as a site to wage an old battle for the reinstatement of eternity in the form of any notion of divinity or even by reinstating "theology," but rather because of its philosophical function: it remains a moment of the constitution of novelty, and conversely, it is here, within the demands of the paradigm of genuine novelty, that traces of this "place" in the evocation of mystical language resurface.

Therefore Whitehead "identifies" the function of novelty *as* novelty in his philosophy with the maybe at first surprising claim that it is that by which "philosophy is mystical" as he defines mysticism as "direct insight into depths as yet unspoken"—that is, as the evocation of the unprecedented (*MT,* 174). Deleuze, on the other hand, addresses these depths of novelty with his concept of "pure difference,"[37] which, in only repeating itself, creates "that which cannot be replaced." It differentiates "non-exchangeable and non-substitutable singularities,"[38] which cannot represent anything given or eternal. Yet, such novelty needs a language that employs the traces of the disappearance of eternity (even in the form of repetition).

In fact, Deleuze articulates novelty in a language with mystical allusions that hardly avoids reminiscing the language of Meister Eckhart, Nicolas of Cusa, and Giordano Bruno.[39] For one, he adopts *their* notion of the divine as "movements in immanence—*complication* and *explication.*"[40] But even more prominently, he grounds his whole book *The Fold* in the underlying mystical concept of the "fold" in order to make novelty feasible in a world of becoming. And it is in the midst of this move that, as we know, Deleuze's Whitehead appears.[41]

A dramatic example of this trace of mysticism of novelty can be found in *Difference and Repetition,* where Deleuze claims "pure difference" in a language that is nothing but an expression of the very function of mystical language—namely, to manifest the very differentiation of the ground (of thinking) *from* any difference that can be named (and hence already "is") and *from* mere non-difference of silence that would not be productive of a world philosophy wants to understand. Hence, in Deleuze's mystical account of pure difference, it means "a ground in relation to which it no longer matters whether one is before . . . a beginning or an end, since the two coincide in this ground which is like a single and unique 'total' moment, simultaneously the moment of evanescence and production of difference, of disappearance and appearance . . . the moment at which difference both vanishes and is produced."[42]

The Dilemma of Infinite Becoming

The connection between novelty and mysticism will become more obvious when we further explore the problem of genuine novelty in a world of infinite becoming. In short, it is the function of the mystical articulation of infinite becoming (which both Whitehead and Deleuze employ) to save its inherent essence of novelty from a twofold neutralization (self-annihilation) into either mere temporality or eternity.

On the one hand, if infinite becoming has no *telos* or final state, every "state of affairs" must, in light of every new becoming, perish. How, in such a world of "perpetual perishing," can genuine novelty be expected when everything disappears in Heidegger's *lethe,* the stream of eternal oblivion?[43] If there is no attainment in becoming, nothing can genuinely become something of importance.[44]

On the other hand, if the world of becoming and perishing is seamless, that is, if it is infinitely becoming and perishing, how can we say that it harbors anything creative at all? This is Nietzsche's problem of the eternal return. If an infinite process of becoming must repeat infinitely what it has created infinitely often already, novelty is just an illusion (working as long as we keep our scope small enough).[45] We may well end up with Ecclesiastes's statement that "What has been is what will be; and what has been done is what will be done; there is nothing new under the sun."[46]

The question is: How can novelty escape these two pitfalls of perpetual perishing and worthlessness, on the one hand, and eternal repetition of the same, on the other? The first neutralization demands an interpretation of novelty as a kind of persistence in the midst of change that allows for attainment; the second neutralization demands an interpretation of novelty as "production of new creatures." While the first qualification of novelty is *importance,* the second one is *creativeness.*

The Paradox of Life and Death

One way of solving these two neutralizations is barred: the invocation of eternity against which the paradigm of novelty was set. This implies that the mystery of genuine novelty in a world of infinite becoming cannot be articulated as a mystery of existence.

The *locus classicus* of this mystery is Wittgenstein's famous dictum in his *Tractatus* 6.44 that "It is not how things are in the world that is mystical, but that it exists." Since for both philosophers "becoming" is ultimate, "being" must always be an abstraction from becoming.[47] Hence, neither of them is interested in dividing reality into existence and essence or into Heidegger's ontological difference, for that matter.

Over against Shakespeare's "to be or not to be," we find that Whitehead and Deleuze focus on novelty in the context of life and death. On the one hand, novelty is the event of life in a world of infinite becoming; on the other hand, however, since becoming is also always an infinite process of passing, it is a world of death. In fact, for Whitehead and Deleuze, the mystery of novelty addresses the coincidence of life and death.

For Whitehead, "Life is a bid for freedom"; the problem it presents is not "endurance" but "How can there be originality?" (*PR*, 104). It gains its pure expression in what Whitehead calls an "entirely living nexus," which is not an enduring structure "at all, since 'life' cannot be a defining characteristic. It is the name for originality, and not for tradition" (*PR*, 104); it constitutes an "element of chaos" (*PR*, 110) in all life-organization; it strives for novelty "along the borders of chaos" (*PR*, 111). This is the paradox of life and death: the more vivacity organic structures develop, the more life becomes destructive of the organization protecting its chaotic nature (see *PR*, 103).

In confessing that his philosophy is about "events, life, and vitalism," Deleuze also emphasizes bursts of "orgiastic" originality over against organic structure. It is "nonorganic life"[48]—rather than being the life *of* organisms, in its pure expression it is their death. In fact, Deleuze acknowledges that "you can't ever reach it, you are forever attaining it, it is a limit,"[49] the very limit where life and death coincide, where difference "*as such* is cruelty"; where "all forms . . . cease," where "the ground rises to the surface" and "the human face decomposes."[50]

In so differentiating the mystery of novelty from the mystery of existence both Whitehead and Deleuze effectively undermine a theological language that unavoidably becomes part of Plato's affirmation of givenness—the divine initiation of existence; preordained order—the divine realization of essence; and determined teleology—a divine set of final aims (see *PR*, 111).

However, in the assessment of this differentiation, Whitehead and Deleuze differ greatly. For Whitehead, embracing the mystery of novelty avoids the identification of the divine with eternity. Although Deleuze has recognized this Whiteheadian shift, in which "God desists from being a

Being" and "becomes Process,"[51] he resists such a move in order to avoid a corruption of novelty. While Whitehead's divinity now names the process of "intensity, and not preservation" (see *PR*, 105), for Deleuze it remains an "*illusion of transcendence*,"[52] tied to the paradigm of existence.

The Mutuality of Persistance and Creativeness

Nevertheless, their different assessment of what follows from the refusal of the mystery of existence does not yet explain their deeper synchronicity in expressing novelty with mystical language. This seems to be related to the fact that, on a deeper level, the extradition of the mystery of existence (the divine gift of existence) leaves a trace in the mystery of novelty that alerts us to the problems of *persistence* and *creativeness*. But, while in the paradigm of eternity they were tied to a divine coincidence of existence and essence and a contingent creation striving for eternity, in a paradigm of novelty they must be articulated in the coincidence of life and death.

If the coincidence of life and death means that it is chaos that "grounds" a world of becoming in which genuine novelty can arise, it must also stand for the death of all organisms that harbor novelty in any meaningful sense.[53] Novelty out of chaos can only avoid this problem if it names something that is neither pure chaos nor pure eternity. That which allows chaos to generate novelty instead of sheer meaningless change or infinite return of the same is the mystery that "defines" novelty as such.

Let me explore what it must accomplish. First, it must avoid *worthlessness* in the event of becoming. Second, it must avoid infinite repetition that equals an eternal sea of the same. Since it must address *creativeness*, the sought "worth" cannot be something that *actually* fulfills it eternally—an *actus purus*.[54] Given these parameters, it must achieve what Whitehead calls "novelty without loss" (*PR*, 340), or the "permanent elements apart from which there could be no changing world" (*RM*, 9).

In other words, if novelty is to be neither change nor repetition, it must be about attainment of worth in the midst of change that is not eternally pre-given. In the midst of the chaos of becoming, it must in a new way address a moment of persistence or importance; and in the midst of the infinity of becoming, it must articulate a moment of creative difference. In the paradigm of life and death, genuine novelty must name a creativeness that generates persistence and a persistence that generates creativeness.

Interestingly enough, both philosophers conceptualize such a medium of "persistent creativeness" or "creative importance" that is neither a permanent loss of the Singular nor a permanent repetition of the Same. Whitehead calls this reality "Value" and Deleuze "Virtuality."[55] Their shared function is to address precisely the horizon of novelty, the possibility of novelty as such, or the transcendental condition of the possibility of novelty.[56]

Value and Virtuality

It is significant that while Whitehead introduces the term "Value" affectively in the context of the concept of "the possible"—his infamous "eternal objects"[57]—Deleuze, from the first appearance of the "Virtual" on, juxtaposes it to "the possible."[58] However, if we follow the respective function of these terms in their philosophies, we will find that Whitehead's "eternal objects" precisely function *as* "virtualities" and conversely that Deleuze's "virtuals" *do not* subsume Whitehead's "eternal objects" under the otherwise rejected "possible." In fact, both Whitehead's "possibility" and Deleuze's "virtuality" address the problem of novelty in such a way that in both cases the *classical* notion of "the possible" is rejected.[59]

Deleuze juxtaposes the virtual to the possible because for him "possibility" is an expression of the paradigm of *existence*—that is, of the divorce of existence from an eternal essence in different modes of existence: it must be; it can be; it is in fact; it might be or is not or will not be. Thereby, the possible preforms novelty by naming an already fixed "form" to which "existence" is added or from which it is subtracted.[60] This is the "possible" of classical universals—that is, representations of the Platonic forms of givenness, order, and preordained aims. Instead, Deleuze's "virtualities" are neither universals nor individuals, neither forms nor structures, but universal singularities, pure differences, multiplicities, infinitely moving, and thereby indicating the novelty of un-preformed events.[61]

Whitehead's "eternal objects," however, although they *seem* to indicate this realm of universals (essences) of which facts (existents) are only actual variations, in fact neither function as "forms" nor do they lack reality. On the contrary, they are "pure possibilities" insofar as they are real in their own right by being "unrealizable" as actualities.[62] Hence they do not repeat the Platonic distinction of Idea and simulacrum, whereby the image appears only as variation of the essence of the Idea (as many still misunderstand Whitehead's possibilities), but invoke a field of instigation of that which is *not* (or other than) a possibility, namely a concrescing actuality of actualities mediated by possibilities, which remain other, different (differentiating), and dispossessed. They can only be invited; they are real, but they do not "become" actual; and they are not (wholly) abstract (mere mental abstractions) either, but the very *relations* mediating actualities (cf. the structure of "subjective forms" in Whitehead, *AI,* 183).

Furthermore, Whitehead's "pure possibilities" are not in any way a master-plan for, or even like, a potential house built up from possible bricks where every free spot is plastered (another misunderstanding of Whitehead's possibilities). On the contrary, as infinity of pure possibilities (and their relations among themselves and to all actualities, as well as being these relationships), they cannot be fixed in any meaningful sense. Although they seem to be "complete," their completion is not finite (countable or uncountable) but comprises an *infinity* (of possibilities) which per definition cannot be circumscribed.[63] Since they cannot represent a pre-given order (which Whitehead secures in the image of a divine act of valuation and ordering), they are among themselves unordered and do not exhibit any "unity" or represent any "entity" or form any "class" of structures; rather they are pure *multiplicities* (see *PR,* 31).

Precisely insofar as the becoming of any actual event includes the "(infinite, chaotic) whole" of this pure multiplicity without unity, it offers *infinite differentiation* of actual events and, hence, the sought creativeness of unprecedented novelty instead of an infinite variability of the eternal.[64] In Deleuze's assessment of Whitehead's "pure possibilities" in *The Fold,* he correctly identifies them not only as "pure Possibilities" but (in Deleuze's critical sense directed against the Platonic possible) *as* "pure Virtualities."[65] This interpretation of "eternal objects" is the reason that Deleuze, in the preface of the American edition of *Dialogues,* can confess that he always has "felt that [he is] an empiricist, that is, a pluralist" who follows Whitehead's "search [that] is not for an eternal or universal, but for the condition under which something new is created."[66]

The Realms of Multiplicity

Although both philosophers develop these concepts over the course of the body of their whole work, their mystical inclination is best observed in their very last works—Whitehead's "Immortality" and Deleuze's "Immanence: A Life." Both works are a résumé of a life's work as they formulate concisely the relationship between mysticism and novelty by way of the very reference of Values and Virtuals as well as events and processes of becoming to their one "essence"—namely, as their folding-together as pure multiplicity, or as the play of multiplicities of interactions (of events, processes, values, and virtuals).[67]

In "Immortality," Whitehead differentiates between two worlds, one of Actuality and one of Value. While the former indicates the processes of the concrescence of actual events (from actual events), the latter names the very medium by which actualities in the "infinitude of possibility"[68] realize themselves as concrete values, instigated by the "World of Value."[69] While Value is an extremely complex notion throughout Whitehead's work, here, it indicates four moments:

1. "Values" are about the importance of actual becoming because they are "not rooted in any passing circumstances." They allow the "World of Activity" to become "valuable because it shares in the immortal of some value."[70] Hence, values cannot "become" actualities. They name a multiplicity of relations (or a relational multiplicity) that *as* multiplicity can instigate novelty when invited into actualization of events.
2. The "World of Value" "has an essential independence of any moment of time" but "it loses its meaning apart from any necessary reference to the World of passing fact."[71] Although a multiplicity of potentials, values can only be generated by processes of valuation, which are actualizations.
3. Because *any* World—the world of "Mortality" and "Immortality"—for "an adequate description . . . includes characterizations *derived* from the other," they are *mutually exploratory* (emphasis added).[72] In this *mutual* "process of modification," they generate creativeness without perpetual repetition.[73] Potential multiplicity and actual multiplicity meet without ever exchanging their respective perspective, necessary to mutually differentiate as multiplicities (instead of unities or many unities, or a unified many).
4. The process of creating Values "includes 'incitement toward' and 'deterrence from,' a manifold of possibility" by an "active coordination of the various possibilities of Value."[74] This activity Whitehead identifies as "the concept of God."[75] Hence, this (concept of) the divine in Whitehead offers a path to the open space in which the sensitivity for multiplicity as relational folding of pre-identical (or not yet identified) processes unfold/fold together in mutual interdependence, immanence, and processual actualization, valuation, and dramatization.

In "Immanence: A Life," Deleuze also relates Virtuality and Actuality in exactly such an intricate manner. Although he could be expected to shy away from any language invoking a divine dimension, he does not, in fact, avoid expressing novelty in terms of a mystical language. This essay shows the traces of theological language, even as it alludes to its very disappearance into apophatic indifferentiation. And it employs the same four moments as Whitehead's text.

1. Virtuality indicates the *medium* and *meaning* of actualization insofar as its multiplicity cannot be unified to any entity (a thing, a person, an actual actor, a god) but is viewed as an (impersonal, non-entitative, non-actual/particular) "transcendental field"[76] by which universal singularity is conditioned and, hence, *only* multiplicity is generated.

2. Yet virtual reality is also independent *from* actualizations since in their "non-actualized (indefinite)" state, the "virtual events" are "lacking nothing"—although they are "engaged in a process of actualization."[77] Hence, its multiplicity can always initiate actual becoming without being "dependent" on it as it generates the unprecedented as its very "nature" as multiplicity.

3. Hence, the virtual "exists" *before* its actualization as *pure* multiplicity, while also coexisting with all creative events of actualization in time. While the virtual initiates actualization, it is not dependent on it and, hence, beyond time-events a multiplicity of events of indifference.

4. Again employing mystical language, this virtual reality can "no longer be dependent on a Being or be submitted to an Act."[78] Its "own" reality is not only beyond actualization, but beyond subject and object, indifferent to these differences (but creative of them). Hence, in the most clearly mystically motivated move in Deleuze's work, he now dares to name this multiplicity (beyond identity and difference, a language he learned from Nicolas of Cusa and Giordano Bruno) as "absolute immediate consciousness," "consciousness without a self," and "pre-reflexive, impersonal consciousness."[79]

In comparing these four moments of Value and Virtuality in Whitehead and Deleuze, respectively, we must first recognize the important resonance: that of the interaction of multiplicities to generate multiplicities, that is, realms of novelty instead of imperial unifications of eternity. Yet we must also realize a subtle but nevertheless ever-growing bifurcation in the progress of the series of their respective four aspects of the two realms of multiplicity. The first moment of (the medium of) "meaning" allows both concepts—Value and Virtual—to rescue the moment of "importance" in their respective thought. Yet the second moment of *independence* and *involvement* already diverts both philosophers. Whitehead understands Value as multiplicity because it is conditioned *by* actualities so that neither can be viewed as a preformation of novelty.[80] Deleuze, on the other hand, is more interested in the *self-sufficiency of the virtual* reality beyond actualization, which comes (much more than Whitehead at this point) close to a classical allusion to the eternal (divine), and is only kept from becoming its revival as long as the Virtual can be shown to indicate a pure multiplicity. The third moment regarding the *interaction* of the two realities (worlds) reifies this difference because where for Whitehead their multiplicity is recurred by their mutual *exploratory interdependence*, for Deleuze their ability to instigate novelty is secured by their mere *coexistence*.

Finally, the fourth moment implies the most obvious manifestation of the employment of a *mystical* move for the uncompromising directedness toward novelty through multiplicity. Yet, in both thinkers, it leads to almost opposite conclusions. Whitehead's *mutual immanence* of both realities allows him to conceptualize the World of Value *in terms of* (its "other," namely) Activity (as the World of Creativity is described in terms of valuation). It is here, in this interaction, that Whitehead sees the necessity to explicate his mystical language of mutuality as inducing divinity (although a very different one).[81] Deleuze, on the other hand, refuses to understand the Virtual in any form as an *act* because he views such a move as a dangerous subordination of multiplicity to (unifying, occupying, imperial) transcendence. Instead, in order to save novelty from occupation, he invokes a *different* mystical image, namely that of the "absoluteness of an immediate consciousness."[82]

The Mystery of Novelty

So what in these explorations of the mystery of novelty (with the allusion of mystical language and as secured by the intricacies of multiplicity) exactly differentiates Whitehead from Deleuze? What differentiates Whitehead's "active coordination" of the infinite manifold of "possibilities of Value"[83] from the "flow of absolute consciousness"?[84] It is not that one "needs" divinity and the other shuns it; it is not that one seeks the eternal and the other the novel;[85] it is *how*, for them both, realities are mutually interwoven.

While both philosophers can use common terms in order to describe *either* reality—Whitehead talks of the act *of* valuation and the value *of* actualities; Deleuze of *virtual* events and actualizations *of* virtualities—Deleuze carefully insists on the saturation of both realities (against the lack of reality of the virtual over against the actual) while Whitehead points to their abstractness in isolation without mutual immanence. Hence, for Deleuze, novelty occurs in the *coexistence* of both multiplicities as processes of differentiation, while for Whitehead novelty occurs in the intricate *mutuality* of these processes (by which they are and remain multiplicity).

Therefore, what Whitehead views as an *act* of synthesis *within* both Worlds is also that *of* both Worlds; Deleuze, on the other hand, views any synthesis *of* both Multiplicities only as one *within* both Multiplicities (by which they do not become unified against possible and actual novelty). What Whitehead considers the condition of novelty—mutual immanence through an act of synthesis, although not as an imperial occupation—Deleuze denounces precisely as that: "a unity that is superior to all things or a Subject as an act that brings about a synthesis of things."[86] This is why Deleuze cannot accept any notion of divinity in addressing novelty—as it would hinder multiplicity—and Whitehead expresses novelty with a notion of divinity—the act of upholding multiplicity. Yet, Deleuze does not indulge in such a negation of "theology" at the heart of philosophy, but, instead, affirms its traces in the form of his embrace of the mystical move of indifferentiation: he *transfers the mystical function of divinity* to the "plane of immanence" to which he attributes its most delicate characteristic—namely, absolute consciousness, undifferentiated by the subject-object split (of ordinary consciousness and naïve notions of god).[87]

Yet, on deeper analysis, we realize that Whitehead's *divine* act of coordinating Value is not so far from Deleuze's *absolute* consciousness. As the latter, the World of Value has no Subject; rather Value is always outside of subjectivity. As in Deleuze, it is a prereflexive and impersonal multiplicity (by all standards of personality Whitehead employs).[88] In this sense, it is also "*pure* consciousness" exactly insofar as is not a subject synthesizing the World of Creativity but names the pure immanence *of* the World of Value itself as it generates it as multiplicity. And in the mutual immanence of the two Worlds, this "divine consciousness" must not be understood as a *synthesis* of them, but as the Eros toward novelty by which these multiplicities remain (never the same) multiplicities that, against meaningless change and the boredom of endless repetition, generate difference in form of novelty.[89]

Ironically, while Whitehead's "immanence" is always *mutual*—and hence is purely relative—Deleuze's immanence is only immanent *to itself*—and hence becomes *absolute.* While Whitehead's "active coordination" of Values is accused as repetition of the theistic past, it is, contrarily, *most immanent* in the production of novelty in the World of Creativity, only producing multiplicity. Deleuze's "flow of immanent consciousness," on the other hand, although one would expect his thought to function as the denial of such a theistic move, is indeed "absolute" and hence, in some sense repeats the classical content of the conceptualization of divinity. It avoids this "classical" implication only insofar as it remains a means to address multiplicity. But it does so with the mystical move for which it is "typical" that its reality does not lack of anything, which makes it indifferent to actualizations.

This presents us with an interesting paradox: the criticism of Whitehead's invocation of the divine in his *philosophy* (not as a reinstated "theology")—a criticism in which Deleuze did not participate—does not appreciate the function it gains as expression of a multiplicity in generation of a chaosmos of novelty. The accusation of a blindness with which Deleuze is seen to repeat Nietzsche's dismissal of divinity, on the other hand, does not take into account the very thinly veiled mystical language with which Deleuze secures multiplicity and novelty by employing one of mysticism's most cherished images: that of the indifferent reality of absoluteness as consciousness, being beyond differences (of subject and object) or not of being or "being" not-being at all.

While I agree that "the issue here is not whether Deleuze should have a place for God in his metaphysics" but "whether his idea of the virtual can provide the kind of permanence sought by Whitehead in the face of perpetual perishing,"[90] I will add that in light of the two "characteristics" of novelty—namely, the sense of *importance* and *creativeness* inherent to multiplicity—both philosophers equally allude to (even have a systematic necessity to refer to) a mysticism in their work that can be acknowledged *philosophically*. Without subscribing to any "theology," their respective articulation (and the tension of their respective approaches) might be vital for any future restatement of the triadic Platonic force field of the relation among philosophy, sophistic/relativism, and poetic/theology.[91]

A Mystagogy of Becoming

At this point—that is, the acknowledgment of a mystical move at the very core of the philosophical conversion of a world of eternity into that of novelty in Whitehead and Deleuze—we may even begin to realize that this common move is not only about "thought"—a reminder of the isolation of the *ego cogito*—but, as Plato imagined himself of the meaning of philosophy, about a *philosophical life*. In this sense, Whitehead's and Deleuze's novelty that is about the novelty of the multiplicity of the chaosmos may initiate nothing less than a *mystagogy of becoming*. That is, in the exploration of the thought of Whitehead and Deleuze regarding the mystery of novelty, we can find hints for a certain *philosophical praxis* by which one can, in a certain way, approach the mystery that makes one (and should never only make one) think. I will name four tentative moments for such a *way into* the mystery.

First, in choosing becoming instead of being, the world we live in becomes overturned. This is an experience of conversion, as Deleuze mentions. In seeking novelty instead of eternity, we become sensitive to the liberating force of life, chaos, creativity, and difference over the forces of Law, order, repetition, and sameness. It will overturn not only our attitude towards Life but also any articulation of a divine dimension: whether and where we seek it, what it implies, and the intention of its invocation.[92]

Second, since this different horizon of life will also change all the categories with which we frame our existence, we will be enabled to confront anew a cruel paradox, the paradox of life and death. Where we hail becoming, we also see perpetual perishing; where becoming is seamless, we should not expect salvation from contingency. Where life and death coincide, the "human face," as Deleuze states, "decomposes."[93]

Third, both philosophies indicate that the only way to live novelty will always lead us beyond the stabilizations we seek to escape into being, permanence, identity, and eternity. While we still might seek attainment in the event and creativeness in restriction, pure life also indicates the death of subjectivity, individuality, personality, and Self. This is what the mystery of novelty shelters: importance *dispossesses* life of subjectivity and objectivity; creativeness is the death of all forms. With Deleuze, we have to find the infinitive of "a Life" in the midst of "the Life"[94] we possess.[95]

Fourth, this reality can be experienced and conceptualized only on the border of language as complication, as in-and-out-folding, beyond difference and indifference (without ever leaving their differentiation of language). In this context, what is conceptualized resembles a mystagogy of the "mystical death" and an absolute immediacy beyond subjectivity and objectivity.[96]

A final thought: whether this mystical move is best conceptualized philosophically with divinity or not is secondary. What remains in question, however, is whether genuine novelty in a world of infinite becoming *must* invoke such a reality as its transcendental condition.[97] In any case, in my view, in the contrast of Whitehead and Deleuze, any future mystagogy of becoming will never be less than the expression of this problem and perhaps never be more than its affirmation.

Notes

1. See Roland Faber, *Prozeßtheologie. Zu ihrer Würdigung und kritischen Erneuerung* (Mainz: Gruenewald, 2000).

2. See Roland Faber, "'O bitches of impossibility!'—Programmatic Dysfunction in the Chaosmos of Deleuze and Whitehead," in *Deleuze, Whitehead and the Transformation of Metaphysics*, ed. André Cloots and Keith Robinson (Brussels: Flemish Academy of Sciences, 2005), 117–28.

3. See Keith Robinson, ed., *Deleuze, Whitehead, Bergson: Rhizomatic Connections* (Houndmills, U.K.: Palgrave Macmillan, 2009); Steven Shaviro, *Without Criteria: Kant, Whitehead, Deleuze, and Aesthetics* (Cambridge, Mass.: MIT Press, 2009); Roland Faber, Henry Krips, and Daniel Pettus, eds., *Event and Decision: Ontology and Politics in Badiou, Deleuze, and Whitehead* (Cambridge: Cambridge Scholars Publishing, 2010); Faber and Andrea M. Stephenson, eds. *Secrets of Becoming: Negotiating Whitehead, Deleuze, and Butler* (New York: Fordham University Press, 2011).

4. See John D. Caputo, *The Prayers and Tears of Jacques Derrida: Religion without Religion* (Bloomington: Indiana University Press, 1997).

5. See James Williams, *Encounters and Influences: The Transversal Thought of Gilles Deleuze* (Manchester, U.K.: Clinamen Press, 2005), ch. 5.

6. See Joseph A. Bracken, *The One and the Many: A Contemporary Reconstruction of the God-World Relationship* (Grand Rapids, Mich.: Eerdmans, 2001), ch. 3.

7. See Catherine Keller, *Face of the Deep: A Theology of Becoming* (New York: Routledge, 2003); Roland Faber, *God as Poet of the World: Exploring Process Theologies* (Louisville, Ky.: WJK, 2008).

8. See Roland Faber, "Bodies of the Void: Polyphilia and Theoplicity," in *Apophatic Bodies: Negative Theology, Incarnation, and Relationship*, ed. Chris Boesel and Catherine Keller (New York: Fordham University Press, 2010), 200–223.

9. See Ramona Naddaff, *Exiling the Poets: The Production of Censorship in Plato's Republic* (Berkeley, Calif.: Zone Books, 2003), 73.

10. See Noburu Notomi, *The Unity of Plato's Sophist: Between the Sophist and the Philosopher* (Cambridge: Cambridge University Press, 2001).

11. See Christopher S. Celenza, "The Revival of Platonic Philosophy," in *The Cambridge Companion to Renaissance Philosophy*, ed. James Hankins (Cambridge: Cambridge University Press, 2007), 73.

12. See Catherine Pickstock, *After Writing: On the Liturgical Consummation of Philosophy* (Oxford: Blackwell, 2000), 47.

13. See Isabelle Stengers, *Thinking with Whitehead* (Cambridge, Mass.: Harvard University Press, 2011), ch. 24.

14. See Jeffrey A. Bell, *Philosophy at the Edge of Chaos: Gilles Deleuze and the Philosophy of Difference* (Toronto: University of Toronto Press, 2006), ch. 6.

15. See Gilles Deleuze, *Difference and Repetition* (New York: Columbia University Press, 1994), 66–69.

16. See Gilles Deleuze, *Two Regimes of Madness: Texts and Interviews 1975–1995* (New York: Semiotext(e), 2006), 262.

17. See Gilles Deleuze, *Expressionism in Philosophy: Spinoza* (New York: Zone Books, 1992).

18. See Lucien Price, *Dialogues of Alfred North Whitehead* (Boston: Little, Brown and Company, 1953), 9.

19. See Roland Faber, "Surrationality and Chaosmos: For a More Deleuzian Whitehead (with a Butlerian Intervention)," in Faber and Stephenson, *Secrets,* 157–77.

20. See Gilles Deleuze, *Negotiations, 1972–1990* (New York: Columbia University Press, 1995), 135–55.

21. See Gilles Deleuze and Félix Guattari, *What Is Philosophy?* (New York: Columbia University Press, 1994), ch. 2.

22. See Deleuze, *Two Regimes of Madness,* 304.

23. See Deleuze, *Difference and Repetition,* 284–85.

24. See Deleuze, *Negotiations,* 143.

25. Gilles Deleuze, *The Fold: Leibniz and the Baroque* (Minneapolis: University of Minnesota Press, 1992), 81.

26. See Roland Faber, "Whitehead," in *The Deleuze Dictionary,* ed. Adrian Parr (Edinburgh, Edinburgh University Press, 2010), 302–4.

27. Roland Faber, "Introduction: Negotiating Becoming," in Faber and Stephenson, *Secrets,* 1–49.

28. See Gilles Deleuze, *Desert Islands and Other Texts 1953–1974* (Paris: Semiotext(e), 2004), 32–51.

29. See Faber, "'O bitches."

30. See Roland Faber, "Whitehead at Infinite Speed: Deconstructing System as Event," in *Schleiermacher and Whitehead: Open Systems in Dialogue,* ed. Katie Goetz, Christine Helmer, Marjorie Suchocki, and John Quiring (Berlin: DeGruiter, 2004), 39–72.

31. Deleuze, *The Fold,* 79.

32. See Deleuze and Guattari, *What Is Philosophy?,* 43.

33. See Gilles Deleuze, *Nietzsche and Philosophy* (New York: Columbia University Press, 2006), 152–56.

34. Deleuze, *Difference and Repetition,* 57.

35. See Faber, *God as Poet of the World,* pt. 3.

36. Deleuze, *The Fold,* 81.

37. Deleuze, *Difference and Repetition,* 42.

38. Ibid., 1.

39. Ibid., 280–81; Deleuze and Guattari, *What Is Philosophy?,* 44–45.

40. Deleuze, *Two Regimes of Madness,* 261.

41. Deleuze, *The Fold,* ch. 5.

42. Deleuze, *Difference and Repetition,* 42. Cf. Faber, "'The Infinite Movement of Evanescence'—The Pythagorean Puzzle in Plato, Deleuze, and Whitehead," in *American Journal of Theology and Philosophy,* 21, no. 1 (2000): 171–99.

43. See Roland Faber, "'Indra's Ear'—God's Absence of Listening" in *The Presence and Absence of God: Religion in Philosophy and Theology,* ed. I. U. Dalferth 42 (Tübingen: Mohr Siebeck, 2010), 161–86.

44. Heidegger's *a-letheia* addresses this rescue from eternal oblivion. Cf. Martin Heidegger, "The Essence of Truth," in *Basic Writings* (San Francisco: Harper, 1993), 111–38.

45. This is the reason that Deleuze reinterprets Nietzsche's *eternal return* (also the "place" of the disappearance of the divine in a world of becoming) as prime expression of difference that aims at genuine novelty. Cf. Deleuze, *Desert Islands,* 117–27.

46. Ecc. 1:9.

47. See Roland Faber, "Tears of God—In the Rain with D. Z. Philips and J. Keller, Waiting for Wittgenstein and Whitehead," in *Metaphysics, Analysis, and the Grammar of God,* ed. Randy Ramal (Tübingen: Mohr Siebeck, 2010), 57–103.

48. Deleuze, *Negotiations,* 143.

49. Gilles Deleuze and Félix Guattari, *A Thousand Plateaus* (Minneapolis: University of Minnesota Press, 1987), 150.

50. Deleuze, *Difference and Repetition,* 28.

51. Deleuze, *The Fold,* 81.

52. Deleuze and Guattari, *What Is Philosophy?,* 49.

53. See Deleuze, *Negotiations,* 143.

54. See Lewis Ford, "Whitehead's Transformation of Pure Act," *Thomist* 41, no. 3 (1977): 381–99.

55. Only recently have scholars of Whitehead and Deleuze realized the close proximity of Whitehead's concept of "Value" and Deleuze's concept of "Virtuality." Regarding their respective function in their philosophies and their mutual connotations, see Roland Faber, "De-Ontologizing God: Levinas, Deleuze and Whitehead," in *Process and Difference: Between Cosmological and Poststructuralist Postmodernism,* ed. Catherine Keller and Anne Daniell (Albany: State University of New York Press, 2002), 209–34; James Williams, "Deleuze and Whitehead: The Concept of Reciprocal Determination," in Cloots and Robinson, *Deleuze, Whitehead, and the Transformation of Metaphysics,* 89–106.

56. See John Marks, *Gilles Deleuze: Vitalism and Multiplicity* (London: Pluto Press, 1998), ch. 4.

57. See Elizabeth M. Kraus, *The Metaphysics of Experience: A Companion to Whitehead's "Process and Reality"* (New York: Fordham University Press, 1998), 28–35.

58. Gilles Deleuze, *Bergsonism* (Brooklyn, N.Y.: Zone Books, 1988), 43.

59. See Roland Faber, "Bodies," in *Apophatic Bodies: Negative Theology, Incarnation, and Relationship,* ed. Christoph Boesel and Catherine Keller (New York: Fordham University Press, 2010), 117–20.

60. See Michael Hardt, *Gilles Deleuze: An Apprenticeship in Philosophy* (Minneapolis: University of Minnesota Press, 1995), 16–17.

61. Besides the classical Platonic instantiation of this scheme of possibility, which *lacks* actuality but in actualization only "realizes" the essence of the possibility actualized, a contemporary affirmation of this "possible" is David Lewis's view of "possibilities" as the *actuality* of all possible worlds. Even if they do not indicate any preformed order, because of the infinity of actualized alternate worlds, they allow for no novelty at all: in this multiverse, every possibility is already realized and actual. In both cases, however, it is crucial that the possible is defined either as "realized" or "unrealized" while this "realization" of the actual possibility executes an eternal essence. Cf. David Lewis, "Possible Worlds," in *Contemporary Readings in the Foundations of Metaphysics,* ed. Stephen Laurence and Cynthia Macdonald (Oxford: Blackwell, 1998), 96–102; and William Lycan, "Possible Worlds and Possibilia," in Laurence and Macdonald, eds., ibid., 83–95.

62. See William Hendrichs Leue, *Metaphysical Foundations of a Theory of Value in the Philosophy of Alfred North Whitehead* (Ashfield, Mass.: Down-to-Earth Books, 2005), ch. 3.

63. See Faber, *God as Poet of the World,* 92–93.
64. See Leue, *Metaphysical Foundations,* 91–106.
65. Deleuze, *The Fold,* 79.
66. Deleuze, *Two Regimes of Madness,* 304.
67. See Faber, "Bodies," 220–21; Williams, *Encounters,* 79–85.
68. A. N. Whitehead, "Immortality," in *The Philosophy of Alfred North Whitehead,* ed. Paul Schilpp (La Salle, Ill.: Open Court, 1991), 689.
69. Ibid., 686.
70. Ibid., 684.
71. Ibid.
72. Ibid., 683–84.
73. Ibid., 685.
74. Ibid., 687.
75. Ibid., 694.
76. Deleuze, "Immanence: A Life," in *Pure Immanence: Essays on A Life* (Brooklyn, N.Y.: Zone Books, 2005), 31.
77. Ibid., 29–30, 31.
78. Ibid., 27.
79. Ibid., 27, 25.
80. See Whitehead, "Immortality," 685.
81. See Faber, "De-Ontologizing God," 217–18.
82. Deleuze, "Immanence," 29.
83. Whitehead, "Immortality," 687.
84. Deleuze, "Immanence," 25.
85. See Faber, "'O bitches," 218–19.
86. Deleuze, "Immanence," 27.
87. Ibid., 31.
88. See Faber, *God as Poet of the World,* § 22.
89. See Whitehead, "Immortality," 687.
90. Williams, "Deleuze," 105.
91. See Roland Faber, *The Divine Manifold* (Lanham, Md.: Lexington Books, 2014).
92. See Faber, "Introduction: Negotiating Becoming," 1–49.
93. Deleuze, *Difference,* 28.
94. Deleuze, "Immanence," 29.
95. See Faber, "Bodies," 222–23.
96. See Faber, *God as Poet of the World,* 112.
97. See Deleuze, "Immanence," 26.

SEVEN

The Event and the Occasion

Deleuze, Whitehead, and Creativity

Keith Robinson

It is now recognized that the philosophical projects of the French philosopher Gilles Deleuze and the British mathematical physicist and philosopher Alfred North Whitehead display remarkable affinities, despite the apparent dissimilarities in disciplinary backgrounds, styles, traditions, and influences. Both philosophers espouse a new metaphysics that is simultaneously a metaphysics of the new. The central category of this metaphysics of the new is "creativity," and for each philosopher temporality is a condition of creativity. I want to explore the idea that Deleuze and Whitehead each emphasize and valorize different modalities of time in the structure of creativity, giving us two approaches to the metaphysics of the new that are at least in tension, if not outright opposition. What is at stake in these differing approaches are assumptions about how certain modalities of time relate to each other and, in that relation, have the power to constitute the experience of movement, change, and difference. The relations between the differing modes of time exposes underlying commitments to the values of transformation, mutation, and the creativity of the new and how these should be conceived. For Whitehead the activity of creativity comes from the power of the past, the self-determinations of the present, and the relative continuity between them. The essential movement of this activity is gathering, synthesizing, and unifying. In this activity the actual occasion is produced, the new is disclosed, and its achievement becomes objectively immortal, "saved" by passing into the "consequent nature" of God. For Deleuze, in contrast, the essential movement of time in creativity breaks and disrupts any gathering, disjoins syntheses, and opens thought to an unknown future. Here the emphasis is toward relative discontinuity, where continuity is ruptured and time is thought as an event that cannot be saved in the actual but must be constantly undergone as the eternal and virtual "wound" of our condition. It is a "time out of joint" that fractures any subject-object equilibrium. In both cases time is a transcendental condition for experience (with the transcendental understood in a new and transformed way), and for both this structure of time is more or less covered over, creating "illusions" (Deleuze) or "fallacies" (Whitehead) relating to experience. In both cases creativity is governed by two "multiplicities" or two aspects of reality, and, although the relation between them is one of reciprocal determination, in each case the temporal emphasis in that determination is different. By contrasting these two approaches to time—summarized here as the event and the occasion—I will highlight internal differences within their metaphysics of the new and uncover what is at stake in their philosophies of creativity. Along the way, I will offer readings of Whitehead's and Deleuze's metaphysics and take up a position in relation to some of the canonical scholarship and contemporary readings of their work, as well as look at Deleuze's own reading of Whitehead. I will begin by describing Deleuze's and Whitehead's shared methodological commitment to metaphysics and their transformation of the philosophical notion of the "category," and then move on to discuss their subtly differing conceptions of creativity and time in the context of their respective concepts of the event and the occasion.

Metaphysics and Categories

In my view, with the philosophies of Deleuze and Whitehead, we move toward "that remarkable point of modern metaphysics which all preceding discourse had indicated like a flickering compass."[1] The "remarkable point" referred to here is the achievement of an immanent or fully differential metaphysics that returns to "life" and the concrete world, a thorough going effort to renew metaphysics in the wake of Kant and then Heidegger. This is what Deleuze recognized in Whitehead, and this is also no doubt one of the reasons why Whitehead, like Bergson, was marginalized by professional philosophy in the latter half of the twentieth century. Although some seem to prefer to talk about "ontology" instead of metaphysics, there may be good reasons to abandon talk of ontology in Deleuze, especially given Deleuze's and Deleuze and Guattari's explicit determination to think outside of "is" and to "undermine being, make it topple over."[2] Deleuze did not have a problem with using the term "metaphysics"; as he declares, simply, "I am a pure metaphysician."[3] In fact, for Deleuze and Whitehead the philosopher is a metaphysician regardless of his or her intent. Metaphysics provides at once both the "system" and the "method," and it involves the positing of an "absolute"—and Deleuze has said explicitly and from very early on that the absolute is achieved when metaphysics pushes all the way to difference. I agree with Arnauld Villani that Deleuze's affirmation of metaphysics is crucial for his entire philosophy, just as it is for Whitehead.[4]

There is much that one could say about this affirmative transformation of metaphysics. Perhaps one of the more important aspects of Deleuze's Whiteheadian inflected renewal of metaphysics is that it operates on the basis of a new yet incomplete system of categories (with a new understanding of "system" and "category")—categories, as Deleuze says, "not in the style of Kant, but in the style of Whitehead," which are drawn and "transposed" from various disciplines and elements of experience. It is directly from Whitehead that Deleuze finds the means to retain and employ a new type of category, a "problematic" or "virtual" sense of category "so that 'category' takes on a new, very special sense."[5] These new categories are no longer tied to structures of rational necessity that represent an essentially complete and unchanging real inevitably suppressing the different, the contingent, and the anomalous. If much of modern philosophy after Kant and culminating with Heidegger simply abandons categorial thinking, Whitehead's singular response is to "reform" or reinvent the category not as a structure of being or of cognition, but as the unique act or event of the self-differentiation of things. Indeed, when Deleuze says in *Difference and Repetition* that "[Whitehead's] *Process and Reality* is one of the greatest books of modern philosophy" it is because Whitehead's categories, or "empirico-ideal notions" as Deleuze calls them, are precisely an effort to move beyond Aristotelian categories of being and Kantian categories of possible experience in the development of something completely new.[6] Categories of the Aristotelian-Kantian type, although very different in themselves, belong for Deleuze to the world of representation where they distribute and partition being according to the laws of "sedentary proportionality." By contrast Deleuze-Whitehead's own "descriptive," "nomadic," or "phantastical" notions are said to be "really open" because they preside over a distribution of difference that is not governed by representational rules. Such notions are said to betray an empiricist or pluralist sense of Ideas collapsing the "transcendent" distinction between existence and essence, thought and being. Thus, rather than presupposing the validity of categorial thinking in the Kantian mode as the epistemological conditions for all possible experience, these "notions" are the conditions of real experience. Deleuze invokes

Whitehead's "empirico-ideal" notions, then, as examples of a nonrepresentational, differential, and metaphysical structure or "open" system of categories where the Kantian map of critical reason is displaced and reworked. Here categories "in the style of Whitehead" become the immanent differences and intensities of the "nomadic" movement and processual distribution of becoming itself. It is in this sense that Deleuze can say "to my mind, the conclusion of *A Thousand Plateaus* is a table of categories (but an incomplete, insufficient one). Not in the style of Kant, but in the style of Whitehead."[7] This new table of categories forms the conditions of real experience, conditions that account for novelty or the creativity of the new.

Creativity in Whitehead: The Occasion

This dynamism and becoming of the real in Deleuze and Whitehead is essentially a movement of creativity, and so we could say that creativity is the "first" and general category of this new metaphysics. Indeed, if there is one designation that accurately characterizes Whitehead's later philosophy, it is that it is a metaphysics of creativity in which becoming, thinking, and creativity are one. For Whitehead the category of the "Ultimate" is "creativity." It is, he says, "the Universal of Universals characterizing ultimate matter of fact" (*PR*, 21). We could claim that Whitehead's metaphysics is in fact the first metaphysics of *creativity* since he actually invented the concept, the English word "creativity."[8] For Whitehead creativity is the fundamental principle that precedes the other categories (*PR*, 31). Creativity is not itself an "entity"; nor is it reducible to entities; yet it is not independent of the activity of actuality. It is, rather, the ultimate genetic factor presupposed by actual occasions. As Whitehead puts it, all of actuality is "in the grip of the ultimate metaphysical ground, the creative advance into novelty" (*PR*, 349).

In several books Whitehead appeals to Spinoza, just like Deleuze, to characterize creativity. Creativity is said to be a general or "substantial activity" that is individualized into modes or actual entities. In *Process and Reality* Whitehead cautions us not to think of creativity as an "external agency" that is more final or "eminent" (Deleuze would say "transcendent") than the "accidents" of actuality, nor should we think that creativity and God coincide (*PR*, 222). Creativity is immanent to actualities, as real as they are. Using one of Deleuze's favorite phrases, we might say that creativity is "real without being actual, ideal without being abstract."[9] Whitehead often talks about creativity as a *principle*. One key phrasing of this principle from *Process and Reality* is that creativity "expresses the general principle presupposed in the three more special categories" (*PR*, 31). The three other categories of existence, explanation, and obligation *presuppose* the category of creativity. This is one reason why creativity is the "Ultimate" principle. But Whitehead insists that, although creativity is the ultimate, it is not more ontologically real than anything else in the universe. For Whitehead all the components of the metaphysical scheme have an equal share in the univocity of the real, although the univocal is distributed across the differing parts of the metaphysical scheme. As Whitehead says, "there is no meaning to 'creativity' apart from its 'creatures', and no meaning to 'God' apart from the creativity and the 'temporal creatures,' and no meaning to the temporal creatures apart from 'creativity' and 'God'" (*PR*, 344). This is the "coherence" of Whitehead's system, wherein each component cannot be separated from the others as each performs its functions as entity, principle, or category.

As the ultimate category, creativity is, in the language of *Religion in the Making*, a "formative element," the element "whereby the actual world has its character of temporal passage to novelty" (*RM*, 90). Creativity is thus, in one of its functions, the condition or formative element for the "temporal passage to novelty." In addition to creativity, the temporal passage to novelty also involves the other notions of "one" and "many" that make up the category of the Ultimate. Whitehead describes the temporal passage as a move from disjunctive multiplicity to conjunctive unity, a movement that gives us the "production of novel togetherness" (*PR*, 21). The temporal passage to novelty aims at gathering a unity and togetherness from disjunction. This unity ends in "satisfaction," and this achievement acquires the status of "objective immortality," saved in the consequent nature of God.

Some interpretations of this movement in Whitehead argue that creativity is at work only in the present, that the past has already become, and the future has not arrived, and so the past cannot act since it is no longer actual and the future cannot act because it is not yet actual. In other words, once actuality is achieved, creativity perishes. A number of well-known interpretations (e.g., Christian, Cobb, Hosinski) follow this path in order to install God as the cause of the new occasion, and others (e.g., Leclerc, Kline) argue that creativity be confined to the actual present with the superject as devoid of activity and creativity.[10] Perhaps the most recent interpretation to offer a variant of the latter view is found in the work of Graham Harman.[11] Much like Kline and Leclerc, Harman wants to distinguish occasions from becoming but instead of locating the actual exclusively in the concrescence (as Kline and Leclerc do), Harman wants to argue that it is the individual entity that is fully actual. On this view, time is a series of discrete cinematic instants that are in "perpetual perishing," and actual occasions are viewed as a string of distinct atomic units. There are numerous problems with Harman's view, including treating "societies" of occasions as actual entities (he says that he thinks this distinction fails in Whitehead, but he does not tell us why) and ignoring the different types of relation that make up actual occasions, especially the difference in temporal relations, preferring instead to talk of "current relations," which is another way of reducing the determination of Whitehead's occasions merely to the "present." But perhaps the most important problem from the perspective of this essay is that he completely ignores Whitehead's ultimate: creativity! As I suggested above, for Whitehead the "ontological principle"—to which Harman rightly appeals in his reading—presupposes the category of creativity. And it is creativity that explains both unity and novelty, continuity and discontinuity, individual existence and relativity. In fact, Whitehead often discusses creativity not just in terms of individual existence but in terms of "the continuity of events," a passage of nature without any cuts or radical breaks.[12] Indeed, Whitehead's philosophy is developed on the basis that any notion of "independent existence" is a "vacuous actuality" or at best an abstraction and needs to be supplemented by a more comprehensive metaphysics that affirms relations of becoming and continuity. Interpretations like Kline's, Christian's, and now Harman's are at least one-sided and tend to ignore the explicit aims of Whitehead's thinking (i.e., the fundamental emphasis on the reality of process and becoming alongside individual existence, the essential distinction between creativity and God, etc.) and the continuing development of his thought (before and after *Process and Reality* Whitehead stresses the importance of the past as active). In various texts Whitehead affirms a "double-aspect" ontology of occasions as both subject and superject, each coextensive with creative actuality. An emphasis on the concrescing occasion as self-determining in the present needs to be balanced with the importance that Whitehead attaches to processes of transition and the continuity of the past such that "the whole antecedent world conspires to produce a new occasion" (*MT,* 164).

Creativity expresses itself, as Whitehead says, through "two kinds of fluency." Creativity is at once an activity "conditioned by the objective immortality of the actual world" (*PR,* 31) and the creative advance into novelty. The two poles of Whitehead's creativity enter into a relation of reciprocal determination and mutual presupposition such that each mode of process and each actual occasion is the general activity of creativity individualized by the imposed conditions. Creativity creates its own creatures and, apart from these "accidents," Whitehead says, creativity is "devoid of actuality." However, apart from the conditions imposed by these accidents there would be no novelty. It is what Whitehead calls the "real potentiality" providing both the objects for a new occasion and the "factor of activity" for the initial phase of the new occasion. Creativity thus serves as the virtual or "transcendental" principle behind the becoming and internal genesis of actuality as well as the principle of movement or extrinsic conditioning between actualities (*AI,* 179). As Whitehead puts it, "creativity is the actualization of potentiality, and the process of actualization is an occasion of experiencing" (*AI,* 179). Thus the creative advance into novelty is the process whereby the many become one and are increased by one, but this one creative process of unification is split into the two "multiplicities" of process.[13]

For Whitehead, like Deleuze, if these creative processes or multiplicities are not properly articulated together, we will be left with a series of "fallacies" regarding the nature of experience ("the fallacy of misplaced concreteness," "the fallacy of simple location," etc.) not unlike the "illusions" that Deleuze diagnoses. Like Deleuzian "transcendental empiricism" and Bergsonian "intuition," Whitehead's method of "descriptive generalization" aims to overcome the spatializing fallacies of consciousness and the "bare" repetitions of habit and memory in order to account for the creative "temporalizing" or processual conditions of experience. As I have argued elsewhere, Whitehead often contrasts what he is doing with Kant's account of the "transcendental aesthetic" in the first critique.[14] Whitehead seeks to invert the Kantian solution since it "assumes the radical disconnection of impressions *qua data*" such that knowledge begins with the bare datum or percept affecting an essentially passive and simple receptivity of intuition (*PR,* 113). Thus, Kant "conceives his 'Transcendental Aesthetic' to be the mere description of a subjective process appropriating the data by orderliness of feeling" (*PR,* 113). This is a false beginning for Whitehead since the data is already an interconnection, and an activity of "feeling" or synthesis of "prehensions" is already in process. Behind the receptiveness of the ego and its perceptions (what Whitehead calls "perception in the mode of presentational immediacy") lies the "causal efficacy" of the past that precedes and conditions the activity of the "I think." In order for the active "I" of the understanding to represent what is given, there must be subrepresentative or nonrepresentative syntheses conditioning its activity, what Michel Foucault would call an "unthought" element that conditions me and that I do not control. The "other" lives in me, or in Rimbaud's formula: "I is another." The "other" lives objectively for Whitehead through the "transference of throbs of emotional energy" passing through the "vector" of time, an experience that Whitehead designates as "the passage of nature" (*PR*, 116). In *Process and Reality* Whitehead names this mode of process *transition* and describes it variously as the "vehicle of the efficient cause," the "immortal past," or the "perpetual perishing" in us (*PR*, 29, 81, 210). As I suggested earlier, many readings of Whitehead tend to downplay or just ignore the role played by "transition" in Whitehead, but it is the key to Whitehead's metaphysics of the new. Without transition, there would be no real creative or differential "repetition" and, as Whitehead says, "tear 'repetition' out of 'experience' and there is nothing left" (*PR*, 206). For Whitehead "what becomes involves repetition transformed into novel immediacy," and this process of transforming the bare, naked, material repetition and clothing it with feelings of novel immediacy is initiated in transition (*PR*, 207). Transition is, then, not just the handing over or "picking up" of already completed occasions. It is both the "perishing," or better, the "immortalizing" or "becoming immortal" of the present, and the power of repetition that originates a new present in conformity with the past. It is the "passing on," as Whitehead calls it, of the creativity into which the actual occasion will infuse its own particularity (*PR*, 213). This unthought or unconscious creative element is, then, more properly understood as a *temporalizing* synthesis in conformation with the past, or as Whitehead says, following Bergson, the synthesis is "unspatialized" (*PR*, 114). These non-conscious and non-spatialized elements or "feelings" exhibit a vector character transforming the past into a merging with the present. As Whitehead says, "The *how* of our present experience must conform to the *what* of the past in us" (*S*, 58). Creativity here is the ever-advancing reality of the world, "the throbbing emotion of the past hurling itself into a new transcendent fact" (*AI*, 227). The processes of transition from the past, then, include an "active" factor of desire, creativity, or power, a "living urge" that, at a critical stage, *changes in kind* and intensifies, forming *concrescences* or modes of intense becoming that precede and enable the formation of things, individuals, or organisms. Whitehead's theory of "objectifications" explains how, in its transitional phase, this activity drives the processes whereby the completed occasions of the past are repeated inside the concrescing occasion. Objectification involves "decisions" that push the datum to a critical or poised threshold, marking points at which the process of transition spontaneously changes its structure, breaks symmetry, and becomes self-organizing. Whitehead describes this self-actualizing nature of concrescence in terms of how the nascent occasion "feels" that datum given in the transition and makes its "decision" with respect to what it has received, "grafting," feeling, and incorporating the data as an increasingly unique individuated "subjective aim." The process of concrescence is, then, properly *causa sui* or self actualizing but it emerges out of the datum given in transition. If the transition is the disjunctive datum stripped bare, with creativity approaching zero, yet still carrying a factor of activity or desire, concrescence is the intensifying subjective form, including the "ingression" of relevant eternal objects, which conjunctively "clothes" itself in its movement of becoming toward "satisfaction": the subject becomes "superject." In any case, the product of transition is the new occasion in its earliest stage, and concrescence is the complex self-directed unfolding, dissociation, and differentiation of transitional components into intensive fields, dynamisms, and interiorities progressively passing through what Whitehead calls the "diverse routes" and "borders of chaos" (*PR*, 111) that eventually determine and compose the extensive organism. As Whitehead says "organism has two 'meanings', interconnected but intellectually separable, namely, the microscopic meaning and the macroscopic meaning" (*PR*, 128–29). The microscopic process is "the real internal constitution" of the organism, enabling its growth from the real to the actual by a complex process of condition conversion. The macroscopic process is the transitional movement from the actual to the real, the "superjective" advance or thrust whereby "the future is merely real without being actual" (*PR*, 214). The actual occasion can be understood as an indissoluble double process with two odd, dissimilar, and dysymetrical "halves" or multiplicities, what Whitehead calls a "subject-superject," a process-product, an organism and environment that are meaningful only with reference to one another.

Thus, both transition and concrescence are distinct yet continuous phases or multiplicities of creativity. Transition *from* concrescence is creativity that is other-caused, and transition *to* concrescence is other-causing. Yet concrescence itself is self-causing creativity. Transition is creativity *that affects and is affected by the other,* and concrescence is creativity that *affects itself.* Transition is creativity of the product to enter into other processes and concrescence is creativity to enter into the product. These modes of creativity together drive the processes of becoming that constitute the real and its individuation.[15]

Thus, creativity in Whitehead cannot be restricted to the concrescing subject; nor can reality be exclusively located in the individual existent. Rather, the actual occasion as a past, "perished," or individually existent object is creatively active just as the occasion as concrescence in the present is active. But these forms of creativity are active in different senses. The object is active in its power to affect others, and the subject is active in its power to affect itself. The essential movement of this double activity is aimed at the continuity between each of its aspects and the gathering, synthesizing and unifying of experience that it produces. The creativity of the occasion resides in these aspects so that the future becomes the relatively open horizon of the integrating and unifying work of the temporal relation between past and present.[16]

Creativity in Deleuze: The Event

With regards to Deleuze, it seems to me that Peter Hallward's basic claim in his book *Out of This World* that Deleuze offers a metaphysics of creativity is just about right, although I think he gets a good deal of the details wrong.[17] In fact, the main problem with Hallward's reading of Deleuze finds a striking parallel with the problem in some of the interpretations of Whitehead that I identified earlier. Hallward's claim that the process of creativity is unilateral and that only the virtual is creative is as reductive as Kline's claim that for Whitehead only concrescence is really actual; it is also as one-sided as Harman's claim that for Whitehead only the individual existent is real independently of its becoming.[18] This is so because for Deleuze, as for Whitehead, becoming, thinking, and creativity are one. Deleuze gives us a metaphysics of creativity in which the fundamental power is a force of creative differing. For Deleuze, being itself is creativity, an unlimited "One All" that differentiates itself into all that is. As Deleuze says, "differentiation is never a negation but a creation, difference is never negative but essentially creative and positive."[19] All of being and life, every "thing" and every activity is creation. Artists create in their medium, with painters, for example, creating the "percept" or the "being of sensation"; scientists are said to create "functions"; and famously it is left to the philosopher—and only the philosopher—to create concepts. Like Whitehead, Deleuze invokes Spinoza to characterize creativity, and, again like Whitehead, Deleuze points out that substance is not to be thought as an eminent term but should be made "to turn around the modes."[20] The activity of differentiation is expressed "in terms of what it creates and its mode of creation," a single activity of individualization with virtual and actual "aspects" or "attributes." Thus, everything that exists exists in the same way but, as Deleuze adds, that existence is "said of difference":

> There are not 'two paths', as Parmenides' poem suggests, but a single 'voice' of being which includes all its modes, including the most diverse, the most varied, the most differenciated. Being is said in a single sense of everything of which it is said, but that of which it is said differs: it is said of difference itself.[21]

Every creation of being is said in the same sense but that of which it is said differs. Much of Deleuze's philosophical effort is devoted to uncovering the genesis of these created differences, dipping beneath the abstract fallacies and "transcendental illusions" that cover over the creativity of things in order not only to describe but to *explain* their genesis. As with Whitehead, we can think of Deleuze as a radical empiricist searching for the conditions under which something new is produced:

> I have always felt that I am an empiricist, that is, a pluralist. But what does this equivalence between empiricism and pluralism mean? It derives from the two characteristics by which Whitehead defined empiricism: the abstract does not explain, but must itself be explained; and the aim is not to rediscover the eternal or the universal, but to find the conditions under which something new is produced *(creativeness).*[22]

The abstract does not explain but must itself be explained through a genesis of its creative conditions. If there is an appeal to "truth" in Deleuze it is this: "truth is not to be achieved, formed or reproduced; it has to be created. There is no other truth than the creation of the New."[23] At the very least, I think we can claim that Deleuze, in appealing to creativity and "creativeness" (which importantly Deleuze writes in English), was thinking with Whitehead (as well as Bergson).

This is borne out by the attention given to the concept of the "event" in Deleuze's metaphysics of creativity and the attempt to align certain aspects of his own thinking with Whitehead's. Deleuze of course discusses the concept of the event explicitly with detailed attention in several books. "I've tried in all of my books," Deleuze says, "to discover the nature of events. It's a philosophical concept, the only one capable of ousting the verb 'to be' and attributes."[24] In his *The Fold: Leibniz and the Baroque,* Deleuze even uncovers a "secret school" devoted to answering the question "What is an Event?" Of course the successor to this secret school, the *diadoche* as Deleuze calls him, who inherits the question of the event is none other than Whitehead.[25] Think of all the philosophers whom Deleuze could have named here. Heidegger immediately springs to mind. Why is Heidegger not the successor, or Derrida, or even Foucault, who devoted a number of texts to the idea of what he called "eventalization"? But Heidegger is after all the thinker of *ereignis,* the veiling-unveiling as the event of Being. It seems to me that Deleuze's naming Whitehead as the successor to the question of the event is important and that it is related precisely to Whitehead's metaphysics of creativity. In any case, it is true that Whitehead also, like Deleuze, spent a good part of his career writing about the event. I want to suggest that what Whitehead offered Deleuze here was a model or "logic" for thinking the event in relation to creativity and the new that would come to inform Deleuze's own conception of the event.

Deleuze's concept of the event receives various formulations in his work but the basic structure is well known: on the one hand, a state of affairs that relates to actualized bodies and individuals and, on the other, an incorporeal reserve of infinite becoming and virtual movement. Treating this structure as a simple hierarchical dualism has been used to give a distorted image of Deleuze's thought in texts by Badiou, Hallward, and Žižek (see note 17). I suggest that a better image is the "between-two" or "fourfold" where each component is internal to and required by the other. In terms of Deleuze's reading of the event in Whitehead, extension, intension, prehension, and ingression each has a virtual/actual side, and the process of conversion between them is carried out by different modes of creativity. Deleuze describes this in his own terms when he refers in both *Difference and Repetition* and *Logic of Sense* to "two dissymmetrical halves." In *Difference and Repetition* Deleuze says that "everything has two odd, dissymmetrical and dissimilar 'halves' . . . each dividing itself in two."[26] The dissymmetrical halves then become the *"entre-deux"* or fold between two that informs his reading of the event in Whitehead.

So, for Deleuze it is Whitehead who is the successor to the question of the event, a question that reaches back, according to Deleuze, at least to the Stoics who first elevated the event to the status of a concept. The second "great logic of the event" comes with Leibniz for whom the event is a relation, a relation to time and existence. What, for Deleuze, constitutes Whitehead's unique contribution to this school, and the third great logic of the event, is to begin to show precisely how the event can be thought in terms of the question of the new. Whitehead's creative advance over Leibniz's event and, for Deleuze, over phenomenology and Heidegger is to lay out the conditions for thinking novelty and the new in itself. Such a thinking of the event would reveal the best of all worlds: "not the one that reproduces the eternal, but the one on which new creations are produced, the one endowed with a capacity for innovation or creativity."[27]

What are the conditions for the event of the new? In *The Fold* Deleuze attributes four conditions or components to Whitehead's event, and I want to suggest that each component finds an equivalent correlate in Deleuze's own event. Whitehead initially conceived of events as "extending over" each other in an infinite relation of continuity between wholes and parts. The unique novelty of an event is given by its "passage" into another series of events either as part or whole. Deleuze makes this concept of "extension" the first condition or component of Whitehead's event. Extensive series have intrinsic properties, "for example height, intensity, timbre of a sound, a tint, a value, a saturation of color."[28] If extension gives us something rather than nothing, then "intension" gives us "this" rather than "that." Matter or what fills space and time always has characters, properties, degrees, or "intensities" of value that determine its texture in relation to other materials that are a part of it. The second component of the event, then, is "intension." A further condition of the event for Deleuze-Whitehead is the "ingression" of eternal objects. Eternal objects are thoroughly indeterminate "pure possibilities" and express a general potentiality unconstrained by any states of affairs, but when actualized or ingressed, they instantiate fully determinate facts or forms of definiteness. However, in addition to these three components there is another. One crucial factor in Deleuze's reading of the event in Whitehead is the appropriation and creative use of the past in the formation of the new individual. The creation of the new is achieved through what Whitehead called *prehension*. Next to creativity, and the three other conditions of the event, this is another element that converges with Deleuze's ontology, and it is perhaps one of Whitehead's most important concepts. Prehension is a noncognitive "feeling" guiding how the occasion shapes itself from the data of the past and the potentialities of the future. Prehension is an "intermediary," a purely immanent potential power, a relation of difference with itself, or pure "affection" before any division into form and matter. Prehension for Deleuze is a passage or folding "between" states, a movement of pure experience or perception that increases or decreases its potential through interaction and communication with those states. As Deleuze says, "everything prehends its antecedents and its concomitants and by degrees prehends a world." "All prehension," Deleuze remarks, "is a prehension of prehension, and the event a nexus of prehensions."[29] The event of prehension is double-sided and "rhythmic" in that it is the objectification of one prehension and the subjectification of another. In *What is Philosophy?* Deleuze and Guattari describe the rhythmic movement of prehension in the context of Whitehead's public/private coupling:

> The ("public") matter of fact was the mixture of data actualized by the world in its previous state, while bodies are new actualizations whose "private" states restore matters of fact for new bodies. Even when they are non-living, or rather inorganic, things have a lived experience because they are affections and perceptions.[30]

Deleuze turns to Whitehead's theory of prehensions here to describe the creative ongoing rhythm of "lived experience" as a unity with two sides or aspects. There is no ontological "gap" or separation in the sides, only a gathering of things into a "prehensive unification," and as the many become one, so the many are increased by one. In *The Fold* Deleuze describes this two-sided rhythm of prehension through the process of perception in Leibniz. For Deleuze each distinguished or clear perception emerges, through a genetic process, from the dark depths of the world that is contained within each monad. Deleuze describes this double process in terms of the "microscopic" and the "macroscopic," terms that Deleuze borrows from Whitehead's *Process and Reality,* where they are used to refer both to the two meanings of "organism" and the two forms of "process."[31] However, for Deleuze the essential difference between Whitehead and Leibniz is that Leibniz's monad operates, famously, according to a condition of closure, whereas for Whitehead "a condition of opening causes all prehension to be *already* the prehension of another prehension."[32] This condition of prehension—the opening onto the new in itself—is a key feature of the event in Deleuze's reading of Whitehead and one that Deleuze does not find in Leibniz, phenomenology, or, indeed, in Heidegger's phenomenological ontology.

The Event of the Future

Although Deleuze's reading of Whitehead remains faithful to many aspects of Whitehead's philosophy, I want to suggest that Deleuze tends in his remarks to align the creativity of Whitehead's occasion too closely to his own conception of the event that affirms inclusive disjunctions, bifurcations, and incompossibilities as a condition of the new. Indeed, Deleuze says that in Whitehead "even God . . . becomes Process, a process that at once affirms incompossibilities and passes through them."[33] Now, although it is the case that for the Whitehead of *Process and Reality* God is the basis of novelty and "apart from the intervention of God, there could be nothing new in the world" (*PR,* 247), the novelty is always qualified and constrained. Although the "Primordial nature of God" in Whitehead does involve "the unconditioned conceptual valuation of the entire multiplicity of eternal objects," the primordial nature "lures" the occasion to concresce in accordance with its "initial aim," an aim that is then taken over by the subject in concrescence. The initial aim is the best actualization for that occasion, an ideal pattern of intensities that gives the most harmonious possible experience for that occasion and for its achievement beyond itself. Both the initial aim of God, which grades the relevance of eternal objects, and the "perished" yet still affective actual occasions made available in transition "jointly constitute the character of the creativity for the initial phase of the novel concrescence" (*PR,* 248).

There are several points to make here about these constraints on creativity. Firstly, this ordering cannot be a pure affirmation of disjunctions and incompossibilities in Deleuze's sense because only one order of possibilities is affirmed by God for the occasion, that is the "best" order, even if the concrescing occasion does not actually take up that order of possibility. Indeed, *any* modification of God's initial aim ought to be seen as a limitation of possible intensities. Secondly, the best of possible worlds here for Whitehead is not one simply endowed with novelty and newness understood as the affirmation of incompossibles, as Deleuze seems to suggest. Novelty is a necessary condition for deepening the intensity of satisfaction in the occasion but not a sufficient condition. The one "best" order requires novelty and a harmony or contrast of intensities in and between occasions that contributes to God's feelings, persuading the world toward what Whitehead elsewhere calls "peace," and beautifully summarized in the final pages of *Adventure of Ideas* as a "harmony of harmonies" (*AI,* 285). This systemic aim is rather different from the crisis and dissolution of harmony that one finds in Deleuze and the affirmation of an infinity of orders of possibility captured in Boulez's phrase: a "polyphony of polyphonies."[34]

Deleuze's own conception of the event and its creativity, first worked out in his texts published in the 1960s, especially *Logic of Sense* and *Difference and Repetition,* is seemingly preoccupied with modes of temporality and forms of genesis that do not appear in Whitehead's accounts of the actual occasion and its relation to creativity. Although there are similarities in that for Deleuze the event never happens and is always that which is about to happen, just as for Whitehead the occasion never really "is" but perpetually perishes, fundamentally, the creativity of the event in Deleuze is conditioned by a future that is always to come and a pure past that never was. In *Logic of Sense* this notion of a future that never arrives and past that has never been is thought through Deleuze's Stoic-inspired reading of events as incorporeal "effects" caused by bodies, mixtures, and their states of affairs. Events are not existent but are said to "insist" or "subsist"; they "hover" above or even "inside" their material actualizations. Events are said to be expressed by verbs in the infinitive, as well as substantives or adjectives that relate to a present, and they are not just active or passive but "impassive," "neutral," and "sterile." The time of the event is given on the one hand by *Aion,* a time that becomes and divides endlessly into the future and the past and, on the other hand, through *Chronos,* a time that measures and regulates the present.

Thus time in the event must be grasped twice: once as the present that regulates corporeal mixtures, bodies, and states of affairs and once again as infinitely divisible in the past and future, divided into the incorporeal effects that result from bodies, yet are "independent of matter." The incorporeal effects play only on the surface and elude the depth and thickness of bodies. These two modes of reality—essentially versions of the virtual and the actual that Deleuze operates with elsewhere in his work—are said to produce a new cleavage of the causal relation. Causes operate on causes in the depth of bodies but produce effects on the surface as "quasi causes." Incorporeal effects do not "cause" each other so much as differentiate, become, or "express" each other. These two aspects of reality produce, then, two "readings of time," both necessary and exclusive.[35] One time is composed of interlocking presents, and the other is continually decomposed into elongated pasts and futures. Although this dualism functions as a reciprocal determination, Deleuze sometimes emphasizes, and on occasion privileges, the expressive creativity of the quasi cause and the surface play of the incorporeals. The power of this creativity comes from the time of *Aion,* an empty form or straight line of time upon which the "eternal truth of the event" is played out. The eternal truth of the event is that it signals a time that is always already passed and forever yet to come. These strange modes of time that Deleuze at one point describes as the "secret" of the event are essentially disjunctive and disruptive, breaking up any gathering, disjoining syntheses, and cutting into the unifying processes that bring the past, present, and future together in a continuum. In other words, if Whitehead's account of occasions shows novelty as a continuity with the emphasis on how creativity joins and associates time and movement, Deleuze's account of the creativity of the event tends to emphasize the discontinuity and disassociation of time and movement in a fundamental ungrounding of temporality.

In *Difference and Repetition* Deleuze's account of this creative ungrounding is given in terms of a transformation and reinvention of the concepts of univocity and eternal return where eternal return appears as a valorization of the future "in the image of a unique and tremendous event, adequate to time as a whole."[36] As I said earlier, for Deleuze a purely affirmative creativity would be the realization of univocity, and univocity can only be fully realized in the form of repetition in the eternal return. Deleuze's criticism of Spinoza is instructive here. Deleuze says that Spinozism only needed to make substance turn around the modes, or "*in other words, to realize univocity in the form of repetition in the eternal return.*"[37] A purely affirmative creativity, or realized univocity, is here figured as a time of the future in which a pure repetition of differences act as a "caesura" that both conditions and ungrounds or cuts into the other modalities of time, opening them fully and once again to genuine novelty. "Eternal return, in its esoteric truth, concerns—and can concern—only the third time of the series. Only there is it determined. That is why it is properly called a belief of the future, a belief in the future. Eternal return affects only the new, what is produced under the condition of default and by the intermediary of metamorphosis."[38]

What is produced under the condition of default are disjunctions and dissociations that create the new. Such disjunctions are the work of an unknown and unknowable future that has ontological priority in disrupting and fracturing the present. Throughout Deleuze's work, the notions of the "eternal return," the third synthesis of time, the time of *Aion*, and so on, refer to a pure past that never was and a future that is always to come and that breaks open the present and fragments any continuity. For Deleuze repetition of an unknown future appears as the most "creative," the most differentiated event since it communicates with a world without identity and without resemblance, a world in which the only ground is difference.

This repetition of a pure futural event in Deleuze is a different kind of genetic and conditioning function for genuine novelty that we do not seem to find in Whitehead's account of occasions, and it might be worth speculating as to why this is the case. For Whitehead the ultimate wounds of time, of "perpetual perishing," are saved in God's "consequent nature." As Whitehead puts it, what is done in the temporal world is "transformed into a reality in heaven" so that nothing is lost, and this reality in heaven then passes back into the world as a fact of experience, qualifying the world and each new temporal actuality (*PR*, 351). For Deleuze, in contrast, the very nature of time and thought requires real loss and destruction, a complete emptying out and ungrounding so that the new may come about. This is the "royal repetition" of the eternal return that strips the other repetitions (the present of habit, the memory of the past) of their autonomy and subordinates them to repetition as the category of the future and the completely novel.[39] As Deleuze puts it:

> The new with its power of beginning and beginning again remains forever new . . . the new, in other words, difference, calls forth forces in thought which are not the forces of recognition, today or tomorrow, but the powers of a completely other model from an unrecognized and unrecognizable *terra incognita*.[40]

In other words for Deleuze the problem is the belief that the wound of time, the "perpetual perishing," needs to be or can be healed, reconciled, or saved since this merely covers over the intensities and forces that come from a "completely other model" and eternally revivify and create new thought and being. In such a "completely other model" of the future, it is only that which is "to come" that returns, that which is unanticipated, the new as the unknown or "difference as the origin, which then relates different to different in order to make it (or them) return as such."[41]

From this Deleuzean perspective, and despite Deleuze's own reading of Whitehead, it may appear that Whitehead could be added to the list of the great philosophers of creative repetition who, in *Difference and Repetition*, finally reconcile us to ourselves, to God, and to the world. Here Whitehead might be placed alongside Kierkegaard and Peguy, who are said to ultimately entrust the supreme repetition of the future to a "faith" in which God and World are rediscovered and saved. For Deleuze, the great repeaters weren't prepared to pay the necessary price (loss of Self, God, and World), and so the novelty of the world is lost, and the rumbling of the most profound intensities in the eternal return are covered over.

And yet, in Whitehead's extraordinary articulation of creativity as the "double problem" in the conclusion of *Process and Reality*, the appeal is not to a future restored through faith as such—even though Whitehead admits "there is nothing here in the nature of proof" (*PR*, 343)—but to the guidance of his system's metaphysical principles, wherever they may lead. In Whitehead's metaphysical construction a Deleuzean future or eternal return as the purely empty and unknown form of time is not necessary either as a formal condition for creativity or for the transvaluation of values. Rather than the dissolution of God and world as the "necessary price" for thinking the truth of the creative, Whitehead proposes instead "the secularization of the concept of God's functions in the world" (*PR*, 207). And what is required for this "secularization," as we saw earlier, is the ongoing reciprocal determination, coupling, and adjustment to each other of the two processes, aspects, or dimensions of creativity that do not accord one process any privilege over the other. For Whitehead there are always at least two multiplicities or "types" needed to express secularization as the power of the creative, and in each antithesis, "there is a shift of meaning that converts the opposition into a contrast" (*PR*, 348) without favoring one side of the opposition over the other. In *Process and Reality* God and the World are the final contrasted opposites "in terms of which Creativity achieves its supreme task of transforming disjoined multiplicity, with its diversities in opposition, into concrescent unity, with its diversities in contrast" (*PR*,

348). God and World stand contrasted in each other expressing the final metaphysical truth that both "appetitive vision and physical enjoyment have equal claim in creation" (*PR*, 348). Neither God nor the World reaches any kind of static completion in this process since "both are in the grip of the ultimate metaphysical ground, the creative advance into novelty" (*PR*, 349). Each is the "instrument," as Whitehead puts it, of novelty for the other. The double problem cannot be separated into two distinct problems since "either side can only be explained in terms of the other" (*PR*, 347), and no two actualities can be torn apart: "each is all in all" (*PR*, 348), or, in Deleuzean terms, "being is univocal."

In *Modes of Thought* Whitehead refers to the two types of "process" and "individuation" wherein each is interwoven with the other and acts as the exemplification of the other. In the same text he refers to "'The Type of Actuality' and 'The Type of Pure Possibility'" (*MT*, 70). Throughout all of these oppositions, types, or worlds, Whitehead insists that they "require each other" (*MT*, 70, 97) such that oppositions are lured into contrasts and "contrasts of contrasts" where each element or type intensifies the satisfaction of its "diversities" only by being submitted to the achievement of the other. Disjoining these elements would be to yield to transcendence, a "bifurcation of actuality" that "involves contradiction at every step. . . . This is the final Platonic problem" (*PR*, 346). What needs to be thought here, as Whitehead states it, is not the "mere problem of fluency *and* permanence ["the Platonic problem"]. There is the double problem: actuality with permanence requiring fluency as its completion; and actuality with fluency requiring permanence as its completion. . . . The double problem cannot be separated into two distinct problems. Either side can only be explained in terms of the other" (*PR*, 347). In his late essay "Immortality," Whitehead refers to the double problem in terms of the "World of Value" and the "World of Fact," which must undergo a "fusion" because each world can be described only in terms of factors that are common to both of them: "such factors have a dual aspect, and each world emphasizes one of the two aspects."[42] Whitehead calls these factors that are common to each world "Ideas." "Each Idea," he says, "has two sides": on one of its sides, the Idea responds to the question "how?," "how much?," "when?," and so on—questions of the accident and fact and not the essence. The other side of the Idea is the response to "value" and valuation and he calls this response "evaluation." Evaluation values the accident, modifies values in relation to it, admits and omits, includes and excludes possibilities. Evaluation functions "actively as incitement and aversion" and yet evaluation cannot be disconnected from the immortal world of value. The "junction" of the two worlds "infuses the unity of the coordinated values into the multiplicity of the finite acts."[43] When we emphasize only one world in one of its aspects, then we are committing the "fallacy of misplaced concreteness" and mistaking our abstraction for the concrete. For Whitehead we overcome this tendency toward "independent existence" only by stressing that the "ultimate character of the universe . . . has two sides—one side is the mortal world of transitory fact acquiring the immortality of realized value; and the other side is the timeless world of mere possibility acquiring temporal realization. The bridge between the two is the 'Idea' with its two sides."[44]

Whitehead's articulation of the "double problem" here and his approach to it suggests that the "wound" of time can be creatively "transvalued" without appealing to the absolute difference of eternal return. Indeed, opposing diversities or differences do not so much conceal or cover over each other, as they are continually transformed into ever new contrasts of intensity. Difference is recuperated and liberated not through repetition in the eternal return but through its conversion in the double problem. There is no need for the complete elimination of the negative and the identical since everything is saved for transfiguration in its other. From this Whiteheadian perspective, the Deleuzian eternal return, as an empty form of time that cracks actuality open, looks increasingly like transcendence compared to the immanence of the double problem. From this point of view, absolute difference or otherness risks separating the double problem of creativity into two distinct problems, thereby effectively becoming an "exclusive disjunction" in the Deleuzean sense. Yet from the Deleuzean side, Whitehead's speculative solution risks importing into his account of the new figures of difference still too bound to the same where otherness is relativized and domesticated. On this view the past is always partially recuperable, and the future only partially unknown. That Whitehead's articulation of the double problem finds its source in what he calls "civilized intuition" can only compound these worries on the Deleuzean side and suggests a reliance upon dogmatic modes of thought that bring diversity under a form of the same and the new into the category of the already known and recognizable (*PR*, 347).

By contrasting Deleuze's and Whitehead's approaches to creativity—summarized here as the event and the occasion—I have highlighted some of the internal similarities and differences within their metaphysics of the new and uncovered some of the stakes in their conceptions of time. As we have seen, the activity of the occasion is one of synthesizing and unifying the real and ideal oppositions that structure the power of the creative. In this activity the actualities are converted into each other as contrasts, and creativity achieves a reconciliation of permanence and flux. For the Deleuzean event, in contrast, the essential movement of "royal repetition" in creativity breaks and disrupts any reconciled gathering, disjoins syntheses, and opens thought to an unknown future. Here the tendency is toward relative discontinuity where continuity is ruptured and time is thought as an event that cannot be saved in the actual but must be constantly undergone as the eternal and virtual "wound" of our condition. It is a "time out of joint" that fractures the equilibrium of the occasion. Arguably any genuine philosophy of creativity or metaphysics of the new cannot do without the insights of both the philosophies of the event and the occasion, and the Deleuzean inspired revival of Whitehead's extraordinary philosophy now underway brings this into clearer focus.

Notes

An earlier version of this paper was presented to the Society for the Philosophy of Creativity, Central Division Meeting, American Philosophical Association, Minneapolis, Minnesota, March 2011. I would like to thank the society for the invitation to speak, and I would like to thank the commentators on my paper—Peter Gunter and John Hartmann—for their thoughtful responses.

1. Vincent Descombes, *Modern French Philosophy,* trans. L. Scott-Fox and J. M. Harding (Cambridge: Cambridge University Press, 1980), 136.

2. The idea that, as Deleuze says, the event "ousts" the verb "to be" is important for my claims here since it suggests an overturning of ontology, or the subordination of "is" to "and." In other words, I'm suggesting that Deleuze offers a metaphysics that, after *Difference and Repetition,* attempts to "twist free" of ontology, a metaphysics of the creative "and, and, and . . ." where the creative event supersedes being. In this respect Heidegger, for Deleuze, remains tied to ontology and never really breaks with the "isness" of things and the verb "to be." That Deleuze's model of the event and its folds is informed by Whitehead, not Heidegger, is explored in more detail in my "Towards a Political Ontology of the Fold: Deleuze, Heidegger, Whitehead and the Fourfold Event," in *Deleuze and The Fold: A Critical Reader,* ed. Niamh McDonnell and Sjoerd Van Tuinen (New York: Palgrave MacMillan, 2010).

3. Gilles Deleuze, "Responses to a Series of Questions," an exchange between Arnauld Villani and Gilles Deleuze, *Collapse* 3 (November 2007): 42.

4. See Arnauld Villani, *La guepe et l'orchidee: Essai sur Gilles Deleuze* (Paris: Belin, 1999).

5. Deleuze, "Responses to a Series of Questions," 41.

6. Gilles Deleuze, *Difference and Repetition,* trans. Paul Patton (London: Athlone Press, 1994), 284–85.

7. Deleuze, "Responses to a Series of Questions," 41.

8. I thank Steven Meyer who persuaded me of this. See his introduction to *Configurations* 13, no. 1 (Winter 2005): 1–33.

9. Deleuze, *Difference and Repetition,* 208.

10. The "classical" representatives of this view are the books published in the late 1950s and 1960s by Ivor Leclerc and William Christian, which arguably establish the first "philosophical" readings of Whitehead's metaphysics in the Anglo-American academy. Cf. William Christian, *An Interpretation of Whitehead's Metaphysics* (New Haven, Conn.: Yale University Press, 1959); John Cobb, *A Christian Natural Theology* (Louisville, Ky.: Westminster John Knox Press, 1965); Thomas Hosinski, *Stubborn Fact and Creative Advance* (New York: Rowan and Littlefield, 1993); Ivor Leclerc, *The Relevance of Whitehead: Philosophical Essays in Commemoration of the Centenary of the Birth of Alfred North Whitehead* (London: Allen & Unwin, 1961); *Whitehead's Metaphysics: An Introductory Exposition* (London: Allen & Unwin 1965); George Kline, "Form, Concrescence and Concretum," in *Explorations in Whitehead's Philosophy,* ed. Lewis Ford and George Kline (New York: Fordham University Press, 1983).

11. Perhaps the most surprising aspect of Harman's claims about Whitehead is the downplaying of the importance of process and becoming in his work. Harman claims, for example, that an emphasis on becoming in Whitehead is "misleading" and that "he should not be seen as a philosopher of becoming." Graham Harman, "Response to Shaviro," in *The Speculative Turn: Continental Materialism and Realism,* ed. Levi Bryant, Nick Srnicek and Graham Harman (Prahran, Victoria: re.press, 2010), 291. For Harman's views on Whitehead, see also *Guerilla Metaphysics* (Chicago, Ill.: Open Court, 2006).

12. Alfred North Whitehead, *An Enquiry Concerning The Principles of Natural Knowledge* (New York: Dover, 1982 [1919]), 203.

13. For more on the event and the need to think it in terms of "two multiplicities," see my "Between the Individual, the Relative and the Void: Thinking the 'Event' in Badiou, Deleuze and Whitehead" in *Event and Decision: Ontology and Politics in Badiou, Deleuze and Whitehead,* ed, Roland Faber (Cambridge: Cambridge Scholars Press, 2010).

14. See my "The New Whitehead? An Ontology of the Virtual in Whitehead's Metaphysics," *Symposium* 11, no. 1 (Spring 2006): 69–80; repr. in *The Intensive Reduction,* ed. Constantin V. Boundas (New York: Continuum, 2009).

15. The Whitehead scholar who has done the most to make this argument and elevate the role of transition as of equal importance alongside concrescence in our understanding of Whitehead is Jorge Luis Nobo. See his "Transition in Whitehead: A Creative Process Distinct from Concrescence," *International Philosophical Quarterly* 19 (1979): 265–83. Also see Nobo's superb monograph on Whitehead, *Whitehead's Metaphysics of Extension and Solidarity* (Albany: State University of New York Press, 1986).

16. In this account of occasions, it seems to me that Whitehead is keen to point to a middle way between an emphasis on reflection and cognition that is discernible in what we can call "intellectualist" accounts of experience (with Kant here acting as Whitehead's example) and empiricist accounts of experience where the "given" is constituted by an atomistic sense data view of perception inscribed upon a tabula rasa. For Whitehead, as for James, there is no perception that is not already thoroughly imbued with associations and connections to an indeterminate and diffuse field of possibilities. Rather than any atomistic or monistic experience Whitehead, like Deleuze and James, supposes the pluralistic nature of experience in which a continuous flux of differences enters into varying degrees of unity.

17. I don't have space to properly defend this here, but I cannot agree with Hallward's insistence throughout his book *Out of this World* (New York: Verso, 2006) on a "unilateral configuration" of creativity such that creativity divides into an "active *creans*" and a "passive *creaturum*" (27). For Hallward, creating is active and virtual and the created is actual and passive. In my view there are different modes of creativity in Deleuze, and it is as true to say that the virtual is active and the actual passive as to say that the virtual is impassive and the actual active. In fact, just as in Whitehead, each half of reality in Deleuze has two sides with each half participating through different modalities and degrees of creativity. In this sense one can only begin to account for Deleuze's thought when justice is done to the constant movement, exchange, translation, tension, struggle, displacement, and conversion between both of these halves and their sides and their ever-shifting degrees of intensity and creativity. In one way or another the effort to attribute simple hierarchical dualisms to Deleuze, and the determination to polarize his thought, characterizes not only Hallward's book but also Badiou's *The Clamour of Being*, trans. Louise Burchill (Minneapolis: University of Minnesota Press, 2000) and Žižek's *Organs Without Bodies* (London: Routledge, 2004). Badiou insists that Deleuze must choose (and has already chosen) between animal or number, one or multiple, Plato or Aristotle (and a bunch of other dualisms), a decision that for Badiou appears to be determined formally by an "axiom of choice." For his part Žižek claims that Deleuze's work rests on "two conceptual oppositions" that are incompatible: the logic of effect and the logic of production. Žižek uses this distinction to divide Deleuze's texts—"*The Logic of Sense* versus *The Anti-Oedipus*"—and to separate Deleuze from Guattari. Although a number of commentators have objected, rightly, to these reductionist and divisive strategies and to their sometimes narrow and misleading emphases (e.g., Hallward on the "theophanic," Badiou on the "One"), one virtue (amongst numerous others) is that both Hallward and Badiou situate Deleuze under the sign of metaphysics.

18. Although I think these similarities are significant, I would not want to exaggerate this resemblance in the debates and literature on Deleuze and Whitehead. These debates can often be found in the scholarship surrounding numerous philosophical figures. For example, one debate in the Kant literature is between those, like Allison, who argue for a "double aspect" one world reading of phenomena/noumena and those, most famously Strawson, who argue for "two worlds" and ontological independence. Decisions about these metaphysical or epistemological questions are then used to make ethical or political claims. Cf Henry Allison, *Kant's Transcendental Idealism* (New Haven, Conn.: Yale University Press, 1983); P. F. Strawson, *The Bounds of Sense* (London: Methuen and Co., 1966).

19. Gilles Deleuze, *Bergsonism*, trans. Hugh Tomlinson and Barbara Habberjam (London: Athlone Press, 1988), 101.

20. Deleuze, *Difference and Repetition*, 304.

21. Ibid., 36.

22. Gilles Deleuze, *Dialogues*, trans. Hugh Tomlinson and Barbara Habberjam (London: Athlone Press, 1987), vii.

23. Gilles Deleuze, *Cinema 2: The Time-Image*, (London: Athlone Press, 1989), 146–47.

24. Gilles Deleuze, *Negotiations*, trans. Martin Joughlin (New York: Columbia University Press, 1995), 141.

25. Gilles Deleuze, *The Fold: Leibniz and the Baroque,* trans. Tom Conley (London: Athlone Press, 1993), 76.

26. Deleuze, *Difference and Repetition,* 279–80.

27. Deleuze, *The Fold,* 70.

28. Ibid., 77.

29. Ibid., 78.

30. Deleuze and Guattari, *What is Philosophy?*, 154.

31. That Deleuze is borrowing these terms from Whitehead is confirmed by a footnote in *The Fold.* See ch. 7, 154, n7.

32. Deleuze, *The Fold,* 81.

33. Ibid.

34. Ibid., 82.

35. Deleuze, *The Logic of Sense,* trans. Mark Lester with Charles Stivale, ed. Constantine Boundas (New York: Columbia University Press), 61.

36. Deleuze, *Difference and Repetition,* 89.

37. Ibid., 304.

38. Ibid., 90.

39. Ibid., 94.

40. Ibid., 136.

41. Ibid., 125.

42. Alfred North Whitehead, "Immortality," in *The Philosophy of Alfred North Whitehead,* ed. Paul Arthur Schilpp (Chicago, Ill.: Northwestern University Press, 1947), 683.

43. Ibid., 682.

44. Ibid., 683–84.

EIGHT

Whitehead and Schools X, Y, and Z

Graham Harman

Alfred North Whitehead is generally described as a "process philosopher." Little wonder, since his major book is entitled *Process and Reality,* it inspired the so-called process theology movement, and kindred phrases such as "process studies" automatically suggest a Whiteheadian influence. The bond between Whitehead and the word "process" is obviously unbreakable, and I will waste no energy attempting to break it. Instead, I want to note an ambiguity in the term "process" that encourages a misleading assessment not only of Whitehead, but of the entire present-day landscape of Continental philosophy. Above all, Whitehead has been linked too closely in recent years with the philosophy of Gilles Deleuze.[1] Without engaging in dispute with individual commentators, I would like to suggest that we now suffer from the conflation of two entirely different philosophical schools.

As I see it, one of these schools includes both Whitehead and the present-day French thinker Bruno Latour.[2] We can call this group "School X" to mark the difficulty of inscribing it in either analytic or Continental philosophy. After all, the analytics and Continentals are both inclined toward Kantian presuppositions in a manner that Latour and Whitehead brazenly renounce. In the first part of this essay, I will show why Whitehead and Latour should not be linked too closely with a second group of powerful thinkers, including such figures as Henri Bergson, Manuel DeLanda, William James, Gilbert Simondon, and Isabelle Stengers. To distinguish this group from School X, we might whimsically term it "School Y." When these two groups are too easily united, with little sense of the friction between them, then we completely miss what ought to be a pivotal debate in present-day Continental philosophy. For whereas School X opposes the traditional philosophy of enduring substance with a relational but ultimately punctiform model of entities, School Y opposes substance in the name of an uncensored form of raw, pulsating, nonstop flux-and-flow action in which becoming is continuous and individual states or moments do not really exist. In what follows, I will assess both of these philosophical schools and oppose them from my own preferred position: "School Z," more commonly known as object-oriented philosophy. Whitehead plays a central role in this essay for the following reason: he deserves praise for defending individual entities against the blend-o-rama of becoming that defines today's fashion, but also deserves blame for reducing entities to their relations. This gives Whitehead a compellingly ambiguous status from the standpoint of School Z.

Process, Becoming, and Relation

We should begin by distinguishing among three different notions: *process, becoming,* and *relation.* Unless these terms are treated separately, the nature of the choice now facing Continental philosophy will be hopelessly obscured. In the present context, the broadest of the three is surely *process.* Although the phrase "process philosophy" often functions as a proper name referring to Whitehead's own philosophy, we might use it more generally to refer to all recent philosophies that emphasize change over stasis. Rather than viewing the world as made up of enduring substances "which enjoy adventures of change throughout time and space," change is now regarded as primary, and the apparent stasis of enduring things must be explained rather than presupposed (*PR,* 35). It is true enough that all of the thinkers listed above in both Schools X and Y (Bergson, DeLanda, Deleuze, James, Latour, Simondon, Stengers, and Whitehead) are philosophers of change. None of them speaks favorably of traditional enduring substance or essence, and all seek a dynamic view of the cosmos in opposition to the supposedly static one of the past.

But not all philosophers of process are philosophers of *becoming.* If "process philosophy" means that underlying substances must be replaced by concrete events, "philosophy of becoming" means that individual entities per se are derivative of a more primordial dynamism, thereby reducing individuals to realities of the second rank. Though process and becoming might seem closely related, process is actually the broader term: some process philosophers *are not* philosophers of becoming. The two shining examples of this are Whitehead and Latour. For Whitehead, it is by no means true that individuals are derivative of a primordial or virtual indeterminate flux; instead, individuals are the very stuff of reality: "'actual entities'—also termed 'actual occasions'—are the final real things of which the world itself is made up. There is no going behind actual entities to find anything more real. They differ among themselves: God is an actual entity, and so is the most trivial puff of existence in far-off empty space" (*PR,* 18). Later, Whitehead draws an even sharper contrast between this principle of actual entities and the view that everything is in continuous flux:

> the extensive continuity of the physical universe has usually been construed to mean that there is a continuity of becoming. But . . . it is easy, by employing Zeno's method, to prove that there can be no continuity of becoming. There is a becoming of continuity, but no continuity of becoming. . . . Thus the ultimate metaphysical truth is atomism. (*PR,* 35)

We should also remember Whitehead's famous "ontological principle," which means "that actual entities are the only *reasons;* so that to search for a *reason* is to search for one or more actual entities" (*PR,* 24). In other words, everything that happens must be explained by the workings of individuals, and by this alone. There is no "pre-individual" realm in Latour or Whitehead,[3] but a world made up entirely of distinct individuals. This is by no means the case for School Y, in which individuals are derivative in comparison with primordial fluxes and wholes, topological structures, attractors, virtualities, and other pre-individuals said to be deeper than fully articulated actors and entities. Latour is entirely Whiteheadian in his tacit embrace of the ontological principle,[4] and Latour's emphasis on real individuals even leads to a candid thesis against the primacy of becoming: "Time is the distant consequences of actors as they each seek to create a fait accompli on their own behalf that cannot be reversed. In this way time passes." In other words, "time does not pass. Times are what is at stake between forces."[5] What this means is that time and becoming are not autonomous forces lying somewhere outside or prior to individually determinate entities. Instead of entities being derivative of a primordial flux, time and becoming are produced by individual actors. In this way Latour can even be viewed as a sort of anti-Bergson. The point has become even more obvious with the publication of Latour's new systematic work, *An Inquiry into Modes of Existence,*[6] which includes REP (reproduction) as one of fourteen modes of existence. The reason REP is a basic category for Latour is that nothing continues inertly in existence through any sort of Bergsonian *élan* or *durée*. Instead each entity is punctiform and passes away in an instant, which entails the need of ontological labor to reproduce it.

This Whiteheadian-Latourian focus on fully determinate individuals would be puzzling to the thinkers I have termed School Y, since none of them places individual entities at the basis of the cosmos. Deleuze tends to treat individuals as sterile efflorescences on the surface of the world, with the deeper "virtual" plane as more vital and less determinate than individuals.[7] Simondon's niche as a metaphysician consists almost entirely in his subordination of fully formed individuals to the *process* of individuation, whereas I will show that Whitehead's use of "process" always goes hand in hand with the absolute supremacy of fully formed (though transient) individuals.[8] James is also a typical School Y figure on the question of individuals. In psychology as in philosophy, James condemns those "oversubtle intellects . . . [who] have ended by substituting a lot of static objects of conception for . . . direct personal experiences."[9] And then we have Bergson, the granddaddy of them all, for whom individuals are carved out of flux by the needs of human practical action. In *Creative Evolution* Bergson makes the typically Bergsonian statement that "the truth is that we change without ceasing, and that the state itself is nothing but change."[10] And as concerns the status of individual things:

> The distinct outlines which we see in an object, and which give it its individuality, are only the design of a certain *kind* of influence that we might exert on a certain point of space; it is the plan of our eventual actions that is sent back to our eyes, as though by a mirror, when we see the surfaces and edges of things. Suppress this action, and with it consequently those main directions which by perception are traced out for it in the entanglement of the real, and the individuality of the body is re-absorbed in the universal interaction which, without doubt, is reality itself.[11]

The concept of "universal interaction" leads us to the third idea I wished to discuss: *relation*. Philosophies of relation are those that hold that the thing is not an autonomous reality apart from its interactions with other things, but is instead constituted by those interactions. Bergson declares this standpoint in the passage just cited, and even more clearly so in his early masterpiece *Matter and Memory*.[12] James and Simondon are clearly practitioners of a relational ontology, though in the cases of Deleuze and perhaps Stengers this may or may not be a point of greater controversy. As for the School X of Whitehead and Latour, they serve up what might be the most relational ontologies in the history of Western thought. Latour tells us bluntly in *Pandora's Hope* that the reality of an entity (an "actor," in his terminology) is defined by nothing more than "what other actors are modified, transformed, perturbed, or created by the [actor] that is the focus of attention."[13] In Whitehead's case, we read in similar fashion that "in a sense, every entity pervades the whole world" (*PR*, 28), and further, that "each atom [i.e., each actual entity] is a system of all things" (*PR*, 36). This all sounds a great deal like Leibniz's hyper-relational manifesto in the *Monadology:* "As a result, every body is affected by everything that happens in the universe . . . 'All things conspire,' said Hippocrates."[14] But whereas Leibniz gave us the monads as underlying substances, Latour and Whitehead give us monadologies without enduring monads—theories in which individuals are entirely reducible to the conspiracies they weave with other things.

Let me now summarize how all these terms play out for the purposes of this essay. The members of both School X and School Y (unlike, say, Aristotle or Aquinas) are philosophers of *process* rather than static things. But only the School Y philosophers are devoted to *becoming* rather than individuals, since in Whitehead and Latour the reason for everything that happens must be found in individual entities themselves. Moreover, these entities are not just derivative outcroppings of some deeper pre-individual becoming—as we find especially in such figures as Bergson, James, Deleuze, and Simondon. As for *relations,* both School X and School Y prefer relations over things, the former more vehemently than the latter. Since School X and School Y both prefer process over stasis, they seem to present a united front against traditional philosophies of substance. In the present day they have much momentum in their favor, since the current fashion is to view substance as rigid, static, reactionary, patriarchal, and oppressive, while dynamic fluxes and flows strike the educated public as innovative, liberating, interactive, holistic, and fresh. The roots of this antisubstance reaction can be found in the idealist or empiricist flavor of modern philosophy, which asks what is directly *accessible* in things, rather than what is arbitrarily posited as lying outside direct access; a commitment to immanence has become fashionable, while any talk of *transcendence* is taken to be a retrograde mark of intellectual shame. In turn, the tendency to define things in terms of their relations *to us* sometimes mutates, among more speculative thinkers, into the habit of defining them by way of their relations *to each other* as well. In our time it is widely believed that only a miserable, Scrooge-like curmudgeon would ever defend stasis over process. Yet this nearly unanimous outcry against traditional substance must not overshadow a deeper schism between School X and School Y on the question of becoming. As we have seen, becoming is by no means defended by Whitehead and Latour, who treat individuals as utterly determinate in each instant. Nor

	Process	Becoming	Relations
School X (Latour, Whitehead)	YES!	NO	YES!
School Y (Bergson, DeLanda, Deleuze, James, Simondon, Stengers)	YES!	YES!	YES
School Z (object-oriented philosophy)	NO	NO!	NO!

Figure 8.1. Though the process philosophy of Whitehead has been conflated with Deleuze's philosophy of becoming, the differences between these two schools—and a third school, object-oriented philosophy—can be sharpened by attending to their positions on process, becoming, and relations.

must this pair of themes (process and becoming) be confused with that of relation, which will turn out to be altogether separate from the theme of process. At this point a diagram may be helpful. (Exclamation marks refer to especial intensity of commitment.)

As is clear from Figure 8.1 and the foregoing discussion, School Y affirms all three principles—process, becoming, and relation—as pillars of its ontology. My own position, object-oriented philosophy, rejects all three.[15] School X is very close to School Y, diverging from it only on the question of becoming. But this divergence has serious implications for present-day Continental philosophy, as the remainder of this essay will clarify.

In passing, it should be noted that there are other possibly useful ways of grouping these authors. For example, Latour and Whitehead agree strongly with object-oriented philosophy in treating all relations in the same manner as the human-world relation: the human relation to a window is no different *in kind* from that of raindrops to the window. Some of the School Y figures might also agree on this point, while others would not, but to decide this question would require a more intricate reading of these figures than the present essay can undertake.

I will now give a brief survey of Whitehead's views on the three notions of process, becoming, and relation, and then conclude this survey with a brief discussion of why all three are unsuitable as foundational principles of ontology.

Whitehead and Process

Yes, Whitehead is a philosopher of process.

It would not be unfair to say that Western philosophy has valued the eternal and unchanging, or at least the durable, over the manifold transient processes unfolding in the world. This is clear enough in Plato and his tradition, so devoted to the eternity of forms—the perfect cat, horse, tree, justice, friendship, or other *eidei* that serve as eternal models for all fleeting, mortal entities. It is true on the other hand that for Aristotle and many of his followers, substance need not be eternal (G. W. Leibniz is a notable exception). Yet Aristotelian primary substance is always somewhat durable, enduring as the same thing for many seconds, hours, days, years, or millennia. Even in the phenomenology of Edmund Husserl, which aspires to be so sensitive to the multiple shifting facets of conscious experience, there are intentional objects that endure over time despite being seen in many different "adumbrations." According to Husserl, a blackbird or mailbox can appear to consciousness in countless different ways, but always as the *same* blackbird or mailbox. In all these philosophers the movement of the world is subordinated to some nucleus of stasis; the adjective and verb are conquered by the noun. In this way, with scattered exceptions (David Hume comes to mind) the Western philosophical tradition through the early nineteenth century shows a marked preference for enduring units that lie beneath the world's surface of transient happenings.

In the late nineteenth century, the tide began to turn. Along with some striking passages in Nietzsche, we find Bergson[16] and James[17] insisting that experience is a ceaseless stream in constant fluctuation. The role of the enduring thing-in-itself, an unchanging subject of change lying beneath all surface fluctuation, is de-emphasized to the point of being abandoned. Throughout the twentieth century, philosophies of substance are widely accused of reactionary archaism and a general opposition to the new. Non-Western cultures are frequently praised for being less beholden to petrified enduring substances and their ostensible counterpart, subject-predicate grammar. One example can be found in Whitehead himself: "the philosophy of organism [i.e., Whitehead's own philosophy] seems to approximate more to some strains of Indian, or Chinese, thought, than to western Asiatic, or European, thought. One side makes process ultimate; the other makes fact ultimate" (*PR*, 7). We find a further well-known example in Benjamin Lee Whorf's praise of Hopi grammar for its superior sense of temporal fluctuation, which in his view makes it better equipped than Western tongues to navigate the mysterious sea of quantum physics.[18] Much of Whitehead's philosophy can be interpreted as belonging to the same recent current of antisubstance sentiment that motivates Bergson and James. For instance, early in *Process and Reality* Whitehead writes as follows: "the philosophy of organism is closely allied to Spinoza's scheme of thought. But it differs by the abandonment of the subject-predicate form of thought. . . . The result is that . . . morphological description is replaced by description of dynamic process" (*PR*, 7). More broadly, Whitehead gives the following condemnation of traditional cosmological speculation:

> the notion of continuous stuff with permanent attributes, enduring without differentiation, and retaining its self-identity through any stretch of time however small or large, has been fundamental [to traditional Western philosophy]. The stuff undergoes change in respect to accidental qualities and relations; but it is numerically self-identical in its character of one actual entity throughout its accidental adventures. The admission of this fundamental metaphysical concept has wrecked the various systems of pluralistic realism. (*PR*, 78)

He attacks those philosophers who go through the motions of critiquing Aristotle even while retaining his traditional subject-predicate grammar. This leads Whitehead to a fairly damning indictment of Aristotle's metaphysics as a whole: "The evil produced by the Aristotelian 'primary substance' is exactly this habit of metaphysical emphasis upon the 'subject-predicate' form of proposition" (*PR*, 30). As Aristotle explains in the *Metaphysics*, the primary substances are individual things that can support different qualities at different times. Socrates can be happy and then sad while remaining Socrates all the while; this is what makes him a substance. By contrast, since happy is always happy and sad is always sad, these terms are never substances. In a grammatical sense, this means that Socrates is a subject while happy and sad are predicates. But Whitehead repeatedly insists that the metaphysics lying behind this grammar is mistaken. As he puts it: "The simple notion of an enduring substance sustaining persistent qualities, either essentially or accidentally, expresses a useful abstract for many purposes of life. But whenever we try to use it as a fundamental statement of the nature of things, it proves itself mistaken" (*PR*, 79). Although Whitehead concedes that there are good pragmatic reasons to speak of enduring substances in everyday language and logic, he holds that "in metaphysics the concept is sheer error" (*PR*, 79). Why sheer error? The reason can be found in Whitehead's personal vision of what an entity is, and that is the topic of the next section. So far, we have seen that Whitehead is undeniably a process philosopher. He does not believe in the primacy of enduring individual things that would serve as the substrate of qualitative surface change. What is primary is change itself.

Whitehead and Becoming

No, Whitehead *is not* a philosopher of becoming.

A philosopher of becoming is one who denies that the world is best understood in terms of individual things or individual instants of time. Instead, the world is a pre-individual field not fully carved up into distinct entities, and time is a continuous duration rather than a series of isolated cinematic frames. We have already seen that neither of these views is affirmed by the School X philosophies of Whitehead or Latour. The Whiteheadian cosmos is governed by the ontological principle, according to which discrete actual entities are the root of all reality. Here we could not be further from Simondon's denunciation of fully formed individuals as the product of philosophical naiveté. Whitehead is not interested in the generation of individuals from a quasi-determinate pre-individual field, but in the generation of individuals *from prior individuals*. The sense of the word "process" in Whitehead is completely different from what it is in Simondon.

Whitehead's world is one of actual entities, which he also calls "actual occasions." The reason for this alternate terminology, "occasion," is the completely instantaneous nature of actual entities: "an actual entity never moves: it is where it is and what it is. In order to emphasize this characteristic by a phrase connecting the notion of 'actual entity' more closely with our ordinary habits of thought, I will also use the term 'actual occasion' in the place of the term 'actual entity'" (*PR*, 73). Latour proposes the similar principle that each thing happens just once, in one place and one time only.[19] Whitehead's actual entity does not undergo adventures in time and space, because it is completely defined by its specific stance in time and space, its relation to all other things. For this reason the entity can only *perish*, not change: "Actual entities perish, but do not change; they are what they are" (*PR*, 35). Aristotle's primary substances also are what they are, but in Aristotle's case this does not include their exact relational dealings with all other entities, whereas in Whitehead's case it does. His actual entities, like Latour's, are so utterly concrete that they cannot endure the slightest shift in their features without dying instantly. "Actual occasions in their 'formal' constitutions are devoid of all indetermination. . . . They are complete and determinate matter of fact, devoid of all indetermination" (*PR*, 29). Whitehead's technical term for this is "satisfaction."

In short, for all his talk of dynamic process, Whitehead's philosophy is one in which entities are so utterly determinate that they can last only for an instant before perishing and being replaced by other actual entities. If School Y defends a dynamism deeper than any individual entities, the dynamism of School X consists entirely in a chain of such entities stretching across time. Consider the two senses in which Whitehead's philosophy continues the occasionalist tradition in philosophy. Occasionalism began as an early Islamic theological school in Basra, upholding the view that God was not only the sole creator in the universe, but the only legitimate causal agent at all. For this reason, even the mere collision between two inanimate objects must be mediated by God. Moreover, since endurance was viewed as an accident of things, the world was made solely of perishing things and time made solely of disconnected instants, so that a continuous creation of the universe was necessary.[20] These ideas later passed into European philosophy through the French Cartesians, though they lost their prestige during the general Enlightenment onslaught against divinity. Whitehead is perhaps the most candid recent defender of *both* senses of occasionalism: the inability of two entities to interact without the mediation of God, and the disjunctions between separate instants of time.

As for divine intervention in the philosophy of Whitehead, it occurs always and everywhere. When actual entities other than God prehend one another, or relate to one another, they do this always in terms of specific qualities ("eternal objects"). God's role in this process is stated clearly enough: "the things which are temporal arise by their participation in the things which are eternal. The two sets are mediated by a thing which combines the actuality of what is temporal with the timelessness of what is potential. This final entity is the divine element in the world" (*PR*, 40). And as concerns the radical disconnection of temporal instants, this is clear enough from the passages in which Whitehead describes the "perpetual perishing" of actual entities. It is true that Whitehead ascribes to these actual entities an appetite, conatus, or drive that pushes them beyond their current instantaneous being: "Appetition is immediate matter of fact including in itself a principle of unrest" (*PR*, 32). Yet this addition of appetite to actual entities seems utterly gratuitous. In speaking of prehensions, Whitehead writes: "the analysis of an actual entity into 'prehensions' is that mode of analysis which exhibits the most concrete elements in the nature of actual entities" (*PR*, 19). In other words, actual entities are nothing more than their prehensions, and this is what makes them actual *occasions* limited to a specific time and place and unable to undergo adventures outside those exact coordinates. The price one must pay for viewing entities as utterly determined by their specific situation, and hence as nondurable, is that it becomes difficult to see how one such self-contained entity could ever link to the next. It is for this reason that Whitehead posits "appetite" as a sort of bonus property of his self-contained actual entities. In doing so, he risks committing a classic *vis dormitiva* maneuver. Just as Molière's physician claims that opium causes sleep by means of a sleeping faculty, Whitehead's "appetite"—despite his explicit critique of the "faculty psychology" (*PR*, xiii)—implies that actual entities change by means of a changing faculty. Or rather, since actual entities are excluded from the possibility of change, they are replaced by new entities by means of a faculty-for-being-replaced. In this respect, Whitehead shows himself guilty of the same incoherence that he says can be found in all philosophies after sufficient analysis:

> Incoherence is the arbitrary disconnection of first principles. In modern philosophy Descartes' two kinds of substance, corporeal and mental, illustrate incoherence. There is, in Descartes' philosophy, no reason why there should not be a one-substance world, only corporeal, or a one-substance world, only mental. . . . The attraction of Spinoza's philosophy lies in its modification of Descartes' position into greater coherence. . . . The gap in [Spinoza's] system is the arbitrary introduction of the 'modes.' (*PR*, 6–7)

By the same token, one of the gaps in Whitehead's system is the arbitrary introduction of appetite as a means of shying away from the radical discontinuity in moments of time that would otherwise be required by the absolute concreteness of actual occasions.

But this is not even the main issue. The main issue is that there are vividly occasionalist elements at the center of Whitehead's thought: the role of God as a relational mediator, and the nature of time as composed of disconnected punctiform instants. Latour is indebted to occasionalism in similar fashion, except that he makes no appeal to God as the mediator of all relations and instead treats mediation on a more secular and local level.[21] But what is most striking is how clearly this separates Latour and Whitehead from the figures grouped here under the title School Y. After all, the problems that motivate Whitehead's use of God as a relational mediator, and appetite as a mediator between instants, would be ridiculed by School Y from the outset as false problems. It is merely comical to imagine James or Deleuze positing God as a mediator between entities, and utterly ridiculous to imagine Bergson viewing time as made up of isolated occasions that would need to be bridged by a forward-looking "appetite" in the heart of each occasion.

Whitehead and Relation

Yes, Whitehead is a philosopher of relation.

Along with opposing durable substances that would persist across time, Whitehead even more famously opposes the notion that entities are self-contained. Indeed, Whitehead is one of the foremost champions in Western philosophy of a *relational* metaphysics, in which entities have no reality apart from their interaction with other entities. In this way, the old Western philosophical cosmos of rigid enduring things seems to be replaced by a dynamic universe of process and relation. We have already seen that Whitehead goes so far as to accept a doctrine of *internal* relations, according to which a thing's relations belong to its inner reality. After praising John Locke as a venerable forerunner, Whitehead adds the following objection: "Locke misses one essential doctrine, namely, that the doctrine of internal relations makes it impossible to attribute 'change' to any actual entity. Every actual entity is what it is, and is with its definite status in the universe, determined by its internal relations to other actual entities" (*PR*, 58–59). Stated differently, "the actual entity, in virtue of *what* it is, is also *where* it is. It is somewhere because it is some actual thing with its correlated actual world. This is the direct denial of the Cartesian doctrine, 'an existent thing which requires nothing but itself in order to exist'" (*PR*, 59).

For Whitehead (and for Latour), the idea that a thing is determined by its relations is a necessary part of the doctrine "of individual actual entities, each with its own self-attainment" (*PR*, 60). Given the commitment of School X to process rather than static substances, we would veer dangerously close to Aristotelian substance if an actual entity were allowed to endure for more than an instant, preserving its reality despite shifting relations and shifting stances in space and time. This explains why School X is so much more vehement about the relationality of the world than School Y, just as the borderlands of a country are often more nationalistic than the capital.

On Behalf of School Z

One purpose of this essay has been to drive a wedge into the crack between two types of "process" philosophers, which I have called School X and School Y. Since both agree on dynamic process over stasis, and both roughly agree on a relational ontology (with School X being far more emphatic about relations), their point of disagreement can be found entirely in the theme of *becoming*. This amounts to the question of whether individual entities are the true engine of the world, or merely a sterile byproduct of deeper dynamisms. What we have found is that Whitehead and Latour stand out from the rest in elevating individual entities or actors to the pinnacle of reality, even to the point that such individuals are the root of everything else. The exact opposite is the case for the School Y thinkers, who do not regard actual individuals as the site where everything of importance occurs.

This difference is so glaring, and of such primordial metaphysical importance, that it remains somewhat shocking whenever attempts are made to synthesize Whitehead (and less often, Latour) with the philosophy of Deleuze, however common these attempts may be. Deleuzean philosophy has been in the ascendant since the mid-1990s, and has even become the standard avant-garde weaponry of Continental thought. It should also be clear to any observer of the contemporary scene that this blurring of boundaries between X and Y is rarely initiated by the former school. We see few attempts by Latourians to colonize Deleuze for Latourian purposes, nor am I am aware of those who are principally Whiteheadians making such attempts with much frequency. Rather, the movement of conquest always seems to proceed in the opposite direction. Since there are few Jamesians anymore, while today's followers of Bergson, DeLanda, Simondon, and Stengers also tend to be followers of Deleuze, it is really the Deleuzian influence that sets the agenda in mixing Deleuze together with Whitehead in a single "process" stew.

When this happens, we lose what is unique to Whitehead in comparison with School Y. In my view, what is unique are the *gaps* in Whitehead's cosmos that must be bridged. We encountered these gaps when considering the two occasionalist elements in Whitehead's philosophy. First, God is needed to mediate the gap between actual entities (things) and eternal objects (qualities). This might also be described as the gap between the actual and the potential, or the discrete and the continuous. And as Whitehead puts it, "continuity concerns what is potential; whereas actuality is incurably atomic" (*PR*, 61). Note that the gap for Whitehead is not just between actualities and potentialities, but also between actualities and other actualities. After all, they encounter each other only by mediation of the eternal objects, being unable to prehend one another with total accuracy in the manner of which God alone is capable. No such puzzling gaps exist in School Y, which tends to view gaps as false problems left over from the bias of Western intellectual tradition, Indo-European grammar, or the *faiblesse* of common sense. Instead, in School Y there reigns a doctrine of continuity—whether of time (Bergson), the interrelation between things

(James), or a pre-individual realm not yet carved into distinct individuals (Simondon). For School Y, it is discontinuity that must be explained rather than continuity.

There is no good reason to accept Whitehead's positing of God as a universal mediator who closes all gaps. I say this not because we must be good post-Enlightenment atheists obliged to ridicule God whenever he is mentioned in public, but because *no* specific entity should be empowered to function as a bridge across all gaps. If actual entities are unable to exhaust others with their mutual prehensions, then it is utterly arbitrary to stipulate that God alone (who is also described by Whitehead as an actual entity) is granted the miraculous ability to prehend other entities to their uttermost depths. Latour avoids this hypocrisy by attempting the first-ever secularized version of indirect causation, though I have argued elsewhere that his solution does not work either.[22] Yet the important point is that they have at least raised the question, which School Y is unable to do. Only a philosophy of actual individuals is capable of seeing that these individuals are individuals only when partly cut off from one another, and that if there are individuals then the world is already not a unified whole in which influence can be transmitted free of charge. Stated simply, either the world is one or it is many. If it is one, then we are in the territory of Parmenides, and there is no way to explain why the many would ever arise from the one. But if the world is many, then communication between this plurality of things poses a problem: they are separate things, there is a gap between them, and communication between one and the other can never be total and never direct, but requires a mediator.[23] On the question of the one and the many, it might seem as though Whitehead is trying to have it both ways: "The many become one, and are increased by one. In their natures, entities are disjunctively 'many' in process of passage into conjunctive unity. This Category of the Ultimate replaces Aristotle's 'primary substance'" (*PR*, 21). But the conjunctive unity to which he refers does not ontologically cancel the disjunctive reality of the many, even if it unifies them. Note that Whitehead's Ultimate simply "increases by one" the army of the many, taking its place as a more colossal entity of the same order of being as their own—unlike the one of Anaximander or Parmenides, ontologically different in kind from any multitude.

Second, the utter determinacy of every entity for both Whitehead and Latour means that there is a gap between any entity at time T and the "same" entity at time T^1. Actually, for Whitehead and Latour they are not the same entity at all, but merely have a close resemblance without being one and the same. Just as Whitehead arbitrarily posits "appetite" in the heart of things so as to link one moment with the next, Latour occasionally flirts with the Spinozist conception of *conatus.*[24] But we have seen that this amounts to nothing more than a new version of the *vis dormitiva* ("an entity changes by means of a changing faculty"), which is posited to address a built-in drawback of the initial theory. That drawback should be obvious enough: there is no reason to adhere to a theory of internal relations, and hence no reason to view things as so utterly determinate in their relations that they are incapable of adventuring from one moment to the next. Stated differently, this is a point on which School Y is closer to the truth, since this group generally insists on something in reality deeper than any current relational configuration between specific things. We find this above all in Deleuze and DeLanda, since for them the virtual is never fully actualized in specific things.

Nonetheless, it is in Whitehead and Latour that we find a closer approach to the truth, thanks to their sharper sense of gaps and discontinuities. Stated differently, what we must embrace is the occasionalist problems they raise—the first by sharpening the problem, and the second by recognizing it as a dead end. The first problem is the need for a mediator between things, for the simple reason that since things are individual and do not penetrate one another to the core, they must meet in some shared third space. It cannot be God, as Whitehead claims it is, because it is unclear why any specific entity should be able to breach the very ontological laws by which all other entities are constrained. Nor can it be Latour's solution of requiring that Actor A (politics) and Actor B (neutrons) must be mediated by Actor C (Frédéric Joliot-Curie), since the same question will arise of how C touches either A or B, and in this way the problem is just pushed back another step further. The second problem is the need to determine the link between an entity at time T and at time T^1 without resorting to convenient but empty stipulations such as those of "appetite" or "conatus." But in this case, unlike the first, the problem seems not worth solving, since it should never have arisen at all. Namely, Whitehead's "appetite" appears on the scene only because he himself has imprisoned his actual entities in a single concrete instant, and "appetite" is then pulled from a hat as a means of escape from that instant.

The point is that there was never any need to imprison entities in an instant at all. That would be necessary only if, like Whitehead, one were committed to *attacking* the Aristotelian model of substance that endures through a variety of changes in quality, accident, and relation. Unless there is such an underlying substance existing as a surplus outside the current state of the world, there is no reason why that state would ever change. In other words, if everything were completely determined by its prehensions of all other entities in the world, all entities ought to be thoroughly exhausted by their current relations. They would harbor no residue crying for the right to assert itself beyond the current state of the world; there would be no cause for rebellion or uprising among things. Harman would *internally* contain the determination "sitting on a brown couch typing on a MacBook," and if that is what Harman is, then that is what he is, and he can never be elsewhere. In a world of exhaustive deployment such as that of Whitehead and Latour, we cannot preserve any possibility of transformation with words such as "appetite" or "conatus." Nor are "subjective form" or "subjective aim" any help in escaping relationism. Once the entity has been defined in terms of its prehensions, once any excess of "vacuous actuality" has been mocked, it does no good to stipulate that entities *also* have some magical urge or drive or freedom that saves them from the relationist trap. For if this extrarelational concession has to be made at the end of the argument, then we might ask why it was not simply conceded at the beginning. And if that had been done, then entities could never have been analyzed into their prehensions in the first place, and the old concept of substance would have seemed much more redeemable than Whitehead wished to believe.

What we need, in fact, is a new *antiprocess philosophy.* We need a renewed philosophy of self-contained entities that may not be "static," but whose dynamism must be explained via the ontological principle and the interaction between actual things, rather than presupposed in the gratuitous concept of "appetite." We need entities that are not thoroughly relational but are so much themselves that they cannot automatically communicate with one another, so that their communication is a puzzle to be solved locally. As a name for this alternative school, I propose School Z. With this name we pay passing tribute to Xavier Zubíri,[25] the most uncompromising defender of nonrelational entities in post-Heideggerian philosophy. What we need, cutting against the grain of our era, is a philosophy that does not worship process, becoming, or relation.

Notes

1. See for example Steven Shaviro, *Without Criteria: Kant, Whitehead, Deleuze, and Aesthetics* (Cambridge, Mass.: MIT Press, 2009). And for perhaps the most prominent example, see Isabelle Stengers, *Thinking with Whitehead: A Free and Wild Creation of Concepts,* trans. Michael Chase (Cambridge, Mass.: Harvard University Press, 2011). The subtitle's reference to the Deleuzian phrase "creation of concepts" is already a giveaway that Stengers reads Whitehead through Deleuzian lenses.

2. For a more complete account of my interpretation of Latour, see Graham Harman, *Prince of Networks: Bruno Latour and Metaphysics* (Melbourne: re.press, 2009).

3. An exception can be found in Latour's recent writings in his sporadic references to a giant unformatted "plasma" lying beneath all individual things. See Bruno Latour, *Reassembling the Social: An Introduction to Actor-Network Theory* (Oxford: Oxford University Press, 2007), 50, 132, 227, 241, 244, 245, 253. For a discussion of why this plasma is inconsistent with the rest of Latour's philosophy see Harman, *Prince of Networks,* 132–34.

4. See especially "Irreductions" in Bruno Latour, *The Pasteurization of France,* trans. Alan Sheridan and John Law (Cambridge, Mass.: Harvard University Press, 1988).

5. Ibid., 165.

6. Bruno Latour, *An Inquiry Into Modes of Existence: An Anthropology of the Moderns,* trans. Catherine Porter (Cambridge, Mass.: Harvard University Press, 2013).

7. Gilles Deleuze, *Logic of Sense,* trans. Paul Patton (New York: Columbia University Press, 1990).

8. Gilbert Simondon, *L'individuation à la lumière des notions de forme et d'information* (Grenoble: Millon, 2005).

9. William James, *Essays in Radical Empiricism* (New York: Longmans, Green and Co., 1958), 50.

10. Henri Bergson, *Creative Evolution,* trans. Arthur Mitchell (New York: Barnes and Noble, 2005), 2.

11. Ibid., 10.

12. Bergson, *Matter and Memory,* trans. Nancy Margaret Paul and W. Scott Palmer (New York: Dover, 2004).

13. Bruno Latour, *Pandora's Hope: Essays on the Reality of Science Studies,* trans. Catherine Porter (Cambridge, Mass.: Harvard University Press, 1999), 122.

14. Gottfried Wilhelm Leibniz, *Monadology* §62, in *Selected Philosophical Essays,* trans. Roger Ariew and Daniel Garber (Indianapolis, Ind.: Hackett, 1989).

15. For the most concise account available at present, see Graham Harman, *The Quadruple Object* (Winchester, UK: Zero Books, 2011).

16. Henri Bergson, *Time and Free Will: An Essay on the Immediate Data of Consciousness,* trans. Frank Lubecki Pogson (New York: Dover, 2001).

17. William James, *The Principles of Psychology,* 2 vols. (New York: Dover, 1950).

18. Benjamin Lee Whorf, *Language, Thought, and Reality* (Cambridge, Mass.: MIT Press, 1956).

19. Latour, *The Pasteurization of France.*

20. For a clear overview of this theme in the history of Islamic philosophy, see Majid Fakhry, *Islamic Occasionalism and Its Critique by Averroes and Aquinas* (London: Allen & Unwin, 1958). A more recent work in German with an even broader theme is Dominik Perler and Ulrich Rudolph, *Occasionalismus: Therorien der Kausalität im arabisch-islamischen und im europäischen Denken.* (Göttingen: Vandenhoeck & Ruprecht Verlag, 2000).

21. For an account of how Latour appeals to local causal mediators, see my summary of Joliot as the mediator between politics and neutrons in Harman, *Prince of Networks,* 73–75.

22. Ibid.

23. See Graham Harman, "On Vicarious Causation," *Collapse* 2 (2007): 171–205.

24. See the exchange found in Bruno Latour, Graham Harman, and Peter Erdélyi, *The Prince and the Wolf: Latour and Harman at the LSE* (Winchester, UK: Zero Books, 2011): 106–9.

25. Xavier Zubíri, *On Essence*, trans. A. R. Caponigri (Washington, D.C.: Catholic University Press, 1980).

NINE

Whitehead's Curse?

James Williams

And I may say in passing that no educational system is possible unless every question directly asked of a pupil at any examination is either framed or modified by the actual teacher of that pupil in that subject.

—Alfred North Whitehead, *The Aims of Education and Other Essays*

The Gift

I will call it Whitehead's gift. In truth, I do not know who delivered it to the class. The contraption appeared one day in the science corner, perhaps another harebrained initiative by the overambitious deputy. But once the time machine began to operate, it became possible to teach according to Whitehead's ideals. Each pupil chose a destination suited to his or her favorite lesson. We devised experiments to test during the voyage. The subsequent lesson lived from the excitement of what we discovered through those one-way windows in our invisibility-cloaked machine: a dinosaur succumbing to fumes in a deep swamp; Roman galleys crossing the Channel; Washington leading his troops; Gandhi urging nonviolence; the final preparations for an Apollo mission; joy around the Berlin wall; celebrations for the end of British rule in Hong Kong; bird species on the Galapagos. Some choices were of course ill-judged and had to be either curtailed or vetoed: Vesuvius erupting over Pompeii; the bombing of Coventry and Dresden. The thrill offered by second choices quickly made up for initial disappointment.

In his work on the rhythms of education, Whitehead calls the excitement of discovery the "Stage of Romance." Each pupil has a different potential for this romance. As we shall see, there is always great resistance to doctrines of equal capacities in Whitehead's work, since for him potential is different for each pupil, because each is a singular set of processes rather than a particular case of a general type: "But for all your stimulation and guidance the creative impulse towards growth comes from within, and is intensely characteristic of the individual" (*AE,* 61). Once singular promise is unlocked, for instance, in witnessing the glory days of Rutherford's Cavendish laboratory or peering over Woolf's shoulder as she allows a sentence to unfold, then each pupil is given a different romantic energy for other more arduous stages. Some initial knowledge must prepare for this excitement and in return romance saves knowledge from a dusty and wasteful barrenness of bare fact, condemned by Whitehead: "Romantic emotion is essentially the excitement consequent on the transition from the bare facts to the first realisations of the import of their unexplored relationships" (*AE,* 28).

For Whitehead, bare facts without live application are a step on the way to inertness, a dynamic property that spreads through education systems, destroying their worth: "Education with inert ideas is not only useless: it is, above all things, harmful—*Corruptio optimi, pessima.* Except at rare intervals of intellectual ferment, education in the past has been radically infected with inert ideas" (*AE,* 2). Whitehead's impressionistic yet wise historical approach informs his work on education, as does his related sense of the historical struggle between living vibrant processes and inert dying ones.[1] This explains his selection of the metaphor of infection. Living processes are dynamic through the progress or retreat of infection and health. Like Derrida, in his work on infection and immunity for democracies or religions, Whitehead denies purity to either movement: "The host is never immune from being scathed."[2] There is no health without infection and decay. There is no decay independent of health. Time machines and other innovations in education such as video or computers are thus neither mere tools for gaining attention or achieving shortcuts, nor technical expressions of an ideal form of learning. They are instead necessary moments of creative novelty and, as such, also subject to a necessary waning of their own, always on the edge of the next invention and excitement.

Even the processes of infection are double-edged, since infection can have a positive effect on later health. Thus, one of the highest values identified in university education by Whitehead is imagination, which is itself contagious: "Imagination is a contagious disease" (*AE,* 145).[3] It is only through contact with teachers in the grip of an imagination virus that the students will themselves contract imagination. The rhythms of education and the duty to nurture romance hence apply as much to the teachers as to the taught. This is a lesson in the process of being lost in the recent drift to separation of teaching from research in university contracts and roles. Division is fostered and welcomed by administrators for ideological and financial reasons—for instance, through the greater distinction of teaching and research funding, and greater focus on specific projects and outcomes of research funding over successive rounds of research assessment in the United Kingdom:

> The binary divide between research active and research inactive staff and institutions in England has widened with a greater separation between teaching and research following the implementation of the Higher Education Act of 2004. Those institutions and departments regarded as largely 'research inactive,' as measured by a low output of publications in high quality peer-reviewed research journals, face the pressure of severe cuts in external funding.[4]

The process and rhythms of infection determine varied and often long time frames, so one of the profound aspects of Whitehead's philosophy is its setting of organisms within history, itself defined according to the rhythms of short and long dynamic historical periods and cycles. For example, given immense advances in biological research, it is a temptation to detach the organism from its history and from the history of its environment except where relevant to the development of the code. The genetic code can hence be seen as self-sufficient, or at least primary, in questions of health and disease. Against this lure, Whitehead is attuned to the deep connections between organic vibrancy and subsequent decay *over many resonating historical ages,* including in education: "In the history of education, the most striking phenomenon is that schools of learning, which at one epoch are alive with a ferment of genius, in a succeeding generation exhibit merely pedantry and routine" (*AE,* 2).[5] This is why the time machine felt such an apt device to bring Whitehead's ideas into the future. Time travel, done well, is not only an exercise in retrieval and learning from the past. It is a lesson from the past about an ineluctable decay in each present. For those pupils it was also an instruction on how to counter this passing, thanks to their singular revaluation of the past.

Thus Whitehead echoes Hume, another philosopher dedicated to learning from history and seeing life as essentially historical, in using the Latin phrase "the corruption of the best for the worst" to capture the negative dynamism of some historical processes: "From the comparison of theism and idolatry, we may form some other observations, which will also confirm the vulgar observation that the corruption of the best things gives rise to the worst."[6] In bare facts, the will to learn of youth is wasted. Worse than this, though, because all events occur in dynamic systems, this waste contributes to further negative energy and even more destruction of potential growth and enjoyment—a destruction Whitehead calls "evil." Following from the inevitable mix of health and corruption, evil is relative. The judgment of evil can hence be ascribed to an apparent good, if later potential is destroyed: "This evil path is represented by a book or a set of lectures which will practically enable the student to learn by heart all the questions likely to be asked at the next external examination" (*AE*, 7).

The contemporary success of hand-outs and aide-memoires, of lecture notes and slide-show presentations, of online tutorials and fact-sheets, repeated by students to the relief of teachers rewarded with high feedback marks and external assessment, is then partly an illusory good when viewed from Whitehead's philosophy of education. These small victories are defeats over time, because they will be undone by the rapid fading of memory allied to the failure of life and history to repeat or to conform to exact learning: "Whatever be the detail with which you cram your student, the chance of his meeting in after-life exactly that detail is almost infinitesimal; and if he does meet it, he will probably have forgotten what you taught him about it" (*AE*, 41–42). So no matter how great your technical tools, even those permitting jumps through time, if assessment remains anchored to bare repetition, then Whitehead's lessons on rhythm and romance will have been betrayed. It is not about the technique, or the experience, but about the later event of reanimation of learning in novel situations.

In place of this detail, Whitehead emphasizes the learning of principles. Again, there is a Humean and Deleuzian bent to this definition and use of principles. A principle is a contracted habit of mind: "A principle which has thoroughly soaked into you is rather a mental habit than a formal statement. It becomes the way the mind reacts to the appropriate stimulus in the form of illustrative circumstances" (*AE*, 42). There is an important symbiosis of principles, knowledge, and the romance of practical encounters, because for Whitehead the acquisition and even application of principles and knowledge become unconscious and habitual.[7] Principles and lasting knowledge therefore depend on intense and engaged practical experience: "But the growth of knowledge becomes progressively unconscious, as being an incident derived from some active adventure of thought" (*AE*, 59). Principles formed through habitual contraction prepare us for the unforeseen, for the event. This is a double process since in order to form principles below or within conscious assimilation, the learning has itself to be an event—that is, a novel experience demanding activity and transformation alongside this derived unconscious preparation.

In this role of preparation through the unconscious, we can see the skill of divination and the demands of risk and experimentation in learning through principles. Were the time machine only used to reinforce factual recollection, then the unconscious and risk would play but minor parts associated with mistakes. You took them to the wrong battle. The exam failed to ask a question about that slightly shocking scene with Cleopatra. However, when shaping pupils for tests by the unknown, by the novel event, the selection of principle and preparatory event is subject to unavoidable chance and, sometimes, disaster. You might have selected travel through peaceful realms, for a class that would know another world war. Or maybe this was the right test, where only exposure to past efforts for peace could prepare pupils to try for a new peaceful event amidst conflict and hatred.

It is this adventure that Whitehead's gift brought to the classroom. Careful preparation could then be secured and challenged through exploration and encounter: "Ideas, facts, relationships, stories, histories, possibilities, artistry in words, in sounds, in form and in colour, crowd into the child's life, stir his feelings, excite his appreciation, and incite his impulses to kindred activities" (*AE,* 34). It had to be a sensual physical gift, not necessarily one devoid of words, but one where the senses played an essential part in infusing ideas with sensual urgency and relevance, against what Whitehead called the danger of recondite knowledge in mathematical education: "The science as presented to young pupils must lose its aspect of reconditeness. It must, on the face of it, deal directly and simply with a few general ideas of far-reaching importance" (*AE,* 119). "Recondite" does not mean difficult here. It means detached from relevance and urgency: "By this word I do not mean difficulty, but that the ideas involved are of highly special application, and rarely influence thought" (*AE,* 117). The gift would have been wasted, then, had we traveled merely for distraction or escapism. Each adventure needed to bring us back to a novel reflection on pressing modern problems.

A Radical Education

It could be claimed that our age has learned Whitehead's lessons about romance well. The best modern curricula pay close attention to group and individual learning through engaged experiences and activities, rendering knowledge live and even imparting it in live situations, as opposed to rote learning. For instance, active participation in lectures and laboratories has become a standard recommendation, if not always a fact on the ground, for science teaching at the university level: "Scientific teaching involves active learning strategies to engage students in the process of science and teaching methods that have been systematically tested and shown to reach diverse students."[8] Of course this standard is not universally upheld, and, even where the curriculum advocates romance, this is often countered through other pressures and doctrines, for instance with regard to universal examination of pupils and objective-based monitoring of teachers and schools, or through the "ultimate" goal of economic growth as set by narrow and dogmatic views about which disciplines and practices benefit growth, competitiveness, and well-being.

Against all these dampers to romance, Whitehead is much more radical than modern orthodoxy. As shown in the chapter epigraph above, he is opposed to general examinations and returns assessment to individual teachers, who must in turn bend it to individual pupils: "every question directly asked of a pupil at any examination is either framed or modified by the actual teacher of that pupil in that subject." This is the language of a radical progressive, a believer not only in the singular promise of each pupil ("that pupil") but also in the singular capacity and judgment of each teacher ("the actual teacher"). Yet he is even more radical than shown in this attention to individual pupils and educators. He is radical about each teaching and assessment *event:* "every question . . . is either framed or modified."

In later works such as *Adventures of Ideas* and *Process and Reality,* Whitehead will define an event as a nexus of actual occasions (*AI,* 201; *PR,* 73). The event is a relation and sometimes a very distant one. It is also a feeling and oneness, with a given date, yet it is open to connection to other events in another nexus. This feeling and relation through a mutual transformation in a singular situation, as opposed to any abstract universal or general concept, is at the core of Whitehead's description of learning and teaching. It is also at the core of his educational principles, because the event is essentially singular yet also essentially a relation. This, then, conditions education in all its manifestations because general concepts cannot be applied alone legitimately without running counter to the singular nature of each event, not only at the point of learning, but also at the points of testing and application. Moreover, since each event is a relation and process with no final boundaries, there are no final legitimate barriers or distinctions to be drawn once and for all on the basis of abstract generalizing theory. This applies not only to history, for instance, against the notion of a pure golden age, or perfect state of education in a given epoch. It also applies to subjects, where Whitehead's philosophy of education stresses the interrelation of subjects in learning events.

Each event, each encounter of teacher and pupil, is a difficult challenge with no simple solutions or straightforward prescriptions or guidelines. This explains his appeal to a novel definition of principles as unconscious and habitual, and hence individual, due to differences in individual circumstances, potential, and habit-forming patterns and events. It also explains why the application of those principles must itself involve romance and adventure, because that unconscious work of principles and ideas needs experienced intensity for its release.[9] The rhythms of education form a circle and not a ladder. Each stage must be present in all the others. Whitehead therefore appeals to individual and necessarily imperfect teaching, balancing exciting initiative and dulling training, as a response to ineluctable difficulty: "It is not a theoretical necessity, but arises because perfect tact is unattainable in the treatment of each individual case. In the past the methods employed assassinated interest; we are discussing how to reduce the evil to its smallest dimensions. I merely utter the warning that education is a difficult problem, to be solved by no one simple formula" (*AE*, 56).

Against the conclusion that this tact shows Whitehead pulling back from radical claims, it is very important to pay attention to Whitehead's prose in the epigraph, and more generally in his more accessible writings, whose conversational and humorous style can lure the reader into an impression of slightly forced common sense or wisdom. The underlying philosophy belies these impressions. It is as original as it is extreme. He does not view the matter of education as a choice between educational systems and forms of assessment, but instead makes the much more sweeping point—the almost nonsensical one—that "no education system is possible" unless it follows his position on assessment. Yet, there have been and are still education systems based on standardized national and international tests, as well as national and international league tables based on these tests.[10] Such general testing, standardization, and ranking is in fact the norm rather than the exception. Indeed, Whitehead was writing against such forms of assessment at the same time that he was denying their possibility. How can such an extreme contradictory and counterempirical claim be defended? Is this not a rhetorical misuse of "possible," and by a philosopher to boot?

The answer to this puzzle is in Whitehead's feel for dynamic processes over time. His deep thesis is that there is no *deep and lasting* learning where teaching lacks romantic adventure, tailored to individual pupils.[11] It is also that there is no such teaching where assessment destroys the ambition and practice of singular attention to the thrill of discovery in practice. Finally, it is that each event plays a part in this dynamic struggle and unfolding. Education, indeed any process, is a continuous process affecting and affected by all events. There are no independent discrete parts. There is no legitimate compartmentalization of, say, learning and assessment, or assessment and development, or development and well-being, or well-being and social and economic goods.

This continuity is reflected in Whitehead's doctrine of rhythm, which defines rhythmic movement in terms of manifold scales and stretches.[12] There are therefore many interrelated rhythms, interacting with one another and forming complex patterns of dynamic growth based on emerging differences:

> Life is essentially periodic. It comprises daily periods, with their alternations of work and play, of activity and of sleep, and seasonal periods, which dictate our terms and our holidays; and it is also composed of well-marked yearly periods. These are the gross obvious periods which no one can overlook. There are also subtler periods of mental growth, with their cyclic recurrences, yet always different as we pass from cycle to cycle, though the subordinate stages are reproduced in each cycle. That is why I have chosen the term 'rhythmic,' as meaning essentially the conveyance of difference within a framework of repetition. (*AE*, 27)

The role of singular difference and variation over cycles is of course reminiscent of Leibniz's *Monadology* and Vico's *New Science*. It is also a forerunner to Deleuze's *Difference and Repetition* and of his study of Leibniz in *The Fold: Leibniz and the Baroque*. Closer to Whitehead in epoch and explicit commitment to the analysis of rhythms, there is also Bachelard (and then Lefèbrve) and Bachelard's interest in Pinheiro dos Santos's work on rhythm.[13]

It would be false to conclude from the disparity between contemporary economic and social erosion of living rhythms and Whitehead's insistence on the importance of lived rhythm that Whitehead is somehow behind the times or, worse, reactionary. On the contrary, his concern with rhythm and more widely with progress in and through education is explicitly aimed at modernity and at the roles of science and technology in the modern world: "The key to modern mentality is the continued advance of science with the consequential shift of ideas and progress of technology" (*AE*, 112). So when he defends the continued teaching of Latin or when he argues for the importance of the arts in education, it is not a nostalgic argument or a claim to superior values, but rather to their importance for scientific and technological education and for the advancement of technological and scientific societies: "The antithesis between a technical and a liberal education is fallacious. There can be no adequate technical education which is not liberal, and no liberal education which is not technical: that is, no education that does not impart both technique and intellectual vision" (*AE*, 74).

The value of art and literature is twofold.[14] On the one hand, they complete and intensify our relation to the world around us. So though science has its romance and imaginative passions, these are completed by the way in which the arts enrich and deepen our senses in relation to the world around us: "Art exists that we may know the deliverance of our senses as good. It heightens the sense-world" (*AE*, 74). Literature completes a scientific approach to language by sharpening our senses around language and allowing for greater "aesthetic appreciation," not for some abstract reason but because this will allow for the "successful employment of language" (*AE*, 75).[15] More broadly, Whitehead associates this development of the senses and of appreciation through the idea of "vision."

This idea of vision must not be confused with a current managerial use of the term, where it is identified with an aim *(the vision of this university is to be an international leader in biotechnology)*. Vision is instead a faculty associated with imagination and the senses, beyond specific outcomes and aims. Vision, then, is an ability to sense what is not directly at stake in an activity and not directly at hand. It is a cultivated capacity to imagine and feel the dynamic and emotional promise and threats around an activity. It is a form of foresight rather than sight-setting: "Art and literature have not merely an indirect effect on the main energies of life. Directly, they give vision. The world spreads wide beyond the deliverances of material sense, with subtleties of reaction and with pulses of emotion. Vision is the necessary antecedent to control and to direction" (*AE*, 91). This antecedence is what is missed when, for instance, managers define vision as an imagined final state. Vision occurs prior to this and stands in a critical relation to it.

On the other hand, the arts and literature matter for moral reasons, which are in turn defended for their moral *and practical* worth. Work and the management of work require a counter to their tendency to drudgery and exploitation: "the essential idea remains, that work should be transfused with intellectual and moral vision and thereby turned into a joy, triumphing over its weariness and its pain" (*AE*, 68). For Whitehead, this moral vision follows only from a passionate experience of the arts and of literature.

The moral side to education culminates in religious education, which can have a secular bent given his emphasis on definitions of the principles of religious education free of theistic references—though these can easily be retraced, for instance to God, through eternity and the whole amplitude of time in the following passage.[16] The principles of "duty" and "reverence" stress our responsibility for the world and others, all of the world, over the whole of time, for all others: "Duty arises from our potential control over the course of events . . . and the foundation of reverence is this perception, that the present holds within itself the complete sum of existence, backwards and forwards, that whole amplitude of time, which is eternity" (*AE*, 23). In this highest stage, though not necessarily the most important one, since rhythm assigns import to all stages through their intertwined relations, we see Whitehead's radical demands and principles at their most extensive, but also most burdensome. Education carries the whole of time in each of its events.

The Curse?

The gift was a curse. Perhaps the deputy knew the exam results would ruin my career. Few of my pupils did as well at the exams as expected, despite their newfound enthusiasm and dedication. Rote learning fails the test of time, but deep learning and adventure fail fact-based questioning, just as Whitehead predicted. It was dangerous to adopt radical and innovative methods within a system maintaining countermodes of assessment and evaluation. My innovations required a system capable of recognizing them rather than one that tested for shallower knowledge and facts the students sought to avoid.

Whitehead's philosophy can be accused of idealism in failing to adjust pragmatically to the demands of established practices and demands. His insistence on the rhythms of education lures pupils and teachers into patterns of learning that fail according to the systems already in place. For instance, these systems might require the comparison and assessment of schools and their students in ways inconsistent with his emphasis on individual learning. The idealism would not simply be a dream of an unattainable future state. It would instead be idealism either with regard to the nature of the extent of the revolution needed to bring in a system consistent with the novel view of the rhythms of learning or with regard to the difficulty of gradually introducing a radical program.

The demands of Whitehead's radical model are such that it seems either to call for a violently rapid root and branch change or for a slower set of steps that necessarily sacrifice a vanguard for future benefits. In both cases of idealism, the deep problem is of time and dialectics. The rhythm of education, for all its complexity, does not seem to take account of the necessary compromises and mediations required over time to bring in a radical rhythm-based system. Whitehead is very convincing in constructing an ideal state of education, but his account looks as if it fails two practical demands. His system appears not to explain how we can move between the old and the new state. His philosophy also seems to lack an understanding of the necessity of mediation between these states, where mediation or dialectics remains conscious of the demands, validity and claims to truth, contradictions and syntheses of all intermediate stages.

These worries and accusations can be dispelled, though, if we turn to Whitehead's account of rhythm in education as depending on a profound reflection on time and practice. He frequently refers to time pressures in his essays on teaching. He also frames practice in relation to time. This is not only due to the concern with historical dynamics and cycles. That wide topic is underpinned by a more precise and detailed understanding of time on a smaller scale. This smaller scale determines the broader cycles of rhythm and history, though they determine it in different ways in return.

At the beginning of "The Rhythmic Claims of Freedom and Discipline" Whitehead reflects on the fading of Classical ideals in education in the shift from an education for wisdom to an education of subjects. But when we might have expected a full endorsement of this earlier ideal, Whitehead instead shows an awareness of the inevitability of these historical movements. His aim is not in fact a return to an ideal but rather how best to foster a different one that comprehends the pressures and logical dialectic that wed early ideals to their replacement by more prosaic approaches. The problem is then not how to return to an earlier state or even to imagine a new one. It is rather how to combine ideas and practice with an awareness of their destructive but also productive calls on one another: "My point is that, at the Dawn of our European civilisation, men started with the full ideals which should inspire education, and that gradually our ideals have sunk to square with our practice" (*AE*, 45). Whitehead's position is indicated by his use of "inspire" here. He seeks guidance and inspiration from ideals and principles in a practical environment tending to decay if it loses this direction.

The key to this combination is in the role of time as a double-headed pressure on practice. Shortness of time forces educationalists into ever more practical forms of education—for instance, when we emphasize specific knowledge or narrow disciplines for competitive economic reasons. Shortness is then not a comparative numerical property of time itself, where sixty minutes would be shorter than two hours. It is a property of the processes measured by time, where these processes tend to run out of time due to ever-increasing demands, such as making gains over others or the need to increase profits through productivity, even in education.

However, time is always short, not only because we lack time relative to external factors, such as the necessary decline of competitive advantage, but because pupils are themselves a source of a shortness of time. In their case, though, the lack of time is about the inherent value of events in time. Time is short because events come and go. We need to strike at the right time. So shortness of time is measured in missed opportunities to enhance wisdom, deep learning, imagination, and excitement. There is certainly shortness of time in responding to a need to achieve a certain type of comparative national standard. There is a different and, for Whitehead, more important shortness of time when a stage of development is missed or damaged. One type of shortness can be used to exacerbate or even excuse the other, as, for instance, when the curiosity and raw enthusiasm of youth is sacrificed to tedious reproduction.

The rhythms of education are not therefore solely historical, as in the decline and fall of systems, or solely natural, as in the life cycles of organisms. They are also, and most importantly, in the rhythmic and dialectical interaction of both types of cycle such that the overall rhythm is neither fully constructed nor natural. Neither is it fully ideal or fully practical. Finally, it is neither fully cognitive nor fully sensual. Whitehead's philosophy of education is deployed as a hybrid of types and of contradictory pressures, based on a careful examination of the role of time across them.

There are two connected manifestations of this examination of time in Whitehead's philosophy of education. On the one hand, he deploys distinctions about processes in time as critical and interpretative tools. On the other, he tries to respond to them through positive principles for education caught in the contradictions, stresses, and opportunities defined by time and process. I want to bring the main body of this chapter to a close through close study of two short passages exhibiting these aspects of Whitehead's thought. The point is not only to show the detail of his arguments and ideas, but to show the sources of his remarks on education beyond what some might see as his personal inclinations and intuitions.

Here is a case of the critical work on time and process in education. It brings together the attention to dynamic process we studied in the opening section of this chapter with the radical thresholds and critical points we presented in the second:

> But when ideals have sunk to the level of practice, the result is stagnation. In particular, so long as we conceive intellectual education as merely consisting in the acquirement of mechanical mental aptitudes, and of formulated statements of useful truths, there can be no progress; though there will be much

> activity, amid aimless re-arrangement of syllabuses, in the fruitless endeavour to dodge the inevitable lack of time. (*AE*, 45–46)

First of all, time here is not defined through movement, but in organic change: "sinking" and "stagnation," where to "sink" is not merely to change position but to change in nature, to fade as ideal. Second, the radical horizon of Whitehead's approach appears in the critical divide determined by the demand for "progress" as distinguished from "activity." The difficult and very deep opposition between two ways of thinking about shortness of time supports this distinction.

Activity is "fruitless" and "aimless" because it fails to respond to an inevitable lack of time, where lack is not a property of activity itself. Instead, to run short of time is the result of a process independent of the activity, such as the way in which pupils grow up through different stages or the way systems and societies enter periods of decadence. So shortness here does not indicate a clock running down on an act within a specified time period. It is rather that the activity is knowingly or unknowingly in a struggle with a changing organism that can either enhance or resist the activity.

The opposition between knowing and not knowing is central to Whitehead's work on education because he writes to make us aware of the reasons for shortness of time so that we can alter our ways of learning and teaching to adapt to the proper rhythms of education. The problem with, for instance, "formulated statements of useful truths" is that they are ignorant of the necessary reasons for their redundancy over time. It is not that truths should not be taught; it is that the timing of that teaching must pay attention to a multitude of rhythms governing the how, when, which, and who of each teaching event: "I am pleading that we shall endeavour to weave in the learner's mind a harmony of patterns, by co-ordinating the various elements of instruction into subordinate cycles each of intrinsic worth for the immediate apprehension of the pupil" (*AE*, 33).

This critical side to Whitehead's work on time and education is complemented by a series of important principles based on time. In my view, the most significant of these concerns the "insistence of the present." Education is not about the preservation of past knowledge; nor is it an aim at a future state of knowledge or ability. Rather, it is an attention to the specific demands of the present: "I would only remark that the understanding which we want is an understanding of an insistent present. The only use of a knowledge of the past is to equip us for the present. No more deadly harm can be done to young minds than by depreciation of the present. The present contains all that there is. It is holy ground, for it is the past, and it is the future" (*AE*, 3–4).

This claim for the present allows us to understand Whitehead's radical progressiveness better. It is radical not through a projected ideal, but through a pragmatic attention to the present as focus of the past and of the present. There is to be no sacrifice of the present for past values or for future outcomes. The "insistence," that is, the intensity of callings and of values—the decision points—must come from present events. This is no bland tautology such that a present act must take place in the present. It is the realization that the particular character of the present event as singular rhythmic collecting of the past and of the future must condition our acts of learning and teaching. Preservation of the past, and every future objective, must stem from attention to an insistent present, to an intense potential so easy to fall short of if we do not open our sense to it.

Radical Enough?

When defending a progressive and liberal education, more so one as radical as Whitehead's, a final criticism must be addressed. Does his attention to individual pupils, teachers, classes, and schools, against general syllabuses and knowledge, not lead to a form of individualism incapable of registering the opportunities, fetters, conflicts, and deep injustices that appertain to social groups and classes over and above individuals? Does this incapacity make a liberal and progressive education concurrent with a liberal and capitalist education system, which, at its limit, in the destruction of centralized and egalitarian education, leads to an education market where the language of singular attention and multiple differences serves as a cover for the distribution of quality and access according to wealth?

Whitehead is well aware of these questions, and he provides some straightforward answers and some less conclusive indications.[17] Straightforwardly, he is not opposed to general syllabuses and to viewing society and pupils as a whole, so long as individual rhythms and particular events are not disregarded. He is not advocating an atomization of education but rather a dialectic between the singular and the general and, in his words, between individual "freedom" and general "discipline."[18] Equally straightforwardly, he is a strong critic of the sacrifice of education for greed and profit: "Desire for money will provide hard-fistedness and not enterprise" (*AE*, 69).

However, his argument against greed is moral and practical rather than based on social justice or a critique of capital: "There is one—and only one—way to obtain these admirable results [men with inventive genius and employers alert in the development of new ideas]. It is by producing workmen, men of science, and employers who enjoy their work" (*AE*, 68). In *Dialogues of Alfred North Whitehead*, Price reports him as setting this moral and practical role within the task of civilizing business or "to get business men to civilize themselves."[19] It would be accurate for Marxists to see this position as opposed to collectivist education associated with political revolution. This opposition to revolutionary upheaval through progressive liberal reform is explicit in Whitehead's works, for instance in his remarks on Marx and *Das Kapital* in *Adventures of Ideas* (*AI*, 35).

Whitehead's aim is for careful reform towards "sympathetic co-operation" thanks to a fostering of a "Benedictine"[20] joy in labor in order to avoid a "savage upheaval" (*AE*, 68).[21] The one universal here is the potential for enjoyment. It can and should be released by education, but Whitehead does not see this potential as essentially limited by social and economic conditions assigned to groups and classes. The deep worry remains, though, that even if those conditions are not necessary fetters on the release of the potential of enjoyment in education, they remain practical ones with a social and political dynamic as powerful or perhaps more powerful than the proper rhythms of education.

Notes

I thank audiences at the Warwick Philosophy Graduate Seminar and Dundee AHRI lecture series for their questions and suggestions on earlier versions of parts of this chapter. In particular, remarks by Martin Warner, Miguel Beistegui, Stephen Houlgate, Keith Ansell Pearson, Nicholas Davey, Rachel Jones, Andrew Roberts, and Jim Tomlinson helped to shape my ideas on the problems of Whitehead's critique of standard objectives and outcomes in education.

1. Though the style of Whitehead's work on education is often impressionistic, it is backed by many years of engaged activity as a teacher, education administrator and advisor, and chair on many committees over his career at Cambridge, London, and Harvard. Thus Brian Hendley refutes claims by Harold Dunkel about Whitehead's relative lack of practical activity in education: "Dunkel ignores the fact that Whitehead took an extraordinary number of educational and administrative duties while he worked in London, serving as Chair of the Department of Applied Mathematics at the Imperial College of Science and Technology at Kensington, governor of the Borough Polytechnic Institute at Southwark, member of the Senate and Dean of the Faculty of Science at the University of London, chair of the Academic Council that managed the internal affairs concerning education in London, and chair of the Delegacy administering Goldsmiths College, one of England's major institutions for the training of teachers." Brian Hendley, "Whitehead and Business Education: A Second Look," *Interchange* 31, nos. 2–3 (2000): 179–95, esp. 180. For Whitehead's comments on this academic

work, see Lucien Price, *Dialogues of Alfred North Whitehead* (Jaffrey, N. H.: Nonpareil, 2001), 247.

2. Patrick O'Connor, *Derrida: Profanations* (London: Continuum, 2010), 127.

3. Attention is drawn to imagination as contagious by Ronald F. Blasius in his "Alfred North Whitehead's Informal Philosophy of Education," *Studies in Philosophy and Education* 16 (1997): 303–15, esp. 309; however, this connection is interpreted more as a poetic moment than one consistent with Whitehead's ideas on rhythm and organisms.

4. Chris Holligan, Michael Wilson, and Walter Humes, "Research Cultures in English and Scottish University Education Departments: An Exploratory Study of Academic Staff Perceptions," *British Educational Research Journal* 37, no. 4 (2011): 717–18.

5. For a far-reaching study of this broad, inclusive, and connective approach to biology and evolution, see Isabelle Stengers, *Penser avec Whitehead: Une Libre et sauvage création de concepts* (Paris: Seuil, 2002), 131–32. Stengers is commenting on the extraordinary passages on perception and objects in *The Concept of Nature* where Whitehead demonstrates the necessarily connective quality of perception within a complex nature: "Nature appears as a complex system whose factors are dimly discerned by us" (*CN*, 163).

6. David Hume, *The Natural History of Religion* (London: A. and H. Bradlaugh Bonner, 1889), 38, http://files.libertyfund.org/files/340/Hume_0211_EBk_v6.0.pdf.

7. This concern with the relation of freedom and discipline in education, as countering tendencies to chaotic indifference or decay in each other, can also be found in the closing sections of *Process and Reality*: "Another contrast is equally essential for the understanding of ideals—the contrast between order as the condition for excellence, and order as stifling the freshness of living. This contrast is met with in the theory of education" (*PR*, 338).

8. Jo Handelsman et al., "Scientific Teaching," *Science*, n. s., 304, no. 5670 (April 23, 2004): 521–22.

9. For a rich practical study of the stage of romance in relation to Whitehead's theory of prehensions, see Adam Scarfe, "Selectivity in Learning: A Theme in the Application of Whitehead's Theory of Prehensions to Education," *Interchange* 36, nos. 1–2 (2005): 9–22, esp. 13.

10. As shown, for instance, by UNESCO's International Standard Classification of Education, http://www.uis.unesco.org/Education/Documents/UNESCO_GC_36C-19_ISCED_EN.pdf, or through the Bologna process in European Union higher education, http://www.ehea.info/.

11. This use of the idea of adventure as counter to decay is also found in the sections in *Adventures of Ideas* where Whitehead discusses business and technology ("Foresight"). In that book, philosophy has the coordinating role allowing adventure to counter decadence: "But when civilization culminates, the absence of a co-ordinating philosophy of life spread through the community spells decadence, boredom, and the slackening of effort" (*AI*, 98).

12. It is interesting to see the continued importance of this complex idea of rhythm in contemporary research inspired by and developing Whitehead's philosophy. Brian Massumi's elegant and sensitive work on dance, art, and music gives an exceptionally tactile and sensual rendering of Whitehead's aesthetic event as essentially rhythmical. Massumi also explains well why Whitehead insists on the bodily and sensual, precognitive, aspect of the stage of romance in education: "The effect wells up from below the threshold of human experience. It comes to pass the threshold in *its* way, following its own

rhythm, when it is ready to set in. *It*—the event-nexus—expresses its own coming together, as it passes through its human channelled bringing-itself-into-perceptual-focus. This makes the experience integrally ecological." Brian Massumi, *Semblance and Event: Activist Philosophy and the Occurrent Arts* (Cambridge, Mass.: MIT Press, 2011), 165.

13. Luciana Parisi and Steve Goodman discuss Whitehead and Bachelard on rhythm in "Extensive Continuum: Towards a Rhythmic Anarchitecture," Luciana Parisi and Steven Goodman "Extensive Continuum: Towards a Rhythmic Anarchitecture," *Inflexions* no. 2 "Nexus" (December 2008), http://www.senselab.ca/inflexions/volume_2/nodes/Inflexions_Goodman_Parisi.pdf. They argue that Whitehead's later work on the extensive continuum goes further than Bachelard and his critique of Bergson: "For us, Whitehead's extensive continuum moves beyond the Bergson and Bachelard deadlock because it accounts for the continual potential relations between discontinuous actual occasions" (4). Irrespective of these distinctions, it is notable how far modern lives have drifted from many senses of natural or created rhythms through our technological control over nature, our nefarious effect on the very seasons, the capitalist drive to deny cycles of rest and recuperation in the name of competitive advantage, and the ceaseless demands of the production of surplus-value. Gaston Bachelard, *La Dialectique de la durée* (Paris: PUF, 1950), 129–50.

14. The reference to romance and to the importance of the arts is echoed in the discussion of the "Romantic reaction" in *Science and the Modern World*. Romantic poetry was a plea for the organic connection of things and for values over and above, and essential to, matters of fact: "the nature-poetry of the romantic revival was a protest on behalf of the organic view of nature, and also a protest against the exclusion of value from the essence of matter of fact" (*SMW*, 94). These arguments are picked up towards the end of the book in a discussion of the importance of art in education that rates among some of Whitehead's most lyrical and inspiring: "This fertilisation of the soul is the reason for the necessity of art" (*SMW*, 202).

15. For an exceptionally lucid interpretation of this understanding of the aesthetic in Whitehead, see Steven Shaviro's *Without Criteria: Kant, Whitehead, Deleuze and Aesthetics* (Cambridge, Mass.: MIT Press, 2009). Shaviro emphasizes the ubiquity of aesthetic "contemplation" central to Whitehead's argument for its necessary role in education: "Even the most utilitarian, result-and-action-oriented modes of perception remain largely receptive and involve a certain 'affective tone' and a certain degree of aesthetic contemplation—and, Whitehead adds, 'thus art is possible'" (68–69).

16. For a comprehensive and rewarding discussion of this "spiritual" side of Whitehead's work on education and its debt to William James, see Jack G. Priestley, "The Essence of Education: Whitehead and the Spiritual Dimension," *Interchange* 31, nos. 2–3 (2000): 117–33, esp. 122–28.

17. For a brief and rather anecdotal set of remarks by Whitehead on the extension of education beyond an elite in the nineteenth and early twentieth centuries, see Price, *Dialogues of Alfred North Whitehead*, 110.

18. Howard Woodhouse makes a similar point regarding the dialectical rather than linear nature of the stages of education in response to critical remarks on the role of knowledge in Whitehead: "By relating abstract principles to concrete facts emergent from human experience, the learner in the cycle of generalisation achieves an inclusive understanding connecting abstract principle and concrete experience." Howard Woodhouse, "Overcoming Tragedy," *Interchange* 31, no. 1 (2000): 79–82, esp. 80. It is the

cyclical and inclusive elements that show the dialectical movement, though I disagree with Woodhouse's characterization of principles as abstract in Whitehead since they are not acquired or held in an abstract manner. It would be better to define them as immanent in the contemporary usage developed around work on Deleuze and others.

19. Price, *Dialogues of Alfred North Whitehead,* 61.

20. For a good account of this reference to Benedictine education, see Sandra Fidyk's article illustrating the potential of Whitehead's account of rhythm and romance, and the stages of education through many enlightening practical teaching examples and cases, many of which stem from the teaching of literature. Sandra Fidyk, "Precision and Craft in Whitehead's Educational Philosophy," *Interchange* 31, nos. 2–3 (2000): 301–17, esp. 313.

21. "Technical Education and Its Relation to Science and Literature" is the title of the essay from which this quotation is sourced. There is a deep and balanced discussion of the relation to market in Whitehead's philosophy of education by Howard Woodhouse. He argues that Whitehead's position is not compromised by its aim of civilizing business, but that nonetheless Whitehead underestimates the conflicts between education and market in terms of aims and values. Woodhouse's argument is not conclusive, though, and ends with exactly the kind of difficult questions and statements that I have wanted to raise here: "was Whitehead's seduction by the market's logic of value the result of its compatibility with certain assumptions of his speculative thought?" Howard Woodhouse, "Was Whitehead Seduced by the Market?" *Interchange* 32, no. 4 (2001): 431–40, esp. 437.

TEN

Cutting Away from Smooth Space

Alfred North Whitehead's Extensive Continuum in Parametric Software

Luciana Parisi

> All mathematical notions have reference to processes of intermingling. The very notion of number refers to the process from the individual units to the compound group. The final number belongs to no one of the units; it characterizes the way in which the group unity has been attained. . . . There is no such thing as a mere static number. There are only numbers playing their parts in various processes conceived in abstraction from the world-process.
>
> —Alfred North Whitehead, *Modes of Thought*

According to Alfred N. Whitehead, there are no numbers without group, no unity without process. But as the quotation above also serves to illustrate, Whitehead believed that there are processes of another kind that do not correspond to the world-process (the actual world). Whitehead is specifically addressing mathematical abstractions. This essay instead will address the mode of abstraction involved in the computational processing of data and in particular in the use of parametric software in architectural design. It will argue that the computational power of parametric software does not simply involve the design of space according to given sets or geometrical points, but also, and significantly for us, it relies on variables open to change in real time. Since these variables are not simply discrete units that represent points in space that are connected together, but are set to evolve in time, they have been said to be generative of space. Much contemporary debate on computational architecture has focused on notions of folding and topological evolution of forms, drawing on ontological premises of continuities and becoming.[1] This essay instead argues that Whitehead's notion of the extensive continuum can help us to rethink parametric design as offering a conception of space based on mereotopological relations between parts and wholes.

Before proceeding to explain the way parametricism and mereotopology may oddly overlap and become the source of new speculations about the relation between discrete and the continuum, it may be useful to immediately clarify here these two key terms.

Within the field of digital design, *parametricism* refers to transformation of digital animation techniques from the mid-1990 towards an increasing malleability of data open to manipulation through scripting (use of computer code). The breaking down of geometrical figures, such as cubes, rectangles, spheres, and so on, into animate geometrical entities such as splines, nurbs, and the like, has led to spatio-temporal forms that become increasingly divided into an infinite number of variations (volume, dimensions, weight, scale, load pressure) and are interdependent and programmed to respond to external elements (such as urban traffic or weather variations) by means of adaptation. Instead of using design software tools such as CAD (Computer Automated Design) to reproduce geometric forms, parametric design starts with maintaining a dynamic link between evolving parameters and their use in form definition, enabling real-time continuous parameter space exploration through scripting. In short, parametric design points to an open mode of quantification of variables, whereby discrete parameters are not simply assembled together to produce a continuously changing form. Instead, these discrete elements are open to real-time updates thus including an infinite variety of code revisions within the computation of form. Parametricism therefore points not at a continual change of form but to a new understanding of the relation between whole—form—and parts—parameters.[2]

A specific articulation of the relation between wholes and parts is put forward by Whitehead's use of the scientific notion of *mereotopology*, derived from a combination of *mereology* (the analysis of parthood relations) and *topology* (the study of a self-connected whole undergoing continuous change). This notion became central to Whitehead's early attempts to characterize his ontology of events and explain their connection. As opposed to the primacy of a continuous becoming of form that would not account for the atomic nature of spatio-temporal actualities, Whitehead used mereotopology to explain how two events, parts (albeit complex and not individual parts), can share the region in which they are located by being co-located (by means of overlapping, conjunctions, line-to-line segmentation) rather than dissolving their parthood relations into one continuous field.

In the first part of this essay, I will focus on Whitehead's understanding of the actual world as being fundamental to his notion of the extensive continuum. This notion, however, cannot be fully grasped without a closer engagement with his mereotopological schema, which explains the fractal relation between parts and wholes. This essay claims that this schema is fundamental to Whitehead's metaphysics in its attempts at considering spatiality, measurement, division, discretization, finitude as an addition to time, temporality, duration, infinity, continuity. The second part of the essay will then address this schema as it offers to us an entry point into the conception of space that is at stake in the pervasiveness of the computational "abstraction from the world-process." The case of parametric design in digital architecture will be used to discuss an abstract form of spatiotemporality that is at once discrete and continuous. I will also suggest that parametric architecture involves not simply the generative design of spatiotemporalities through the qualitative transformations of the architectural shape, but also reveals the persistence of parametric quantities, thereby disclosing how spatio-temporalities cannot be fused together. I argue that by programming relations between spatio-temporal parts and wholes, parametricism uses a mereotopological and not simply a topological mode of design. The essay will conclude by suggesting that parametric abstraction does then not simply reduce lived temporality to coded spatiality. Instead it points at the advance of algorithmic actuality, an automated mode of prehending data defining a new form of digital spatio-temporality.

Discrete Infinities

For Whitehead, the actual world is composed of actual occasions. These actualities are grouped in events, which become the nexus of actual entities "inter-related in some determined fashion in one extensive quantum" (*PR*, 73).[3] Events therefore explain the togetherness of actualities, which Whitehead calls the "nexus." But every nexus is a component part of another nexus. The latter emerges as an unalterable entity from the concrescence of its component elements, and it stands as a fact, possessed of a date and a location (cf. *PR*, 230). Whitehead points out that the individual particularity of an actual entity, and of each nexus of entities, is also independent of its original percipient and thus "enjoys an objective immortality in the future beyond itself" (*PR*, 230). From this standpoint, Whitehead confutes the primary notions of space and time, and argues that only events, as nexuses of actual entities, are able to remain unrepeatable places with dates. In other words, actual entities are events because objects have time and space, and yet as a nexus of entities, events go beyond this space and this time.

Whitehead's metaphysics of events does not determine objects by rendering them as the synthesis of the qualities that are projected onto them.[4] If, as Whitehead explains, each and any actual occasion is an assemblage of prehended data and prehending activities, then an assemblage is composed of parts-objects, which constitute an enduring object that acquires an epochal singularity. This singularity—which might be referred to as eventfulness—cannot be repeated, because the objects that define this singularity are partial, contextual, historical actualities. At the same time, however, if an event is a nexus of actual objects, and not the result of projected qualities, it is because it corresponds to the eventuation of unprecedented qualities that go beyond the direct projection of the actual data. But is it possible here to understand relations to be both more than effects and less than the projections of a perceiving subject? How does Whitehead avoid equating relations with projections? In particular, can the notion of prehension sustain the reality of objects without reaffirming the subjective (and phenomenological) experience of objects?

According to Whitehead, prehensions are first of all mental and physical modalities of relations by which objects take up and respond to one another. As he puts it, "prehensions are concrete facts of relatedness" (*PR*, 23). Whitehead does not start with the substance of an object or with the perception that one has of it, but confers autonomy to an actual entity's constitutive process of acquiring determination, completeness, and finitude from indeterminate conditions (cf. *PR*, 45). Although for Whitehead, prehensions are external fact of relatedness, they are not mental projections, but rather conceptual and physical relations (cf. *PR*, 245). In other words, prehensions are not only concrete ideas, but also concrete facts. This means that the actual prehension of another actual object, or of its elements, changes the internal constitution (the mental and physical tendencies) of the prehended actuality.[5] From this standpoint, prehensions also account for how actual entities acquire determination or completeness from an indeterminate process of mental and physical contagions, or from the intrusions of elements from other actual entities. Whitehead calls this process a "concrescence of prehensions" (*PR*, 24–26).

Actual entities, therefore, are not substances or indissoluble objects. On the contrary, they can become indivisible only once the concrescence of prehensions affords an actual object that then becomes the subjective form of the data prehended. This process of prehensions is thus a process of determination, and what it determines is the actuality of data defined by the concrescence of prehensions. This is why an actual occasion is not eternal, but rather an event. It happens and then perishes. It acquires a subjective form of the prehended data and at once reaches objective immortality: it becomes an indissoluble event in time. From this standpoint, actual occasions are not effects of prehensions or mirrors of perceptions. On the contrary, they are led by their final cause to transform prehended data into a subjective form and into objective actuality (cf. *PR,* 19). The subjective form of the actual entity thus remains an objectified real potential that can be prehended anew by other actual entities. From this standpoint, the process of prehension is not a relative mechanism by which no object can as such be defined autonomously; instead, this process explains how actual entities become events, and thereby new spatio-temporal objects on the extensive continuum (cf. *PR,* 64–65).

Whitehead's process metaphysics is concerned with how indivisible or discrete unities can exist in the infinity of relations with other events, or with other actual occasions. This metaphysics does not offer us the option of simply merging or separating abstract and actual objects, but rather explains how infinity, indetermination, and abstraction infect actualities. As Whitehead puts it, "The true philosophical question is, how can concrete fact exhibit entities abstract from itself and yet participated in by its own nature?" (*PR,* 20). Each and any bit of an actual occasion strives for its own individuation by selecting or making a decision about the infinite amount of data (the qualities and the quantities) inherited from past actual occasions, from contemporaneous entities, and from the pure potentials of eternal objects. Yet prehensions are always partial, since all actual objects at once select and exclude, evaluate and set in contrast all of the inherited data. In other words, prehensions do not at all coincide with a direct downloading of data on behalf of an entity, and do not constitute objects by projecting data onto them. If, according to Whitehead, actual prehensions are the conditions of space and time,[6] and are the markers of events, it is because the indissoluble atomic architecture of each and any actual occasion is imbued with indetermination. Whitehead's process metaphysics therefore suggests that events are a nexus of actual objects. These are unrepeatable events, and yet they remain incomplete, because their objectified real potential can be prehended by any other actual entities and thus become other than it was.

From this standpoint, even if an actual object is what it is and cannot be another, it remains an unsubstantial entity. An actuality cannot therefore remain unchanged from the material corrosions of its parts; it cannot stop bursting into a sea of entropic chaos. Similarly, an actual object cannot remain an eternal form (the form of the apple) that physically reenacts itself, and that self-reproduces itself, as does an autopoietic system. Instead, an actual occasion maintains its objective determination, involving the prehension of both actual and abstract data. To put it otherwise: actual objects are not simply dissolved into a seamless process of projections, but are instead forms of processes, forms of infinity.

Whitehead in fact rejects the idea that processes involve the continual variation of a self-modulating whole. There could be no process without forms of processes, without conceptual and physical objects prehending the infinity of actual and abstract data. According to Whitehead, a form of process precisely responds to the question: "How does importance for the finite require importance for the infinite?" (*MT,* 86). A form of process therefore explains how "each fully realized fact has an infinity of relations in the historical world and in the realm of form" (*MT,* 89). In other words, a form of process defines how an actual object reaches its completion and becomes individualized, and how infinite potentialities, or eternal objects, enter the actual spatio-temporality. A form of process explains how unexpected worlds become added to already existing objects. But this form does not correspond to the sum of objects and the accumulation of qualities and quantities of data. The concrescence of the universe involves the concrescence of actual worlds that are imbued with eternal objects. Actual objects could not become complete and there could be no event without the capacities of actual objects to fulfill the potential content of selected (or prehended) eternal objects, through which actual qualities and quantities can become other than what they were.[7]

Whitehead's metaphysics does not simply substitute empirical with transcendental causality, actualities with process, or facts with forms. Instead, it insists that there are at least two coexisting—and immanent—causes at work within an actual object: *presentational immediacy* and *causal efficacy.* Whilst the former explains how prehensions are immediately taken by the present, causal efficacy refers to the reality of the past data that lurks in the background. If causal efficacy is "the sense of derivation from an immediate past, and of passage to an immediate future" (*PR,* 178), presentational immediacy, the sense-perception of things as they are presented here and now, is what is felt at the instant of prehending. Whitehead explains that the present locus is a datum for both modes of prehension: it is an object of direct prehension according to the cause of presentational immediacy, and an object of indirect prehension through causal efficacy. In other words, the double causality does not exclude the potential in favor of the actual, and yet does not simply merge the two causes together through material empiricism or transcendent idealism.

The two causes are two ontologies of infinity: eternal objects correspond to the infinity of ideas, and actual objects deploy the infinity of matter. It is when an actual entity selects certain ideas that a nexus becomes an event, and another actual object is added onto the extensive continuum. As Whitehead puts it, "For a continuum is divisible; so far as the contemporary world is divided by actual entities, it is not a continuum but is atomic" (*PR*, 62). In other words, for extension to become, it has to be interrupted, broken down, infinitely divided by the infinity of actual occasions selecting the infinite variations of infinities that are the eternal objects. Eternal objects, therefore, do not glue actual entities together, merging all individualities into one continual process. On the contrary, the extensive continuum as the general relational element of actual occasions is defined by "the process of the becoming of actuality into what in itself is merely potential" (*PR*, 72).

From this standpoint, the relation between eternal objects and actual entities is not simply a matter of coevolution or structural coupling, as might for instance be claimed by an autopoietic approach establishing the reversible correlation between the abstract and the concrete. Similarly, eternal objects do not generate actual occasions, but are instead "potentials for the process of becoming" of actual occasions (*PR*, 29). Eternal objects, therefore, are part and parcel of any actual entities, since the latter are precisely forms of process, and spatio-temporal structures of data. Eternal objects are intrinsic to actualities, no matter how small and how inorganic these latter might be.

Eternal objects are not the ideal continuity that link all actualities, but are indeed objects, despite being infinite varieties of infinities. Whitehead's metaphysics thus offers us an original view of infinity, which does not correspond to infinitesimal continuity between two objects, but which instead explains that eternal objects are discrete infinities nested within any nexus of actualities. It is this nesting and grappling of eternal objects inside spatio-temporal actualities that deploy the workings of a mereotopological schema, wherein actualities are hosts to an infinite number of infinities (without reaching an ultimate whole).

To reiterate: eternal objects are pure potential objects that are transformed into a real potential in time and space. Inasmuch as actual entities are causes of themselves, so too are eternal objects *causa sui*. This also means that their eternality is not grounded in substance, spirit, or life. Similarly, eternal infinities cannot be derived from finite actualities because eternality is not flattened onto here with actual spatio-temporality. At the same time, however, eternal objects are not simply to be thought as universal qualities through which actualities relate. For Whitehead, eternal objects are ideas that are as real and as effective as any other physical thing. These ideas are at once discrete and infinite, since eternal objects are not equivalent to each other, but are instead defined by their own uncompressible infinity. Each eternal object or each idea is therefore not simply different from another. This is not simply a world of ideas: instead, each idea is constituted by infinite data that cannot be contained by a smaller entity. Eternal objects are incomputable infinities that cannot be compressed by actual quantifications (rational numbers). Instead, these nonactual worlds explain how deep connections of ideas occur between the most varied objects.[8] This is why the relation between objects is not simply given by an ideal fusion, but rather implies a fractal architecture of actual entities (indivisible sets) imbued with eternal objects (infinite quantities), worlds belonging to irreducible orders of reality, magnitude, and complexity. Eternal objects, therefore, do not simply guarantee continuity between actual occasions, because they are permanent unsynthesizable infinities that enter into, infect, and abduct actualities. Ultimately, eternal objects are not there to guarantee a continual flow or smooth connection between actualities. Instead they involve an irreversible contagion, an outburst in the continuous flow of actual relations, which corresponds to the formation of new discrete infinities on the extensive continuum of actualities.

Extensive Abstraction

Whitehead's notion of mereotopology[9] will contribute towards explaining how the computation of spatio-temporal data now includes relations among wholes, parts, and parts of parts. This implies that computational forms of abstractions are not only set to design the becoming of continuity itself, but importantly, they are also exposing new forms of becoming. In other words, the question of computational abstraction is now as follows: How can that which relates to itself become? To put it crudely, computational abstraction is now concerned with production of events: with the nexus of spatio-temporalities as these become irreversibly infected with eternal objects.

But before explaining this form of computational abstraction in the context of parametric design, it is important to clarify what is at stake in Whitehead's notion of mereotopology vis-à-vis his conception of extension and of spatio-temporal relations. In particular, it is possible to suggest that the notion of mereotopology, because of the relation between parts and parts and wholes, can also be seen to lie at the core of Whitehead's notion of extensive continuum.

Whitehead used the notion of mereotopology to address the problem of abstraction and spatial measurement.[10] He used a nonmetrical logic to define the relations between extended parts and wholes, starting from concrete actualities.[11] Since all metrical relations involve measurement (and to measure or quantify involves a method of abstraction), Whitehead developed a new notion of extensive abstraction to problematize the general theory of relativity and the theory of measurement, which, he complained, seemingly collapsed physics and geometry into one another, ultimately ignoring the distinction between the abstract and the concrete.[12]

Whitehead used the notion of mereotopology to argue that space is composed of actual entities that connect. These entities are atomic occasions and constitute discrete events, and according to Whitehead, they explain not continual becoming but the becoming of continuity itself. Zeno's paradox of discrete units and infinitesimal divisibility is not addressed here through the Bergsonian metaphysics of a continual duration, or *élan vital,* where all quantity amounts to a difference in kind.[13] Instead, the mereotopological relation between atomic spatio-temporality reveals that continuous connection is interrupted by actual regions and subregions of relation. According to Whitehead, Leibniz's infinitesimal divisions could not define the reality of events on the plane of continuity (or the continual chain of cause and effect determining the sequential relations between actualities) because the distance between actualities could not be filled by the infinitesimal continuity of percepts and affects (cf. *PR,* 332–33). On the contrary, the distance between actual entities had to be considered in its own right: as actualities of connection, overlapping, inclusion, juxtaposition, disjunction, and intersection defined by points and lines. In other words, according to Whitehead there are always actualities amid actualities.

If Bergson's *élan vital* is a virtual continuum that is ceaselessly divided by perceptual selections or material actualities, Whitehead seems to claim that this correlation between one time (the topological invariant continuum of indiscernible, undifferentiated duration) to many spaces precludes any event from ever occurring on the extensive continuum of actualities. Similarly to Henri Poincaré's view of an infinitesimal curving space or a topological continuum of uncut forms, Bergson was seeking a temporal invariant between events.[14] From this standpoint, only *virtual* time (uncoordinated intensive time) can *amodally* link two causally connected actualities (or parameters). Such virtual time is a real interval that exposes the plenitude of cosmic time, and has no intrinsic measure except a continual variation of differential relations.

Whilst rejecting the idea that infinitesimals could be used to explain the relation between actualities, Whitehead also argues that these relations should be compared not to the infinite lines of the Euclidean parallel axiom, but rather to finite segments (cf. *PR,* 328). Each actual occasion is finite, and does not change or move. Actual entities are real potentialities, determined by what Whitehead called causal efficacy: the sequential order of data defined by the physical prehensions of past data from one entity to the next (cf. *PR,* 169). From this standpoint, continuity is explained by the connection between entities, which are not geometrical points, but rather "spatial regions" with semi-boundaries (e.g., volumes, lumps, spheres) (cf. *PR,* 63; 121–25; 206). Hence, continuity is not given by the convergence of two parallel infinite lines touching infinity, but by the actual relation between spatio-temporal regions of objectified real potentialities (actual entities): slices of time, atomic durations.[15] Instead of infinitesimally divisible points of perception and affection, Whitehead believes that there are an infinite number of actual entities between any two actualities, even between those that are nominally close together. This is why Whitehead rejects Zeno's paradox of infinitesimal small points and argues that continuity is not a ground to start from, but something that has to be achieved as a result of the extensive connections of actual entities (cf. *PR,* 97–97; 294).

In "The Relational Theory of Space"[16] Whitehead explained his method of extensive abstraction as the interconnection of different levels and scales of actualities. With the concept of extension, as opposed to notions of absolute space,[17] Whitehead claimed that relations were part of the concrete order of things. But how does a connection between actualities become a relational actuality, a blind spot or space-event? To answer this question, we need to delve deeper into Whitehead's mereotopological schema. According to the latter, actualities, in the process of their formation, select eternal objects or pure potentialities. Through doing so, they cause the continuum of actualities (or the extensive continuum) to split into events: atomic occasions of experience that change the nature of the continuum itself. In other words, the continuum becomes other than it was each time actual entities prehend eternal objects, the ingression of which corrupts their structure and organization. This is how actual entities become objects of contingency. As Whitehead specifies, "in the essence of each eternal object there stands an indeterminateness which expresses its indifferent patience for any mode of ingression into any actual occasion" (*SMW,* 171). Eternal objects are internally determined by infinity, but are externally related to actual entities, as the latter's indeterminate possibilities (cf. *SMW,* 160).

It may be important to specify here that eternal objects are not an undifferentiated pool of qualities that are divided or spatialized by actual entities. On the contrary, it is important to rethink eternal objects in terms of discrete infinities, which do not define the external relation between actual entities in terms of infinitesimally smaller points of conjunction (e.g., Leibniz's percepts and affects, Deleuze's differential or intensive gap, or Bergson's duration or virtual time). Eternal objects, therefore, are not temporal forms of relations, but are permanent and infinite quantities that are isolated from their individual essences. They are relata in the uniform schema of relational essences, where each eternal object is located within all of its possible relationships (cf. *SMW,* 164). Whitehead explains that there is a uniform scheme of relationships between eternal objects, which is precisely defined by the impossibility of reducing their infinite quantities by subsuming them under a smaller or integral cipher (i.e., the one, God, or being). Instead, eternal objects remain isolated from each other, embedded as they are in their own infinity. Nevertheless, whilst eternal objects are indifferent to the extensive continuum of actual entities, from whose standpoint eternal objects are pure indeterminacy, they nonetheless acquire an unprecedented togetherness once they are included in an actual entity, and thus gain an individual essence—a certain quality of infinite quantities. This means that for any actual occasion "a," there is a group of eternal objects, which are, as it were, the ingredients of that actual occasion. Since any given group of eternal objects may form the base of an abstractive hierarchy of relation, there is an abstractive hierarchy associated with any actual occasion "a." This associated hierarchy is "the shape, or pattern, or form, of the occasion, insofar as the occasion is constituted by what enters into full realization" (*SMW,* 170). This formal hierarchy thus defines the unity of eternal objects in actualities.

Despite the fact that the order of eternal objects, as pure relata, is not open to modification by spatio-temporal actualities, these objects are nonetheless part and parcel of the eventful becoming of such actualities. In particular, and insofar as these otherwise noncommunicating eternal objects are selected by actual entities to accomplish their "subjective aim," they also acquire unrepeatable unity in actual entities. This unity reveals how eternal objects are also subjected to the irreversible formation of events (or nexuses of actualities) and, indeed, change within the order of actualities (where pure potentiality or indetermination becomes real or determinate potentials). This also means that space-events are at once disjunctions of actual data and conjunctions of eternal objects.

According to Whitehead, eternal objects are internally related to each other only in terms of "a systematic mutual relatedness" wherein each eternal object has a particular status in relation to other objects (*SMW*, 161). Therefore an eternal object "stands a determinateness as to the relationship of *A* [an eternal object] to other eternal objects" (*SMW*, 160). This determinateness suggests that these objects are not fused into one continual eternal form. On the contrary, they are eternal only because they are infinite. Yet they do not share the same kind of infinity. There is no equivalence between the status of an eternal object and another eternal object. Eternal objects are not externally related to each other but only to actual entities, which select them as they grow and change. However, eternal objects also explain the atomistic character of actual entities: their nonrecursive spatio-temporality, which constitutes a slice of duration. The relations between actual entities therefore neither correspond to a mechanical chain of cause and effect and nor can they simply be granted by a metaphysical continuum, a transcendental time described by the infinitesimal degrees of being. Instead, relations are spatio-temporal actualities, and define events as an irreversible disjunction within the order of actualities and a unilateral conjunction of eternal objects. From this standpoint, the extensive continuum of actualities that determines their material ground of sequential connection and recursive calculations splits itself into thousands of quantities, the asymmetrical reassemblage of which becomes a nexus of actualities or a space-event. The extensive continuum is, to say it with Deleuze and Guattari, schizophrenic.

Computational Quantities

Whitehead's mereotopological schema can thus contribute to seeing the computational abstraction of concrete relations under this new light. I will now discuss how this mode of abstraction has become central to digital design, and in particular, to *parametricism,* which Patrick Schumacher has claimed to be the new global style for architecture and design.[18] As an instance of computational abstraction of concrete relations, I argue that digital parameters need to be conceived in terms of actualities, spatio-temporal divisions that are forming a new algorithmic matrix. In particular, Whitehead's mereotopological schema offers us an entry point into the increasingly smaller divisions or partitioning of time, a micro-quantification that is able to calculate the gap between one state and another, or the relation between states. Whitehead's mereotopology resolves the question of partitioning of continual temporality by suggesting that between states there are always an infinite number of actualities, actual regions and subregions of actualities. With parametricism, the dynamic partitioning of the gap between points exposes the persistent function of parts and of the relations between parts, in which wholes are nothing more than parts that connect. These parts—in this case, parametric quantities in computational programming—are discrete entities that change values at different places according to different degrees of relations established by the program and the environmental input, due not only to their capacity to select data that come from the actual ground, but also to their capacity to be infected by data that they are not able to compute. As noted above, this aspect of parametricism can be explained through Whitehead's notion of mereotopology, because the relation between parts and parts and wholes can be seen to lie at the core of his notion of extension or extensive continuum.

Whitehead's mereotopological schema rejected the Leibnizian infinitesimal series and questioned Bergson's predilection for temporal continuity by arguing that what connects points are actual entities on an extensive continuum. Whitehead's mereotopological schema provides an apposite means of suggesting that there is no ontological or metaphysical equivalence between computational abstraction and the world-process. Instead, Whitehead's mereotopology also serves here to suggest that algorithmic parameters, like numbers, are dynamic agents playing their parts in the formation of an algorithmic matrix of infinite spatio-temporalities. The latter are not representations of an actual world of data or of actual spatio-temporal experience that can never be fully quantified. Instead, the digital—and parametric—process of abstraction of physical data cannot but correspond to proliferation of algorithmic or parametric actual entities that cannot be fused with or incorporated by what we know of space and time.

At the core of the mereotopological view of the extensive continuum, there is a persistent nonreciprocal relation between parts and the whole, so that the continuous partitioning of the continuum on behalf of increasingly smaller actualities imposes the view of a constant fractional matrix, never coinciding with its parts. To this end, mereotopology does not reject but insists on the significance of division and quantification in the production of spatio-temporal actualities and new occasions of experience.

Whilst topological continuities are expressions of large assemblages, and these assemblages are able to incorporate discontinuous events into a stream of infinitesimal variations, mereotopology instead accounts for the unalterable encounter between parts and between parts and wholes. From this standpoint, an algorithmic parameter is not only the transduction of physical qualities (such as the volume of a space, gravitational forces, the circulation of air, the movement of people, the shades of light, the sonic frequencies, electromagnetic vibrations, etc.) into finite quantities, but is an actual object itself. Furthermore, the relation between parameters is itself a spatio-temporal actuality that is not visible to the terms of the relation. This is because the abstract potential between parameters cannot be grasped at the level of sequential sets, but needs to be explained as the infinite quantities of abstract relations that infect and add novelty to the actual order of parameters. This means that topological continual relation is only one way of articulating the relation between parts and wholes. The mereotopological schema between eternal objects and actual entities offers another way.

The dominance of topological approaches to explain the relations between parameters is demonstrated for instance by Lynn's calculus-based architectural forms. Here it is that the qualitative relations of vectors constitute space as a fluid environment of forces. Yet this insistence on the capacity of parametric design to account for the dynamic and infinitesimal relations between points, resulting into the proliferation of curving surfaces and morphogenetic forms, corresponds to the temporal design of space, where the capturing of movement defines digital architecture in terms of time. This anti-Euclidean proposition of space has led to the formation of "parametric urbanism" concerned with the inclusion of approximations and emergent qualities that cannot be exactly measured (i.e., approximations to a point) into planning. By conferring fluctuation and movement to the geometrical form as a whole, digital architecture has incorporated the qualitative dimension of the gap between points, the percepts and the affects, into the digital design of temporal space. The ingression of topological connectedness between points has thus resulted in an automated process, whereby algorithms are constantly transducing temporal qualities—affects and percepts—into approximate quantities, thus developing an aesthetic of continual quantities of qualities.

The critique of computational modes of quantification contends that instances of the latter (such as parametricism) are yet another form of measuring the qualitative character of relation. Nevertheless, to argue that computation mainly entails a transduction of qualities into quantities (albeit approximate quantities) is to deny that quantities could ever be more than finite sets of instructions. Yet Whitehead's mereotopological schema adds an abstract schema of infinite objects to the actual continuum, so that the infinite quantities cannot be discerned from qualities. Points of connection are not only finite parts that overlap: the process of overlapping includes the selection of abstract quantities that add a new quantitative character to parts that are already overlapped, and thus reveals the formation of a new actual entity. From this standpoint, I want to suggest that parametric relations are not only transductions of qualities into quantities. They are infected with abstract, non-denumerable quantities, or rather eternal objects: discrete yet permanent infinities that add novel data to the relation between existing parametric processing. From a mereotopological point of view, each parametric extensive relation is hosting another order of quantities that cannot be contained by the number of its actual members.

The topological model implies the permanent ground of movement from which events emerge qua events only when it becomes possible for actualities to jump out of the spatio-temporal grid into the infinity of virtual time. The mereotopological schema suggests instead that events are the cumulative order of spatio-temporal actualities hosting an unrepeatable togetherness of eternal objects. Therefore it is not the formal hierarchy of eternal objects that determine actual events. Instead, events are the result of the actual accumulation of physical data, the causal chain, which is interrupted by the irreversible ingress of eternal objects. These objects are not simply selected by actualities to manage orders of behavior or action, but are prehended for the pure chance or potentialities that these objects offer. Actualities therefore do not simply operate a probabilistic calculation about which eternal object to select. On the contrary, the selection for nonactual ideas involves the ingression of chance into what has happened, what may happen, and what could have happened. This is how contingency becomes intrinsic to the formal architecture of eternal objects: a process by which existing relations can change and fashion themselves anew. This means that the indeterminacy of eternal objects is prehended like the irreversible reality of chance; they offer pure potentialities, and thereby determine the atomic (and eventful) character of actual relations.[19]

If the topology of parametric design implies the continuous calculation of variables, Whitehead's mereotopology, by contrast, always subtracts actual events from overall continuity. Mereotopology therefore suggests that underneath continual morphogenesis there lies a space of random quantities or infinite numbers that cannot be counted as such. These are the black holes that are inherent within probability and statistical calculation and that remark the occurrence of *an infinite variety of infinities* immanent to the actual regions of a nexus of occasions. In parametric design, this space perforated with holes is defined by the intrusion of parasitic data, the surplus of codes that are unable to be united under a morphogenetic continuity.

The parametric design of buildings, cities, environments, and objects does not simply involve the algebraic manipulation of physical data. Instead, the computational abstraction of the extensive continuum of actualities (resulting in parametric relations) involves the addition of chance to actual relations. Parametric design thus confronts those discontinuous infinities constituting finite quantities. This discontinuity explains how the spatio-temporal continuum can become other to the actual relations that compose it. Here, the introduction of novel configurations of space is not derived from the continual variations of form, but from universes of infinite quantities that abduct the actual relations of data, infecting any set of probabilities. If topological continuity involves qualitative transformations, mereotopological discontinuities expose the eruption of uncompressible quantities breaking through any smooth surface. Instead of criticizing computational abstraction as the mere (and reductive) measuring of qualities, this essay suggests that parametric design deals with unsynthesizable orders of quantification (finite and infinite relations), and in consequence it cannot avoid becoming a channel for the proliferation of indetermination within the programming of extensive relations.

Whitehead's mereotopological schema of parts and wholes thus offers another view of the computation of relations that lies at the heart of digital design, and of parametricism in particular. The relational space of data processing is defined by the actuality of the relation, whereby the sequential order of actualities is infected with abstract objects, the indeterminate reality of which adds new character to existing patterns of actual relations. This is not to say, however, that contingent physics is ontologically grounded in the order of eternal geometry.

Mereotopology exposes parametricism to the indeterminate, contingent infinities of urban programming, where abstract quantities add a new level of determination to parametric relations. From the standpoint of mereotopology, these infinite quantities are parts that connect or disconnect with the processing of sequential parameters (considered as a whole). At the same time, this whole processing can also be a part that connects to another. Parts therefore are not the components of a whole, but remain random objects that have the power to change the extant order of actualities.

Following the logic of cause and effect, the relation between parametric data involves a movement from past spatio-temporalities to those of the present and future, all of which are restricted by the physical level of parametric design. Here extension, as Whitehead reminds us, is not the realm of measure, but "the most general scheme of real potentiality" (*PR*, 67), since "all actual occasions are internally and externally extensive,"[20] and are related by means of extension—or, in this case, by parametric quantities, which are veritable actualities amidst the others.

For instance, multi-agent systems,[21] such as BDI (Belief-Desire-Intention) agents,[22] are probability models that operate not through pattern recognition (or according to the connectionism of neural networks), but by developing tendencies and attitudes that lead to thought-actions. Multi-agent systems are not only informed and generated by the interaction between agents and by their local capacities to learn and adapt, but are able to evolve certain inclinations instead of others. These systems can be conceived as forming a nexus of actual entities,[23] and as thereby crafting new possibilities of actual relations. Multi-agent systems are able to prehend[24] (to borrow a term from Whitehead), select, and reactivate variable quantities (changeable and evolving parametric relations) derived from past and simultaneous parameters. In short, multi-agent systems are finite entities composed by the prehensions of both their internal relations (defined, for instance, by the evolving dynamics of genetic algorithms using past data to reengender information) and their external connections, which determine the extensive relationship between parameters. Multi-agent systems are therefore proactive entities that select and rearrange their internal relations and acquire a subjective unity (a subjective form in Whitehead's terms) by which they can ingress the world's external relations by prehending other elements and entities. It is precisely this process of prehension, selection, activation, and assemblage of data that links Whitehead's mereotopological schema of extensive relations to parametric urbanism.

Multi-agent systems for instance point out that endorelations within systems already enjoy a series of external relations of variables. Here a variable becomes part of another cluster of variables, which in turn changes the pack of variables it originated from. In other words, parametric design exposes how endorelations within sets of variables and series of exorelations are faced with irreducible subvariables, which are those irreducible parts that can be detached from the computational design of the whole. Therefore, if we take the relation between a set of parameters A and a set of parameters B, the subsets of A and B are not simply fused in the relation C, but become a new object: a new parametric set equipped with new tendencies, singularities, and powers proper to C. C is not simply the link between relata, but becomes a set of data itself, autonomously establishing new conditions of possibilities not only for C but also for the autonomous subsets of A and B. This is why the coming of C does not mark the disappearance of the A and B subsets, but the extension of their real potentialities in C. If the individual and autonomous subsets of A and B become part of C, because their potential tendencies exceed the local connection between A and B, they are however not neutralized in the whole object C, but retain their unaltered indivisible singularity (or subatomicity). It is however important to bear in mind that according to Whitehead, actual entities—the regions and subregions of A and B—do not endure forever. These entities must exhaust their own set of relations, reach completeness or satisfaction, and thus perish in order for C to become objective data for another set of variables—just as C inherited objectified data and the real potentialities of relations from A and B.

Similarly, the parametric software adaptive structure corresponds to the physical, extensive connection between actual entities, the fusion and integration of parts into wholes. But, this is only the topological level of parametric design. However, a mereotopological reading will have to include another level of relationality, the overlapping and intersection of subatomic parts by means of other parts *(mereology).* In other words, the relation between the distinct planes of actuality implies not their merging but rather their simultaneity as revealed by the actual regions and subregions of intersection, that is, the actuality of the relation itself.

It could be argued that parametric design involves at least two modes of potentialities that define each and any level of actuality. These modes correspond to Whitehead's distinction between the real potential of each actual entity to become the datum of another and the pure potentials (or eternal objects) that enter actual occasions at many points (*PR,* 23). From the standpoint of mereotopology these modes imply at least two orders of magnitude: the order of finite quantities and the order of infinite quantities. This is to say that Whitehead's distinction between the real potential of actual entities and the pure potentials of eternal objects returns in parametric design as the automation of actual relations, as finite and infinite quantities.[25] The computation of relations therefore reveals the presence of an alien spatio-temporal system that intersects the digital design of spatio-temporalities: the advance of space-events or new actual forms of infinite quantities as internal conditions of the parametric order. It is therefore possible to argue that there are computational events corresponding to the actuality of spatio-temporal systems that are irreducible to both the physical and the digital binarism of extension. In the next section, I will discuss the event in terms of automated prehensions and thus clarify what a computational event—or nexus of actualities—can be.

Automated Architecture

Drawing on Whitehead's method of abstraction, it is possible to consider parametric design in terms of an algorithmic process of prehension by which space and time are derived from the ordered world of parametric programming through the transmission of data from the past to the present. From this standpoint, a programmed environment is entangled in a process of parametric prehension, whereby past data enter into a relation with the data of the present. This defines the arrival of novelty not as something that depends on the subjective impressions of interactive users, but rather as involving the parametric prehension of data—a prehension that derives its own regions and spatio-temporal extensions from already programmed sequences.

If parametric urbanism marks the programming of extensive relations, it truly involves the automation of prehensions, and thus a new level of determination of space and time. In other words, digital urbanism is adding a new spatio-temporal system onto the extensive continuum of actualities. Parametric urbanism includes rules for selecting, contrasting, and adopting data from previous sets so as to calculate present and future quantities of relations. It thus entails that parameters can become calculative engines relying on their prehensive capacities to connect variables across different orders. This is not due to a free, unbounded power that parametric design has to generate change in architectural models (i.e., the generative evolution of genotypes forming infinite versions of the same shape). On the contrary, if parameters are not simply executors of commands, it is because they are prehensive operators nesting data within a set, selecting and transforming quantities, and establishing actual nexuses between parameters of various scales and dimensions.

Digital parameters therefore are automated modes of prehension insofar as they are also modes of decision-making that do not simply correspond to the binary states of 0s and 1s. On the contrary, parametric design now implies the computation of continual or topological relations, according to which relations have become objectified, datified as actual entities. Parametric design thus requires no preplanned modeling, but step-by-step procedures of decision-making, according to which the path of the sequence can be reordered in real-time. The prearranged order of parameters therefore remains open to counterdirections derived from the short-term power of decision acquired by automated relations in the process of computation. The computation of relations thus requires that preplanned decisions become substituted by prehensive capacities of decision-making, which afford the parametric system the freedom to establish unintended connections between parameters within the constrained conditions of sequential programming.[26] As Whitehead argued, freedom derives from the power of decision, which implies that an actual entity (a parameter or nexus of parameters in this case) reaches its final cause (or subjective form) by transforming the data received into finite sets of rules. Actual entities can decide the extent to which they can enter in a relational composition with other entities, and in doing so, they exercise a power of freedom or autonomy. This means that not all sets of variables must enter into relation with all parameters encountered in the process, or that some changes in their arrangement are negligible and do not lead to a space-event. In other words, parametricism maintains no overall dictum according to which everything must be connected or kept in a constant state of change. Whilst it is true to say that there is no emptiness between parametric sets, there are at the same time indeterminate degrees of relatedness depending upon the actual prehensions involved.

From this standpoint, one could argue that parametric urbanism may be conceived as a mode of programming extension that is driven by software-prehensive capacities of spatio-temporal division, and not by the topological invariant that gathers all spatio-temporalities into a continuous varying whole. The parametric automation of prehensions does not simply quantify urban qualities of relations, but is set to design the quantitative relation between parameters involving the selection of abstract quantities in the construction of a soft urbanism.[27] Thus the parametric programming of temporal and environmental changes—physical variables, such as humidity, temperature, wind, air circulation, the movement of people, and so on—also involves the design of the causal efficacy of actual entities, the prehension of the physical data of the past that is inherited by the present sequential processing of variables. Even when physical data are introduced into the program in real-time, it is still a matter of how these data from the past are prehended by parameters within the present. This is because the parametric programming of weather variables, for instance, organizes the prehensions of spatio-temporal configurations precisely as the registering of change from one state to another. In short, I suggest that the programming of physical variables coincides with the automated prehension of variables, which result in the registering of change from the past to the present. On the other hand, however, parametric probabilities are not mere representations of physical variables, but rather become a present counteraction on the inherited past.

Parametric design thus also implies the automation of both physical and conceptual prehensions through which data from the past is not simply inherited but transformed in the present. As such, conceptual prehensions define the mental pole of an actual entity (in our case, a parameter or a set of parameters) and its power of decision-making. This latter is informed by the selection of eternal objects, indeterminate quantities infiltrating the arrangement of probabilities in the process of computation. Since parametric relations coincide with spatio-temporal forms of process, potentialities and possibilities built upon regions and subregions of relations, the sequential calculation of probabilities cannot but admit indeterminate quantities in a programmed sequence of rules. These quantities define the actuality of the relation not only in terms of temporality but also, and importantly according to Whitehead's mereotopological schema, as extension. The relation therefore corresponds to an invisible space split from point A and B and yet it explains how A and B can be simultaneous without becoming fused into one. The computation of relations therefore involves the constitution of a new actuality that is reducible neither to the combinatorial mode of digital parameters nor to the interaction of physical variables within digital programming.

From this standpoint, the mereotopological schema offers a strange understanding of parametricism, according to which the latter corresponds to the computational abstraction of relations showing that parameters themselves acquire actuality as they enter into a spatio-temporal nexus. These actualities can be understood here as computational space-events. Events, according to Whitehead, involve the capacity of any actual entity to select and become affected by pure data-objects (or eternal objects in Whitehead's terminology), which define how the indeterminate becomes determinate in any actual entity.

Whitehead's mereotopological schema implies that events come first. Events are the summation of actual entities in a nexus of actualities, which has been infected by an infinite variation of data that have come together for the first, unique, and unrepeatable space-time. From this standpoint, it is possible to contrast the topological view of parametricism, which assumes that variations are to be derived from the relational or *infinitesimal space* of contingencies that lie outside the system (and are then programmed within the urban model, for instance), with the mereotopological insistence that parts, quantities, and discontinuities exist not only at the level of actualities, but also at the general level of formality. This means that Whitehead's mereotopological schema forces us to revisit the computational significance of formal hierarchies in relation to actual contingencies. Contingencies are no longer to be conceived as external to the formal schema (i.e., as a mere factor of extrinsic force); instead, it is here argued that contingency or chance are in fact internal to any formal processing—that they are parts of that formal process that nonetheless remain incompatible with the whole process. This means that patternless quantities—incalculable data—are the unconditional matrix of any logic of computation. As a result, they define the incomputable starting point of any mathematical, physical, or biological order, as well as of the order of culture.

From this standpoint, parametricism can be criticized not for being too abstract, but for not being abstract enough to accommodate the view that indetermination is to be found first of all at the level of formal computation, because it is there that parameters encounter the indeterminate conditions (patternless data) for which they can become eventful. This idea of computational indetermination is based on the mathematical logic of randomness (i.e., lack of structure), whereby "something is random if it can't be compressed into a shorter description. In other words, there is no concise theory that produces it."[28] This notion of randomness is strictly derived from Gregory Chaitin's algorithmic information theory, pointing at the centrality of infinite infinities or of incompleteness within axiomatics to show that randomness corresponds to the maximally unknowable data within computation. Since it is impossible to calculate the size of the smallest program, as Turing and Gödel demonstrated, Chaitin concludes that computational logic implies a program-size complexity, whereby it is the program (the software, the theory, or formalism) and not just its application that shows the existence of patternless infinities, which drive decision-making within any algorithmic set.

Similarly, I have not used the example of parametricism to claim that novelty in computation is to be derived from external factors, or for instance from means of interaction between software and hardware, which supposedly explains, according to some designers, how digital urbanism can develop dynamic planning able to adapt to infrastructural variations. This is not what is argued here. Instead, my argument is driven by the possibility offered by the mereotopological schema of finding the conditions for novelty in the digital conception and programming of spatio-temporality. I suggested that the discontinuous architecture of eternal objects corresponds to the infinite varieties of infinities (whereby there is no ultimate plane to engulf them all) and not to the continuous variations of a whole (as represented by the topological model of continuous transformation of shapes). Eternal objects therefore are not just eternal qualities of objects, such as the intensive qualification of a chair that constitutes *chairness* (the capacity of the chair to function as a seat). On the contrary, taking inspiration from Whitehead's mereotopological schema, I argue that eternal objects are infinite varieties of parts that acquire relational continuity only once they enter, are selected by, or infect actualities. Hence, a whole as a relational continuity is a discrete unity, a part that exists in this actual entity and not in any other. In other words, a whole is neither smaller nor bigger than its parts but is split into parts that do not necessarily communicate with one another (i.e., they do not communicate by means of a principle of sufficient reason).

This essay has perhaps forced an unnatural juxtaposition of the formal level of randomness (patternless data) with the formal schema of eternal objects. But this forcing is not arbitrary. It is simply a means of arguing for the underestimated significance of infinite varieties of quantities in the computational method of abstraction and in particular in the programming of spatio-temporality in digital architecture. It is suggested here that the nonnegotiable power of random data (i.e., data that cannot be compressed in an elegant theory, theorem, or program) is the very unconditional condition for a novel formalism of digital space that does not simply extend software to an interactive relation with hardware or with the physical environment. From this standpoint, mereotopological discontinuity is not conceived as an alternative to the topological transformation of space, which is ontologically grounded in relational continuity. If anything, the mereotopological schema of discontinuous data can help us to address the randomness of a computational event. The latter instead requires that indeterminate data become decisional quantities in the cumulative processing of nonequivalent actualities. These indeterminate data are not simply subsumed within an extant (albeit changing) process. Instead, they define spatio-temporal events, which arrive and perish, without constituting a continual surface of variation.

To put it in another way: the topological ontology of parametricism implies that the event is programmed before it can happen, thus flattening novelty (or event) onto a topological matrix of continual coevolution, reciprocal presupposition, or structural coupling. Yet against this, and whilst borrowing from Whitehead's mereotopological schema of relation, it is possible to suggest that parts do not become a whole: instead, parts (e.g., eternal objects) are infinite infinites that join together and become a whole (the unity of eternal objects in actual entities) that itself remains a part (an actual entity) that connects to another (actual entity). This is also to say that if the topological aesthetics of parametricism harnesses events in its own morphogenetic body, mereotopology reveals that the computational abstraction from the world implies the eventuation of new actualities, breaking spatio-temporalities that characterize the becoming of the extensive continuum: the arrival of a new spatio-temporality out of sync with the entire system of relations *qua* smooth variations.

Against the metaphysics of the whole (Being, Time, or God), Whitehead's mereotopology suggests that the relations between actualities are to be explained by other spatio-temporal parts. Similarly, I propose that the critical reading of digital architecture cannot reduce computational abstractions to already programed and finite productions of spatio-temporalities. Instead, I claim that the digital parts are derived from the unconditional non-denumerable infinities or by the ontological power of randomness. Since digital architecture capitalizes on the capacity of relations to smooth edges and permeate boundaries, it seems important to engage with the question of relationality itself in order to demystify the dominant role that topological continuity has acquired in describing the ontology of extension. In particular, I argue that the insistence on the temporal quality of relations and thus the inclusion of real-time and contingent variations within planning through parametric software is being underdetermined by the infinite quantities that disrupt the order of parametric relations.

From this standpoint, parametricism (or the computational abstraction of relationality) is not simply another instance of the smooth environment of ubiquitous digitality. On the contrary, parametricism can instead be taken to suggest that the smooth surface of continuous variations is in fact exposed to computational interferences, blind spots, or space-events that cannot be compressed in finite quantities.

Events, therefore, do not grant continuity between entities, but on the contrary are the occasions for the discontinuous becoming of the continual order of actualities. This explanation however only helps us to describe the actual level of novel spatio-temporality. Actual novelty instead does not come from nowhere, and does not exclusively concern the physical realm. Novelty must also be explained at the level of abstraction, or in our case computational abstraction. The mereotopological schema of eternal objects and actual entities proposed by Whitehead affords metaphysical support to what in information theory is increasingly becoming unavoidable: the presence of the randomness at the heart of formalism. This formal reality of randomness (the fact that non-computable data are now an 'unknown probability and not an impossibility for computational programming) is here taken as the unconditional condition that makes any mode of computation (analog or digital) possible.

This unconditional stance has to be found within the computational processing of algorithms, at the formal and axiomatic level. It is suggested here that random data can reveal a strange contingency within form, or indeterminate chance within programming. From this standpoint, randomness interrupts the topological coevolution and interactive modes of continuous adaptation between the use of urban software and urban behavior. Far from establishing a continuous feedback or reversible function whereby software takes command over urban behavior or the latter acts back on the program, the sequential running of algorithms instead inevitably confronts the infinite quantities of rules for each quality of behavior, which result in the proliferation of unprovable and inapplicable computational spatio-temporalities. It is my argument that randomness triggers contingency within computational rules and, in the particular case of parametricism, in the digital design of urban space.

This new dominance of contingency within programming demarcates the unquantifiable reality of an abstract space-event and the impossibility for physical space to be one with these events. In particular, digital urbanism is invaded by computational events that are at once discovered and constructed by the software programming of actual spatio-temporalities. From this standpoint, parametricism is a case in which the digital design of time and space is not simply set to program the emergence of events, but is instead unleashing unlived spatio-temporal relations into the urban worlds of the everyday. These space-events are symptoms of the concreteness of digital architecture, which, it is now clear, can never absolutely match the physicality of actual space. I do not consider this mismatch to be a failure. Instead, it points at a schizophrenic and nonreversible situation whereby the programs used to organize urban infrastructure are constructing and/or revealing an infrastructure of another kind, thereby exposing the all too real realm of data-volumes, data-density, and data-architecture.

Notes

1. Greg Lynn, "Architectural Curvilinearity: The Folded, the Pliant and the Supple," *Architectural Design* 63, nos. 3–4 (March–April 1993): 22–29. Kipnis Jeffrey, "Towards a New Architecture," in *Space Reader: Heterogeneous Space in Architecture,* ed. Michael Hensel, Christopher Hight, Achim Menges (London: John Wiley & Sons, 2009), 112. Giuseppa Di Cristina, "Topological Tendency in Architecture," in *Architecture and Science,* ed. Di Cristina (New York: Wiley, 2001).

2. For specific examples about parametric architecture see "Digital Cities," special issue, *Architectural Design* 79, no. 4 (July–August 2009): 1–135, i–iii; "Material Computation: Higher Integration in Morphogenetic Design," special issue, *Architectural Design* 82,

no. 2 (March–April 2012): 1–144, i–iii; "Computation Works: The Building of Algorithmic Thought," special issue, *Architectural Design* 83, no. 2 (March–April 2013): 1–152, i–iii.

3. For instance, a molecule, as a moving body, experiencing local changes is not an actual occasion, but a nexus of occasions and thus an event.

4. This argument against Whitehead's process metaphysics can be found in Graham Harman, *Guerrilla Metaphysics: The Carpentry of Things* (Peru, Ill.: Open Court, 2005), 82–83.

5. Ibid.

6. As opposed to the universal and absolute conceptions of space-time, Whitehead argues that the mutual prehension of things defines the very condition for spatiality. For instance, in the concert hall, the mutual prehension of the volume of sound, the forms of instruments, the distribution of the orchestra, the mathematical analysis of each momentary sound, the musical score are all implicated in the experience of an immediate specious present. See *MT*, 84.

7. Whitehead points to a double movement (and causality) of form and process, which requires actualities to become infected with potentialities, atomic entities to be related by means of potential divisions of their continual relations (*MT*, 96–97).

8. Whitehead specifies that an eternal object is "any entity whose conceptual recognition does not involve a necessary reference to any definite actual entities of the temporal world" (*PR*, 44).

9. Whitehead used mereotopology to explain the spatialization and temporalization of extension. See *PR*, 294–301.

10. The analysis of parthood relations (*mereology*, from the Greek *mero*, "part") was an ontological alternative to set theory. It dispensed with abstract entities and treated all objects of quantification as individuals. As a formal theory, mereology is an attempt to set out the general principles underlying the relationships between a whole and its constituent parts, as opposed to set theory's search for the principles that underlie the relationships between a class and its constituent members. As is often argued, mereology could not however explain by itself the notion of a whole (a self-connected whole, such as a stone or a whistle, as opposed to a scattered entity of disconnected parts, such as a broken glass, an archipelago, or the sum of two distinct cuts). Whitehead's early attempts to characterize his ontology of events provide a good exemplification of this mereological dilemma. For Whitehead, a necessary condition for two events to have a sum was that they were at least "joined" to each other, that is, connected (despite being or not being discrete). These connections, however, concerned spatiotemporal entities, and could not be defined directly in terms of plain mereological primitives. To resolve the bounds of mereology, the microscopic discontinuity of matter (and its atomic composition) had to be overcome. The question of what characterized an object required topological, and not mereological, analysis. From this standpoint, two distinct events could be perfectly spatiotemporally colocated without *occupying* the spatiotemporal region at which they are *located*, and could therefore share the region with other entities. The combination of mereology and topology contributed to Whitehead's articulation of the notion of the extended continuum. See Roberto Casati and Achille C. Varzi, *Parts and Places: The Structures of Spatial Representation* (Cambridge, Mass.: MIT Press, 1999), 13–17, 51–54, 76–77; and *PR*, 294–301.

11. An occasion of experience, according to Whitehead, implies a certain unique togetherness in experience. See *PR*, 189–90.

12. In particular, Whitehead used the notion of mereotopology to suggest that the mathematical-geometric order had to be separated from the physical world so as to explain their relations formally, by making measurement as determinate as possible. According to Whitehead, the general theory of relativity equates the relational structures of geometry with contingent relations of facts, and thus loses sight of the logical relations that would make cosmological measurement possible. This is why Whitehead's mereotopological approach insists on the spatialization and temporalization of extension, whereby "physical time is the reflection of genetic divisibility into coordinate divisibility" (*PR*, 289). Whitehead argued that the solution to this problem was to separate the necessary relations of geometry from the contingent relations of physics, so that one's theory of space and gravity could be "biometric," that is, built from the two metrics of geometry and physics. See *PR*, 283–87; 294–301; 327–29.

13. In particular, and contrary to Whitehead, Bergson's theory of time, the qualitative time of the *élan vital,* is opposed to the metric time of scientific epistemology, thus identifying the necessity of abstraction with the imperatives of the scientific enterprise. Whitehead, on the contrary, seeks to separate geometrico-mathematical abstraction from physical actualities to propose a more rigorous metaphysical schema of relations. See Henri Bergson, *Creative Evolution,* trans. Arthur Mitchell (New York: Random House, 1994), 358–65, 374–80.

14. Henri Bergson, *Matter and Memory,* trans. N. M. Paul and W. S. Palmer (New York: Zone Books, 1991), 133–78.

15. As Whitehead explains, each actual entity is atomic as it is spatiotemporally extended. See *PR*, 77.

16. Alfred N. Whitehead, "The Relational Theory of Space," trans. P. J. Hurley, *Philosophy Research Archives,* no. 5 (1979): 712–41.

17. In the relational theory, Whitehead discussed the connection between points and objects as a causal action occurring between atomic units not in the spatial dimension, but only in the temporal (*PR*, 37). However, the method of extensive abstraction or the extensive continuum mapped the interrelated structures of events according to a geometry that deployed the uniform relatedness of nature, especially of spatio-temporal relations and the topological priority of events. Modern topology distinguishes between many different types of connectivity (connected, locally connected, pathways connected, and so on). Whitehead's mereotopological model of the extensive continuum instead specifically concerned the interrelation between the actual occasions that define the spatio-temporal order of nature. See *PR*, 148.

18. Patrick Schumacher recently claimed that parametricism is the dominant style of today's avant-garde, characterizing the power of large-scale urban schemes. See Patrick Schumacher, "Parametricism: A New Global Style for Architecture and Urban Design," *Architectural Design* 79, no. 4 (July–August 2009): 14–24.

19. As Whitehead specifies, "In the essence of each eternal object there stands an indeterminateness which expresses its indifferent patience for any mode of ingression into any actual occasion" (*SMW*, 171).

20. As Whitehead observed, actual occasions are the entities that become and thus constitute a continuously extensive world. In other words, whereas extensiveness becomes, "becoming" is not itself extensive, but atomic. The ultimate metaphysical truth

is atomism. The creatures are atomic. In each cosmic epoch, according to Whitehead, there is a creation of continuity. See *PR*, 35, 77.

21. Multi-agent systems are composed of interactive intelligent agents used to solve problems and make rational decisions spanning from online trading, disaster response, and the modeling of social structures. See Ken Binmore, Cristiano Castelfranchi, James Doran, and Michael Wooldridge, "Rationality in Multi-Agent Systems," *Knowledge Engineering Review*, no. 3 (1998): 309–14.

22. The Belief-Desire-Intention (BDI) software model is a program for Intelligent Agents using the notions of belief, desire, and intention to solve problems in agent programming. Chang-Hyun Jo, "A New Way of Discovery of Belief, Desire, and Intention in the BDI Agent-Based Software Model," *Journal of Advanced Computational Intelligence and Intelligent Informatics* 7, no. 1 (2004): 1–3. Inspired by Michael Bratman's theory of human practical reasoning, where intention and desire are considered as pro-attitudes (mental attitudes concerned with action), the model focuses on problem-solving concerned with plans and planning, and does not just allow the programming of intelligent agents. Michael Bratman, *Intention, Plans, and Practical Reason* (Cambridge Mass.: MIT Press, 1999). According to Manuel DeLanda, these multi-agent systems develop an attitude towards the meaning of sentences, propositions, and semantic content. For instance, the belief and desire of agents can change and develop a new attitude towards sentences, which leads to a new set of consequences for the workings of the system. BDI agents, as opposed to neural nets that operate on pattern recognition and extraction, are susceptible to language. The field of parametric design, according to DeLanda, needs BDI agents to model complex urban conglomerates, but it can also benefit from cellular automata to model specific and complete levels and scales of spatio-temporal interaction. Hence, it is only through the interaction of a population of models that specific domains and their singular levels and scales of interaction can be fully designed. See Manuel DeLanda "Theorizing the Parametric," paper presented at University of Southern California conference on "Intensive Fields—New Parametric Techniques in Urbanism," Los Angeles, December 12, 2009; see podcast at http://arch-pubs.usc.edu/parasite/intensive-fields/video-archive/.

23. Whitehead's notion of a nexus of actual entities may be particularly relevant to describe the architecture of multi-agent systems, which is based on the nexus between variable quantities composed by internal relations and external connections. In particular, actual entities are finite units and have an extension in space and time. Whitehead also calls actual entities "microscopic atomic occasions" (*PR*, 508), by which he means that actual entities enter a process of concrescence moving from an initial status or facts (or for instance an initial variable quantity) coinciding with a macroscopic view to a final status or fact (or a changed quantity) defining the microscopic view. In other words, an actual occasion reaches a subjective unity, becoming a final fact through its concrescence. Thus actual entities are divisible but undivided. Actual entities perish, terminate, and become complete quantities through a process of internal division and external connection that forms the architecture of a nexus, involving the development of actual entities in time with all their changes. Similarly, multi-agent systems can be conceived as a nexus of finite actual entities, variable quantities acquiring a microscopic unity.

24. Whitehead's abstract scheme defines prehension (or relation within actual entities) as marking the genetic division of the extensive continuum. This means that pro-

cesses are generated by relations within actual entities via the notion of inclusion (or genetic division) and between actual entities via overlapping or external connectivity (coordinate division and strains). See *PR*, 114–15.

25. On the categorical distinction between pure and real potentialities, see *PR*, 23.

26. The divergence in the trajectory of a path from its initial conditions characterizes the physics of chaos and complexity theory. Whilst deterministic chaos is, like every empirical phenomenon, entirely determined in principle by linear cause and effect, chaos physics has pointed out that the cause of chaos cannot be traced back in a linear fashion. From the standpoint of far-from equilibrium dynamics, there is no deterministic efficient causality for all the particles in the universe. As Shaviro points out, such a position violates Whitehead's ontological principle (that everything actual must come from somewhere) and the reformed subjectivist principle (that everything actual must be disclosed in the experience of some actual subject). Hence, even God is not omnipotent, but subjected to restrictions. Steven Shaviro, *Without Criteria: Kant, Whitehead, Deleuze, and Aesthetics* (Cambridge Mass.: MIT Press, 2009), 17.

27. Marco Vanucci, "Open Systems: Approaching Novel Parametric Domains," in *From Control to Design: Parametric/Algorithmic Architecture*, ed. Michael Meredith, Tomoto Sakamoto, Albert Ferre (New York: Actar D USA, 2008), 118.

28. Gregory J. Chaitin, *Exploring Randomness* (London: Springer-Verlag, 2001), 18.

Part III

PROCESS ECOLOGY

ELEVEN

Possessive Subjects

A Speculative Interpretation of Nonhumans

Didier Debaise

Translated by Thomas Jellis

Whitehead's philosophy can be renewed in the context of a reconstruction of the thought of the subject. This is the hypothesis to which I would like to give sense by starting with a proposition: "apart from the experiences of subjects there is nothing, nothing, nothing, bare nothingness" (*PR*, 167).[1] If we make an immediate abstraction of the repetitive form that gives it a particular status, this proposition at first seems to smoothly extend some of the principal events of contemporary philosophy. Let us limit ourselves to one of the major references constituting the interior space from which Whitehead constructs his own philosophy, the philosophy of Bergson. Had he not already affirmed, two decades before Whitehead, that the most certain point of an investigation of nature should necessarily go by the analysis of a privileged perspective—namely, our own? The first phrases of *Creative Evolution* go in this direction: the "existence of which we are most assured and which we know best is unquestionably our own, for of every other object we have notions which may be considered external and superficial, whereas, of ourselves, our perception is internal and profound."[2]

Whitehead himself, a few years before his proposition, affirmed in his book *The Concept of Nature,* without apparent reservation, that the notion of nature should be entirely reconstructed on the basis of a perceptive, human experience. To the question "What is nature?" Whitehead therefore proposed a definition that recentered the concept on our perception: "Nature is that which we observe in perception through the senses. In this sense-perception we are aware of something which is not a thought and which is self-contained for thought" (*CN,* 3). We have, with sense perception, a vague awareness of something that exceeds our thought and does not depend upon it. What we experience is the existence of events that indicate others more or less confusedly: we perceive a room indicating the existence of a building of which it is a part and, more vaguely, the existence of other buildings, other events. The objects of our perception are sections, blocks, bits, cut-outs, and partial events that point toward others with which they are linked. In the end, it is all a complex system of events that is indicated in our immediate perception, events that are at once relative to these and independent, as they maintain direct relations with each other. In the end, "the immediate fact for awareness is the whole occurrence of nature" (*CN*, 14).

But why then does Whitehead insist so strongly, several years later, on asserting that beyond subjective experience there is *nothing?* Why, if this proposition only extends to previous axes of contemporary philosophy, does Whitehead announce this as a point of bifurcation, the sign of a new orientation or a new philosophical scene? Can we see only the simple radicalization of an already started trajectory in which this proposition came to insert itself? On the contrary, it seems to me that by simply holding on to what is said, in the literality of this proposition, we cannot maintain the idea of continuity. This is because Whitehead does not limit himself to affirming the central position of the subject or of sense-consciousness in the experience of nature; he goes much further by adopting a position on nature in general. Alongside Bergson and his previous works, there is certainly a comparable extension, an "effort to go beyond the human state,"[3] in a passage on which Gilles Deleuze comments by affirming that this consists of opening "up to the inhuman and the superhuman (durations which are inferior or superior to our own), to go beyond the human condition: This is the meaning of philosophy."[4] However, one way or another, this experience of the infra- and the suprahuman should, according to Bergson, necessarily pass through this mixed situation of the human as the bearer of dimensions that go beyond it in the both directions. Whitehead's proposition is by contrast, as I wish to show, directly ontological, or more precisely, according to his own terms, cosmological. This is not an affirmation that we cannot go beyond our own experience as subjects, but the adoption of a position on the reality of nature as such.

The hypothesis that I wish to defend here, as it seems to actualize Whitehead's philosophy and rejoin its linked tendencies to a pluralist vision of nature, is that the question of the subject acquires a novel dimension by becoming an ontological question, a question of nature itself, independently of a perceiving, exclusively human, subject. Put simply, I think that

Whitehead's proposition can be taken up as part of an investigation into nonhuman subjects of nature, or what I would call more generally, the "subjects of nature." Ultimately, the question to which this work gives meaning could be formulated in the following way: what is a nonanthropological subject?[5]

A World of Possessions

Therefore, the first task of a metaphysics of subjects consists in problematizing approaches that would prioritize human beings. For this, one needs to rethink the notion by provisionally bracketing out all the categories that tend to obfuscate its current usage, and have overdetermined the meaning. The question one needs to pose in the framework of a metaphysical restoration is thus: Does a notion of the subject preexist its attachment to categories such as intentionality, consciousness, or representation? What would be the main components and their number? If the problem is effectively formulated by Whitehead, the question remains without an unequivocal answer from him. We can simply try to pick up the heterogeneous lines of conceptual developments that cross his philosophy and meet where the notion of the subject could acquire its own consistency. By first approximation, I would propose to define the Whiteheadian subject as a beam of "feelings." Here, "feeling" alludes to notions such as "sensation," the "sentiment of something," the "impression," a "vague conscience," "emotions," but also the verb to sense or, more precisely, "sentient being." Whitehead attributes it to all the forms of subjective experience in nature. In this way, for example,

> a jellyfish advances and withdraws, and in so doing, exhibits some perception of causal relationship with the world beyond itself; a plant grows downwards to the damp earth, and upwards towards the light. There is thus some direct reason for attributing dim, slow feelings of casual nexus, although we have no reason for any ascription of the definite percepts. (*PR*, 176–77)

We can inscribe the project of a general theory of feelings in an ongoing polemic against Kantian philosophy:

> The philosophy of organism aspires to construct a critique of pure feeling, in the philosophical position in which Kant put his *Critique of Pure Reason*. This should also supersede the remaining Critiques required in the Kantian philosophy. Thus in the organic philosophy Kant's "Transcendental Aesthetic" becomes a distorted fragment of what should have been his main topic. The datum

includes its own interconnections, and the first stage of the process of feeling is the reception into the responsive conformity of feeling whereby the datum, which is mere potentiality, becomes the individualized basis for a complex unity of realization. (*PR*, 113)

The notion of feeling would thus become the first term of a new "aesthetic"[6] and, with it, as the subject is nothing more than a multiplicity of feelings, an "aesthetic" redefinition of subjects of nature. Whitehead is rather elusive as to this rethinking *[reprise]* of the aesthetic. However, it seems possible to me to extend the elements given in the preceding quotation and to imagine the limits that Whitehead would express on the aesthetic project, in the Kantian sense, and with it, most of its future inheritance. Therefore, the main limit would be that while the aesthetic continues to be thought within a framework of a theory of faculties, as pointing to one among several, it is the "capacity (receptivity) to obtain representation through the way in which we are affected by objects."[7] Indeed, the aesthetic tends to designate a subject's modes of receptivity, the manner in which it is affected by sensory data *[les doneeés des sens]*. When we limit the aesthetic by inscribing it within a human faculty, we risk subtracting all aesthetic dimensions that are immanent to it, as if nature was not already populated by a multiplicity of ways of being affected, of feeling, of hoping, or of fearing. This complex operation by which nature is emptied of all its aesthetic qualities—or, in a less radical reading, made opaque to its aesthetic dimensions, to then attribute these to a perceiving subject that would project them beyond itself—is an expression of what Whitehead calls the "bifurcation of nature." It is in a different context, notably in the analysis of the emergence of the modern sciences, that Whitehead develops this critique of the bifurcation of nature, but it could also very well be applied here in the context of the limitations of the aesthetic:

Another way of phrasing this theory which I am arguing against is to bifurcate nature into two divisions, namely into the nature apprehended in awareness and the nature which is the cause of awareness. The nature which is in fact apprehended in awareness holds within it the greenness of the trees, the song of the birds, the warmth of the sun, the hardness of the chairs, and the feel of the velvet. The nature which is the cause of awareness is the conjectured system of molecules and electrons which so affects the mind as to produce the awareness of apparent nature. (*CN*, 30–31)

Against this bifurcation between "real nature" and "apparent nature," Whitehead affirms that "the red glow of the sunset should be as much part of nature as are the molecules and electric waves" (*CN*, 29). The "aesthetic" must not be displaced from the way in which nature is experienced, but must be replaced as a factor of existence. It is no exaggeration to affirm that for Whitehead it becomes "ontological." All beings should have their own aesthetic, a singular way in which they are affected by nature, a particular form of expression. It is a theory of expressive modes in nature that Whitehead, implicitly, aims at by attempting to generalize the aesthetic, to displace it from the oppositional space between nature and the perceiving subject, in order to make it the first term of the very existence of nature. Each "fact" is already inside, at the center of an aesthetic, already animated by "interconnections," "conformities" to other experiences, already profoundly relational.[8]

The question that I was initially posing—"what is a nonanthropological subject?"—has transformed into a new question, highlighting the constitutive operation of such a subject. It becomes instead: What is a feeling? It is the notion of feeling that we must now specify. By taking this in its most habitual form, it will thus be possible to extract the more ontological dimensions. What do we wish to mean when we say, for example, that an animal senses a danger that suddenly disturbs its milieu or when we have the feeling that a situation could change, could become dangerous or enjoyable? Is it the same experience as that of a body affected by diverse sensory impressions expressing that it feels its milieu? In its most general form, the feeling means at once the fact that the data of the world are "integrated," taken into account, and that the data are under a particular mode. If a particular milieu becomes disturbing, it is because the data that constitute it have become partially disturbing in the perspective of an experience that is in the making. In the same way, if the body feels its environment, it is across sense organs that integrate the facts under a particular form, according to a singular filter: it is through the eye that things are seen, and it is with the hand that tactile sensations are experienced.[9] Other senses are equivalent to other ways of polarizing the data of the world.[10]

In one sense, all the experiences express, according to an extremely wide variety of processes of integration or capture: nutrition, tactile impressions, sight, or even predation. Call it what you will, a feeling is above all a capture, a particular way of possessing,[11] an activity through which something "appropriates the datum so as to make it its own" (*PR*, 164). We can go further in taking from the preceding examples the ontological characteristics that are implicated therein, by affirming that all centers of experience are the capture of immediate data that form the environment, and, step by step, the universe in its totality. What the alert animal senses is not a particular datum that would confirm the reasons for a danger; it is the entire universe under the modality of danger; everything becomes expressive of danger. In its ontological form, we would therefore say that each feeling is the totality of the universe that is felt: the aesthetic becomes cosmological. Whitehead here extends the project of a monadology, where monads are all centers of experience, of perspectives, and are composed of all the others. Or as Leibniz puts it, "every substance is like a complete world and like a mirror of God or of the whole universe, which one expresses in its own way, somewhat as the same city is variously represented depending upon the different positions from which it is viewed."[12] Thus the traces of all events are found in each individual subject, and "when we consider carefully the connection of things, we can say that from all time in Alexander's soul there are vestiges of everything that has happened to him."[13]

By affirming that the history of the universe, without exception, is felt, that each event, as insignificant as it may be at first, leaves a trace that marks all the others, this theory of feeling seems to go very far. Yet, despite this unprecedented enlargement, it is not sufficient for Whitehead. Strangely, this still overly limits feeling. To say that all the universe is felt, that is to say captured or possessed, according to a perspective, is not enough. For Whitehead it is missing a fundamental dimension: the trace of all the possibilities that accompany a feeling.

> A feeling bears on itself the scars of its birth; it recollects as a subjective emotion its struggle for existence; it retains the impress of what it might have been, but is not. It is for this reason that what an actual entity has avoided as a datum for feeling may yet be an important part of its equipment. The actual cannot be reduced to mere matter of fact in divorce from the potential. (*PR*, 226–27)

This is what Peirce calls in his "*Pragmatism*," a "would be,"[14] a possibility. What could have been, the choices made and the selections that took place, define a subject as much as what it actually is. The feeling carries with it all the "would bes," the eventualities that the subject had to dismiss in its actual existence, all the alternatives that were presented to it. The fact that Caesar may not have crossed the Rubicon—that another world than the one that we have inherited could have existed, linked to this act that it excluded—gives all its importance and its singular form to the fact that he did actually cross it. The hesitation within a particular action shows that possibles are envisaged, all of which form trajectories of existences left in suspense to the benefit of one of them. If they are actually excluded, they remain no less crucial to the acts performed. In this way, all positive feeling, all capture, is permanently accompanied by a constellation of feelings of avoidance, of refusal, of rejection of the possible that amplify their importance. This is what Whitehead means when he writes that the "actual cannot be reduced to mere matter of fact in divorce from the potential" (*PR*, 227).

However, the importance of these feelings of the possibilities that are not actualized should not be exaggerated. If the possible worlds, felt, attached to each of our actions, to each feeling, are constitutive of these, they would be only pure abstraction, undone of all real inscription, if they were not directly linked and engaged in the actions-in-act, in the making. The eventuality, the hesitation when faced with a choice and the traces left behind by the rejection of a possibility, are only real through the acts that actually happen. There is certainly a primacy in the experience, a primacy that we could take as ontological, of effective feelings on the possible, of the act on power. This point seems to me to be fundamental as it marks Whitehead's refusal of all evaluation of the possibles released from their real action; what interests him are the possibles crystalized in the acts, incarnated in actual subjects. Whitehead provides a historical example: the battle of Waterloo.

> This battle resulted in the defeat of Napoleon, and in a constitution of our actual world grounded upon that defeat. But the abstract notions, expressing the possibilities of another course of history which would have followed upon his victory, are relevant to the facts which actually happened. We may not think it of practical importance that imaginative historians should dwell upon such hypothetical alternatives. But we confess their relevance in thinking about them at all, even to the extent of dismissing them. (*PR*, 185)

In a more or less intense way, according to the situations in which we are engaged in our actual world, we inherit the possibilities linked to another course of history than that of Napoleon's defeat. All feeling relative to that event carries with it the trace of the fact that it may not have taken place, and that eventuality does not float in an ethereal world of abstractions but is inscribed, almost corporeally, in feeling.

Modes of Existence of Subjects

So what exactly is the relation between feelings and the subject? If the aesthetic, and with it the question of an ontology of feeling, becomes paramount and extends to all aspects of nature, the fact remains that there is indeed, at one time or another, a "subject" that feels. This raises the question of primacy: Is it the subject, now designating all centers of experience and no longer only the anthropological subject, which we can say feels, experiences, or is affected by the world? Or, by contrast, do we have to postulate that feelings are primarily without subject? To answer this, Whitehead distinguishes between two meanings of the word "subject,"[15] which are drawn from two distinct traditions of the history of philosophy and which he tries to reunify:[16] the subject can be thought either as *subjectum*, or as *superjacio*. Let us start with the first meaning. The subject as "subjectum" highlights notions such as "to be placed below," "to be put beneath something." If we link such a meaning to the question of feelings, then we can say that the subject, in this first form, appears as the "support" or the "base" for feeling, at once set back, placed behind, and what gives them sense. Everything happens as if the subject was in complete possession of "its" feelings, which would be, with more or less force, like accidents affecting the identity or expressing superficial aspects. If this vision of a possessive subject of its feelings has imposed itself, especially in modern philosophy, it is because it effectively manifested certain fundamental traits of the experience. It expressed the sentiment that all experience is polarized, oriented toward a subject that is at the center and from which emanate expressive qualities: affective tonalities, sounds, colors, tactile sensations, and so on. To the extent that these feelings seem to indicate a subject toward which they tend, the subject can indeed appear as the support from which feelings originate.

How, then, does Whitehead manage to take on as his own this first vision of the subject? Quite simply, by inverting the order of causes. This impression of a support or a foundation for feelings, the sense that there is a subject from which feelings seem to derive—these common and indisputable impressions to which philosophies of the subject have tried to give a theoretical basis—are the effect of a process and not its end. Whitehead provides an example: "Descartes in his own philosophy conceives the thinker as creating the occasional thought. The philosophy of organism inverts the order, and conceives the thought as a constituent operation in the creation of the occasional thinker. The thinker is the final end whereby there is the thought" (*PR*, 151). Most of the time, thought by no means requires that we connect it to any subject, but if, in retrospect, we attempt to chart the stages of development of these thoughts, we would add the subject that actually derives from the thought. In this way, the subject is understood as being in full possession of itself and, by derivation, of its feeling (or, as Whitehead would say, of its thoughts); seemingly beneath its affections and supporting them, the subject must not be considered as a first reality but on the contrary as the retroactive term of a "series of experiences,"[17] the moment where this becomes fully itself, acquiring its own fullness. The subject appears as the moment where the feelings are crystalizing in a unified experience, a complex of feeling having become a singular experience.

We can very easily generalize this inversion and redeploy it to all centers of experience in nature: an animal, for example, is a multiplicity of centers of experience, which are "the various parts of its body" (*MT,* 23) with their feelings, their particular ways of being affected and of putting themselves in relation with the wider environment of their experience. Yet these multiple centers of experience, which are the parts of its body, are no less related to each other as "one centre of experience" (*MT,* 23) that enables communication within this multiplicity of corporeal centers and forms a complex unity, living and manifesting itself as *this* sentient animal. Each center of experience of its body is a subject, in the sense that it expresses a plurality of feelings situated in one point of experience, but the ensemble of these "centres of experience," as much as they converge towards a superior unity, also form a subject that is the animal as a complex unity of experiences. Such a superior unity is not always required; for example, "in the case of vegetables, we find bodily organizations which decisively lack any one centre of experience with a higher complexity either of expressions received or in-born data" (*MT,* 24). Certainly we find a multiplicity of small centers of experience, but it is not necessary that these are subordinated to a superior center. As Whitehead puts it, a "vegetable is a democracy; an animal is dominated by one, or more centers of experience. But such domination is limited, very strictly limited. The expressions of the central leader are relevant to that leader's reception of data from the body" (*MT,* 24). Thus, this vision of the subject as "subjectum" reflects an important part of the experience of feelings but as an effect (the final phase) of their consolidation,[18] the final term of a process where the feelings, step by step, condense *[se densifient]* into a unified experience, an experience of self: *this* part of a body, *this* animal, *this* thinker.

Yet by itself, this understanding of the subject is, even if redeployed within a new logic of its relation to feelings, insufficient. It does not dispense with the argument that although we can go as far as we wish in displacing the reemergence of the subject, putting it at the beginning or at the end, it still remains that at one moment or another, a subject is constituted and distinguishes itself from its feelings. How can we avoid the vicious circle implied by the fact that the subject, even taken to its most minimal form, can be explained only by something that would already be subjective? It is here that Whitehead takes another meaning of the notion of subject, affiliated with another tradition: the subject as "superjacio." We can translate this with a series of expressions such as "throw over," "throw towards," but also "to exceed" or "to cross." It is a subject of which we can say that it is in some ways in advance of itself, virtually already there in each feeling. It is less a fully realized subject than a tendency: the "aim is at that complex of feeling which is at the enjoyment of those data in that way" (*MT*, 152). Everything is in the way, in the manner or mode: the way in which experience is made, the way in which something is felt, the way of experiencing. This constitutes the precision of the aesthetic that I was describing earlier: each center of experience is characterized by its own way, a tonality that distinguishes it from all the others.[19] There is no need to postulate an autonomous subject and possessor of its experiences to see that already the thoughts, the sensory impressions, what Whitehead also calls visceral experience, are common to most living things, putting to work as many singular ways of being related to data as obtained from their environments. This way is the aim, the orientation in which what is felt is engaged or mobilized. Therefore, we would say that "feelings are inseparable from the end at which they aim; and this end is the feeler. The feelings aim at the feeler, as their final cause" (*PR*, 222).

The two meanings of the term subject—*subjectum* and *superjacio*—are not in opposition; on the contrary, they can be taken together in a renewed thought of subjects detached from all exclusively anthropological inscription. If indeed we pose the question by beginning from feelings, it becomes evident that there are two moments of a feeling to which correspond two subjective phases. First of all, in its initial state, the feeling tends to merge with what is felt, that is to say the facts, sensations, ideas, general impressions. However, this immanence of feeling to the facts is already inhabited by a subjective form. In this sense, as much as the feeling is, in this first phase, almost indistinct from that which is felt, the way, the polarization of the facts, is already the expression of a virtual subjectivity *(superjacio)*, a style separate from the feeling. It is in terms of the activity of an experience of self, what Whitehead also calls "self-enjoyment," that the feeling as such, of its own style, emerges. It thus becomes a subject in its own right *(subjectum)* possessor of itself through data from which it comes. As summarized by Gilles Deleuze,

> *self-enjoyment*, marks the way by which the subject is filled with itself and attains a richer and richer private life, when prehension is filled with its own

data. This is a biblical—and, too, a neo-Platonic—notion that English empiricism carried to its highest degree (notably with Samuel Butler). The plant sings of the glory of God, and while being filled all the more with itself it contemplates and intensely contracts the elements whence it proceeds. It feels in this prehension the *self-enjoyment* of its own becoming.[20]

Conclusion: A Universe of Subjectivities

I have proposed a possible heritage here, by recentering it on the question of feelings and of the implementation of an aesthetic, which would become the initial term of a cosmology, of Whitehead's proposition: apart from the experiences of subjects there is nothing, nothing, nothing, bare nothingness. This proposition indicates a whole program seeking to redefine the modern conception of nature. Nothing obliges us to oscillate perpetually between two conceptions of nature that are combined in a multiplicity of variables more or less near to their original form, with one approach being what Whitehead calls "romantic" and the other "scientific." The first, notably expressed by Shelley and Wordsworth, affirms that "nature cannot be divorced from its aesthetic values, and that these values arise from the cumulation, in some sense, of the brooding presence of the whole on to its various parts" (*SMW,* 87)—that is to say, of the insistence of the universe in each particular case. The second approach affirms that "Nature is a dull affair, soundless, scentless, colourless; merely the hurrying of material, endlessly, meaninglessly" (*SMW,* 54), where the aesthetic and axiological expressions only appear as "psychic additions" (*CN,* 29), simply added by the perceiving mind. This opposition, inherited from the "bifurcation of nature" in operation in the seventeenth century, continues to move without losing any of its efficacy in contemporary thought, and the oppositions between philosophies of the subject and those of nature seem only to redeploy the components of a problem that they never truly succeed in undoing.

Whitehead's gesture consists of not making these "aesthetic values" a supplement added to nature by a perceiving subject, but to make them the most fundamental factors of nature. With Whitehead, the aesthetic becomes the site of all ontology, the plurality of ways of doing, ways of being, capacities to be affected—in a word, the modalities of "feeling" are at the heart of a theory of subjects of nature. We do not have to renew the opposition between "reality" and "perception," between "being" and "aesthetic values," to then try to reunify the terms, as nature can be directly considered as a multiplicity of centers of experience, all directly expressive. Whitehead's philosophy is indeed a cosmology, and it can be characterized as a universal mannerism *[maniérisme universel]*. Being and the manner of being are indistinguishable; they form the conditions of existence for all subjects, human and nonhuman.

Notes

1. For a very long time, this proposition was ignored by most readers of Whitehead. Indeed, in the French inheritance of his philosophy, there is no mention of it: e.g., see Henri Bergson, *Durée et simultanéité* (Paris: Quadrige, 2009); Maurice Merleau-Ponty, *La nature: Notes, cours du Collège de France* (Paris: Seuil, 1995); Émile Meyerson, *Du cheminement de la pensée* (Paris: Vrin, 2011); Jean Wahl, *Vers le concret. Études d'histoire de la philosophie contemporaine* (Paris: Vrin, 1932); Gilles Deleuze, *Le pli: Leibniz et le Baroque* (Paris: Minuit, 1988). Only recently has Isabelle Stengers, in *Penser avec Whitehead: Une libre et sauvage creation de concepts* (Paris: Gallimard, 2002), announced the importance of this proposition for the very first time.

2. Henri Bergson, *Creative Evolution*, trans. Arthur Mitchell (Mineola, N.Y.: Dover Publications Inc., 1998), 1.

3. Henri Bergson, *The Creative Mind: An Introduction to Metaphysics*, trans. Mabelle L. Andison (Mineola, N.Y.: Dover Publications Inc., 2007), 163.

4. Gilles Deleuze, *Bergsonism*, trans. Hugh Tomlinson and Barbara Habberjam (New York, N.Y.: Zone Books, 1991), 28.

5. I call the "anthropological paradigm" the affirmation that a proposition has legitimacy and consistency if and only if it can be linked, by generalization or analogy, to a human experience. The project of "subjects of nature" aims to break radically with this paradigm. In this sense, I completely agree with Quentin Meillassoux and his critique of correlationism in *Après la finitude* (Paris: Seuil, 2006), 18. However, I think that the question is more general than the relation, as Meillassoux claims, between being and thinking.

6. On this topic, see the excellent book by Steven Shaviro, *Without Criteria: Kant, Whitehead, Deleuze, and Aesthetics* (Cambridge, Mass.: MIT Press, 2009).

7. Immanuel Kant, *Critique of Pure Reason*, trans. Marcus Weigelt and Max Muller (London: Penguin Books, 2007), 59.

8. Whitehead develops the ground of a relational ontology through his "principle of relativity," and in this regard he can be linked to contemporary philosophers who are today objects of rediscovery, such as Gilbert Simondon, *L'individuation à la lumière des notions de forme et d'information* (Paris: Jérôme Millon, 2005) and Gabriel Tarde, *Monadologie et sociologie* (Paris: Les Empêcheurs de penser en rond, 1999).

9. See, for instance: "the *hand* is the *reason* for the projected touch-sensum, the *eye* is the *reason* for the projected sight-sensum" (*PR*, 176).

10. The most patent examples of such a plurality of worlds linked to diverse forms of experience are found in Jakob von Uexküll's notion of *umwelt* in *Mondes animaux et monde humain* (Paris: Editions Gonthier, 1956).

11. This is one of the main metaphysical propositions of Tarde in *Monadologie et sociologie*. For more, see Bruno Latour, "Gabriel Tarde. La société comme possession," in *Philosophies des possessions*, ed. Didier Debaise (Dijon: Presses du réel, 2012).

12. Gottfried Leibniz, *Discourse on Metaphysics and Other Essays*, trans. Daniel Garber and Roger Ariew (Indianapolis, Ind.: Hackett Publishing), 9.

13. Ibid., 8.

14. Peirce, "Pragmatism," in *The Essential Peirce,* ed. the Peirce Edition Project (Bloomington: Indiana University Press, 1998), 2: 410–11.

15. For a more complete analysis of this double meaning of the subject, see Didier Debaise, *Un empirisme spéculatif* (Paris: Vrin, 2006).

16. See Alain De Libera, *Archéologie du sujet* (Paris: Vrin, 2007).

17. On the questions of series and transitions of experiences, see William James, *Essays in Radical Empiricism* (London: University of Nebraska Press, 1996), principally ch. 2, "A World of Pure Experience."

18. This is inspired by the theory of consolidation developed by Eugène Dupréel in "Theorie de la consolidation. Equisse d'une théorie de la vie d'inspiration sociologique," *Revue de l'institut de sociologie* 3 (1931): 473–530.

19. This theme seems to me to be in a striking proximity to the philosophy of Étienne Souriau and principally what he calls the "solliticitudinary" *(sollicitudinaire).* See on this subject, Souriau, *Avoir une âme. Essai sur les existences virtuelles* (Paris: Les belle letters, 1938), and Souriau, *Les different modes d'existence* (Paris: Presses Universitaires de France, 2009), as well the magnificent introduction to that work, written by Bruno Latour and Isabelle Stengers and titled "Le Sphinx de l'œurve." Étienne Souriau, *Les différents modes d'existence* (Paris: Presses Universitaires de France, 2009), 1–75.

20. Deleuze, *The Fold: Leibniz and the Baroque* (London: Continuum, 2006), 89.

TWELVE

Another Regard

Erin Manning

The gorillas regarded me. To them, I had never been away, because I had really been there once. Time is different to the gorillas. It is about being together, not about being apart. I am content to feel that kind of time, and I close my eyes and smell deeply the hot lemon smell of gorillas and the thick sweet smell of the hay.

—Dawn Prince-Hughes, *Songs of the Gorilla Nation: My Journey through Autism*

First Movement: Are You a Gorilla?

In a piece entitled "The Silence Between," Dawn Prince-Hughes writes of an encounter with a bonobo chimpanzee, Kanzi, which sets the stage for a rethinking of the deep "regard" Prince-Hughes shares with apes of all kinds. Having flown to Decatur, Georgia, at the invitation of primatologist and linguist Sue Savage-Rumbaugh, Prince-Hughes finds herself alone with Kanzi. She writes:

> Naturally, I fell into the gorilla language I knew, a language of body, mind, and spirit. Kanzi and I played chase up and down the fence line, both of us on all fours, smiling in a sea of fun and deep breaths.

Then something uncanny occurred:

> He stopped suddenly and grabbed his word board off the ground. He pointed to a symbol and then pointed to me and made a hand gesture with his eyebrows raised. It was clear that he was asking me a question. He repeated this series of words and movements over and over, until I said, out loud, "I'm sorry, I can't understand, Kanzi. Let me get Sue and maybe she can help me." At first, she was at a loss. Then after asking him to point to the word again, she realized he was pointing to the word "gorilla" on his board and making the American Sign Language sign for question after pointing to me. It was clear he was asking me

> if I was a gorilla. What was amazing, though, is that he didn't know American Sign Language: he had seen a video of the gorilla Koko using it and must have not only remembered the signed words, but, not having known other gorillas, assumed that all gorillas understood sign language. If I was a gorilla, he thought, this must be a way of communicating that I would understand.[1]

Before I turn to the story in detail, I want to begin with the quotation above where Prince-Hughes writes, "The gorillas regarded me." This regard of which she speaks is how I want to frame the engagement with Prince-Hughes's story, beginning right away with the speculation that this regard sets the stage for the encounter with the bonobo Kanzi, shifting it from one of detached observation to one of concern. For Whitehead's notion of concern, as outlined throughout *Adventures of Ideas,* is very much about the emphasis on a different notion of regard, regard not of the subject for the object, or of one individual for another, but of the occasion for its own unfolding.

The notion of concern is one way of reworking the dichotomy of subject and object, reinserting them in the event. "The occasion as subject has a 'concern' for the object. And the 'concern' at once places the object as a component in the experience of the subject, with an affective tone drawn from this object and directed towards it." The subject does not begin the process; it is the process that activates the subject. "The subject-object relation can be conceived as Recipient and Provoker, where the fact provoked is an affective tone about the status of the provoker in the provoked experience," Whitehead writes, adding that "the word 'recipient' suggests a passivity which is erroneous" (*AI,* 176). "Concern" is not an intersubjective term, but rather the basis for understanding that experience emerges through "the rise of an affective tone originating from things whose relevance is given" (*AI,* 176).

This is relevant to the story Prince-Hughes recounts for two reasons. First, as I mention above, the framing of the event is built on a notion of regard, which foregrounds less an interpersonal stance than an affective tonality. Second, in the event of the regard, there is a slippage in time that undermines a static positioning of subject and object. Whitehead's notion of concern gives us the tools to understand this crafting of time in the relation. Prince-Hughes writes: "To them, I had never been away, because I had really been there once." In the event of relation, a concern is emergent that alters the conditions for a regard that "will always have been there once." Recipient and Provoker are not to be confused simply with "Dawn" and "the gorillas" or "Dawn" and "Kanzi." Recipient and Provoker are the myriad affective tonalities of an encounter that stages time and event such that "to have really been there once" is to have set into motion the conditions for an activation of regard—of concern—which is capable of outliving the immediate occasion.

The challenge here is to understand that regard is not something that flows unidirectionally between the human and the animal. What is happening in the first quotation is the setting into place of a dynamic relation that foregrounds the movement of time, emphasizing how time is itself a dynamic form that recasts how relation is conceived. When Prince-Hughes writes that "To them, I had never been away, because I had really been there once," it is of course her interpretation of the event, but nonetheless it sets into motion an interesting provocation to the relational field that continues to be foregrounded in the story Prince-Hughes then tells about her encounter with Kanzi. I want to suggest that this notion of "regard" allows us to reposition the ultimate question—"Are you a gorilla?"—away from the interpersonal toward an emphasis on the relational movement that frames the second encounter—"Kanzi and I played chase up and down the fence line, both of us on all fours, smiling in a sea of fun and deep breaths"—where movement itself becomes the way the event has concern for its unfolding.

Let us replay the event: Dawn and Kanzi run along a fence, goading one another, moving one another forward in an eight-footed play. First, Dawn moves with what she knows: "Naturally, I fell into the gorilla language I knew, a language of body, mind, and spirit." Dawn is not mimicking. Her movement comes from an affective attunement based on a long-standing connection to nonhuman languages: "When I was young I talked to animals in that language of silence. I knew what trees and streams were saying because they told me. I knew what sow bugs and snakes were saying because they molded me. . . . Sometimes my grandfather would ask me in the garden, 'What are the worms saying today,' 'Fine fine slither dirt push good rotting green,' I would answer, smiling."[2] This, the language of the nonhuman, is a language that already tunes, for Dawn, to her movement. She listens with movement, listens to how it expresses in the now of the encounter. She knows the welling event has regard for this movement, this expression in the moving of the more-than of human experience. Kanzi, in turn, plays with the language of movement she proposes, "both of us on all fours, smiling in a sea of fun and deep breaths."[3] Dawn and Kanzi, cueing, aligning, creating a rhythm, in counterpoint. Gorilla-like.

Counterpoint

William Forsythe defines counterpoint as "a field of action in which the intermittent and irregular coincidence of attributes between organizational elements produces an ordered interplay."[4] This definition of counterpoint emphasizes the relationship between movement and time. Forsythe speaks of choreographing the future *in the present-moving,* asking his dancers to "dance where the other dancer is going" to "meet him there."[5] Dancing in an alignment with futures in the making suggests a structured improvisation that is attuned to the incipient more-than of movement—movement's technicity. To move into the technicity of movement is not to mimic or predict: there is no standing back from the event-in-the-moving. It is to move—with the movement's excess of position. It is to craft movement—moving in the more-than of movement's taking-form. This happens in counterpoint as dancers "shift each other's time." Forsythe explains: "syncing is not what's important, in the sense of matching an already known timing." Move in the time-frames of the becoming-movement, preaccelerate into the relational field activated by movement-moving, move with the affective tonality, with future time presenting. "This can operate in different time frames: go slower, be in another's past right before they catch up to you, then move past them to their future—look for the moment—aim at it rather than going directly to it."[6] Counterpoint is not the activity of an individual body—it is the activity of a relational field through which movement moves. Movement-moving is intensively distributed—always beyond its simple location, as Whitehead would say.[7] In counterpoint, the movement exceeds the frame—the frame of time, the frame of the skin-envelope—activating an inframobility that tunes to a relational movement. As collective movement becomes attuned to this relational field, time folds, individual movements no longer abstractable from the whole. One movement-moving, in difference. Counterpoint.

The one is of course always more than one. It is an infinity of movement-speciations. Speciations make a dancing-body, not the other way around. We no longer have one, two, three bodies dancing. We have an affective attunement. This affective attunement cannot be measured in linear time. It happens in a time continuously folding into the intervals created by the moving field. This time of movement-moving is felt by the dancers as a moment of uncanny synchronicity. Synchronous because the movements create a collective experience of time-shaping. Strange because the collective movement is slightly off, attuned to but in the difference of movement's capacity to invent, creating "an ordered interplay," yes, but also something more: a sense of having been transported into the more-than by the event. A field in counterpoint has been created. Any repetition of the exercise of counterpoint will necessarily create a different field. Each counterpoint-event makes its own time.

Counterpoint's intermittent and irregular coincidence of attributes agitate the field of action at the level of speciations. In the case of Dawn and Kanzi, it is not two fully constituted body-envelopes that dance, but a multiplicity of body-tendings moving in their difference. Speciations in the moving: finger-ground-spine, extension-rotation-bend, metal-fur-breath. What agitates is a body-likeness, a field of relations that does not mimic a body, but creates a body*ing* in a shifting co-composition of experiential spacetimes. Von Uexküll speaks of spiders that are fly-like, of cups that are coffee-like. These are speciations—compositional tendencies active in the relational field their coming-into-eventness calls forth. "To be fly-like means that the spider has taken up certain elements of the fly in its constitution. . . . Better expressed, the fly-likeness of the spider means that it has taken up certain motifs of the fly melody in its bodily composition. Everywhere it is the counterpoint which expresses itself as a motif in such configurations."[8] The dancer's movement was perhaps spiral-like, wall-like, sound-like, connecting not directly to another body, but to a sounding, a spiraling, a levitating gravitational field. Heavy-to-the-ground meets laughter-in-movement: gorilla-like.

Speciations are rhythmic activations of a body-morphing that never precede the event of their coming-into-relation. They give rhythm, give tone, to the how of the event's in-forming, cutting across species fully-formed, connective as they are in the milieu of their relational activation. In the event of Dawn and Kanzi, to take these two first as the bonobo and the human would be to engage in the practice of placing the subject outside the event, ignoring the force of speciation. It would be to take the notion of species as given, and assume that all encounters are framed by species already fully-formed. This is a brand of identity politics: before we can know how to approach the question, "are you a gorilla?" we must know who you really are, a captive gorilla? an autistic woman? a philosopher? an animal activist? a zoo-keeper? an anthropologist? While all of these criteria make a difference to how the event unfolds—there is no suggestion here that there are not asymmetrical power relations[9]—to posit identity politics as the starting point of the process is to background in advance the activity of the milieu's rhythmic in-forming, and, even more importantly, to undermine the potential of coming, if not to a different answer, at least to a different way of framing the question. For to begin with identity politics is always to assume to know in advance how to frame an answer to a question of belonging, of territory, of identity. To frame the event in advance of its unfolding with markers of identity ("obviously" she is not a gorilla, "clearly" Kanzi is misrecognizing) is to sidestep the act of the event's unfolding *as event:* for who can know yet what constitutes gorilla in this context of movement counterpoint?

All movement is, to some degree, counterpoint. Movement rhythms: it connects, prolongs, undermines, subverts, dances. It never stops. Movement is always of multiple valences. There is absolute, or total movement—the durational field of movement-moving—which envelops all worldings. Counterpoint cuts into total movement to create an actualizable field—"an ordered interplay." In doing so, counterpoint touches on both registers of movement, virtual and actual, tapping into the field of total movement to create an opening for this or that movement-quality in the realm of the actual. This allows the milieu of movement to resonate with the more-than. This more-than is the counterpoint-event's motif. This motif is a likeness. It gives the milieu a singular tonality. This tone in turn tunes the milieu to certain tendencies. A milieu with a springing motif tunes to air-likeness, for instance. Or, as in von Uexküll's example, fly-likeness tunes not to fly-as-species but to a qualitative likeness of a fly-movement intensively in rhythm with the spider's web. This likeness is first and foremost affective—it is an attunement not simply to the fly in its quantitative dimensions, or in its behaviors, but to the way its singular movement-tendencies affect the speciation spider-like. "The web—but never the fly—can be called the goal of forming the web. But the fly does indeed serve as the counterpoint . . . for the formation of the web."[10]

A speciation is not, as such, organic. It is not made up of separately definable human and animal components in a metonymic relation to an organic whole. This very idea of the organic whole is a misnomer: both "body" and "species" are general categories that can be conceived as such only by divesting them of the relational field that co-constitutes them.[11] To posit such a notion of the whole is to have separated out the event of bodying from its activity. Speciations are how to think this activity, the in-act of body-world constellations in all their organic and inorganic intermixings. These in-acts are not strictly physical—they are a conglomeration of physicalities with affective tonalities that emerge from the very necessity of the milieu: it is the milieu that fashions them. Speciations body in the event of their direct co-relation to the event, they are not body-species pre-formed, and are never finally formed—they are bodyings. An event has concern for the bodying. And there is no body that is not infinitely more than one.

An autonomy of expression is at work in the relational field that speciations call forth. We are not talking of relations that exist outside of the event of their emergence. The relational field of movement-moving activates the distributed field in which the dancers dance, and in the dancing, they move with it, aligning to it, moving *it*. The *field* expresses, the field dances to attention, not the dancers as individuals. And what it expresses is a relational movement that exceeds the terms of the dancers' individual body-ness, bringing into complex constellations a rhythm that in-forms the speciations their movement-moving creates.

The culmination of the movement-moving is a territorializing. Something has come to form, and with the coming-to-form, a certain casting into itself of movement has emerged. "An ordered interplay." From here, techniques can be abstracted, and positions extracted. Territories are short-lived, however: movement keeps moving, occasions keep perishing. So what is left? Motifs, expressive tendencies. These motifs are the mode of appearance of a vacillating territorialization that is an abstraction of a subjective form. With them comes the tonality of the event's form-taking.

Style

"Expressive qualities entertain variable or constant relations with one another (that is what matters of expression *do*); they no longer constitute placards that mark a territory, but motifs and counterpoints that express the relation of the territory to interior impulses or exterior circumstances, whether or not they are given. No longer signatures, but a style."[12] Style can never be pinned down to form. It is a mode of existence always intimately tied to the event of its expression. And yet there is a certain consistency to style across occasions. A style can be recognized, in the feeling—we know-feel the languid grace of a cat, the frenzied disappearance of a cockroach, even before we quite see them. Style happens in this "not quite," in the movement of expression before it takes its form as this or that. Style is always in the moving.

Style connects with the event's affective tonality. It is movement quality carried forth into an event through the force of its reactivation from relational field to relational field. It is chiefly non-sensuous, as Whitehead would say, activating for the event a certain quality of past occasions. This quality is always a renewal of itself for the present occasion. Style is therefore never quite the same for two occasions. A moving-body's expressivity will carry the force of an attunement that can be aligned to. This aligning will express a certain style that can be connected, transversally, to other events of its kind. A movement, Forsythe-like. The how of the aligning as style is not a question of connecting to a certain superficial quality but of moving with the movement's movement such as to captivate the movement's very potential for expression. Moving gorilla-like.

Second Movement: At Play

The dynamic form gorilla-like is bred in play. Dawn and Kanzi run, on all fours, along a fence, laughing, grunting. There is no outside to their game: it is not meant for anyone else. Play is unselfconscious. Improvisation, spontaneity, mixed in with the constraints of incipient territorializations—the fence, the time of day, the newness of the encounter with gestures no doubt at first quizzical, careful, and then perhaps engaged, untroubled even, at times. Instinct, some people would say. Art, others would respond.

Counterpoint is creative. It proposes an assemblage, and this assemblage is always, to a degree, a territorializing platform. But what counterpoint also does is keep that territory moving, active, transductive. For counterpoint activates the associated milieus of the territory, the milieus that cross through it and are always, to some extent, in excess of it. This is the paradox of counterpoint: it must remain territorial to the degree that it can be accessed and returned to. But what is returned to is always, to a certain degree, difference. The field of counterpoint is dynamic, its movements local insofar as they co-constitute the singular expression of emergence their in-concertness calls forth, and global to the degree that they can be recaptured for future events in the making. Counterpoint produces not positions as such, but the more-than of position on its way to activating times as yet unseen, unfelt. Positions outdoing themselves, in concert.

Territory's play undoes the dichotomy between speciations and species, locating them not as opposites but on a continuum. For speciations are complex aggregates—they affect on a multitude of strata, including that of the species, elasticizing the territory even as they move in concert with it. It is not that there is no longer a bonobo and a human; it is that the event never begins there. It begins in movement, in the mobility of relation where there is always more-than this particular species-combination. For as soon as the territory becomes an active milieu, it becomes a field of movement constellations. Species is a general category always abstracted from the movement of the event.

What is concretely in-act is never the general category. This is why starting with a general category cannot not yield nuanced results. Take, for instance, the question of gender. While (en)gendering—as speciation—has many roles to play in an event such as that between Kanzi and Dawn, "gender" posited as a pre-formed category cannot make sense of their encounter without imposing a framing device onto the event from the outside. This has the effect of backgrounding the in-act of the event, losing sight of the intricate complexities of the event's acting-out. For instance, a general statement about the general category "woman" in relation to Dawn would immediately connect her body to a certain set of qualities or criteria that would mediate the event of her encounter with Kanzi, who, as a "male" would then be expected to respond in certain, often stereotyped, ways. To posit the genders male-female as the framing device would also ignore the fact that gender identification tends to be speculative at best for many autistics, for whom having a fixed body, let alone a fixed gender, is one of the most abstract of all abstractions.[13] What is concretely in act, I want to suggest, is never a "gender," but an *engendering*, a coming-into-itself of a singular set of relations, of which male-likeness and female-likeness may be defining elements, but always only in their in-actness, in tandem with co-constitutive elements active in the associated milieu. This engendering opens the field to new constellations, some of which may be allied to gender, others of which may constitute forms of speciation not yet defined and categorized.

Back to the fence, and to the art of play. "We consider that an animal, in a complex and accidental milieu, would have few chances of survival if he could only use stereotyped behavior, even if more or less corrected by orienting stimuli. Much more important are the improvised responses directed to the stimuli . . . that act as a sort of irritant, not as a signal."[14] Animals play, and play is an art, as Brian Massumi underlines, precisely because instinct, conceived as artless, is "downright maladaptive"—its stereotyping forbids a response tailored to the singularity of the situation.[15] Following Ruyer, Massumi suggests that, at play, a processual trigger spurs a creative advance, an "immanent modification." "The stimulus irritates, provokes, stirs. It is a processual inducer. What it most directly induces is an integral modification in the tendencial self-consistency of animal experience, correlated to the externality of an accident-rich environment but governed by its own stirring logic of qualitative variation."[16] Instinct, as Bergson writes, is *played* more than it is represented.[17]

It is too simplistic, then, to suggest that what moves Kanzi, or what moves Dawn, is simply behavior pre-dating the event, such as instinct tied to gender or species categories. They are not imitating or responding to something that pre-defines them—they are creating play. Gorilla-like is an art.

No gorilla has actually entered the scene. What has entered is a movement-constellation that has taken both Dawn and Kanzi by surprise. Gorilla-like is the more-than of their coming-together, the style, the motif of the event's counterpoint. And although it is spoken in the language of the third—the sign-language "of" the gorilla—it erupts in the language of counterpoint, the language of movement's possession by itself. The movement moves the gorilla-like speciation of which Kanzi and Dawn (in a million variations) are part. Paw-earth, foot-air, laughter-dirt, grunt-metal, all of these speciations are at work in dancing the emergent counterpoint. A speciation: a bloc of sensation, as Deleuze and Guattari might say. A desiring-machine. "Deleuze and Guattari have a favourite word to designate the affective force that pulls deformationally forward toward creativity: desire."[18] Desire as a transformational pull that activates a relational field.

There is no purpose to play, except to create more play, to create more desire for play. "Are you a gorilla?" is this event of play's postscript, not its mandate. If we take it as the starting point, the question of subjectivity will become the framing device for the event. I am, you are: a question of species. Play will be undone of precisely what makes it play: it will become a rehearsal for something that exceeds it in advance. This is not what happens here. Play between Kanzi and Dawn is the fielding of a relational movement, and it is out of this improvisatory field that the question "are you a gorilla?" emerges, not the other way around. It is not a general category "gorilla" that is at stake here, but the gorilla of play's motif, and the way the motif makes ingression into the newly formed constellation: gorilla-like.

"Play is the abstractive suspension of a vital context."[19] It bursts open the frame of expectation. It intuits, activating a consciousness not of, but with—a regard in the playing that defies the extraction of movement from the event at play. This regard creates incipient territories never before moved in the playing. Not "are you a gorilla?" but "how do you move me?" or better, "how does our movement move us?" Play as the bringing into focus of an affective force of relation that reinvents, in its small way, the relational how of life-living. A constellation-machine for movement-invention and for time looping. Counterpoint.

Third Movement: On Novelty

"Life means novelty," writes Whitehead (*PR*, 104). Life is appetition, appetite for the more-than. Life always in tune with *a life*—the force of life-living across the organic and inorganic realms where speciations converge to create territories of difference. To restrict life to the physical plane, as Whitehead notes, is to starkly underestimate the play of its capacity for invention.

Whitehead has a strange name for the force of appetition that activates the more-than of life-living: he calls it *reason*. Reason, for Whitehead, is another word for the force of thought that is immanent to the event. This force of thought is never thought as that which lands onto the event from outside its concrescence. It is the reason *of* nature, in nature, a concern with the very edges of the thinkable in its nonalignment to consciousness. For Whitehead, nature thinks.

When Whitehead says that nature "is impenetrable by thought," what he means is that thought does not enter into nature from the outside to orchestrate it from without (*CN,* 13). Nature is not a passive element to be mediated. Nor is thought a mediating activity. Nature *creates* thought—a thinking *in* the event. This thinking makes ingress into the event in large part through the constellations speciations take. Nature and speciations are cocombinatory—they cannot be taken separately. The question is never, as Whitehead underscores, "what is in the mind and what is in nature?" (*CN* 30). The question is "*how* is gorilla-like?": how does nature's play move life-living, creating thought?

Nature's play is never separate from the event of its coming into being in the same way that the occasion is never preceded by an already-composed notion of space or time. Nature *is* its speciations, active, always, in the time of the event's making. Nature is thus never in-itself, in the same way that a species, a body, an individual, are never solely in-themselves. Nature is a relational field through which certain motifs become active, motifs that in turn activate new fields of relation in the time of the event. It is, in all of its eventness, a multitude of modes of existence, a field of creativity.

Key to what Whitehead calls "the creative advance" is what he terms *self-enjoyment*, the concern the event has for its coming to subjective form: "The notion of life implies a certain absoluteness of self-enjoyment" wherein each occasion of experience is "an individual act of immediate self-enjoyment" (*MT,* 150–51). Self-enjoyment is not a moral category. It is not about the enjoyment *of* this or that. Not the enjoyment of the subject for life, but the enjoyment of life in the event of life-living. Life-living, it bears reminding, as the continuous outdoing of any notion of life in-itself or nature in-itself.

Self-enjoyment is the occasion's concern for its own process, a process that always includes a certain more-than. This more-than, as mentioned above, is brought forth by the event's capacity to exceed its physical pole. The physical pole is a concept in Whitehead that denotes the most bare aspect of the occasion, a concept that is inseparable from the adjacent notion of the mental pole (or "reason"), which he defines as the *how* of the creative advance.

Mentality—"a factor of intensity in experience"—moves the event beyond its physical pole (*PR,* 101). "When the species refuses adventure, there is relapse into the well-attested habit of mere life. . . . Varied freshness has been lost, and the species lives upon the blind appetitions of old usages" (*FR*, 19). If the physical pole were all that were at stake, and if life were merely about a passive overcoming in the interests of self-preservation, there would be no creativity, and certainly no reinvention of life. Again, it is necessary to move beyond the thought of this or that human or animal life: life here touches on all that has the capacity for transition. It is life-living, *a life:* speciation in exquisite more-than human configurations.

Novelty abounds, a novelty spurred by the complex of self-enjoyment, appetition, mentality. Think mentality as the event's thinking-feeling, as Massumi might say,[20] a feltness in the thinking resonant at the edges of experience. Each occasion dances with this not-yet, its becoming always in counterpoint with the more-than of its will-have-been. Time folding: recall Forsythe's "Dance into future movement!"

"Mentality" is perhaps the wrong word for this intensive process, this "organ of novelty," or "urge beyond," for despite this not being the case, mentality, like its earlier counterpart, reason, still sounds as though it is in the mind or of consciousness (*FR*, 33). We might therefore simply call it "thinking-feeling," emphasizing how it is an activity in the event that co-composes with the occasion's physicality to create, in the act, a contributory more-than that emphasizes how novelty is a process of thought in the doing. "[Mentality] seeks to vivify the massive physical fact, which is repetitive, with the novelties which beckon" (*FR*, 33). The force of appetition, as mentioned above, could be another good term for mentality in that it emphasizes the hunger of a process that opens the occasion to novel motifs, activating in the occasion a "factor of anarchy" (*FR*, 34).[21]

This is not to say that creative advance is active all the time under all circumstances. It is to emphasize that the force of appetition and thinking-feeling are always present in germ and contributory in the dynamic form of events concrescing. Whitehead writes: "The quality of an act of experience is largely determined by the factor of the thinking it contains" (*FR*, 80). As soon as a process falls into general categories, its capacity for creative advance is stunted, for general categories do not think. Creativity is always in the dynamic details of a process. These details are played out at the level of the emergent occasion, in the constellation of the event. They are its speciations, its technicities, its overarticulations, its preaccelerations. They are the event's more-than. This is where the thinking-feeling happens, in the in-act of the event's outdoing of form, in the in-act of the event's outdoing of simple location. Movement-moving.

Fourth Movement: An Incompletion

Whitehead writes: "The community of actual things is an organism, but it is not a static organism. It is an incompletion in process of production" (*PR*, 215). Kanzi and Dawn meet. Play ensues. Their movement moves them, connecting them at the level of speciations that exceed them as individuals. In the speciation, a counterpoint emerges. This emergent counterpoint is a structured improvisation: it moves into the habitual movements brought into play at the same time as it connects to a generative field of movement-moving. The generative force of movement in counterpoint activated in the moving creates a motif. This prolongs the dance, giving it a style all its own. This style exceeds Dawn or Kanzi as individuals, exceeds their habitual ways of moving—a relational movement has emerged. This relational movement is a field experience. Everything is concretely at play—the quality of air, the sound of breath on metal, on fur, on skin, the feel of paws on earth, on cement, the heaviness of limbs at play, the grumblings of stomachs, the pull of muscles, the rustlings of fallen leaves. Everything singularly contributes. And in this field teeming with activity, a question is drawn: "Are you a gorilla?" This is not a question intended to be answered; it is a motif. It is a platform to spring from through which new movement-constellations can take flight. Gorilla-like is a new concept.

New concepts, when they really do their work, activate speciations, which, in turn, affect how societies evolve. A society: "A type of order. . . . A nexus. . . . Endurance. . . . An animal body is a society involving a vast number of occasions, spatially and temporally coordinated. . . . Each living body is a society" (*AI*, 203–5). What we usually call a body, a body in the narrow sense, is a knot of speciations (a nexus), a society. This is the force of concepts, that they insist, they irritate, they agitate in the cross-fertilization of occasions and societies. These agitations play out on the level of the occasion, but as the occasion perishes onto the nexus, they also affect the contributive realm—for they continue to make ingress. Concepts resonate transversally, creating a vibratory field that affects how future events are composed. They feed the future-presenting with their appetite for more. They are counterpoint-machines: they create a field of action that provokes a coincidence of attributes to produce the excess of an ordered interplay. Gorilla-like.

The complex relational field of movement-moving courses across the societies "Dawn" and "Kanzi." These societies are altered by the process, as are all of the contributory forces that have made their way into the event. These contributory forces touch on the many stories the event calls forth, each one of them now tainted by the motif, gorilla-like. Take the story of Kanzi, born October 28, 1980, a bonobo chimpanzee raised in captivity, for whom contact has been for the most part restricted to the human. Infuse this story into the event and consider how gorilla-like reframes it, foregrounding, perhaps, the fact that Kanzi's "advanced linguistic aptitude"[22] has made language the vehicle for communication since he was a baby. For not only does he use lexigrams, but he can also understand aspects of spoken language and associate it with the lexigrams. No surprise, then, that gorilla-like emerges in the speaking as much as in the moving. Take the story of Dawn Prince-Hughes, born January 31, 1964, an autistic fighting for a place in a world tuned to neurotypical modes of encounter that continuously, painfully, set her apart. Infuse this story into the event and consider how gorilla-like speaks to the force of "another regard," something Prince-Hughes has honed in her years of working with gorillas, gorillas who she feels have offered her a place in the world. These are some of the societies, in brief, that meet on that fateful afternoon to play along the fence.

The contributory force of a society (a nexus of occasions) on an individual occasion is not quantitatively measurable. Ingression is not about quantitative content per se: it is about the tuning of an occasion toward certain kinds of activations of the past in the present for future-presenting. Style. Style carries across occasions, giving them a sense of consistency. The relational field as it emerges through Kanzi and Dawn's play is imbued with style, marked and fashioned by modes of thought—mentalities—already in counterpoint with their wider comings-to-be. With this in mind, in the spirit of incompletion, I want to turn briefly to one key element of style that I believe makes the question "Are you a gorilla?" far less strange than we may at first have assumed it to be.

This element of style is what I have elsewhere defined as "autistic perception," a style of perception wherein an encounter with the world does not begin by sorting the field into objects or subjects. I bring this up here specifically in relation to the notion of regard, tuned as it is to a relational field that exceeds categorical preconceptions.

Autistic perception is a tendency in perception on a continuum with all perception, *not a definition of autism*. It is a style that has been remarked upon by autistics Tito Mukhopadhyay, DJ Savarese, Amanda Baggs, Jamie Burke, Dawn Prince-Hughes, Dawn Corwin, and many others. In their varied and intricate attempts to define their modalities of engaging the world ecologically, they have not coined the phrase, but they have repeatedly described a mode of existence wherein there is a direct perception of the more-than of experience in-forming. This perceptual style, described speculatively by autistics always to some degree as alien to neurotypical experience, suggests a way of engaging the world through an active thinking-feeling of the edgings and contourings of fields of relation that coagulate into instances of shaped experience. This is similar to what Francis Tustin dismissively calls "autistic shaping."

I want to suggest that this direct experience of the in-actness of worlding results in an ecological sensibility to life-living. But let me be clear: while all autistics I have encountered prize this mode of perception, none of them would ever create a simplified relay between autistic perception and the everyday experience of an autistic. Like the activist movement for neurodiversity, their descriptions of the richness of perception do not disqualify the horrors of trying to attune to neurotypical speeds of existence, to neurotypical expectations in relation to spoken language, to neurotypical ableist arrangements for life-living. Autism is never described by autistics as easy or straightforward, and never do they deny that autism brings with itself painful misalignments to everyday neurotypical existence, many of them of the motor variety, that make independent living if not impossible, then very difficult.[23] Nor I am suggesting that there is a "single" autism. Autism is a spectrum, with as many infinities of perceptual difference as within the misindentified "neurotypical" group.

What I am suggesting is that we can learn from a mode of perception described by autistic Anne Corwin as a "different kind of chunking." She explains: "I often tend to sit on floors and other surfaces even if furniture is available, because it's a lot easier to identify 'flat surface a person can sit on' than it is to sort the environment into chunks like 'couch,' 'chair,' 'floor,' and 'coffee table.'"[24] All perception involves chunking, but what autistics have access to that is usually backgrounded for neurotypicals is the direct experience of the relational field's morphing into objects and subjects. Experientially speaking, there is never—for anyone—the direct apprehension of an object or a subject. What we perceive is always, first, a relational field. It is a key contribution of Whitehead to have created a whole philosophical vocabulary of process to make this clear. Still, given the quickness of the morphing from the relational field into the objects and subjects of our perceptions, many of us feel as though the world *is* "pre-chunked" into species, into bodies and individuals. This is the shortcoming, as autistics might say, of neurotypical perception (that we are simply too quick to chunk), and it is certainly one of the things that makes many autistics feel lost in a world overtaken by normopaths.

The foregrounding of the world in its morphability as experienced in autistic perception opens experience to a level of relation with the world that is rare. This level of relation is an ecological attunement to the multiplicity that is life-living, for it attends, always, to the dynamic details of a process: autistic perception never begins with the general attribute, never assumes integration over complexity. It prehends, always, from the middle, with an active regard for the emergent field's environmentality. In the register of autistic perception, the world is experienced always as an ecology of practices in the complex relations of its emergent unfoldings. This is a language of experience that moves not from self to self, or self to other, but from dynamic constellation to dynamic constellation. As Mukhopadhyay writes: "Maybe I do not have to try very hard to be the wind or a rain cloud. There is a big sense of extreme connection I feel with a stone or perhaps with a pen on a tabletop or a tree. . . . There is no separation."[25] Cloud-like. Rock-like.

If we ignore the non-human-centered valence of Prince-Hughes's or Mukhopadhyay's approach and persist in placing the human at the forefront as the motivating force of all events, their words will seem anthropomorphic. We will read Prince-Hughes's encounter with Kanzi simply as a human once more telling the story of an animal, in human terms; we will interpret Mukhopadhyay as giving a human face to the pen, to the tabletop, to the tree. Autistic perception warns us against this approach, however, persistently reminding us not to begin with the pre-chunked. Begin in the middle! it says. Do not assume to know in advance how the chunking will resolve! It seems to me that we should heed these words and learn from them, with them. That we might listen more intently to how the world composes itself in a mode of perception that does not privilege the human in any of its pre-composed guises, or any other general categories.

But let us not stop there. The accusation of anthropomorphism whether misplaced as in the case of Kanzi and Dawn, or fitting in other instances, need not be a reason for us to return to our old habits of generalizing and categorizing. For is it not true that the accusation of anthropomorphism has become one more way of not attending to the complex counterpoint of the creative advance? As Jane Bennett writes, "a touch of anthropomorphism . . . can catalyze a sensibility that finds a world filled not with ontologically distinct categories of beings (subjects and objects) but with variously composed materialities that form confederations. . . . Maybe it is worth running the risks associated with anthropomorphizing . . . because it, oddly enough, works against anthropocentrism: a chord is struck between person and thing, and I am no longer above or outside a nonhuman 'environment.'"[26]

There is counterpoint in infinite abundance, and we are not hearing it, let alone dancing it. Ecologies of perception are backgrounded by an overarching emphasis on general categories. New modes of attention are needed, and persistent efforts to experience the novelty of life-living are essential to enjoying the complexity of worldings that populates us. The more pressing question is not whether or not an engagement with the more-than human is anthropomorphic but what exactly it is that has led us to the certainty we seem to have that the world *can* be parsed out into subjects and objects, and how intertwined this assertion has become with a notion of interactivity that sets itself up not as a radical empiricism but as a mediating interplay between already-existent terms. James's mantra bears repeating: "The relations that connect experiences must themselves be experienced relations, and any kind of relation experienced must be accounted as 'real' as anything else in the system."[27] There is no object "in-itself" just as there is no subject only "for-itself." To cite Whitehead again, "the occasion has a 'concern' for the object. And the concern at once places the object as a component in the experience of the subject, with an affective tone drawn from this object and toward it" (*AI,* 176). Subjects and objects edge into experience, relationally. Not human-relationally, but in an incipient relation that speciates.

The in-itselfness of the object (or the animal) must be resisted as strongly as the in-itselfness of the human. Neither human nor object nor animal comes to experience fully formed. It is the counterpoint of their speciations that is at stake in experience. This, it seems to me, is what can be taken wholesale from Kanzi's and Prince-Hughes's dance: speciations connect, cutting transversally across all genera, meeting at the level of intensities, motifs, creating styles, in the moving. An ecology of practices. A mode of existence. An activist philosophy.

Dawn Prince-Hughes writes: "I hope that autistic people, and others that have been beyond understanding until recently, will be the natural interpreters of an important patois."[28] The patois of which Prince-Hughes speaks is a language replete with the sensitivity of autistic perception, thick with a force of thought in the middling of its expressibility, textured by a more-than of future movements and un-chunked experiences, ripe for the infra-linguistic telling. The incomplete answer to "Are you a gorilla?" is spoken in such a patois, a language that can only be heard in the moving, in the infra of positioning, in the choreographic thinking that is always in the beyond of subject and object.

This is the challenge: to move in counterpoint with a language that trembles on the edges of understanding. To become as "autistically perceptive" as possible, even at the risk of losing our footing in a species-oriented world—and gaining our footing in a world of speciation. To participate in the concern for another regard.

Notes

1. Dawn Prince-Hughes, "Cultural Commentary: The Silence Between: An Autoethnographic Examination of The Language Prejudice and Its Impact on the Assessment of Autistic and Animal Intelligence," special issue on Autism, ed. Ralph Savarese and Emily Savarese, *Disabilities Studies Quarterly* 30, no. 1 (2010), http://www.dsq-sds.org/article/view/1055/1242.

2. Ibid.

3. Ibid.

4. This definition was coined by Norah Zuniga Shaw with William Forsythe for the Synchronous Objects website, www.synchronousobjects.org.

5. Forsythe, rehearsal, November 2010.

6. In *Science and the Modern World,* Whitehead writes: "To say that a bit of matter has simple location means that, in expressing its spatio-temporal relations, it is adequate to state that it is where it is, in a definite finite region of space, and throughout a definite finite duration of time, apart from any essential reference of the relations of that bit of matter to other regions of space and to other durations of time" (SMW, 58).

7. Jakob von Uexküll, *A Foray into the Worlds of Animals and Humans: With a Theory of Meaning,* trans. Joseph D. O'Neil (Minneapolis: University of Minnesota Press: 2010), 190–91.

8. One response might be: "but these asymmetrical relations are so dominant that to sidestep them is to not even begin to address the place whence such an investigation can begin!" A film like *Project Nim* (James Marsh, 2011) makes this abundantly clear. It seems to me that this issue is nonetheless best returned to through other means than those of identity politics. For movements are restricted in an infinity of ways, and while the fence that separates Kanzi and Dawn is a blatant case of the imposition of controls on animals, the more interesting question is how speciations open the way for a different ecology of freedom of movement that affects the human constellation as well, albeit in different ways. Once the question of speciation has unfolded and the counterpoint has been explored, questions of power (and the fact, for instance, that there are asymmetrical notions of freedom that frame the event) become all the more complex. In other words, to not settle the distinction in a vocabulary based only on species might allow us to understand better the complexities—the ecologies—through which to better take care of notions such as freedom of movement, leading, perhaps, to a stronger notion of an ecology of practices that might at the very minimum lead to different practices of animal internment.

9. In "The Thinking-Feeling of What Happens," in *Semblance and Event* (Cambridge, Mass.: MIT Press, 2011), Brian Massumi develops a concept of semblance that emphasizes the notion here developed of "likeness." He writes: "The 'likeness' of things is a qualitative fringe, or aura to use a totally unpopular word, that betokens a moreness to life."

10. Deleuze and Guattari write: "Once again, we turn to children. Note how they talk about animals, and are moved by them. They make a list of affects. Little Hans's horse is not representative but affective. It is not a member of a species but an element or individual in a machinic assemblage: draft horse-omnibus-street. It is defined by a list of active and passive affects in the context of the individuated assemblage it is part of: having eyes blocked by blinders, having a bit and a bridle, being proud, having a big peepee-maker, pulling heavy loads, being whipped, falling, making a din with its legs, biting, etc. These affects circulate and are transformed within the assemblage: what a horse 'can do.'" Gilles Deleuze and Félix Guattari, *A Thousand Plateaus: Capitalism and Schizophrenia,* trans. Brian Massumi (Minneapolis: University of Minnesota Press, 1987), 257.

11. Ibid.

12. There is a large literature on "gender dysphoria" and autism. This literature tends to take gender identity as a given, ignoring the rich autistic literature on their experience of gender's complexity and autistics' experience of not adhering to pre-fixed categories. In *Women from Another Planet? Our Lives in the Universe of Autism,* Kearns Miller writes: "For some of us here, our lives, outlook, and behavior don't have much of a sense of gender at all. I myself live a somewhat femme life but it feels in some sense detachable, like a costume. I was an androgynous kid and most clearly perceive the world in a non-gendered way." Jean Kearns Miller, ed., *Woman from Another Planet—Our Lives in the Universe of Autism* (Detroit, Mich.: Dancing Mind Books, 2003), 38. See *Woman from Another Planet* for a variety of perspectives on gender and engendering.

13. Raymond Ruyer, *Genèse des formes vivantes* (Paris: Flammarion, 1958), 149, quoted in Brian Massumi, "Animalité et abstraction: Ecrire comme un rat tord sa queue," in *Philosophie* 112 (2011), my translation.

14. Brian Massumi, "Ceci n'est pas une morsure: Animalité et abstraction chez Deleuze et Guattari" in *Philosophie;* my translations throughout.

15. Ibid.

16. Henri Bergson, *L'évolution créatrice,* (Paris: PUF, 1941), 180. The French "jouée" is translated to "acted" in the English. See Ibid., 181.

17. Massumi, "Ceci n'est pas une morsure."

18. Ibid.

19. Brian Massumi, "A Thinking-Feeling of What Happens," *How Is Research-Creation, Inflexions: A Journal for Research Creation,* no. 1 (2008). See also Massumi, *Semblance and Event.*

20. In Whitehead, mentality and appetition are two different concepts, though aligned. He writes: "In physical experience, the forms are the defining factors: in mental experience the forms connect the immediate occasions with occasions which lie beyond. The connection of immediate fact with the future resides in its appetitions" (*FR,* 32). I reduce the concept here to the force of appetition simply to foreground how mentality is not of the mind but of the "hunger" of the process.

21. http://en.wikipedia.org/wiki/Kanzi.

22. Jim Sinclair writes: "In my own experience, sensory sensitivities can be painful and can prevent enjoyment of some aspects of normal social involvement—but I gain so much beauty and meaning from the way my senses work! My hearing is oversensitive and this is bothersome at times, but I wouldn't change it because I don't want to lose the colors of voices and the tactility of music. My vision is not just oversensitive

but is scrambled and difficult to use. I would be cautiously interested in exploring therapies to enable me to have more functional use of my vision. The reason for caution was illustrated a couple of years ago when I tried wearing Irlen lenses. After an adjustment period, I found that the tinted lenses did indeed make certain utilitarian visual tasks easier—but they also messed up my hearing. I couldn't see sounds anymore. I came up with the compromise solution of getting the tinted lenses put in flip-up frames, so I could have them flipped down when I needed efficient vision to do mundane things, and flip them up out of the way when I wanted to focus on something personally meaningful without being distracted. This still seems to me like it would be the best solution, but unfortunately the flip-up frames are not sturdy enough to withstand being used by a person with my motor planning problems. After the fourth or fifth time that I broke them, I decided it wasn't worth the hassle anymore. For me, it is more adaptive to find ways to compensate for my poor visual processing than to sacrifice meaning in perception by wearing the lenses all the time." http://www.jimsinclair.org/.

23. http://www.existenceiswonderful.com/.

24. See Ralph Savarese, "More Than a Thing to Ignore: An Interview with Tito Rajarshi Mukhopadhyay," in Savrese and Savarese, special issue on Autism, *Disabilities Studies Quarterly,* http://www.dsq-sds.org/article/view/1055/1242.

25. Jane Bennett, *Vibrant Matter: A Political Ecology of Things* (Durham, N.C.: Duke University Press, 2010), 99, 120.

26. William James, "A World of Pure Experience," in *Essays in Radical Empiricism* (Lincoln: University of Nebraska Press, 1996), 42.

27. Prince-Hughes, "Cultural Commentary."

THIRTEEN

Of "Experiential Togetherness"

Toward a More Robust Empiricism

Steven Meyer

The little words "is," "and," "or," "together,"
are traps of ambiguity.
—Alfred North Whitehead, "Analysis of Meaning"
in *Essays in Science and Philosophy*

Veritable High Priest of Togetherness

Let me begin by invoking an occasion deep within the Whitehead archive, the publication of an article titled "E Pluribus Togetherness," by one Hugh Rodney King, which appeared in the August 1957 issue of *Harper's Magazine*.[1] Whitehead was hardly unknown to the editors of the journal—Jacques Barzun, author of the wonderful *Stroll with William James* a quarter century later and already a Columbia institution, supervised the book reviews, and the same issue contains an article by the management-guru-to-be Peter F. Drucker on "The New Philosophy Comes to Life," touting a "new emphasis on process"—yet little has come down to us about the redoubtable Mr. King.[2]

I say redoubtable because what I have been able to track is impressive: a 1946 graduate of the University of Oregon, King was awarded a Rhodes scholarship in 1948. His essay "A. N. Whitehead and the Concept of Metaphysics" had appeared in the April 1947 issue of the journal *Philosophy of Science*,[3] and in 1949 King published an essay on "Whitehead's Doctrine of Causal Efficacy" in the *Journal of Philosophy*.[4] There followed two years later a lengthy evaluation of Gilbert Ryle's *The Concept of Mind* in the same journal[5]—the byline still locating the author in "Oxford, England." In addition, King published a pair of essays on Aristotle: "Aristotle and the Paradoxes of Zeno," again in 1949 in the *Journal of Philosophy*,[6] and "Aristotle without Prima Materia," in the June 1956 issue of the *Journal of the History of Ideas*[7]—the byline now transferred to New York City.

Certainly, a very promising start for a young academic, yet in the end only a start. For we are informed in *Harper's* that besides his Oxford studies, King was "formerly a graduate student in philosophy at Harvard"—no doubt accounting for his whereabouts during the missing years between 1951 and 1956—and "is now doing public relations in New York."[8] After 1957 King, who mentions a wife and three-year-old child in the *Harper's* piece, vanishes from the public record, consumed, it would seem, by the world of *Mad Men.* Yet, even so, the Aristotle essays, with their patina of Whitehead, provoked their fair share of controversy. Thus the Harvard philosopher Donald C. Williams remarked in a famous 1951 essay, "The Myth of Passage"—like "Aristotle and the Paradoxes of Zeno" published in the *Journal of Philosophy*—that in his essay King had offered "an exceptionally ingenious, serious, and explicit statement of the philosophy which I am opposing."[9] Did this response account for King's admission into the Harvard program? Did it subsequently account for his departure? Then in 1958, the Cornell classicist Friedrich Solmsen published a ten-page rebuttal in the *Journal of the History of Ideas* of "Aristotle without Prima Materia."[10] An allusion to the controversy still popped up in *Mind* fifteen years later.

So King had serious if somewhat disputed credentials when in 1957 he challenged the right of the women's magazine *McCall's* to the term *togetherness.* Several years earlier *McCall's* had adopted the slogan "The Magazine of Togetherness," and the term had become so closely identified with the magazine in the American mind that King could complain with some justness that *McCall's* was taking too much credit not just for the association but for the word itself. ("As late as March 15, 1957," King writes, "the veteran *Advertising Agency Magazine* stated editorially, '*McCall's* . . . has added a new word to the vocabulary.'") Conversely, "the man who has probably done more than anyone else to put the word on its feet, the veritable high priest of togetherness," none other than "Alfred North Whitehead (1861–1947)," had been given too little credit, or if the *Oxford English Dictionary* was any measure, none at all.[11]

Here is a passage from King's article, including an extensive quotation from Whitehead that offers a handy measure of the feet with which the philosopher had furnished the term. "I'd hate to think," King ventures, "that my wife and I and five million other readers of 'The Magazine of Togetherness' might bring up a whole generation who couldn't understand page 48, for example," of *Process and Reality,* where Whitehead wrote that "relevance must express some real fact of togetherness among forms," and continued:

> The ontological principle can be expressed as: All real togetherness is togetherness in the formal constitution of an actuality. So if there is relevance of what in the temporal world is unrealized, the relevance must express a fact of togetherness in the formal constitution of a non-temporal actuality. But by the principle of relativity there can only be one non-derivative actuality, unbounded by its prehensions of an actual world.

"Such a primordial superject of creativity," Whitehead went on to assert, "is the ultimate basic adjustment of the togetherness"—and with that King closes the citation.[12] The *ontological principle* and the *principle of relativity* are technical terms of Whitehead's, as are the *subjectivist* and *reformed subjectivist doctrines* (brief discussion to follow)—likewise *prehension, primordial, superject, creativity.* And *real togetherness.*

For an additional turn of the screw, consider the following remarks by George H. Allen, assistant publisher of *McCall's,* in a letter to the editor of *Harper's.* King had alluded in his essay to the conclusions of "legal friends" that the failure of *McCall's* to have "printed on its editorial product—or, for that matter, on any product—the official signs of the Registered Trademark, either after, near, by, or in a footnote to 'Togetherness' . . . might seem to indicate a casual, indeed, a flagrant disregard for the hoary traditions of trademark protection."[13] Allen responds:

> As our legal friends will tell you, in this country rights in a trademark arise from use and not from registration. "Togetherness" actually is registered by us to have a formal record of our claims. But it is the continuous identification and association with *McCall's,* "The Magazine of Togetherness" as stated on each cover of our magazine, in our advertising and promotion, and even through such articles as yours, which give us a right to regard "Togetherness" as something which cannot be used commercially without our permission.[14]

Trademarking "Togetherness" may be the height or depth of something, particularly *in this country,* as Allen insists, with its motto "e pluribus unum."[15] Thankfully, such curtailing of the public domain does not extend to uses like Whitehead's, owing to the philosopher's patent lack of venal motivation. This is no less obviously the case in the following set of observations—the third of the trifecta of quotations I am laying out in the first section of this essay—again from *Process and Reality* and cited in part by King in the earlier essay on Whitehead's doctrine of causal efficacy. (It also serves as the source of my title.) "There is *a togetherness of the component elements in individual experience,*" Whitehead remarks:

> This "togetherness" has that special peculiar meaning of "togetherness in experience." It is a togetherness of its own kind, explicable by reference to nothing else. For the purpose of this discussion it is indifferent whether we speak of a 'stream' of experience or of an 'occasion' of experience. With the former alternative there is togetherness in the stream, and with the latter alternative there is togetherness in the occasion. In either case, there is the unique "experiential togetherness." (*PR*, 189, emphasis added)

At this point King adds his voice to what thus becomes a passage that the three of us—Whitehead; King, quoting Whitehead; me, quoting King and Whitehead—can be viewed as conjointly uttering. (Whitehead has just referred to a pair of metaphysical difficulties; King cites the reference, I shall not.) *We* continue:

> The consideration of experiential togetherness raises the final metaphysical question: whether there is any other meaning of "togetherness." The denial of any alternative meaning, that is to say, of any meaning not abstracted from the experiential meaning *[here King briefly falls silent]*, is the 'subjectivist' doctrine. This reformed version of the subjectivist doctrine *[here King joins in again]* is the doctrine of the philosophy of organism—

—as Whitehead termed the philosophical scheme he sought to elucidate (*PR*, 190).[16]

Whereas King avoids any reference in his recital to the so-called subjectivist doctrine or to Whitehead's alternative to it, I shall take a contrary tack and cite several additional observations by Whitehead that build on these references, in order to set up a further observation of my own. In the first place, Whitehead remarked of Kant in the same extended passage that "he adopted a subjectivist position, so that the temporal world was merely experienced. But according to [Kant's] form of the subjectivist doctrine"—nothing less than the subjectivist doctrine proper—"no element in the temporal world could itself be an experient" and so responsible for any actual experiencing. "The difficulties of the subjectivist doctrine arise when it is combined," as Kant proceeded to do, "with the 'sensationalist' doctrine [of Hume] concerning the analysis of *the components which are together in experience*" (*PR*, 190, emphasis added).

In returning here to the juxtapositon of togetherness and experience, albeit in a slightly different formulation, Whitehead has arrived at the crux of his argument. "With the sensationalist assumption, or with any generalization of that doctrine, so long as . . . the only elements not stamped with the particularity of that individual 'occasion'—or 'stream'—of experience are universals such as 'redness' or 'shape,'" the subjectivist philosopher is left with two alternatives: "either Bradley's doctrine of a single experient, the absolute, or Leibniz's doctrine of many windowless monads." "In his final metaphysics," Kant "must either retreat to Leibniz, or advance to Bradley. Either alternative stamps experience with a certain air of illusoriness" (*PR*, 190). By contrast, an analysis like Whitehead's own, starting out from the "togetherness of the component elements in individual experience" rather than from "the components which are together in experience," offered a third alternative unavailable to Kant (or Leibniz or Bradley)—and, clearly, an alternate understanding of experiential togetherness as well. Although the philosophy of organism, Whitehead noted in conclusion, "admits the subjectivist doctrine," it "rejects the sensationalist doctrine: hence its doctrine of the objectification of one actual occasion in the experience of another actual occasion. Each actual entity is a throb of experience including the actual world within its scope" (*PR*, 190). Several more "trademarked" terms of Whitehead's are introduced—technical terms like *actual occasion, actual entity, objectification* (albeit suggestive today of non-Whiteheadian "brands" of analysis), even *throb of experience* (admittedly possessing a strongly Jamesian flavor)—and reference has been made to one of the proximate sources of Whitehead's penchant for *togetherness*, F. H. Bradley.

The question sometimes arises as to just how different the author of *Process and Reality* actually is from the author of *Appearance and Reality*, and Whitehead all but dares us to compare (and contrast) his understanding of *togetherness* with Bradley's.[17] In this context it is fitting that two prominent uses by William James of the term—there is also an earlier use with reference to Hegel and a subsequent one regarding Kant—occur in a pair of passages James cites from *Appearance and Reality* in the course of one of his major criticisms of Bradley. As so often occurs, James and Whitehead are walking along the same path—Whitehead is *thinking with* James, as Isabelle Stengers might put it—in the process together transforming Bradley's idealist *togetherness* into its radical or robust empiricist counterpart.[18]

Togetherness and "Togetherness"

It will be recalled that King found "the entry under 'togetherness' in the eleventh volume of the *Oxford English Dictionary*" wanting:

> [It] says, among other things, that the first recorded usage of the word dates back to around 1656, or about the time the Commonwealth cracked up and

> Cromwell's star was burning itself out in the thickening atmosphere of English anarchy—an opportune hour for togetherness if there ever was one. Yet I gather that the word never really took hold, since the *O.E.D.*'s next reference is well over two centuries later in the *Monist* (1892), a periodical of limited circulation and virtually no advertising budget. After this date, unfortunately, the *O.E.D.* is not of much help. It does make a few curt remarks about togetherness's sister word "togetherhood" (now that's a word with some *real* overtones), but then the writer goes off onto another subject without so much as mentioning the man who has probably done more than anyone else to put the word on its feet, the veritable high priest of togetherness.[19]

In point of fact, the failure of the *O.E.D.* to mention Whitehead is hardly surprising, as the eleventh volume (Ti–U) was only published in 1926. The 1933 *Supplement*, added upon the occasion of the republication of the entire twelve-volume work, actually does cite one of several uses in *Science and the Modern World* (1925): "Cognition discloses an event as being an activity, organizing a real togetherness of alien things."[20] This sentence is one of four added to the entry, alongside the immortal "A piece of string is a thing that, in the main, makes for togetheriness" of Samuel Butler, to illustrate a cognate term that died on the vine. One of the interesting things to be observed in comparing the 1926 entry to the 1933 supplemental entry is that as of 1926, or whenever the initial entry was composed—likely several decades earlier insofar as the only contemporary reference is to the *Monist* of 1892—"togetherness," together with "togetherhood," is classed as a "nonce-wd [word]" and appears only within the entry for the adverb "together." The separate 1933 entry, by contrast, begins with the following instructions: "Delete *nonce-wd* and add examples."

When a second edition finally came out more than half a century later, in 1989, the instructions had indeed been followed. "Togetherness" had long ceased to be the sort of word devised for a single occasion, and the entry contains fifteen broad-ranging examples of the term's use. Unfortunately, in a decision calculated to disappoint King and any number of Whitehead-fanciers, neither the sentence from *Science and the Modern World* nor any other sentence by "the veritable high priest of togetherness" was included. Yet all was not lost. For, as I shall argue, one may elicit the lineaments of Whitehead's own characteristic practice from several of the term's earliest uses. Three quotations, selected from works published between 1892 and 1920, tell the story among them of how Whitehead came to use "togetherness" with such abandon—how shifting philosophical usage would have made the term so appealing to him even as he prepared to apply one more turn of the screw.[21]

These are the quotations:

> 1892, *Monist* 2:218: Even if the link is a feeling it cannot be less than a feeling of the togetherness of two other feelings.[22]
>
> 1912, *Mind* 21:2: The togetherness or compresence of the perceiving and the table is the perception *of* the table.[23]
>
> 1920, A. S. Pringle-Pattison, *Idea of God,* 354: Our primitive and basal experience of time is thus characterized by a togetherness of parts or elements.[24]

The first of the three illustrations is culled from an article entitled "Professor Clifford on the Soul in Nature," which appeared in the important American philosophical journal the *Monist,* then just in its second year. That this use of "togetherness" would have come to the attention of a reader for the dictionary is less of a stretch than one might imagine, given the American provenance. For the author, Frederick Cornwallis Conybeare, was an Oxford-affiliated scholar writing about William Kingdon Clifford (a famous Cambridge man), best remembered today as the object of William James's withering criticism in "The Will to Believe" and as one of a handful of truly brilliant and original nineteenth-century British mathematicans.

Like Max Müller—Oxford Sanskritist, professor of comparative religion, and translator into English of the first edition of Kant's *Critique of Pure Reason* (1881), who was also Conybeare's father-in-law—the editor of the *Monist,* Paul Carus, was a German émigré, and the preceding issues of the *Monist* had included an essay by the non-Darwinian Müller "On Thought and Language," followed by a response from George John Romanes, the important British evolutionary biologist and friend of Darwin who coined the term "neo-Darwinism," a further response by Carus to both Müller and Romanes, and a follow-up by Müller in the same issue containing Conybeare's essay.[25] At the same time, Carus was involved on the pages of the *Monist* in an ongoing exchange with the Austrian physicist and philosopher Ernst Mach regarding the nature of feeling and sensation, and more generally the viability of several variations on the originally Kantian notion of things-in-themselves. This particular controversy had its source in a two-part essay by Carus in another publication he edited, the weekly *Open Court,* in which an argument concerning "feeling and motion" was framed chiefly in terms supplied by Clifford "in his excellent essay on the 'Nature of Things' in themselves."[26] No doubt Conybeare's article, which focuses on the same essay by Clifford, was passed along to Carus by Müller.[27]

One additional feature of the intellectual setting remains to be sketched before I turn directly to Conybeare and the sentence the compilers of the *O.E.D.* abstracted from his essay on Clifford. It so happens that William James's only substantial contribution to the small empire of publications Carus managed for the Open Court Publishing Company immediately followed the second and concluding part of the essay on feeling and motion. James had penned "The Importance of Individuals" a decade earlier in response to criticisms of the *Atlantic Monthly* article "Great Men, Great Thoughts, and the Environment," in which, as he remarked in a headnote in the *Open Court,* he had attempted "to defend the Great Man Theory of History from the attacks of Messrs. Spencer and Grant Allen" (2438).[28] (Despite "the *Atlantic's* publisher" having "declined to print" it at the time, James now proposed that "as the quarrel between Hero-worship and Sociology is always going on in some form or other it may be that remarks on the subject are always in order." Apparently he had promised Carus something else, and offered the newly recovered essay in its place.[29]) I am not concerned here to evaluate James's evolutionary defense of "hero-worship" and more generally of the role of the individual in history (including intellectual history); yet as I shall indicate in the remarks that follow, in his own multiple uses of "togetherness," James shadows each of the three disparate entries selected for the *O.E.D.*, effectively triangulating, and strengthening, what might otherwise seem a fairly capricious argument leading directly from dictionary to Whitehead. James took much the same route as Whitehead did, and did so in conversation with many of the same or equivalent figures.[30] As a term of art in Anglo-American philosophical discourse, thus expanded to incorporate James's practice, "togetherness" provides evidence for a larger claim regarding which the present essay makes no more than a down-payment—namely, the breadth of James's anticipation of Whitehead's "flux-philosophy," in detail and in the aggregate.

Now back to Conybeare, whom Carus presents as "a personal disciple of Professor Green"—referring to T. H. Green, generally credited with having inaugurated the British Idealist movement in the second half of the nineteenth century.[31] After complimenting Conybeare for his "lucid presentation of the transcendentalist position," Carus summarizes the essence of the argument as follows: "Mr. Conybeare, like Prof. F. Max Müller, assumes a Self independent of the reality from which the idea of self has been abstracted, and he attempts to prove the existence of this self."[32] Elsewhere Carus proposes that both Müller and Green ("the founder of the Oxford transcendentalist school")—and by extension Conybeare, son-in-law of one, disciple of the other—"start from this assumption, that man's mental activity is performed by a something which is quite distinct from it."[33] "This something," Carus adds, "is the thing in itself of the human soul"; it is "'the worker who does the work of the mind,'" in Müller's phrasing (cited by Carus); it is "the self-perception of the ego, the sense that in all my various feelings it is *I* who am conscious, this 'unity of apperception,'" in Conybeare's (and Kant's).[34]

The intricacies of Conybeare's and Carus's arguments do not need rehearsing in the present context—neither Conybeare's criticism of Clifford's postulate that an "elementary feeling" possesses an "absolute and unrelated existence," and so is, Clifford insists, "'*Ding an sich*,'" nor Carus's criticism of Clifford's and Conybeare's divergent stances regarding the precise nature of things in themselves (214, 223). The general summary should suffice to bring out relevant aspects in the two passages that follow. The first contains Conybeare's complete sentence, of which only a segment survived the transition to the *O.E.D.* The second is Carus's response:

> If feelings are joined by links of what nature are these links? Clifford does not say that they also are feelings, so presumably they are not; in that case no link is left save a connecting self. But even if the link is a feeling it cannot be less than a feeling of the togetherness of two other feelings, but such a feeling would involve memory of those feelings and memory involves self-hood. It is really, however, an abuse of words to apply the term feeling in such a case. We might with Hume ask of this feeling which links other feelings, "Is it a taste, a smell, a sound, an impression of sight or touch?"[35]

> Mr. Conybeare speaks of the self as *having* memory, while in fact, memory is one of the features, indeed the most important feature, of mind-activity.
>
> Says Mr. Conybeare:
>
> "Such a feeling [of the togetherness of two feelings] would involve memory and memory involves self-hood."
>
> Memory does not involve any transcendental self-hood. True self-hood, viz. that which can reasonably be understood by self-hood, is not prior to, not the cause of memory; self-hood, i.e., the personality of a man, the organized unity of the psychical aspect of a human organism, is consequent upon, it is the effect of, memory. Self-hood is the product of memory.[36]

Speaking broadly, a number of diverse monisms are in play here—idealist monisms of differing sorts (Clifford, Green) and a non-idealist or positivist monism (Carus), a perfectly fitting mix in a journal titled the *Monist*. None of these appeals as such to the richly pluralistic approaches of either James or Whitehead (*pace* Bertrand Russell), which combine features distributed among the several monisms. Still, Conybeare's distress at what he takes to be the thoroughly incoherent phrasing of "a feeling of the togetherness of two other feelings" is instructive. (The distress does not register at all in the manner in which the sentence is cited in the *O.E.D.*)

This second-order feeling, Conybeare proposes, cannot be any particular sensation; hence, it cannot properly speaking be called a feeling at all. As such it confirms that "the togetherness of . . . feelings" is a product of *something else,* and as a disciple of Green's, he knows just what this is. Clearly, Carus offers an alternate rendering, although one may suspect it is perhaps a little *too* efficient—after the example of the baby and the bathwater. So, it is left to James and Whitehead to hesitate at the ready identification, common practice in British philosophy since Locke, of *feeling* with *sensation.* Instead they will variously propose that phrasing like *a feeling of the togetherness of other feelings* may indicate a different and more satisfactory way of combining empiricist and rationalist intuitions (to introduce a contrast Whitehead and James, among many others, inherited from Kant), one that does not result in such phrasing striking one as hopelessly oxymoronic, which is its effect on thinkers who take their guidance directly or even ultimately from Kant.

Quite famously, James did not set much store by Kant. Here is a late reference:

> The account I give directly contradicts that which Kant gave which has prevailed since Kant's time. Kant always speaks of the aboriginal sensible flux as a "manifold" of which he considers the essential character to be its disconnectedness. *To get any togetherness at all into it* requires, he thinks, the agency of the "transcendental ego of apperception," and to get any definite connections requires the agency of the understanding, with its synthetizing concepts or "categories." (Emphasis added.)[37]

And here, lacking the "togetherness" only in name, is an earlier reference:

> Both agree that the elements of the subjective stream are discrete and separate and constitute what Kant calls a "manifold." But while the associationists think that a "manifold" can form a single knowledge, the egoists deny this, and say that the knowledge comes only when the manifold is subjected to the synthetizing activity of an ego. Both make an identical initial hypothesis; but the egoist, finding it won't express the facts, adds another hypothesis to correct it. Now I do not wish just yet to "commit myself" about the existence or non-existence of the ego, but I do contend that we need not invoke it for this particular reason—namely, because the manifold of ideas has to be reduced to unity. *There is no manifold of coexisting ideas;* the notion of such a thing is a chimera. *Whatever things are thought in relation are thought from the outset in a unity, in a single pulse of subjectivity, a single psychosis, feeling, or state of mind.*[38]

Almost forty years later Whitehead would write that *"the difficulties of the subjectivist doctrine arise when [as in Kant] it is combined with the 'sensationalist' doctrine [of Hume] concerning the analysis of the components which are together in experience"* (*PR*, 190, emphasis added).

And here is the inaugural reference to "togetherness" in *Process and Reality:*

> Philosophical thought has made for itself difficulties by dealing exclusively in very abstract notions, such as those of mere awareness, mere private sensation, mere emotion, mere purpose, mere appearance, mere causation. These are the ghosts of the old "faculties," banished from psychology, but still haunting metaphysics. *There can be no "mere" togetherness of such abstractions.* The result is that philosophical discussion is enmeshed in the fallacy of "misplaced concreteness"—the all too common attribution of unwarranted concreteness to what are actually abstractions. (*PR*, 18, emphasis added)[39]

"There is no manifold of coexisting ideas." "There can be no 'mere' togetherness of such abstractions." The parallel is even sharper: for where Whitehead immediately alluded to the fallacious effect of "misplaced concreteness" (and directed the reader to an earlier extended consideration of the fallacy in *Science and the Modern World*), James with equal dispatch explained that "the reason why this fact [that things "thought in relation are thought from the outset in a unity, in a single pulse"] is so strangely garbled in the books seems to be what on an earlier page . . . I called the psychologist's fallacy."[40] Whitehead and James are certainly not talking about the same thing—Whitehead was offering an account of the *effects* of faulty philosophical reasoning; James was giving one concerning the *causes* of faulty psychological reasoning—yet Kant's role in each argument indicates the extent of the overlap. One effect of faulty philosophical reasoning has been to encourage faulty psychological reasoning, even as, from Whitehead's perspective, the ghosts of psychologies past continue to haunt the metaphysical present.

By 1912, when the original of the second *O.E.D.* quotation appeared in the British journal *Mind: A Quarterly Review of Psychology and Philosophy,* where James had been so frequent and valued a contributor, the peripatetic American had been stopped in his tracks, transformed into a peculiar mix of psychologist past and metaphysician present. "The unexpected death of Prof. William James," Paul Carus informed his readers in the October 1910 issue of the *Monist,*

> has caused grief in the wide circle of his friends. . . . Professor James will be missed by friends and antagonists for with all his faults as a thinker he was a

> man of unusual genius, who by the very way in which he attacked the problems in which he was interested stirred the imagination and quickened the spirit of inquiry.[41]

Some Problems of Philosophy[42] had appeared posthumously in 1911, and *Essays in Radical Empiricism*[43] would come out in 1912, so the full measure of the metaphysician was still to be taken; indeed, it is fair to say that the full measure of the metaphysician-cum-psychologist is still in the process of being taken a century later.

As for Whitehead, it is no less fair to observe that, despite the publication in 1912 of the second of three volumes of *Principia Mathematica*, no one except perhaps Whitehead himself foresaw the philosopher of science and metaphysician who was to emerge in the decade following World War I—out of nowhere, it would seem. Certainly not his collaborator Russell, in the midst of making a name for himself as a modern philosopher and soliciting ideas from Whitehead, among others, as to how best to proceed. Certainly not Samuel Alexander, author of "The Method of Metaphysics; and the Categories," which appeared in the January 1912 issue of *Mind*[44]—and who a decade later would pair himself and Whitehead among the few philosophers prepared to "take Time seriously."[45]

Alexander had been a student at Balliol College, Oxford, where it is likely that Green and a student of Green's, Henry Nettleship, tutored him, in addition to the Shakespearean and Hegelian A. C. Bradley, younger brother of F. H. Bradley. In 1882, the year of Green's death, he was elected a fellow at Lincoln College, Oxford, where he taught on and off for the next decade, before being appointed professor of philosophy at Owens College (subsequently the University of Manchester). Alexander was the first Jew to obtain a fellowship at either Oxford or Cambridge. Although he cannot strictly be called an Idealist, even in his early, more Hegelian years, when he was concerned to interpret Hegel within a Darwinian framework, the description Dorothy Emmet supplies in an essay comparing Alexander with Whitehead seems just:[46] "Alexander's background was the Oxford Idealism of which F. H. Bradley was the most distinguished figure. He developed his views in a struggle against Idealism, particularly against its theory of knowledge, and he ended with a naturalistic realism."[47]

Space, Time, and Deity (1920), Alexander's Gifford Lectures, proved of great import for Whitehead's *Science and the Modern World* and his own set of Gifford Lectures, *Process and Reality,* as the two men readily acknowledged. Whitehead thus offered to send Alexander "a copy of my 'Gifford's.' I believe them to be in general agreement with your 'Space, Time and

Deity'"; and Alexander in a letter to Emmet enthused, "I read Whitehead naturally not only to understand him but to save my own soul. I think of myself only as having done what Burke said he did for [Samuel] Johnson in conversation—'rung the bell for him'"—although Alexander did admit he was more of a Spinozist than Whitehead and Whitehead more of a Leibnizian. "So there is a side to me which has to be either lost by obstinacy or saved by surrender to Whitehead (or of course the other way about)."[48]

Victor Lowe, Whitehead's biographer, recalled Whitehead having told him "that Samuel Alexander was the philosopher of his time from whom he got most. But he gave me no details, saying only that he and Alexander 'conceived the problem of metaphysics in the same way,' that is, as reconciliation of the unity of the universe (emphasized in Spinoza's metaphysics) and the multitude of individuals (emphasized by Leibniz)."[49] To this Lowe adds: "Whitehead also remarked to me that Alexander, almost alone among their British contemporaries, did not, implicitly at least, assume that our experience is basically an experience of sense-data.[50] Perception, for Alexander, consisted in the 'compresence' of an object and a subject who 'enjoys' a 'togetherness' with the contemplated object." "This is not far from Whitehead's notion of prehension."[51] It is also the gist of the *O.E.D.* citation.

To be sure, many significant differences arise between Whitehead and Alexander. Lowe notes that Whitehead "did not agree with the hypothesis of Alexander's Giffords—th[at] 'Space-Time is the stuff of which matter and all things are specifications.'"[52] Similarly, Emmet remarks that

> the cardinal difference between Whitehead's view and Alexander's is that the former's view is an explicitly relational one, in which Space and Time are derived from relations between events, and the fundamental ontology is one of events. Alexander, on the other hand, absolutizes Space-Time, and even speaks of it as a "stuff" of which things are made.[53]

Finally, one may observe that despite Whitehead's having, in his copy of *Space, Time, and Deity,* "underscored" the proposition that "the relation of a conscious subject to the object which transcends it is not unique, but is 'found wherever two finites are compresent with each other'"—even going so far as to write "Yes" in the margin and thereby permitting the ever-cautious Lowe to venture that "Whitehead sympathized with Alexander's generalization of the subject-object relation"—it is also the case that "when Whitehead started to develop his metaphysical system, he would deal primarily with the transition from object to subject, and the concrescence of the subject."[54] "There is none of this in *Space, Time, and Deity,*" Lowe comments.

In a statement like the one cited by the *O.E.D.*, "The togetherness or compresence of the perceiving and the table is the perception of the table," Alexander is describing the cognitive experience of perception in terms of compresence and togetherness much as Whitehead describes it in terms of what he calls "prehension"—but as Lowe notes, it is not quite the same ("not far"). In a second essay, published in *Mind* the following summer and titled "On Relations; and in Particular the Cognitive Relation," Alexander elaborated: "This relation of knowing an object occurs when a thing called the subject, which possesses the property of consciousness, being stirred by some means or other (of which more hereafter) into consciousness of a certain 'direction' finds itself in the presence of an object, not itself, appropriate to that condition of consciousness."[55]

"Let us abstract from the manner in which the consciousness is evoked," Alexander continued—hence ignoring whether "the act of consciousness is evoked by the object itself," as "in the case of sensation or perception," or "indirectly" by "images, memories, thoughts"—

> and we have in all cases of cognition of an object *the compresence of two things*, the subject in a condition of apprehension, and the object revealed to the extent to which it is apprehended. The relation is thus the whole situation constituted by *the togetherness of these two things*, so far as it connects them. The percipient enters into the situation as the act of, say, perception the object, as perceived, that is in the form in which it is perceived. The relation is that of *this togetherness*. (Emphasis added.)[56]

The appeal of Alexander's line of reasoning for Whitehead lies in the way it is generalizable from the cognitive relation to relations between objects as such, and that Alexander does in fact so generalize it.[57] "Thus the table and I are together in precisely the same sense as the table and the chair are together."[58] "There is nothing in the compresence between the mind and its objects to distinguish that relation from the compresence between any two objects which it contemplates, like the tree and the grass."[59] A much less appealing aspect of Alexander's approach, as Lowe suggests, is that he appears to limit his analysis to the generalized subject-object relation (the subject's experience of an object) understood as equivalent to the generalized object-object relation (objects' experiences of one another), while leaving out of his account several different sets of relations no less integral to what Whitehead conceptualized as prehension—namely, "the transition from object to subject" (past to present experience) and "the concrescence of the subject" (the experience of the present).[60]

In January 1903 James reviewed a volume for *Mind* with the title *Personal Idealism: Philosophical Essays by Eight Members of the University of Oxford.* The interest of the volume lay in part in its contribution to "the sense," as W. J. Mander has observed in a recent history of British idealism, that "something akin to a *school* of like-minded philosophers" had "c[o]me to obtain," and in part in the evidence it supplied that their presence was registered even at the seat of Absolute Idealism.[61] For our purposes, however, the interest of the volume lies elsewhere, quite literally, pointing toward James as well as the philosopher whom Mander characterizes as "in a sense the 'head' of the Personal Idealist thinkers" and still another philosopher whom Whitehead recalled as "an intimate friend . . . almost from the very first day he came to the University."[62] Even as the volume self-consciously pointed inwardly, it unself-consciously pointed away from Oxford in the several directions of the two Cambridges and Edinburgh.

"A re-anthropomorphised Universe," James explained, "is the general outcome of this philosophy, which on the whole continues Lotze, Sigwart, and Renouvier's line of thinking, although it is so much more radically experiential in tone."[63] However much he may have disagreed with particulars of the arguments made by this band of Personal Idealists (including F. C. S. Schiller, whose "humanism" and James's pragmatism would remain closely allied), James was determined to keep his eyes on the prize:

> I add no criticism—although I think that every essay calls for some objection of detail—because I think that the important thing to recognize is that we have here a distinct new departure in contemporary thought, the combination, namely, of a teleological and spiritual inspiration with the same kind of conviction that the particulars of experience constitute the stronghold of reality as has usually characterized the materialistic type of mind.[64]

In his urgent quest for a "revised empiricism" James was ever on the lookout for peers who combined empiricism and rationalism in the non-Kantian order he found temperamentally, and intellectually, congenial; and if they wished to call their worldview "empirical idealism," he was not going to nitpick.[65]

In any case, the *Personal Idealism* volume provided James with a terrific opportunity to redescribe his radical empiricism, ever in the making:

> If empiricism is to be radical it must indeed admit the concrete data of experience in their full completeness. The only fully complete concrete data are, however, *the successive moments of our own several histories,* taken with their subjective personal aspect, as well as with their 'objective' deliverance or 'con-

> tent.' *After the analogy of these moments of experiences must all complete reality be conceived.*

To this asseveration James immediately added:

> Radical empiricism thus leads to the assumption *of a collectivism of personal lives (which may be of any grade of complication, and superhuman or infrahuman as well as human),* variously cognitive of each other, variously conative and impulsive, genuinely evolving and changing by effort and trial, and by their interaction and cumulative achievements *making up the world.* (Emphasis added.)[66]

It is precisely this combination of "moments of experiences," providing a necessary model for "fully complete concrete data," with "the assumption of a collectivism of personal lives"—"of any grade of complication" whatsoever—that Whitehead would unpack in the intricately designed speculative philosophy he delivered in his Gifford Lectures at Edinburgh twenty-five years later.[67] There, he elucidated the complex "experiential togetherness" already introduced above, which similarly combines "the concrescence of the subject" (in moments of experiences) and "the transition from object to subject" (in societies or organisms, as Whitehead alternately called them, offering as much evidence as one might ask for of the thoroughly robust collectivism of personal lives—by no means limited to human beings but operating at every grade of complication, from higgs bosons to neurons to black holes).

I wonder whether Andrew Seth Pringle-Pattison was able to attend Whitehead's inaugural lecture in Edinburgh.

Mander's account of Personal Idealism begins with Pringle-Pattison—former Chair of Logic and Metaphysics at the University of Edinburgh, four-time Gifford lecturer, "Border laird" (on account of an inheritance that required him to change his name from Seth to Pringle-Pattison), "arguably, the culmination of the Scottish philosophical tradition," inarguably, "the first philosopher to give sustained critical scrutiny to that tradition under the label 'Scottish Philosophy,'"[68] author among many other works of the 1887 *Hegelianism and Personality,*[69] which established Personal Idealism as a viable alternative to the Absolute Idealism of Green and his disciples, and author of the third *O.E.D.* citation, "Our primitive and basal experience of time is thus characterized by a togetherness of parts or elements."[70] In Pringle-Pattison's sentence "thus" refers to a page-long quotation from James's *Principles of Psychology,* beginning with the frequently-cited observation that "the practically cognized present is no knife-edge, but a saddle-back with a certain breadth of its own on which we sit perched, and from which we look in two directions into time."[71] Pringle-Pattison was not especially interested in James, however, but rather in the related proposition by James's beloved colleague in the Harvard philosophy department, and neighbor in Cambridge, the Absolute Idealist Josiah Royce, who held, as Pringle-Pattison paraphrased him, that "in the compresence which is thus an essential feature of our consciousness of time we therefore already realize, though doubtless on an infinitesimal scale, the nature of an eternal consciousness."[72]

In a review in *Mind* of the same work Pringle-Pattison was referring to, the second volume of Royce's *The World and the Individual* (yet another set of Gifford Lectures), J. Ellis McTaggart had called this conception of eternal consciousness "the Specious Present of the Absolute[,] an all-embracing Specious Present."[73] With this we return to Whitehead's Cambridge (on the Cam), having first passed, ever so briefly, through James's Cambridge (on the Charles) and Pringle-Pattison's Edinburgh, each locale supplying the academic setting for interrelated if largely uncoordinated responses to the internecine controversies among the Oxford Absolute and Personal Idealists. It was of McTaggart, charismatic Cambridge Hegelian and Idealist, that Whitehead remarked: Despite "hav[ing] never read a page of Hegel"—a proposition the delight in which only increased for Whitehead when he corrected it, as he did immediately: "That is not true. I remember when I was staying with Haldane at Cloan I read one page of Hegel"[74]—it was nonetheless "true that I was influenced by Hegel. I was an intimate friend of McTaggart almost from the first day he came to the University, and saw him for a few minutes almost daily."[75]

From here, it requires just a small interpretative effort to observe that what I am calling the robust empiricisms of James and Whitehead compelled them to take seriously the beliefs and arguments of their Idealist acquaintances and antagonists—especially the acquaintances who functioned as prized intellectual antagonists—a seriousness they have not always been accorded in return. McTaggart offers a good example of the complexities involved in such interactions, especially insofar as one is prepared to take both James and Whitehead into account. Neither McTaggart nor James possessed sympathy for the other's work, a mutual distrust registered in the inadequacy of their published remarks. James would have been most surprised to find McTaggart classed by Mander as a leading Personal Idealist, on a par with Pringle-Pattison; he had always treated McTaggart as an Absolute Idealist and Monist, and a pretty hard-core one at that.[76] At the same time, the care Whitehead displayed in attending to both James's and Royce's speculations concerning not just the specious present but also how it might conceivably be enlarged permitted him to "think with" his close friend McTaggart (in ways I have not discussed here) even as he disagreed with the "feeling of the illusiveness and relative unreality of the temporal world" that motivated McTaggart famously to argue for "the unreality of time" in the pages of *Mind.*

I hope to have shown in this essay that the strongly empiricist manner in which James and Whitehead responded to (some of) the arguments of their Idealist peers, thereby accommodating certain intuitions concerning "togetherness" that did not come natively to them as empiricists, illustrates one sense of the more robust empiricism that attunement to "experiential togetherness" permits. A second sense concerns the way that Whitehead and James were able to address claims made on behalf of the "unreality of the temporal world" in a manner, and with an efficacy, unavailable to traditional British empiricism, precisely because they could avail themselves of arguments that came together under the heading of "togetherness" as the term was used by nineteenth-century British and American Idealists. One can argue, although again I do not do so here, that in the decades following *The Principles of Psychology* James was concerned, with increasing urgency and speculative rigor, to elucidate exactly what it was that "taking time seriously," in Alexander's phrasing, entailed, as Whitehead was in equal measure in the two-plus decades he was able to devote exclusively to philosophical inquiry. In Whitehead's case, such elucidation required the complex understanding of "experiential togetherness" he ultimately arrived at, as something applying to the transitions from object to subject that permit the development of organisms or societies as well as to the concresence of the subject. In this regard although Alexander's empiricism, with its acknowledgment of the insufficiency of sensation as an adequate basis for a truly realist empiricism, proved more robust than that permitted either by Humean empiricisms or the assorted British idealisms, nevertheless insofar as he failed to attend sufficiently to processes of concresence and hence to what James in "A World of Pure Experience" termed "the instant field of the present," it remained less robust than the empiricism James and Whitehead, separately and together, aspired to and accordingly achieved.[77]

Notes

1. Hugh Rodney King, "E Pluribus Togetherness," *Harper's Magazine* 215, no. 1287 (August 1957). Of course, there is no extant Whitehead archive—Whitehead's widow burned his papers at his request. The following essay aims at imagining how one might go about recreating a corner of the archive by situating the emergence of a technical term within a nexus of practices of like- and un-like-minded thinkers.

2. Peter F. Drucker, "The New Philosophy Comes to Life," *Harper's Magazine* 215, no. 1287 (August 1957): 38. After contrasting "the first 'modern' generation[,] that of Newton, Hobbes, and Locke," with "us—the first 'post-modern' generation"—Drucker goes on to locate "anticipations" of processual thinking "in numerous thinkers—for example, in Whitehead, Bergson, Goethe, Leonardo, or Aristotle." Closer to hand, "within the past twenty or thirty years[,] the earliest to expound the new vision in our time was probably that astounding South African, Jan Christiaan Smuts, with his philosophy of 'holism.'" Finally, Drucker mentions "pronounced reflections" of this vision "in the work of two physicists, Lancelot Law Whyte . . . and Erwin Schroedinger," as well as in that of "the distinguished economist Kenneth Boulding," and in the best-selling "paper-back editions" of "the late Ernst Cassirer" (36, 39). Drucker's placement of Whitehead among the anticipators of the new process philosophy rather than among its expositors, like his slightly younger contemporaries Smuts and Cassirer, either indicates ignorance on Drucker's part or worse—namely, an active participation in the broad misrepresentation and repression of the significance of Whitehead's investigations that in the United States took on steam following his death in 1947. (In England it had begun two decades earlier.) To an extent King's article in the same issue of *Harper's* must be read as a last hurrah by a young scholar whose academic profile proved too closely tied to a style of philosophical thought that was suddenly, and perversely, held to be out of date despite its acknowledged anticipation (or more) of "the new world view" (38).

3. Cf. Hugh R. King, "A. N. Whitehead and the Concept of Metaphysics," *Philosophy of Science* 14, no. 2 (April 1947).

4. Cf. Hugh R. King, "Whitehead's Doctrine of Causal Efficacy," *Journal of Philosophy* 46, no. 4 (February 17, 1949).

5. Cf. Hugh R. King, "Professor Ryle and the Concept of Mind," *Journal of Philosophy* 48, no. 9 (April 26, 1951).

6. Cf. Hugh R. King, "Aristotle and the Paradoxes of Zeno," *Journal of Philosophy* 46, no. 21 (October 13, 1949).

7. Cf. Hugh R. King, "Aristotle without *Prima Materia*," *Journal of the History of Ideas* 17, no. 3 (June 1956).

8. Drucker, "The New Philosophy Comes to Life," 20.

9. Donald C. Williams, "The Myth of Passage," *Journal of Philosophy* 48, no. 15 (July 19, 1951): 461.

10. Cf. Friedrich Solmsen, "Aristotle and Prime Matter: A Reply to Hugh R. King," *Journal of the History of Ideas* 19, no. 2 (April 1958).

11. King, "E Pluribus Togetherness," 51.

12. Ibid., 52. Of course, King's "page 48" refers to the original edition of *Process and Reality: An Essay in Cosmology* (New York: The Macmillan Company, 1929). In the revised edition the cited material occurs on page 32.

13. Ibid.

14. George H. Allen, letter to the editor," *Harper's Magazine* 215, no. 1290 (November 1957): 8.

15. As it happens, less than a year earlier—in 1956—"In God We Trust" had replaced "E pluribus unum" as the motto of the United States on order of Congress.

16. King, "Whitehead's Doctrine of Causal Efficacy," 96.

17. In remarks delivered on the occasion of his seventieth birthday, Whitehead offered a fairly precise measure of the complexity of his intellectual ties to Bradley: "[A]s

I said in my book [*Process and Reality*], I admit a very close affiliation with Bradley, except that I differ from Bradley where Bradley agrees with almost all the philosophers of his school and with Plato, insofar as Plato was a Hegelian. I differ from them where they all agree in their feeling of the illusiveness and relative unreality of the temporal world." Alfred North Whitehead, "Process and Reality," in *Essays in Science and Philosophy* (New York: Philosophical Library, 1947).

18. For a compelling meditation by Stengers on what it means to "think with James" in addition to, or besides, thinking with Whitehead, see "William James: An Ethics of Thought?" as well as the comments on James added by Stengers to the English-language translation of her indispensable *Penser avec Whitehead: Une Libre et Sauvage Création de Concepts* (Paris: Éditions du Seuil, 2002); in English, *Thinking with Whitehead: A Free and Wild Creation of Concepts*, trans. Michael Chase (Cambridge, Mass.: Harvard University Press, 2011). For reasons I will not get into here, in the years since my 2001 study, *Irresistible Dictation: Gertrude Stein and the Correlations of Writing and Science* (Stanford, Calif.: Stanford University Press, 2001), I have come to prefer speaking of robust empiricisms in place of James's "radical empiricism." However, as I understand the two phrases, they tend to refer to the same thing.

19. Among the "real overtones" of *togetherhood* one might include *motherhood, brotherhood,* perhaps even *Robin Hood.* King, "E Pluribus Togetherness," 51.

20. *A Supplement to the Oxford English Dictionary* (Oxford: Oxford University Press, 1933), 286.

21. Of the initial examples in the second edition, I exclude the presumably nonce instantiation of 1656 and the self-conscious sentimentalizing of "Having been apart for a little while seemed to make this curious feeling of 'togetherness' deeper and sweeter than ever," dating from 1909.

22. Frederick Cornwallis Conybeare, "Professor Clifford on the Soul in Nature," *Monist* 2, no. 2 (January 1892): 218.

23. Samuel Alexander, "The Method of Metaphysics; and the Categories" *Mind,* n.s., no. 81 (January 1912): 2.

24. Andrew Seth Pringle-Pattison, *The Idea of God in the Light of Recent Philosophy,* 2nd ed. (New York: Oxford University Press, 1920), 354.

25. See Max Müller, "Comment by Prof. F. Max Müller Concerning the Discussion on Evolution and Language," *Monist* 2, no. 2 (January 1892); Max Müller, "On Thought and Language," *Monist* 1, no. 4 (July 1891); George John Romanes, "Thought and Language," *Monist* 2, no. 1 (October 1891); and Paul Carus, "The Continuity of Evolution. The Science of Language versus The Science of Life, as Represented by Prof. F. Max Müller and Prof. G. J. Romanes," *Monist* 2, no. 1 (October 1891).

26. Paul Carus, "Feeling and Motion," *Open Court,* no. 153 (July 31, 1890), 2424–25. For Carus's other articles, see "Feeling and Motion [Concluded]," *Open Court,* no. 154 (August 7, 1890), as well as "Some Questions of Psycho-Physics: Feelings and the Elements of Feelings," *Monist* 1, no. 3 (April 1891) and "Are There Things in Themselves?" *Monist* 2, no. 2 (January 1892); and for Mach's see "Some Questions of Psycho-Physics: Sensations and the Elements of Reality," *Monist* 1, no. 3 (April 1891) and "Facts and Mental Symbols," *Monist* 2, no. 2 (January 1892).

27. Where the Lutheran Müller produced a critical edition of the Rig-Veda, to great acclaim, and sought to demonstrate a continuity between the Veda and Kant's *Critique,* the Catholic Conybeare moved from the study of Armenian translations of Aristotle

and Plato to ancient versions of the Bible and the study of Christian sects as well as "the historical Christ." Conybeare in fact came from a long line of important figures in the Church of England, and his grandfather, William Conybeare, in addition to being Dean of Llandaff in Wales, was a significant paleontologist and geologist in the first half of the nineteenth century. The younger Conybeare was also a leading British Dreyfusard and wrote an important early defense of Dreyfus.

28. William James, "The Importance of Individuals," *Open Court* no. 154 (August 7, 1890): 2438. Both articles were reprinted in *The Will to Believe* (1897) in *Writings 1878–1899* (New York: Library of America, 1984). James's dispute with Herbert Spencer and Grant Allen was of course a dispute among Darwinians, or more exactly between James and Spencer with regard to long-term teleological claims advanced by Spencer that James quite properly viewed as insufficiently Darwinian. Robert Richardson observes of "Great Men" that "its argument had a neat Darwinian twist. 'The relation of the visible environment to the great man,' said James, 'is in the main exactly what it is to the 'variation' in the Darwinian philosophy. It chiefly adopts or rejects, preserves or destroys, in short selects him'" (210).

29. In the headnote to "The Importance of Individuals" James observed, "I had to express my regret to the Editor of *The Open Court,* a few days since, at not being able at present to furnish the article of which it had been question between us. The very next day, in opening a drawer full of antiquities, I came across the accompanying manuscript" (2437). James's inability to produce a new copy may be explained by the fact that he was just then putting the finishing touches on the manuscript of *The Principles of Psychology,* which would appear in the fall. It is likely that Carus (or James) had proposed an essay somewhat along the lines of James's piece on "The Hidden Self," *Scribner's Magazine* 7, no. 3 (March 1890), which addressed work by Alfred Binet and Pierre Janet on dissociation and "the comparative science of trance-states" (363). In that essay James noted that "M. Binet has contributed some of his facts to the Chicago Open Court for 1889," and Binet's important volume, *On Double Consciousness* (Chicago: The Open Court Publishing Co., 1890)—a compilation of "original contributions made to The Open Court during 1889–1890" (2)—also came out from the Open Court Publishing Company in 1890. Indeed, the article that immediately *preceded* the first part of Carus's "Feeling and Motion," on the topic of "The Origin of Reason" and concerning Romanes's 1888 volume on *Mental Evolution in Man: Origin of Human Faculty* (London: Kegan Paul, Trench & Co., 1888), itself concluded with a note regarding Binet's "most ingenious little essay, *La Psycholgie du Raisonnement*" (Paris: Félix Alcan, 1886), 2424. Finally, I should observe that when, two decades later, James mischievously directed a "psychological analysis" of himself to the *Monist* ("Letter to Paul Carus, *Monist* 19, no. 1 [January 1909]) in the wake of an article by Carus highly critical of Jamesian pragmatism—in which Carus acknowledged that "Professor James is a fascinating personality" yet insisted that "in the philosophy of a man like William James the personal equation is the most important item" at a sharp cost to the philosophy ("Pragmatism," *Monist* 18, no. 3 [July 1908]: 359–60)—he was, willy nilly, returning to the earlier polemics regarding "the importance of the individual." "I have read with great relish your diagnosis of my case," James observed in a letter published in the *Monist* along with Edwin Tausch's "William James the Pragmatist—A Psychological Analysis," *Monist* 19, no. 1 (January 1909). "My *flux*-philosophy may well have to do with my extremely impatient temperament. I am a motor, need change, and get very quickly bored" (156).

In the same issue Carus continued his unrelenting criticism of James's pragmatism under the heading, "The Philosophy of Personal Equation," even as he observed that it was "Professor James himself, who advised" Tausch that his "analysis of 'the great pragmatist' . . . might be a welcome contribution to *The Monist.*" "We wish to express our indebtedness for this suggestion to Professor James publicly," Carus concluded. "We take it as an evidence that our critical review of pragmatism has not been [taken] amiss but is received in the spirit in which it was written" (156). For additional consideration of "the Carus-James controversy," see Donald H. Bishop, "The Carus-James Controversy," *Journal of the History of Ideas* 35, no. 2 (July-September 1974); for more on Carus and the *Open Court,* see Constance Myers, "Paul Carus and the *Open Court*: The History of a Journal," in *American Studies* 5, no. 2 (Fall 1964).

30. Unfortunately, extended considerations of James's several uses would lengthen this essay beyond reasonable limits; so I have elected merely to indicate where in a larger account I would discuss the second and third instances much as I do the first.

31. Conybeare's single direct reference to Green in the essay bears this assertion out: "Mr. Green has shown that all theories of the object which ignore the workmanship of thought manifest therein and identify the *esse* of things with their *percipi* lead straight to nihilism. To such nihilism Clifford's doctrine, like Hume's which it resembles, immediately bring us" ("Professor Clifford on the Soul in Nature," 221).

32. Carus, "Are There Things in Themselves?," 247.

33. Ibid., 246.

34. Ibid.; Conybeare, "Professor Clifford on the Soul in Nature," 214.

35. Conybeare, "Professor Clifford on the Soul in Nature," 218.

36. Carus, "Are There Things in Themselves?," 249 (emphasis and bracketed phrasing in original).

37. James, *Writings 1902–1910,* 1009. Even as Conybeare spoke of "a stream of feeling" and the circumstances that prevail when "the stream is called a consciousness" (Conybeare, "Professor Clifford on the Soul in Nature," 218), James invoked "the stream of feeling" as well as "the flux of feeling," "the immediate life of feeling," "the 'immediate flow' of conscious life" (James, *Writings 1902–1910* [New York: Library of America, 1987], 1007)—yet here the resemblance ceased: "No matter how small a tract of [the perceptual flux] be taken, it is always a much-at-once, and contains innumerable aspects and characters which conception can pick out, isolate, and thereafter always intend. . . . Data from all our senses enter into it, merged in a general extensiveness of which each occupies a big or little share. Yet all these parts leave its unity unbroken. Its boundaries are no more distinct than are those of the field of vision. Boundaries are things that intervene; but here nothing intervenes save parts of the perceptual flux itself, and these are overflowed by what they separate, so that whatever we distinguish and isolate conceptually is found perceptually to telescope and compenetrate and diffuse into its neighbors. The cuts we make are purely ideal. If my reader can succeed in abstracting from all conceptual interpretation and lapse back into his immediate sensible life at this very moment, he will find it to be what someone has called a big blooming buzzing confusion, as free from contradiction in its 'much-at-onceness' as it is all alive and evidently there." "Out of this aboriginal sensible muchness," James continued, "attention carves out objects, which conception then names and identifies forever—in the sky 'constellations,' on the earth 'beach,' 'sea,' 'cliff,' 'bushes,' 'grass.' Out of time we cut 'days' and 'nights,' 'summers' and 'winters'" (1008). So it goes with "togetherness" as well. Who

was it, then, who first wrote decades earlier regarding what he called *a big blooming buzzing confusion?*

38. Ibid., 267–68. The following observation sets up the reference to Kant in *The Principles of Psychology* (Cambridge, Mass.: Harvard University Press, 1983): "The ordinary associationist-psychology supposes . . . that whenever an object of thought contains many elements, the thought itself must be made up of just as many ideas, one idea for each element, and all fused together in appearance, but really separate. The enemies of this psychology find . . . little trouble in showing that such a bundle of separate ideas would never form one thought at all, and they contend that an Ego must be added to the bundle to give it unity, and bring the various ideas into relation with each other. . . . Now most believers in the ego make the same mistake as the associationists and sensationists whom they oppose" (267).

39. I recognize that the italicized sentence is a particularly difficult utterance of Whitehead's. King, in his 1947 essay on "A. N. Whitehead and the Concept of Metaphysics," wisely juxtaposes this passage with another in which Whitehead had explained the desired connections among his own famously (if not actually the least bit) idiosyncratic "fundamental notions." The philosophical "requirement" of coherence "does not mean," Whitehead proposed, that the notions "are definable in terms of each other; it means that what is indefinable in one such notion cannot be abstracted from its relevance to the other notions. It is the ideal of speculative philosophy"—at least as he conceived it!—"that its fundamental notions shall not seem capable of abstraction from each other" (*Process and Reality,* 3). King explains that "the 'indefinables' are philosophy's intuitional footholds" (143). The whole point of the so-called *meres*—mere sensation, mere emotion, and the like—is that although they thus "seem capable of abstraction from each other," their very distinguishability permits them (mistakenly) to appear all the more concrete. The problem Whitehead was alluding to when he observed that "there can be no 'mere' togetherness of such abstractions" was that on his analysis it was impossible to combine highly abstract notions like these on the same level of abstractness exhibited by the notions themselves. As we have already observed, and will see again below, "togetherness" for Whitehead is always experiential. This is of course exactly the opposite of Conybeare's argument, and suggests that however profoundly rationalist Whitehead's means, he will always in the end side with the empiricist (although not just any empiricist). It also means that insofar as one chooses to treat what King terms "high abstractions" (143) as the basis for philosophical reasoning, there is no way to avoid the fallacy of misplaced concreteness in one's reasoning. Whitehead circumvented this perplexity by starting with differently configured fundamental notions—the examples he gave were "actual entity, prehension, nexus," *generalizations* of experience rather than abstractions *from* it—that would "not seem capable of abstraction from each other," or to put it the other way around, that would permit him "to base philosophical thought upon the most concrete elements in our experience" (18).

40. James, *The Principles of Psychology,* 268.

41. Paul Carus, "Professor William James," *Monist* 20, no. 4 (October 1910): 638.

42. William James, *Some Problems of Philosophy (1911)* in *Writings 1902–1910* (New York: Library of America, 1987).

43. William James, *Essays in Radical Empiricism,* ed. Ralph Barton Perry (Lincoln: University of Nebraska Press, 1996).

44. Alexander, "The Method of Metaphysics."

45. Samuel Alexander, *Spinoza and Time* (London: George Allen, 1921), 15.

46. A leading Whitehead scholar in England, one of very few, Emmet was also a colleague of Alexander's at Manchester.

47. Dorothy Emmet, "Whitehead and Alexander," *Process Studies* 21, no. 3 (Fall 1992): 138. In a discussion of "the form of idealism which, under the usual name of absolute idealism, has been and is so influential on thinking in this country," Alexander acknowledged being "all the more anxious not to overestimate differences from a school of thought in which I was myself bred, and to whose leaders, Mr. Bradley and Mr. Bosanquet, I owe so much of whatever capacity I may have attained, however unable I may have proved myself to see things with their eyes." Alexander, *Space, Time, and Deity* (London: Macmillan & Co., 1920), 7. Bradley, for instance, read over Alexander's first book, *Moral Order and Progress: An Analysis of Ethical Conceptions* (London: Trübner & Co., 1889), prior to publication. Although the essay on which it was based had been awarded the Green Moral Philosophy Prize, the volume was fairly critical of Green's idealist ethics where it failed to accord with an evolutionary ethics based on natural selection.

48. Emmet, "Whitehead and Alexander," 100. Emmet indicates that Whitehead's letter is undated; the reference to *Process and Reality* suggests it is after 1929.

49. Victor Lowe, *Alfred North Whitehead: The Man and His Work, Volume 2: 1910–1947* (Baltimore: Johns Hopkins University Press, 1990), 360. Lowe dates the conversation "August 1942."

50. Here Lowe refers to Whitehead's still-controversial account of perception, as involving what he characterized as direct perception in the mode of causal efficacy together with perception in the mode of presentational immediacy (limited to sense-data). In the introduction to *Space, Time, and Deity,* Alexander thus writes of sensations: "though integral parts of experience [they] are not the only ones. Thoughts are experienced as much as sensations, and are as vital to experience. It may even appear that there are experiences simpler and of a lower order than sensation itself; and it may be possible to indicate the precise relation of these various forms of our experience in the economy of things. A philosophy which pursues an empirical method"—or, as he described the method he believed philosophy ought to share with science, "taking it as self-evident that whatever we know is apprehended in some form of experience" (4)—"is not necessarily a sensationalistic one" (5).

51. Lowe, *Alfred North Whitehead,* 173–74.

52. Ibid., 174; Alexander, *Space, Time, and Deity*, 2nd imp. (London: Macmillan & Co., 1927), 1: vi.

53. Emmet, "Whitehead and Alexander," 139.

54. Lowe, *Alfred North Whitehead,* 175; Alexander, *Space, Time, and Deity,* 2: 15–16. Lowe describes "the checkmarks, scorings, and detailed comments in Whitehead's copy of *Space, Time, and Deity,* which he read in 1924, [p]robably . . . before he left England" (174). This may stand for a token of the missing Whitehead archive. (Even this copy is now scattered.) Here is an additional sample of Lowe reading Whitehead reading Alexander: "In a passage that Whitehead marked in his copy of *Space, Time, and Deity,* the author, explaining that in his remarks on the interconnection of time and space he was not trying to prove the existence of space, wrote, 'There is no room for "must" in philosophy or in science, but only for facts and the implications of them.'

How different this man was from Bertrand Russell! In place of Russell's hard, logical atomism there was a judicious chapter on 'The One and the Many.' Reading Alexander's philosophy instead of Bertie's must have been a great relief to A. N. W." (175).

55. Samuel Alexander, "On Relations; and in Particular the Cognitive Relation," *Mind*, n.s., no. 83 (July 1912), 316.

56. Ibid. See also Alexander's description of "the experience of togetherness" in *Space, Time, and Deity*, where he explains that "the horses's togetherness with me is experienced by me as my togetherness with the horse; which I express by saying I see a horse. . . . I experience the string which unites us only, as it were, from my own end" (1: 20–21).

57. Admittedly, in contemplating the relation of compresence or togetherness that holds between objects, Alexander is obligated to do so from one perspective or another. He thus imagines the relation as viewed from the perspective of what he terms "angels," who contemplate the viewer as being no different in kind than the object viewed, hence together comprising several objects in some relation or other. "[T]here is no difficulty in supposing higher forms of existence than our own to which our minds would be contemplated objects. Let us call such beings angels" ("The Method of Metaphysics," 4). "In recognizing that in the cognitive relation to the tree, the tree and I are distinct and relatively independent existences compresent with each other, I am, under the limitations imposed on me, anticipating the angel's 'vision.' . . . Hence I have sometimes allowed myself playfully to speak of what here I call seriously the empirical method in philosophy as the angelic method. What the angel sees as the compresence of two objects I experience as the compresence of an enjoyed mind and a contemplated non-mental object" (*Space, Time, and Deity*, 1:20). Alexander's deity is no more actual than his angels are. As Lowe remarks, "Alexander's subject was not God, but the quality of deity. He identified it as, for us, 'the next higher empirical level than mind'" (*Alfred North Whitehead*, 176). Clearly, where Whitehead might be concerned Alexander did not take his angels seriously enough. This raises the question of the extent to which Whitehead's complex reconceptualization of God serves as a corrective of the infinite regress threatened by Alexander's angels. Lowe makes several observations of considerable interest in this regard.

58. Alexander, "The Method of Metaphysics," 3.

59. Alexander, *Space, Time, and Deity*, 1: 26.

60. In fact, Alexander does hint at these two forms of relation in the third variety of togetherness he lists in the "Introduction" to *Space, Time, and Deity:* "Not only is there a togetherness between the enjoyed and the contemplated, which is the same as that between two objects contemplated, but there is a togetherness in enjoyment, as when two acts of mind are distinguished by us as enjoyed, whether at the same time (*e.g.*, I see a friend and hear his voice) or in succession" (1:27). But this is the barest of hints, not yet distinguishing between the additional forms of relation. (By "enjoyment," Alexander means something comparable to James's "knowledge of acquaintance"; contemplation is comparable to "knowledge-about.")

Because the essay is already straining at its word-limits, I leave out two stages in the present argument. The first puts flesh on Whitehead's notion of prehension on the basis of several remarks concerning "terms expressive of the connectedness of things" in the chapter on "Philosophic Method" in *Adventures of Ideas* (230). Here Whitehead focuses on his use of "prehension" and "feeling" in light of what he takes to be Bradley's and James's similar generalizations of "feeling." He also makes relevant observations concerning "togetherness" and the frequent "misuse" of "the term 'together'" (236). Secondly, I am leaving out any discussion of the corresponding use by James of the term "togetherness" which occurs in his essay on "The Thing and Its Relations," *Journal of Philosophy, Psychology, and Scientific Methods* 2 (January 19, 1905), later included as an appendix to his *Pluralistic Universe.* The two instances of "togetherness" in this essay are in fact quotations from a key essay by Bradley, on "The Contrary and the Disparate," which appeared in *Mind* in 1896 and was included ("with omissions") in the appendix to the second edition of *Appearance and Reality* as "Note A. Contradiction and the Contrary." The dueling appendixes return us to Alexander, who in the second of his 1912 essays in *Mind* ("On Relations") includes footnotes both to Bradley's appendix (albeit to "Note B. Relation and Quality") and to James's "The Thing and Its Relations," about which Alexander observes: "Since I corrected this paper for the press, I discover that I have neglected to read James's paper on *The Thing and its Relations* printed as Appendix A of *A Pluralistic Universe.* What is said above and in the remainder of the section as to the continuity of the terms and their relation does not add anything to what is said by James in that paper" (307).

61. W. J. Mander, *British Idealism: A History* (Oxford: Oxford University Press, 2011), 366.

62. Ibid., 409; Whitehead "Process and Reality," 116.

63. William James, review of *Personal Idealism: Philosophical Essays by Eight Members of the University of Oxford,* ed. Henry Stuart, *Mind,* n.s., no. 45 (January 1903), 94. Compare this with the opening of Alexander's 1914 address to the British Academy; see Samuel Alexander, *The Basis of Realism* (London: Oxford University Press, 1914). "The temper of Realism is to de-anthropomorphize," he announced: "to order man and mind to their proper place among the world of finite things; on the one hand to divest physical things of the colouring which they have received from the vanity or arrogance of mind; and on the other to assign them along with minds their due measure of self-existence" (1). Whitehead demonstrated in a manner that neither the Personal Idealists nor Alexander could that such de-anthropomorphizing required a concomitant re-anthropomorphizing and vice versa. "Dear Dr. Carus, the world is wide enough for both you and me to live on our differing philosophies," James might propose—such is the pluralism embraced by Whitehead as well, and it was certainly not limited to persons (Bishop, "The Carus-James Controversy," 520).

64. James, review of *Personal Idealism,* 97.

65. Ibid., 94. For the immediate context of "revised empiricism" in *A Pluralistic Universe* (1909) in *Writings 1902–1910,* see below; also see the excellent essay by Alexander Klein, "On Hume on Space: Green's Attack, James' Empirical Response," *Journal of the History of Philosophy* 47, no. 3 (July 2009).

66. James, review of *Personal Idealism,* 97.

67. Albeit correcting James's "cognitive" with the more general relation of prehension. "I will use the word *prehension,*" Whitehead would explain in *Science and the Modern World,* "for *uncognitive apprehension*; by this I mean *apprehension* which may or may not be cognitive" (69).

68. According to the International Association for Scottish Philosophy website; see http://www.scottishphilosophy.org/andrew-seth-pringle-pattison.html.

69. Reviewed by none other than James for the *Nation* (review of *Hegelianism and Personality,* by Andrew Seth, *Nation,* no. 1186 [March 22, 1888]) and with great

enthusiasm. In the course of a generation, James proposed, "the indigenous form of empiricism" of the "English-speaking lands" had been "outgrown," with Mill and Bain overthrown by the "critical work" of "Anglo-Hegelianism." Yet little in the way of "constructive work" had hitherto been achieved. In *Hegelianism and Personality* (Edinburgh: Blackwood, 1887) "Professor Seth inflicts what are pretty sure to be mortal wounds, and overtly arrays himself against that saintly man, but strenuously feeble writer, Green, the leader of the school." Moreover, the disciple-turned-critic offers intimations of a more constructive project: "Professor Seth plants himself squarely on experiential and pluralistic ground, refuses to interpret as a universal consciousness that 'ego' which (as analysis shows) is involved in the nature of knowledge." It was with this pleasing image still before him that James concluded by inquiring: "Why, with all the spoils of the enemy's camp to enrich him, will he not now set forth empiricism in an adequate and modern way?" (246). Alas it was not to be, and James was himself obliged to make the great effort. Twenty years later in the opening lecture of *A Pluralistic Universe,* delivered at Oxford, James almost exactly repeats the description of this "school of thought, which, on the whole, has reigned supreme at Oxford and in the Scottish universities til the present day." "But now there are signs of its giving way to a wave of revised empiricism" (633). A final rhetorical question in the review of Pringle-Pattison's book, which James directed no less at himself in reviewing the book (and in endlessly reviewing the contemporary psychological literature) than at Pringle-Pattison, proved all too prescient of the author of a subsequent work on "the idea of God *in the light of recent philosophy*": "Can it be that he, too, finds this sorry writing of books about other books, which is the bane of our generation, so much the easier task?" (246). Here is Mander's somewhat more tempered assessment of *Hegelianism and Personality:* Pringle-Pattison "objects that the idealism of Green and his followers errs grievously in turning Kant's *theory of knowledge into a metaphysic of existence* . . . . The principal cause of this error . . . is the Hegelian lens through which they read Kant. . . . . Worst of all, Pringle-Pattison objects, Hegel speaks throughout his writings of self-consciousness, spirit, or intelligence *in general* without, apparently, appreciating that these are just abstractions, and that only *individual* spirits or intelligences are real" (Mander, *British Idealism,* 257–58.)

Again, due to limitations of space, I must set to one side the next stage of the present argument, concerning James's own use of "togetherness" in a note to his essay "On Some Hegelisms," *Mind,* no. 26 (April 1882), which appeared a decade *before* Conybeare's usage in *The Monist.* (The essay was reprinted, fifteen years later, in *The Will to Believe.*) Unsurprisingly, the sense of "togetherness" James associated with Hegel along with the American Hegelians who formed the backdrop of his essay was entirely different from the Whiteheadian understanding of the term. Equally to the point is the introduction of "togetherness," used in this Hegelian sense, into translations of Hegel's *Phenomenology of Spirit* (or *Mind*), particularly the 1910 translation by James Black Baillie, a product of Trinity College, Cambridge (*The Phenomenology of Mind,* trans. J. B. Baillie [London: Swan Sonnenschein, 1910])—and whom Mander describes as the "most conservative of all the British Idealist commentators[,] tend[ing] always to go back to the historical Hegel himself; whose very idiom also he swallowed, much detracting from the overall clarity and coherence of his writing." ("After the First World War," however, Baillie "rejected Hegelianism," replacing it with a variant of Personal Idealism [Mander, *British Idealism,* 48].) This stage in the argument concludes with a three-way contrast of (1) the Hegelian sense of togetherness as James criticized it in his discussion of Hegel in *A Plu-*

ralistic Universe (without actually using the term); (2) Bradley's sense in the passages James cites from him in the same work, where the term *is* used; and (3) the various alternate terms James used in *A Pluralistic Universe* and other works (such as "co-conscious," "interpenetrate," "self-compound") to describe the "modern" empiricist views he sought to formulate.

70. Pringle-Pattison, *The Idea of God in the Light of Recent Philosophy,* 354. Here is an interesting fact: although the three citations from the *O.E.D.* are dated between 1892 and 1920, the birth dates of their authors were all between 1856 and 1859. Whitehead was born in 1861. So Conybeare, Alexander, and Pringle-Pattison were his exact contemporaries.

71. James, *Principles of Psychology,* 574.

72. Pringle-Pattison, *Hegelianism and Personality,* 354.

73. J. M. E. McTaggart, review of *The World and the Individual* by Josiah Royce, *Mind,* n.s., no. 44 (October 1902): 558–61. McTaggart's review appeared in the issue of *Mind* immediately prior to that which contained James's review of *Personal Idealism.*

74. Elsewhere Whitehead suggests that although this may have been strictly true, it was by no means the whole truth. When young, he had taken a look at Hegel's *Logic,* and finding it nonsense mathematically-speaking, dismissed the philosopher. Many years later in recounting the tale, he disapproved of the response but noted that it was just the sort of thing a young man might be expected to do.

75. Whitehead, "Process and Reality," 116.

76. It is true that James did not have the benefit of McTaggart's magnum opus, *The Nature of Existence,* 2 vols. (Cambridge: Cambridge University Press, 1921, 1927), which as Mander observes, "did not appear until the end of his life"; still "McTaggart arrived early on at his basic metaphysical system to which, despite considerable change in the argument he offered for it, he adhered throughout his life" (Mander, *British Idealism,* 370).

77. William James, "A World of Pure Experience," in *Essays in Radical Empiricism,* ed. Ralph Barton Perry (Lincoln: University of Nebraska Press, 1996).

FOURTEEN

The Order of Nature and the Creation of Societies

Michael Halewood

> It is relevant to point out, how superficial are our controversies on sociological theory apart from some more fundamental determination of what we are talking about.
> —Alfred North Whitehead, *Adventures of Ideas*

To state, as seems to be done in the title of this essay, that there is an order to nature that is distinct from an active social realm runs the risk of painting Whitehead as a somewhat traditional thinker. It is to situate him as an advocate of the abiding split between the hard natural sciences, which are concerned with the blind, mechanistic laws of the physical world, and those softer sociocultural analyses, which deal with the contingent patterns of human behavior. Even if it is agreed that the study of the social is indeed scientific, there are few who would nowadays maintain that the laws that supposedly govern the objects and subjects of the social arena can be delineated with the same kind of certainty as that which physicists claim for themselves. There remains, therefore, an apparent gulf between the kind of order to be found in nature and that which might be tentatively traced in the political, economic, or cultural realm. Is this Whitehead's position? The answer is certainly "no." But it is the way in which he produces this "no" that is of interest. For, Whitehead does not simply dismiss nature or science, and he also refuses to accept that the social is something that immediately makes sense on its own terms.

Most importantly, he challenges us to ask what it is that we think we are talking about when we use the word "social" or "society." Those working within sociology, social theory, and the social sciences tend to use the word "social" a lot. This is quite understandable. But do we always know what we mean by the term? Often we use it in its adjectival form, when we talk of social relations, social networks, or social media, for example. Yet, we also like to talk of *the* social; we are happy to treat it as a noun. Alongside such notions, the term "society" is also often evoked. Though we might be more wary than we used to be with regard to such a concept, it still lurks within our thoughts and our writings. Bruno Latour[1] has made much of the difficulties involved in current conceptions of the social and society as well as the way that these are studied by sociology. Indeed, he has expressed his wish to replace the last of these terms with that of "associology."[2] While I am sympathetic to much of Latour's critique, I do not want to go as far as he does. My aim, in this essay, is to use the work of Whitehead to make some moves in clarifying "what we are talking about" with regard to the social and societies. This will also involve an important reconsideration of both the social and the natural.

To point ahead to one of Whitehead's most potent claims: he suggests that to assume that the social is solely or primarily a human affair is unwarranted and presumptuous. As will be seen, Whitehead neither accepts nor disregards either nature or society. Instead, he initially complicates but then clarifies the situation with regard to the thorny problem of their interrelation, as will be discussed throughout this essay.

Whitehead on Order and Disorder

Talcott Parsons (1902–1979) was probably the most influential, though not the best, American social theorist of the twentieth century. It was certainly he who made the question and concept of *social order* central to sociological theory.[3] By "social order," Parsons meant those on-going elements that enable a society to endure. It does not necessarily mean that such a society is internally regimented, cohesive, or smooth-running. Rather, social order refers to the wider social structures, and the relations between these, which means that the same society could be said to exist over time. Nevertheless, his concept of social order is one that tends to emphasize continuity and conformity at the expense of innovation or creativity. Interestingly, Parsons's career at Harvard overlapped with that of Whitehead and there was certainly some influence between them even if Parsons sometimes misunderstood Whitehead.[4] One example of this was precisely the question of social order. For Parsons tends to assume that the socialness of such social order is self-explanatory; it involves the institutions, values, and behavior of humans in social groups. This is more of a description than an explanation as it invokes the very term social (as in "social groups") to justify its account of social order. It is just this kind of approach that lays Parsons (and others) open to Whitehead's charge, as cited at the start of this essay, with regard to "how superficial are our controversies on sociological theory apart from some more fundamental determination of what we are talking about."

Such a "fundamental determination" is precisely what Whitehead sets about in his elaboration of his concept of societies in *Process and Reality.* His fullest discussion of these entities is to be found in part 2, chapter 3 of the text, which, notably, is titled "The Order of Nature." This should alert us immediately that Whitehead has no truck or need for a simple division between nature and society. Indeed he leaves the very status of nature open at this stage, for his concern in these passages is the very concept of order. "The present chapter is wholly concerned with the topic of 'order'" (*PR,* 83). Didier Debaise has made an in-depth and convincing account of Whitehead's development of his concept of order in *Process and Reality,* and it should be noted that the reading that I offer below relies heavily upon his account and analysis.[5]

Whitehead's first point is that there is no such substantive thing as order and, consequently, that order cannot be understood without reference to its corollary, namely, disorder.[6] Order is real and so is disorder, but they can only occur in relation to each other: "Order is, above all, a relative term."[7] But this is not to completely relativize these notions, for there is a major difference between relativism and relationism, and Whitehead is speaking of the latter. In doing so, he uses a term that, as Stengers points out, has great importance for him, namely, that of "contrast"[8]: "the correlative of 'order' is 'disorder.' There can be no peculiar meaning in the notion of 'order' unless this contrast holds" (*PR,* 83).

Whitehead goes on to say, "'Order' is a mere generic term: there can only be some definite specific 'order' not merely 'order' in the vague" (*PR,* 83). That is to say, despite the high level of abstraction at which Whitehead is working, he is aware that, in order to have purchase, his concept of order must not attempt to capture some general realm of orderliness that is dislocated from, or prior to, actual manifestations of order. Indeed order makes sense only in reference to specific occurrences of orderliness. That which is orderly about such occurrences is what Whitehead refers to as "adaptation for the attainment of an end" (*PR,* 83). By this he reasserts a vital element of his philosophy, that of "process" (as in the title of his major work—*Process and Reality*). For, the orderliness of order is not simply a repetition or reaction to that which comes before, to "givenness." Givenness certainly plays a role; however "'order' means more than 'givenness,' though it presupposes 'givenness'" (*PR,* 83). If this were the case, if order were simply the replication of the past, even if in a different form, then Whitehead would remain within the grips of a philosophy of necessity and fixed, immutable laws or logical possibilities. And, as Shaviro has pointed out, the major aim and accomplishment of Whitehead's philosophy is precisely to place genuine novelty at the heart of his conceptual scheme and of existence itself.[9] The notion of an "attainment of an end," as referred to above, is how Whitehead achieves this shift. For, each occasion of orderliness is constituted by a novel incorporation of that which is given, along with a self-generating aim at being something different. To put it another way, the orderliness of an occasion equally involves establishing a past (constituting certain elements as given) and promulgating a future (that which is aimed at).

This introduction of "ends" that are to be attained might, to some, smack of teleology with all the associated problems of ideal goals that supposedly give reason and purpose to all existence—fixed or eternal ideals to which all things and people are inexorably drawn. This is certainly not Whitehead's position.

> There is not just one ideal 'order' which all actual entities should attain and fail to attain. In each case there is an ideal peculiar to each particular actual entity. . . . The notion of one ideal arises from the disastrous overmoralization of thought under the influence of fanaticism, or pedantry. (*PR*, 84)

Whitehead further distances his position from any traditional concept of teleology through the emphasis that he places on "failure." Whilst the aim at the attainment of an end is a real motivational element of each orderly occasion, the actual attainment or realization of such an end is always doomed to failure. This is for two reasons. First, as the ends to be attained do not exist in some separate realm prior to the specific bid for their attainment, then there is nothing (no thing) to attain, as such. Each end is generated anew on each occasion. Secondly, each occasion of order is a specific occasion which occurs in relation to a specific occurrence of givenness; givenness is not a substratum of existence. Instead, the givenness out of which the bid for novelty arises has the more limited role of partially comprising the environment within which such a bid plays out. Givenness, thereby, both enables and inhibits the end that is being aimed for. This inclusion of that which enables and inhibits is Whitehead's definition of "disorder":

> every definite total phase of 'givenness' involves a reference to that specific 'order' which is its dominant ideal, and involves the specific 'disorder' due to its inclusion of 'given' components which exclude the attainment of the full ideal. The attainment is partial, and thus there is 'disorder'; but there is some attainment, and thus there is some 'order.' (*PR*, 83–84)

This returns us to one of the initial points made in this section, namely, the correlation of order and disorder. At first sight, Whitehead's statement—though I paraphrase—that "there can be no order without disorder, and vice versa" might have seemed like a rather general, even banal, aphorism with little critical insight. It should now be clear that Whitehead's insistence upon the contrast between order and disorder as integral to all occasions of existence is a bold philosophical statement. It asks us to think these two terms together without reducing one to the other. This will enable them to keep their conceptual and practical force. But it is quite a demand to envisage such a non-relativized doublet as inhering in all existence.

It should be noted, at this point, that no mention has yet been made of either nature or society, even though these terms were set up as the main concerns of this chapter. The reason for this is that while Whitehead does mention these in section 1 of chapter 3 (*PR*, 83–89), he does so only in passing, turning to a full consideration of them only in section 2.[10] This careful procedure might be seen as a case of Whitehead taking his own advice regarding the need to undertake a "more fundamental determination of what we are talking about." There is no point in talking about the "order of nature" if we are unsure of what order is. So, with this notion of order now established, it is possible to move on to the status of nature and societies.

Order and Disorder in Nature and Society

The nature of nature is, of course, hard to ascertain. And Whitehead does not attempt to provide a once-and-for-all definition. Instead, he is interested in an elaboration of the "order of nature," which he approaches thus: "We speak of the 'order of nature,' meaning thereby the order reigning in that limited portion of the universe, or even of the surface of the earth, which has come under our observation" (*PR*, 89). As will be clear, Whitehead is *not* attempting to provide a concept of nature at this point; this is no philosophy of nature.[11] It is, rather, an outline of the problematic that he wants to address at this juncture—that is, how order (and disorder) manifest themselves in existence. What is striking, for philosophers, scientists, and social theorists, is that his first move is to introduce his own specific concept of "society" or "societies." As Debaise puts it: "What are the 'orders' at the heart of nature called? To what does this notion refer? Essentially, it refers to societies."[12] Or, as Whitehead writes: "The term 'society' will always be restricted to mean a nexus of actual entities which are 'ordered' among themselves" (*PR*, 89). The use of inverted commas should warn us that Whitehead is aware that neither "societies" nor "order" have been fully explained here. But it does point to Whitehead's distinctive position, that the order of nature (whatever that is) can only be understood with reference to "societies." There is to be no utter gulf between the natural and the social, nature and nurture, the individual and society. Societies are those elements of existence that exhibit and express the orderliness of existence and that therefore comprise those enduring things of the world that are encountered by the other enduring things of the world (be they humans, plants, galaxies, rocks, molecules, or televisions).

The important distinction between the purely metaphysical account of existence that Whitehead develops in *Process and Reality,* when he is concerned with discussing "actual entities," "eternal objects," "actual occasions," "prehensions," and so forth, can, and must, be distinguished from his "cosmological" discussions of how the processes and principles that inhere in such entities are displayed in those enduring items of the world—items that encounter each other and that we, as humans, encounter: namely, societies. "It is the mistake that has thwarted European metaphysics from the time of the Greeks . . . to confuse societies with the completely real things which are the actual occasions" (*AI,* 204). Unfortunately, this confusion has also dogged many commentators and commentaries on Whitehead, as Debaise[13] and Stengers[14] have pointed out. As stated previously, Debaise's text[15] stands out as an important marker of the need both to focus on the role of societies within Whitehead's work and to draw out its consequences.[16]

For the moment, and for the purposes of this essay, there are two points that need to be made. The first is that Whitehead has managed to introduce both nature (or, more precisely, the order of nature) *and* societies without mentioning humans. As I have discussed elsewhere,[17] the fact that Whitehead is able to develop an account of societies and the social that is not predicated on the relation between humans, but that does not exclude specific human societies, as usually conceived, is a radical but productive challenge to sociological and social theory; it is one that must be taken seriously and that could offer new approaches to some thorny old problems (such as those of structure and agency, "sex" and gender). Secondly, Whitehead does not try to define or substantiate his concepts of nature and society. They are correlative, in a similar way to that in which order and disorder are correlative. That is to say, he is not relativizing them, he is not dismissing them, he does not want to deny all elements of our usual understanding of these terms. But he does want to foreground that they derive their specificity not from some kind of internal essence but from the *contrast* and *contrasts* upon which they rely and which they produce. It is these that enable them to be what they are, to endure and to have effects. I will return to this point below.

At this stage, however, it might be objected that Whitehead has not really told us what is "social" about societies. What makes them exhibit the order of nature? His intriguing answer is that societies are social insofar as they express an orderliness within nature. Unlike Parsons,[18] who starts by assuming that there is a self-sufficient realm of the social that is utterly human and is, in some ill-defined, yet implacable and resolute way, divorced and different from the natural, Whitehead places the social at the heart of the natural. For, as far as nature is ordered, it is social; it exhibits a "social order."

> A Society is a nexus which 'illustrates' or 'shares in,' some type of 'Social Order.' 'Social Order' can be defined as follows:—'A nexus enjoys "social order" when (i) there is a common element of form illustrated in the definiteness of each of its included actual entities, and (ii) this common element of form arises in each member of the nexus by reason of the conditions imposed upon it by its prehensions of some other members of the nexus, and (iii) these prehensions impose that condition of reproduction by reason of their inclusion of positive feelings involving that common form . . .' (*AI*, 203)

What is social about *social* order therefore involves the notions of *form* and *prehension*.

The term "form" refers not to some realm of ideal Platonic forms (which actual entities or societies aim at) but the *manner* in which actual entities mutually prehend or grasp each other, thereby establishing a consistency that enables them to be, to endure, and to be recognized as a coherent "individual." As Debaise puts it: "That which Whitehead calls an element of form is none other than that which, at the level of actual entities, refers to the *manner* or the *how*, that is to say, the mode of prehension."[19] As has been discussed elsewhere,[20] the manner and mode of activity introduce the notion of the "adverbial." That is to say, rather than being substantive things in the usual sense (objects), societies derive their "thingness" through the way in which their constituents cohere. Societies should not be considered as primarily noun-like—that is, as having some inner core of which qualities are predicated.[21] Instead, societies come to be and endure through the shared manner in which their constituents regard each other.[22] As such, quality is dominant over quantity, and the best way to understand and describe societies is to conceive of them as primarily adverbial.

The importance of the manner in which the components of a society regard each other and thereby hold themselves together refers to Whitehead's specific rendering of the term "prehension." If the "identity" of a society is constituted by the common manner of prehension of its members, then that which does not prehend in that manner will be excluded from that society. The word "excluded" is, however, too strong, as it invokes notions of an active form of negation carried out by a traditional kind of agent. This is not Whitehead's point. Rather, he emphasizes the notion of "likeness." "The members of a society are alike . . . by reason of their common character" (*PR*, 89). The different characters of different societies are to be understood in terms of their likeness of character. The differences between societies are not to be thought of as divisive (though they are decisive) or exclusionary (though the members of one society will exclude those of others). The likeness of character once again brings the notion of quality to the fore, with regard to the existence of a society. And this, in turn, returns us to the notion of "contrast." For, it is the very contrast between the adverbial manner in which the members of one society commonly prehend and the different (contrasting) adverbial manner in which the members of another society commonly prehend that makes each society a definite individual. This contrast is not simply *between* societies; it inheres within the society, thereby making it what it is. A hot stone and a cold stone are not different because there is some secret core of an implacable stone lying in wait to sometimes take on the quality of being hot, sometimes that of being cold, while somehow, mysteriously, remaining the same underneath. Instead, the mutual feeling of hotness by the component parts that make up that society that we call "this hot stone" are in contrast to the mutual feeling of coldness by the component parts of another society that we call "this cold stone." To put it another way, one stone feels itself hotly and the other feels itself coldly.

To sum up: Whitehead's concept of societies is one that places the social, in terms of social order and societies, at the heart of existence, at the heart of nature. He also manages to elaborate his concept of the social without reference to, and without predicating it upon, the existence, intentions, beliefs, thoughts, actions, or prejudices of humans. In doing so, he avoids the otherwise seemingly unavoidable split between the concerns and approaches of the harder sciences and those of social and cultural theory. There is no need to "bring things back in" to social theory since they were always already there. At the same time, it may be felt that Whitehead, despite his detailed analysis of the sociality of the social, has not told us much about the sociological (whatever that might be). This will be addressed in a later section, following a discussion of the creation of societies.

The Creation of Societies

To speak of "the creation of societies" quickly raises the question of who or what does the creating. Is it some external force that creates societies? Or, do they forge themselves out of nothing? For Whitehead, to frame the question in such ways is to limit the possible responses. Before proceeding to an outline of Whitehead's own formulation of a response, it is worthwhile pointing out that his concept of *creativity* is very particular. More than that, and surprising as it may seem, Whitehead coined the word "creativity" in the late 1920s as a technical, philosophical term to explicate a vital element of his philosophy.[23]

In terms of the role of creativity within the formation of societies, a crucial aspect is provided by what Whitehead calls, deploying another of his technical terms, "eternal objects." The status and efficacy of these, within *Process and Reality,* are complex, and there is not space here to fully discuss them. For the purposes of the present argument, eternal objects can be considered as having two major roles.

1. Insofar as societies gain individuality through a shared mode of prehension, so that *how* this prehending occurs makes that society what it is, then eternal objects express this "how," this manner of becoming. But, this "how" is not a simple reaction to the past: "the *how* of feeling . . . is not fully determined by the data." (*PR,* 85)
2. Given that order is not merely a replication or repetition of the past and that there is always an "attainment of an end," eternal objects characterize this aim at the future. (see *PR,* 85–6)

To return to the question of "creation," it should first be noted that there is a distinction to be drawn between *creativity* and *creation.* The first is a general, metaphysical category, designed to express the fluency of existence; the latter is concerned with the specific occurrences of creativity that inhere in existence. Yet, Whitehead does not discuss the coming-to-be of societies in terms of creativity or creation, as such. To do so would be to invite us to rely upon the usual categories of thought whereby something is created by something or someone else. But Whitehead is attempting to elicit a new mode of thought. To this end, he writes: "The point of a 'society' as the term is used here, is that it is self-sustaining, in other words, that it is its own reason" (*AI,* 203). To search for a reason external to that society is to posit an external creating force where there is none. "Outside" of the society, prior to the society, there is only what might be called "undetermination"[24] or disorder. "Beyond these societies there is disorder, where 'disorder' is a relative term expressing the lack of importance possessed by the defining characteristics of the societies in question beyond their own bounds" (*PR*, 92). It might be said that the reason for a society comes-to-be with the coming-to-be of that society; a society's reason does not exist before the creation of that society; it is an outcome of that society's self-creation. "Thus in a society, the members can only exist by reason of the laws which dominate the society, and the laws only come into being by reason of the analogous characters of the members of the society" (*PR*, 91). Whitehead does not deny regularity or law-like behavior, but he does refuse to posit societies as simply examples of already existing reasons or laws. Societies are not derived from more fundamental conditions; they establish the conditions for their own existence and, thereby, impose conditions upon the rest of existence. What is creative about a society is the specific, adverbial, manner in which it establishes these conditions, as opposed to the alternative ways in which it could have established itself (the stone feels itself hotly, not coldly). "Each task of creation is a social effort" (*PR*, 223).

There is, therefore, a creativity inherent in the self-identity of each society, which is precisely that which differentiates it from other societies; this provides the society with its definiteness of individuality. It is in this respect that a society could be referred to as "self-creating," self-caused or *causa sui*. "The self-identity of a society is founded upon the self-identity of its defining characteristics, and upon the mutual immanence of its occasions" (*AI*, 204). Whitehead's use of the phrase "mutual immanence" is crucial. It reminds us of one of the most important aspects of his very definition of a society: namely, that the manner of the mutual regarding of each member of that society makes that society what it is. "The members of the society are alike because, by reason of their common character, they impose on other members of the society the conditions which lead to that likeness" (*AI*, 204). As Debaise[25] makes clear, in order to approach a full understanding of Whitehead's point, it is necessary to conceive of his notion of existence as a mode of "possession"; existence is a matter of "having" rather than simply "being": "The notion of 'societies' develops further the primacy of having *[l'avoir]* over being *[l'être]* by placing identity within having *[l'avoir]*."[26] This is why societies are their own reason. It is the similar mode of membership of that society that enables its members to cohere and inhere, to create the specificity that is that society. It is the novel manner of this coherence that establishes their specific identity. There is no identity prior to that coherence. This enables a full definition of a society, finally, to be given, which Debaise does in the following way: "We now obtain the conditions for a definition of societies, in the form of a precise question which must be asked of each of them: what does a society *possess* in terms of its components and how do these *hold* themselves together?"[27]

Whitehead's account of the creation of societies challenges us to rethink the relations between an individual and society, its members and the environment: "a society is, for each of its members, an environment with some element of order in it, persisting by reason of the genetic relations between its own members. Such an element of order is the order prevalent in the society" (*PR*, 90). This reference to "order" neatly links to the initial discussion of this chapter, where order was established as that relative and relational term whereby nature organizes itself into particular moments of specificity; it is thus creative insofar as there is the creation of a society. There is, therefore, no problematic distinction between the natural and the social, the real and the artificial, the genetic and the cultural. This mention of the cultural is one that leads to a phrase that Stengers regards as one of the most important elements of Whitehead's account of societies, indeed, of his philosophy as a whole, namely that of "a culture of interstices."[28] This entails that it is not objects or things that are externally related; rather, it is the junctions within things that constitute such objects and such things. To put this important point another way: interstices should be given analytical priority over objects and subjects. For objects and subjects are outcomes of a manner of combination. It is this "manner of combination" that constitutes a culture (rather than some enduring "way of life." Hence, insofar as all that we normally consider to be objects are really societies, Stengers further points out that "Everything is sociology."[29] Whitehead would agree, and would do so in a dual manner. Firstly, at the metaphysical level, all enduring existence is a matter of societies. This condition also applies at the "human" level, in that what is normally considered to constitute a human society does not escape the demands of Whitehead's metaphysics. Sociology, as the study of human societies, has its place, though it is a very specific one, as will be discussed in the next section.

Whitehead's "Sociology"

As has been discussed elsewhere,[30] Whitehead was very careful with his use of words with regard to the distinction between the dual terms of *society* and *the social* as opposed to *sociology* and *the sociological*. The first two of these refer to the metaphysical aspect of his argument, and, as discussed above, they demarcate the manner in which the things of the world come to endure. Such societies and their enactment of the social are widespread and are not premised on, or limited to, the activity of humans. Having said this, that which applies to wider modes of existence will also apply to that which is normally considered to be human societies. However, a word of warning must be given here. Although Whitehead does not always make it as clear as he might, when he discusses human societies and deploys the words "sociology" and "sociological" to do so, he is not referring to the usual conception of human societies.

His longest consideration of the status of human societies is to be found in part 1 of *Adventures of Ideas* (*AI*, 3–100), which is aptly titled "Sociological." This can, at first sight, appear to be a slightly traditional, old-fashioned, even limited account of the development of Western "civilization," given that it seems to trace the history of mentalities from Greek philosophy to the early twentieth-century United Kingdom and United States via the rise of the early Christian Church, the Reformation, and positivism, amongst other factors. It is not my aim here to defend the content of Whitehead's account. But I do wish to draw out the kind of sociology that he attempts to develop, with a view to clarifying its challenge to contemporary understandings of the remit of this discipline.

While dictionary definitions are not always helpful, the broad statement that sociology is "the study of the development, organization, functioning and classification of human societies"[31] might offer a reasonable starting point when trying to approach contemporary renditions of this term. This is not, however, how Whitehead uses the term—though he does not offer an alternative definition. Instead, his sense of the word needs to be derived from his usage of it.

The following discussion might appear to "list" the different ways in which Whitehead uses the term "sociology" but it is intended as more than that. By identifying the shared concern that runs through these diverse usages, I think it is possible to eke out a clearer and deeper understanding of his concept of sociology. To jump ahead, sociology has something to do with understanding *how* humans are, and have been, made human. This search for the "how" is in sharp contrast to any search for "what" makes humans human. A search for a "what" is liable to fall into essentialism. The search for a "how" will provide a fuller grasp of what we have become and what we might yet be.

Although Whitehead uses the adjective "sociological" roughly twenty times in part 1 of *Adventures of Ideas,* to my knowledge, he resorts to the specific word "sociology" only three times. On the first occasion, he states: "The religion of Plato is founded on his conception of what a God can be . . . and his sociology is derived from his conception of what a man can be"

(*AI*, 12). Here "sociology" is not "the study of" something; it is more of a theoretical description of what *could be* rather than what *is*. There is some resonance with Whitehead's description of his own philosophical approach as "speculative" as set out in chapter 1 of *Process and Reality* (*PR*, 3–17). Here, the emphasis is not on listing the facts of existence (or, by analogy, the social world) but of carving out a forward-looking conceptual scheme that is coherent, adequate, and applicable to that which exists, has existed, and will come to exist (*PR*, 3). Sociology, therefore, clearly has something to do with humans but it is not simply an analysis of what humans are, in terms of their relations with each other. It is both more and less than that. It is the attempt to draw out what it is that makes us what we are and points to what we could be.

In his second reference to sociology in *Adventures of Ideas*, Whitehead states:

> There were great civilizations. But they became arrested, and the arrest is the point of our enquiry. We have to understand the reasons for the greatness and the final barriers to advancement. Of course, such an ambitious design is absurd. It would mean the solution of the main problem of sociology. What can be done, is to note some indications of relevant tones of mind apparently widely spread in various districts at different epochs. (*AI*, 79)

On this occasion, there does seem to be a nod toward sociology as the study *of* something. Yet, that which it studies is not human societies as such. Rather, that which is of interest is the process of the rise of "civilizations"[32] and equally that which inhibits this. There is also the indication that it is impossible to provide a once-and-for-all account or reason for this. Sociology can never be complete. What can be offered, however, is an analysis of the "relevant tones of mind" that manifest themselves throughout history. It is not that there are simply states of minds or sets of ideas that are to be discovered. Rather, there are the manners, the modes, in which minds operate, which again signals the importance of the notion of the adverbial.

This links to Whitehead's third reference to sociology in *Adventures of Ideas*. Building on the declaration that it is "tones of mind" that are of interest, Whitehead asserts that he wishes to identify how those factors "which were present sporadically and as the dreams of individuals, or as a faint tinge upon other modes of mentality, received a new importance. . . . The question is to understand how this shift of emphasis happened, and to recognize the effects of this shift upon the sociology of the Western World" (*AI*, 8). Here "sociology" seems to refer to a way of being— to the way of being of a certain epoch or "civilization." The task that Whitehead sets himself is to analyze this in terms of the changing "modes of mentality" that suffuse different epochs.

As will have been noticed, there is a different emphasis in each of Whitehead's three deployments of "sociology"; yet running through all of them is an interest not so much in what makes humans human but in *how* humans have been made human, and the role of mentality within this. Such concerns and interest might appear, to many, to be a form of philosophical or sociological idealism—what makes us human are our ideas; what makes us social humans is our shared ideas and ideas of each other. Such a charge might seem to be substantiated by Whitehead's general description of his aim in writing the first section of *Adventures of Ideas*. "The first part of this book is occupied with the most general aspect of the sociological functions arising from, and issuing into, ideas concerning the human race" (*AI*, 9). Such a reading can only be made if it is assumed that we already know what ideas are—they are that which humans have, and, more importantly, they are that which humans generate. But this is not the case for Whitehead. As Isabelle Stengers pointed out in an interview with Steven Meyer in Buffalo on September 26, 2011, "Ideas are things."[33]

We must pay attention to what it would mean to take seriously the phrase that "ideas are things." Indeed, it could well be suggested that this is exactly what Whitehead is trying to do throughout part 1 of *Adventures of Ideas*, and that this is key to what he understands by sociology and the sociological. As he himself says: "I propose to consider critically the *sort* of history which ideas can have in the life of humanity" (*AI*, 3, emphasis in original). This clearly lays out his position that it is ideas that are the focus of his interest; the "life of humanity" is, in a sense, secondary. For Whitehead, it is possible, indeed it is vital, to analyze how ideas intersect with humans and what they can do for them. This is no simple "history of ideas," for two reasons. First, ideas have been dislocated from being either the products of a specific social or cultural epoch or, alternatively, simply the products of "great minds." Second, Whitehead's is not a history in the usual sense, as his phrase "the *sort* of history" makes clear. He is attempting to map out a new approach to history that does not posit ideas as self-sufficient entities that can be studied on their own terms. At the same time, they are not reducible to the isolated creations of humans. Ideas play themselves out in and through humanity. This is why we must take literally the title of his 1933 work, *Adventures of Ideas*. Ideas have their own adventures, though these adventures are only to be discovered within the history of humanity. Ideas have their own lives but do not exist outside of humanity. Whitehead makes a similar point in *Modes of Thought* (1938) when he is discussing consciousness, as opposed to ideas:

> Clear, conscious discrimination is an accident of human existence. It makes us human. But it does not make us exist. It is of the essence of our humanity. But it is an accident of our existence. (*MT*, 116)

Again, there is an important distinction made between humans and humanity. We could have existed, in some sense, as physically human, as just another kind of ape, without clear, conscious discrimination. But we would have lacked humanity. Intriguingly, Whitehead dips into the lexicon of scholastic philosophy to make his point, by drawing a distinction between "essence" and "accident." Conscious discrimination is essential for our humanity but it is not necessary for our simple existence as humans; it is, in this respect, accidental. Its role is to make us human insofar as we have humanity rather than to make us "ape-ity."

> Fragmentary intellectual agencies co-operated blindly to turn apes into men, to turn the classic civilization into mediaeval Europe, to overwhelm the Renaissance by the Industrial Revolution. *Men knew not what they did.* (*AI*, 7, emphasis added)

Ideas, as intellectual agencies, did not have foresight—they did not, in and of themselves, decide to invent humans, to mold them out of apes—but they were still the primary affective factor in this process. Conversely, humans did not generate their ideas out of nothing; humans were, rather, the vehicles that enabled ideas to come into efficacy. A record of the ways in which humanity and ideas combine is precisely the "*sort* of history" that Whitehead wants to elicit.

Conclusion

It is now possible to incorporate the earlier discussion of the status of societies, considered as elements of the general ordering of existence, with Whitehead's "sociology." It will be remembered that each society requires a common mode of prehension, the shared manner in which each individual within that society regards all other members thereby constituting the society as a specific society. The same applies at the human level. "In any human society, one fundamental idea tingeing every detail of activity is the general conception of the status of the individual members of that group, considered apart from any pre-eminence" (*AI,* 10). So, it is an idea that is grasped by each member of a society, even if it is only grasped obliquely, unconsciously, that enables each individual to consist[34] as both an individual and as a member of that society.

Further, it will also be remembered that the mode of analysis required for an understanding of the constitution of each society, and a comparison of societies, is that of contrast. The specificity and definiteness of a society comes from the contrasts within it and between it and other societies. Whitehead calls upon various contrasts throughout *Adventures of Ideas.* There is the contrast between "force and persuasion" (*AI,* 69–86) and that between "freedom and compulsion" (*AI,* 65–58). It is not so much that either of these exists separately or in its own terms. Rather, it is the contrast between the two different dynamic aspects of these contrasts that each express that which is of importance. It is a matter of productive tension, and it is in this respect that Whitehead can, finally, offer a definition of sociology and sociological theory.

> The foundation of all understanding of sociological theory—that is to say, of all understanding of human life—is that no static maintenance of perfection is possible. This axiom is rooted in the nature of things. Advance or Decadence are the only choices offered to mankind.[35] The pure conservative is fighting against the essence of the universe. . . .
>
> [For] the very essence of real actuality—that is, of the completely real, is *process.* (*AI,* 274)

This observation ties together many of the themes that have been raised in this essay. Sociological theory, as an account of "human life," will look at human societies, but in doing so, it cannot separate itself from the wider principles that apply to all societies and that derive from "the nature of things." The key to understanding this is to realize that all existence is a matter of process. However, such process is not mere flux or becoming. The solidity that appears within existence, its enduring elements, are always social (in the widest sense of the term), in that it is only societies that manage to cohere and endure. In one sense, all societies are inherently "conservative" insofar as they constantly attempt to maintain themselves as they are. But, an overemphasis on such conservation, at the expense of reinvigoration, will lead to decay and decadence.

Within human societies, ideas, as things, play a crucial role but not the only role. "Men are driven by their thoughts as well as by the molecules in their bodies, by intelligence and by senseless forces" (*AI*, 46). As will by now be clear, such thoughts are not to be viewed as the creations of humans (to be studied by sociocultural analyses); they are, rather, that which enables us to develop our humanity. The ways in which this has happened is what constitutes history. Thoughts are aspects of the differing careers of ideas as they adventure throughout existence. Equally, senseless forces are not merely the deterministic, iron-clad laws of nature that dictate an uncomprehending but unstoppable rolling-out of existence along a preordained path (and that hard science studies). Senseless forces exhibit the unrelenting process of existence, no matter what we think of it, or how we try to ignore it: "life is an offensive, directed against the repetitious mechanism of the Universe. It is the thesis of this discussion that a policy of sociological defence is doomed to failure" (*AI*, 80).

Whitehead was a philosopher and not a sociologist, but his distinction between the twin couplets of society-social and sociology-sociological seems an important one that enables accounts of the humanly social to take their place within or beside other accounts of existence, and does not relegate sociocultural analyses to the sidelines, leaving the so-called hard sciences to take on the real reality. Yet, Whitehead provides a set of warnings to social theory as well as avenues for developing novel concepts and approaches. One of the starkest of these warnings is not to take anything for granted, be it a general theory of human societies or the existence of the social as a discrete realm. Other terms that sociology, especially, takes for granted, such as "social action," "social facts," "social relations," must also be treated with suspicion, and jettisoned if necessary. Yet, Whitehead also offers some challenging but productive suggestions: that we investigate, without any prior judgement, how it is that the societies that we encounter (which might be anything from a transport system to a door, to a website, to a riot) manage to come to be, to hold together, sustain themselves, or not. This will involve a reorientation of our concepts and less surety in those explanations that many social theorists hold dear. But if social theory, considered as some kind of a society, is not to perish entirely, it must grasp the nettle of novelty, leave behind its comforting but outdated concepts and procedures, and seize some kind of a future, whatever the cost. For

It is the first step in sociological wisdom, to recognize that the major advances in civilization are processes which all but wreck the societies in which they occur:—like unto an arrow in the hand of a child. The art of free society consists . . . in fearlessness of revision. (*S*, 88)

Notes

1. Bruno Latour, *We Have Never Been Modern* (Harlow: Prentice Hall, 1993); Bruno Latour, *Reassembling the Social: An Introduction to Actor-Network-Theory* (Oxford: Oxford University Press, 2005).

2. Latour, *Reassembling the Social*, 9.

3. Talcott Parsons, *The Structure of Social Action: A Study in Social Theory with Special Reference to a Group of Recent European Writers* (New York: Free Press, 1968).

4. See Michael Halewood, introduction to a special section on Whitehead, in *Theory, Culture and Society* 25, no. 4 (2008): 1–14.

5. See Didier Debaise, *Un empirisme spéculatif. Lecture de Procès et réalité de Whitehead* (Paris: Vrin, 2006), 161–72 ff.

6. Ibid., 162–63.

7. Ibid., 164. All translations from Debaise (2006) are my own. They may be a little rough and ready but they are faithful to the original, I hope.

8. Isabelle Stengers. "A Constructivist Reading of *Process and Reality*," *Theory, Culture and Society* 25, no. 4 (2008), 104, 114 (also reprinted as chapter 1 of this volume); Isabelle Stengers, *Thinking with Whitehead: A Free and Wild Creation of Concepts* (Cambridge, Mass.: Harvard University Press, 2011), 313, 513.

9. Steven Shaviro, *Without Criteria: Kant, Whitehead, Deleuze, and Aesthetics* (Cambridge, Mass.: MIT Press, 2009), 71–72.

10. Whitehead uses the word "societies" once in Section I, on page 84, but puts it in inverted commas as it is a technical term which he will introduce fully in Section II. He uses the word "nature" four times but only when discussing the "nature" of God, not nature as usually conceived.

11. See Debaise, *Un empirisme spéculatif*, 161–62.

12. Ibid., 162–63.

13. Ibid., 137–40.

14. Stengers's discussion of Whitehead's "sociology" will be taken up in the next section. Stengers, *Thinking with Whitehead*, 17–18.

15. Debaise, *Un empirisme spéculatif*, especially ch. 3.

16. Such a focus and drawing out of consequences is what is being attempted in this chapter; for this, I am much indebted to the work and ideas of Didier Debaise.

17. Michael Halewood. *A. N. Whitehead and Social Theory: Tracing a Culture of Thought* (London: Anthem Press, 2011), 86–9.

18. Parsons, *The Structure of Social Action*.

19. Debaise, *Un empirisme spéculatif*, 139.

20. Halewood, *A. N. Whitehead and Social Theory*, 27, 29, 98, 162; Shaviro, *Without Criteria*, 38, 56.

21. See Debaise, *Un empirisme spéculatif,* 141. In this passage Debaise is analyzing Locke and his influence on Whitehead. As such, Debaise's commentary, at this juncture, cannot be directly applied to Whitehead's text but it does offer a genuine insight, for example in the following remark: "It is as if the order of predication is inverted: no longer are qualities to be predicated of a subject but, on the contrary, qualities are attributed as subject."

22. Stengers, *Thinking with Whitehead,* 321.

23. See Steven Meyer's introduction, *Configurations* 13, no. 1 (2007): 1–33, and Halewood, *A. N. Whitehead and Social Theory,* 35–38 for a discussion of the extraordinary fact that the nowadays rather commonplace term "creativity" was invented only around eighty-five years ago, within a very abstract metaphysical treatise.

24. I am no fan of unnecessary neologisms. But I have used the word "undertermination" here to differentiate it from "indetermination," which, to my mind, has negative connotations along the lines of uncertainty or inconclusiveness. I envisage "undetermination" as a much more neutral term.

25. Debaise, *Un empirisme spéculatif,* 70–71.

26. Ibid., 70–71, 145.

27. Ibid., 145.

28. Stengers, *Thinking with Whitehead,* 328.

29. Ibid., 325.

30. Halewood, *A. N. Whitehead and Social Theory,* 84–86.

31. *Collins English Dictionary,* ed. Patrick Hanks (London: Collins, 1986), 1447–48.

32. I note the problematic status of the term "civilization" but will not expand on this here as it is not relevant to the argument being made.

33. I attended this occasion, at the kind invitation of Jim Bono. I made a note of this remarkable statement at the time as I was immediately seized by its potency and possibilities. I believe that a transcript of this interview is to be made available at some point in the future.

34. For the importance of the notion of "consisting" to the formation of societies, see Debaise, *Un empirisme spéculatif,* 145.

35. Whitehead's old-fashioned use of "mankind" and masculine pronouns, here and elsewhere, to indicate "all" persons should be noted.

FIFTEEN

Imaginative Chemistry

Synthetic Ecologies and the Construction of Life

A. J. Nocek

> The doctrine I am maintaining is that neither physical nature nor life can be understood unless we fuse them together as essential factors in the composition of 'really real' things whose interconnections and individual characters constitute the universe.
>
> —Alfred North Whitehead, *Modes of Thought*

Artificial Life is alive and well. Despite the perception, ALife was not simply a late-twentieth-century silicon-based fad, with over-ambitious goals of creating life *in silico.* In fact, the discipline may be closer to synthesizing life from the bottom-up than it has ever been. In the twenty-first century, ALife has set its sites on the "holy grail," the synthesis of *wet* life, from chemical building blocks to living systems. The protocell, or the minimal synthetic cell, seems to no longer be a question of if, but of when it exists.[1] This latter point is itself highly contentious, since there is no scientific consensus on what exactly a protocell is, and as such, whether or not it might already exist. So for example, while some claim that a protocell must constitute a minimal form of biological life, and so does not yet exist because it does not meet generally recognized biological life criteria,[2] still others, such as Martin Hanczyc and Takashi Ikegami, do not seem as beholden to this biological definition. They suggest that the protocell already exists, and it exists as a primordial molecular globule formed from both organic and inorganic compounds, and capable of self-organization and dynamic behavior. Protocells, according to the latter definition, do not reproduce minimal, biological life, but are self-organizing processes subject to the laws of physics and chemistry. They are terrestrial agents that possess some but not all of the properties of biological life.[3]

Whether or not these protocells are instances of life *as such,* and not the mere exemplification of certain life processes, is a difficult question. But it is a difficulty that exposes the anthropocentrism of excluding self-organizing processes from being instances of "life." As recent debates in artificial life, origins of life, and astrobiological communities have exposed, defining life as a natural kind with any set of functional[4] and material properties[5] is based on familiar forms of life on earth; it is anthropocentric, and is therefore insufficient for defining life *as such,*[6] since it might limit the possibilities of discovering genuinely "weird" forms of life, terrestrial or otherwise.[7]

Given that life may now even be instantiated in inorganic materials, as Leroy Cronin contends—by means of what he calls iCHELLs, examples of "inorganic biology"[8]—means that known biological or even terrestrial life may be fundamentally insufficient for capturing the full range of existing or possible life. Experiments in wet ALife seem to testify to this biocentrism—to the fact that an ontology of life must be fundamentally more and not less inclusive, capable of accounting for the diversity of actual and potential life, both organic and inorganic; it is a challenge that points us both as far back as Aristotle's *De Anima,* as Eugene Thacker has recently shown,[9] and also forward to some of the most exciting work coming out of the contemporary, neovital materialisms in Continental philosophy. Jane Bennett, for one (who borrows from the rich tradition of vitalism, extending from Kant, Driesch, and Bergson to Deleuze and Guattari, as well as Bruno Latour's actor-network theory, and Spinoza's theory of affect), makes a compelling case for the non-teleological vitality of things. By giving back the life that is proper to things—exemplified in the inorganic world of "metal"—Bennett challenges the post-Cartesian conception of nature as mechanistic and lifeless, and champions a "political ecology of things,"[10] wherein life is immanent to material, instead of added to it according to the "hylomorphic model."[11]

By this account, the achievement of motility from dynamic oil and water-based chemistry (the protocell) seems like just the kind of experimentation that testifies to the need for such an inclusive conception of life, to an ontology of life that is nonanthropocentric and capable of giving voice to all potential witnesses of vitality, whether organic or inorganic. For her notion of vitality, Bennett draws heavily on the work of Gilles Deleuze and Félix Guattari, specifically, the latter's "prodigious idea of *Nonorganic Life*" that is developed out of their interest in metallurgy: "what metal and metallurgy bring to light," they explain in *A Thousand Plateaus,* "is a life proper to matter, a vital state of matter as such, a material vitalism that doubtless exists everywhere but is ordinarily hidden or covered, rendered unrecognizable, dissociated by the hylomorphic model."[12] Metallurgy, they continue, is the "consciousness or thought of matter-flow, and metal the correlate of this consciousness. As expressed in panmetalism, metal is coextensive to the whole of matter . . . even the waters, the grasses and varieties of wood, the animals are populated by salts or mineral elements" (*ATP*, 411).

In this chapter I intend to defend a vital materialism in which there is a "life proper to matter," as Deleuze and Guattari suggest. My claim is in part a challenge to Eugene Thacker's suggestion that, far from needing a new conception of life, what we need is a "critique of life."[13] I will not suggest that we have ever gotten close to a concept of life in-itself, nor that we ever could. Rather, my argument will be that a speculative concept of nonorganic life is meaningful insofar as it is eminently practical, insofar as it can transform our experience of human practices. My claim will unfold in a number of steps.

I look to contemporary wet-life synthesis as exemplary of a scientific practice that raises the question of the ontology of life. I argue that the way it does so obscures the much more radical metaphysics of nonorganic life to which its materials testify. In the opening sections of this essay, then, I take seriously the idea that there is a "metallurgical" aspect to wet-life synthesis, and consider the conditions for it subsisting, or insisting, within the norms of the practice; I do so, however, if only to problematize this hypothesis in the following sections by analyzing a series of key presuppositions undergirding the perspective of Deleuze and Guattari, ones that ultimately challenge the legitimacy of my hypothesis. My suggestion will be that the speculative pragmatics of Alfred North Whitehead act as an important supplement to Deleuze and Guattari's perspective, by demonstrating the *pragmatic* conditions under which the practice of wet-life synthesis would testify to the speculative concept of nonorganic life.

Vital Molecules

It may seem of course that I am exaggerating the importance of the wet synthesis of life, since its practitioners rarely seem, if ever, to be doing anything analogous to the metallurgy Deleuze and Guattari have in mind. Recall that metallurgy is significant for Deleuze and Guattari because it opposes the hylomorphic model of vitality, which asserts—in various guises throughout the history of philosophy—that matter is essentially inert, and is given life by means of a nonmaterial force applied to it from without.[14] But as metallurgists know all to well, vitality insists within matter itself. Metallurgy testifies to the vitality of the inorganic, to the fact that its "operations are always astride the thresholds, so that an energetic materiality overspills the prepared matter, and the qualitative deformation or transformation overspills the form" (*ATP*, 410).

The point to appreciate here is that metallurgy exemplifies nonorganic life for Deleuze and Guattari because metal is a nonhomogenous material, structured by irregularly shaped crystals in continuous variation. The microstructure of metal, as Jane Bennett makes clear by drawing on the historian of science Cyril Smith, is protocrystalline. There is a wide variety of shapes and sizes to crystal grains, determined primarily by their spatial relation to their neighbors. And while the atoms of a single grain, according to Smith, are "arranged on regular array on a space lattice,"[15] there are still imperfections, "loose atoms," located at the "interfaces of the grains" that belong to none of the grains, and so make the boundaries between grains imperfect, or as Bennett insists, "porous and quivering."[16] The structure of a grain is not therefore homogeneous but "full of holes"; it is precisely these "dislocations" in the lattice that allow for change.

These defects are also what make metal exemplary of the nomadism of matter: it is the "atomic quivering" at the fringes of its protocrystalline structure that is the non-place of its vitality, the non-spatial location of its potential for dynamic change. The metallurgist exploits the indeterminacy of metallic structure when, for example, he or she anneals (softens the metal by heating and then cooling slowly), or quenches (a high-carbon steel is cooled quickly after heating in order to harden it). Metal is no longer a trope of inert matter,[17] but is the model for the vitality of the material world, exemplary of how the organic and inorganic are in vital communication. There is *a life* to metal, explain Deleuze and Guattari, one that extends to the entire material world, and it is one "that doubtless exists everywhere but is ordinarily hidden or covered, rendered unrecognizable, dissociated by the hylomorphic model" (*ATP*, 411).

It is important to note here that this conception of life—as what traverses both the organic and inorganic, as what signals the creative advance lurking within a structure, and as what is fundamentally irreducible to that structure—has deep resonances with the notion of life Whitehead develops in *Process and Reality*.[18] Significantly, though, Whitehead's notion of life deepens our appreciation for its immanence to all orders—organic and inorganic—and its nonopposition to the ecologies that support it. In Whitehead's view, life is neither reducible to order (as many functional definitions of life would maintain—see below), nor is it the negation of order; it is rather the indeterminacy insisting within order, or what he calls a society: "life lurks in the interstices of each living cell, and in the interstices of the brain" (*PR*, 105–6). Life "is the name for originality" in Whitehead's metaphysical scheme; it is "a bid for freedom" from the repetition of the past in the present enjoyment (*PR,* 104). Societies neither justify nor account for life, because life is a pure feeling of "anarchic" disorder within every occasion of experience. Life is therefore antisocial, or disorderly, as it resists the genetic "inheritance" of a social order's "defining characteristic" from the other occasions in a nexus the positive feelings of which are what allow a nexus of occasions to enjoy social order (cf. *PR,* 34). A social order, such as a biological order, is therefore

> only to be termed living in a derivative sense. A 'living society' is one which includes some 'living occasions.' Thus a society may be termed more or less 'living,' according to the prevalence in it of living occasions. Also an occasion may be more or less living according to the relative importance of the novel factors in its final satisfaction. (*PR,* 102)

There is not a difference in kind or nature but a difference in degree between living and nonliving societies (bacteria and metal); it is just that "for certain purposes," Whitehead maintains, "whatever life there is in a society may be important; and for other purposes unimportant" (*PR,* 102). But the difference in degree between metal and bacteria, for example, is a consequence of all occasions, at least to some degree, resisting the inheritance of the past (after all, creativity is the "universal of universals," in Whitehead's scheme; cf. *PR,* 21, 31–32). The degree to which a society is living is really a question of how much novelty, or "social deficiency," an order can handle before it will undergo structural change.

In this view, metallurgy is really an ecological practice that experiments with the interstices lurking within crystalline structure—for example, steel is a metal alloy more adaptable than iron, its major component. The issue is not whether there is life in this or that molecular environment (organic versus inorganic chemistry); rather it is how much life, how much originality, an environment can withstand before it undergoes transformation. Life is more of an ecological question than a biological one.[19]

The majority, if not all, of the scientists trying to synthesize life *de novo,* or at least creating the first steps toward it,[20] operate under the following assumptions: (1) that life is a set of predetermined functional properties emergent from a potentially broad range of nonliving chemical constituents,[21] although these constituents are nevertheless limited by the functional definition of life proposed (oil and water chemistry, as I discuss below, may produce the "first cell," but not the first minimally *living* cell); and (2) that the emergence of life from nonlife can somehow be understood or explained, which is to say, there cannot be "truly" emergent phenomena (perhaps only "weakly" emergent),[22] since this would undermine the epistemological constraints of the practice of ALife itself: to know how to produce life from nonlife.[23] At the outset, two main tensions arise with the ecological experimentation on nonorganic life proposed above: (1) there are only certain chemicals productive of life; and (2) irreducible instances of creativity within matter need to be explained away. By this reasoning, the wet synthesis of life seems far indeed from exemplifying the characteristics of metallurgy that Deleuze and Guattari celebrate.

And yet it is critical to recognize that "minor science" ("Metallurgy is minor science in person, 'vague' science, or phenomenology of matter" [*ATP*, 411]) is not a stable goal or end opposed to its royal formalization in state science.[24] There is no doubt that nomad or minor science must be "ideally" distinguished from royal science. Where the latter involves "reproduction, iteration and reiteration" so that "differences of time and place [are] so many variables, the constant from which is extracted precisely by the law" (*ATP*, 372), the former is characterized by "following," not in order to "reproduce" (e.g., the exact chemical conditions required for the emergence of life), but in order to "search for the singularities of a matter, or rather of a material, and not out to discover a form" (*ATP*, 372). The latter is an ambulant procedure for setting variables in "continuous variation" instead of the royal procedure of extracting constants from them. The opposition between the two procedures is far from absolute, however: "more virtual or ideal than real is the opposition between the two kinds of science," insists Eric Alliez in *The Signature of the World*.[25] Deleuze and Guattari explain that ambulant processes are inseparable from their formalization by royal science. Primitive metallurgy, for example, is not divorced from its royal formalization since it is just as easily conceived as a "question of going from one point to another (even if they are singular points) through the intermediary of channels" (*ATP*, 372).

In this perspective, scientists trying to synthesize life *de novo* may indeed be guided by the norm of reproduction so that "for the same phenomena [life] to recur in gravitational and striated space it is sufficient for the same conditions to obtain" (*ATP*, 372). But our question is: does a nomadicism not have to insist within the royal practice of wet-life synthesis? And under what conditions is it achieved? In the next section, I review an experiment performed by Hanczyc and colleagues in 2007 on oil and water chemistry in order to explore the potential for a nomadic space to be generated within the norms of royal formalization.

Case Study

In their article, "Fatty Acid Chemistry at the Oil-Water Interface: Self-Propelled Oil Droplets," Hanczyc and colleagues describe a self-propelled oil droplet based on fatty acid chemistry. In their experiment, they add oleic anhydride oil phase to alkaline water phase (pH 12) on a glass slide in order to see what results from the hydrolysis of the anhydride. The oil reacts to the water immediately: the oil droplets break apart into smaller spherical droplets, begin to move and respond to their environment. Observationally, these self-propelled oil-droplet systems display a maintenance of their own boundaries over time; but because their interface boundaries are extremely sensitive to their chemical environments, the cells are able to respond to chemical gradients in the environment resulting in a behavior known as "chemiotaxis," or directional movement as a result of chemical gradients, a behavior typical of living cells. What is even more surprising, though, is that as these artificial cells move, they remodel their environment to create the conditions for their own movement: "the movement of the oil droplets is governed by a self-generated pH gradient."[26] In other words, *protocells structure their own chemical environment with gradients to which they are sensitive.* Protocell environments are "radically self-constructed."[27]

The interpretation these experimenters offer for the self-propelled oil-droplet system is telling of how observations are "royally" explained within scientific practice. First, they posit that symmetry must be broken so that a "completely symmetric oil droplet" may begin to move directionally. In their system, they note four asymmetric processes: "convection in the oil phase, water rushing into the leading edge, accumulation and expulsion of lipids from the trailing edge, and the self-generated pH gradient."[28] Their challenge is to find the cause for each of these symmetry-breaking events. Why is it, for example, that when *x* chemical conditions obtain, symmetry is broken, and *y* results? "The initial symmetry-breaking event," they conjecture, "*may* be caused by random oscillation at the interface"; if this is the case, then "when a patch of fresh oil becomes exposed to the water during a local oscillation, the Marangoni effect causes a flow of material at the interface toward the zone of high surface tension. This flow then causes the movement of fresh oil from the interior to move to the interface."[29] The Marangoni effect, which is essentially the idea in physics that surface tension gradients determine the transfer of mass along the interface of two systems,

> *may* explain not only the convection within the oil phase of the droplet but also the movement of the droplet. Theoretically, the Marangoni effect *may*

> spontaneously initiate motion and allow for self-sustained autonomous movement of a droplet in a surfactant-rich environment with enough force to create movement.[30]

What is important to appreciate is that the explanation offered for why this chemical system breaks symmetry is no more than a hypothesis. This is certainly something that Hanczyc and colleagues would themselves acknowledge: even though oil-and-water–based chemistry may reliably produce cells that self-construct their environment, and this may indeed be an important first step on the way to synthesizing life,[31] there is still a gap in their ability to understand why this happens. This is why Hanczyc in his article on "Structure and the Synthesis of Life" recently speculated that

> a scientific dichotomy may exist between understanding life and synthesizing it. . . . To synthesize life, perhaps a chemical system too complex to understand must be created and tested. If a chemical system is too complex, then a concise and comprehensive understanding of the system may not be attainable, even if synthetic life is created therein.[32]

And yet that Hanczyc and his fellow scientists nevertheless offer this hypothesis is more telling than it may seem: it is indicative of the epistemological desire for explanation (of chemeotaxis) that animates their practice; it commits them, as Deleuze and Guattari might say, to the royal procedure of tracing emergent phenomena back to their conditions. The well-known emergence cliché, "the whole is greater than the sum of its parts," is a whole whose explanation, and not its inexplicability, animates the hopes of those scientists who dream of synthesizing life from its chemical constituents. Compellingly, this point may also be stated in the terms of strong and weak theories of emergence, wherein a strong theory of emergence—that is, one in which the cause of the emergent property cannot be isolated—is "uncomfortably like magic," and whose embrace would seem to conflict with the passions that animate the practice of ALife: to *know* how to synthesize life from *nonliving* components.[33] Strongly emergent phenomena, or phenomena whose existence is autonomous from and irreducible to the more basic phenomena that give rise to it, are generally deemed undesirable for scientists, since they "risk associating emergence with mysticism."[34] Analytical philosophers have done important work in trying to manage these risks by formulating more palatable versions of emergence, from theories of "weak emergence," where macro-phenomena are "*ontologically* dependent on and reducible to micro phenomena,"[35] to the ever-popular "supervenience" approach to emergence, where, in certain versions, there is dependency of the macro on the micro without reduction.[36]

From this perspective, it seems clear that the theory of emergence endorsed by practitioners of wet-life synthesis covers over what nomadicism celebrates: the irreducible interstices that are productive of an emergent product. Life, write Deleuze and Guattari, is "germinal, and intensive, a powerful life without organs, a Body that is all the more alive for having no organs, everything that passes *between* organisms" (*ATP*, 499). Life is not the cell, but the "interstices," according to Whitehead, that lurk within in the cell.[37]

These conflicting notions of life (product versus process) result, I want to suggest, from a metaphysical presupposition of ALife generally: namely, that there is a difference in kind or nature between the living and the nonliving. And yet this is an assumption that cannot be easily discarded since it is required for the practice of ALife as such: there is nonliving matter (metal, silicon, molecules) that may become living.[38] What I want to insist on, however, is that this is not a harmless assumption; it has consequences for the ontology and epistemology of life that the discipline produces. Life must now be an emergent some-thing, a product that differentiates itself in kind from what is not-life, the emergence of which it is the scientists' job to account for epistemologically. The interstices that are generative of emergent products are covered over by the practice.[39] Opposed to this concept of life founded, as Whitehead would insist, on a "substance metaphysics," stands Deleuze and Guattari's pure productivity of the "prodigious idea of *Nonorganic Life.*"

But if we grant that life-as-(weakly-emergent-)product is the assumption required for the discipline of ALife, then it is the norms of practice and not the experimentation itself that reduces the generative interstices. What it conceals, in the register of Deleuze and Guattari, are the creative processes (life-as-pure-productivity) that undermine the division of the living from the nonliving. Metaphysically, all such divisions abstract from a more primary, impersonal vitality. This is the impersonal *life* in Deleuze's last essay, "Immanence: A Life," that must be distinguished from the "lives" of individuals, from subjects and objects, or from the lives of organisms; *a life* is what gives rise to *lives*.

In this perspective, coextensive with the goals of wet ALife is the experience of the "metallurgic following" of the pure productivity immanent to matter, the impersonal vitality that gives rise to individuated macro phenomena—individuated *lives.* Nomadic following is not of course a new method that could ever have a stable goal or end, but is rather the insistence of a nomadic practice within royal science[40] that discovers a "life proper to matter, a vital state of matter as such, a material vitalism, an ambulant one that doubtless exists everywhere but is ordinarily hidden or covered, rendered unrecognizable" (*ATP,* 411). Hiding within the royal formalization of protocell construction, where emergent properties are mapped back onto more basic phenomena, there insists, within Deleuze and Guattari's register, an ideal, or virtual, point of nomadicism. This is the pure flight of the scientist, not characterized by predetermined conditions, but by the pure following of the life of matter. So in this perspective, the symmetry-breaking events in the oil and water experiment might very well be an important achievement for the eventual synthesis of life defined according the norms of the experimenters' practice; but more than this, these events are indicative of thresholds crossed, of vitality generated from the immanent conditions of matter itself, and are incapable of being recuperated into an end product or goal.[41]

Scientists such as Hanczyc, Ikegami, and Cronin who are experimenting with the dynamic interactions of inorganic compounds, are facilitating the productivity of the inorganic world in their chemical test tubes. That oil and water chemistry is generative, that it is productive of an emergent product, a synthetic cell, is certainly worth celebrating—and scientists certainly do. But the process of chemical productivity itself, I would argue, is something worth celebrating as well. These are the individuating processes generative of the product major or royal science isolates. It is the latter's virtual, or nomadic, condition that is then covered over and reduced to what can be explained away. What is deeply metallurgical about this practice, then, is that it is an exploitation of the indeterminacy that insists within the chemical world.[42] These wet-life scientists become *cosmic artisans,* in Deleuze and Guattari's view, who "follow the matter flow as pure productivity," and whose artisanal following then testifies, if virtually, to the "prodigious idea of *Nonorganic Life,*" but in so doing undermine the metaphysical commitments of royal formalization: that there is a difference in kind between the living and nonliving.

Subjectivist Impasse or Constructivist Absolutism?

While this essay has proposed a nomadicism of wet-life synthesis that testifies to nonorganic life, it still has done little to clarify what it means to testify on behalf of this principle. This is no simple matter. For instance, does it mean that this science, at least in its nomadicism, discovers the absolute, or "vague essence," of matter qua life? And what might it mean to give life such a privilege? A metaphysics of life brings up any number of questions vis-à-vis the justification for its absolutization,[43] not to mention the added, though not insignificant, problem of whether science exceeds its own warrant for success by venturing into metaphysics. So to hazard that this science supports such a metaphysics of life, even in spite of itself, is to raise a host of problems that one must be willing to take on board. It is to take a substantial risk, as Whitehead might say of all true metaphysical interpretation, but it is a risk worth taking when the payoff is so great: that the productivity of matter exploited within the scientist's test tube might be celebrated in nonreductive terms, in terms that resist the tendency to see absolute divisions in nature, the living and the nonliving, and affirm, instead, the conditions for chemical experimentation to facilitate the vitality of matter.

To begin, let me say that it has been taken as axiomatic that there is a metaphysical equivalence between matter and life: life-matter is the creative principle of the universe that exceeds organismic form qua organized body. While this is certainly true of the Deleuze and Guattari of *A Thousand Plateaus,* it would be a mistake to assume that the concept of life does not undergo substantial mutations throughout their coauthored and singly authored texts.[44] What is significant for us is that life, in its various mutations, is consistently taken to be the creative principle that is immanent to matter and cuts across all physical, biological, social, and technological thresholds. And in certain texts, life is taken to be *the* ultimate metaphysical principle. In Deleuze's last essay, "Immanence: A Life," for example, he writes that life is that by which even immanence is defined: "The transcendental field is defined by a plane of immanence, and the plane of immanence by a life."[45] Pure immanence, according to Deleuze, is "A Life, and nothing else. It is not immanence to life, but the immanent that is in nothing is a life. A life is the immanence of immanence, absolute immanence: it is complete power, complete bliss."[46] Life is the achievement of immanence's immanence to itself. That life assumes the power of the absolute is detectable even as early as his 1968 work, *Expressionism in Philosophy: Spinoza:* "Life, that is, expressivity is carried to the absolute. There is a unity of the divine in substance, and an actual diversity of the One in the attributes . . . it amounts to the life of substance itself, the necessity of its a priori constitution."[47]

That there is a "life of substance" in "*excess of* being—including its own being,"[48] is something for which Alain Badiou is well known for criticizing Deleuze,[49] and to which Eugene Thacker has recently drawn attention as well. While my own interest in the absolutization of life is ultimately less contentious, it will be no less rigorous in interrogating the conditions of possibility for such absolutization. My suggestion is that we take seriously the impetus behind many of the recent criticisms of Deleuze and Guattari's metaphysics—namely, that their concepts are still too "subjectivist," issuing from thinkers working, however loosely, under the banner of speculative realism.[50] If we are going to claim that our science testifies to a metaphysics of life in the style of Deleuze and Guattari, then the critique of subjectivism would be a damaging blow to our thesis indeed, since nomad science would testify to a vital universe that is reducible to what Kant, in the *Critique of Pure Reason,* would call a mere "transcendental illusion": the tendency to "take the subjective necessity of a connection of our concepts . . . for an objective necessity in the determination of things in themselves."[51]

In his 2010 work, *After Life,* Eugene Thacker highlights this problem in Deleuze and Guattari's metaphysics by drawing on what Quentin Meillassoux claims is the latter's (along with Nietzsche's and Bergson's) disavowal of "correlationism"—"the idea according to which we only ever have access to the correlation between thought and being, and never to either term considered apart from the other"[52]—which ultimately subtends their position.[53] According to Meillassoux, it is not that Deleuze and Guattari circumvent correlationism; it is that they are bad correlationists for not respecting the post-Kantian asymmetry of the self-world correlation: for while there is no world without a subject who thinks it, there is also no subject without a world in which it is "in" (e.g., Husserl: consciousness is always consciousness of something; Heidegger: Dasein is being-in-the-world; and so on), but this world remains inaccessible; while the latter is necessary, it remains an "in-itself" that forever withdraws from view qua "unthought." What Deleuze and Guattari and others fail to appreciate, however, is the correlational inaccessibility of the in-itself, which culminates in what Meillassoux calls "subjectivist metaphysics" (of which vitalism is a species), or the idea according to which the "in-itself is devoid of truth because it is unthinkable," and so the correlation itself is absolutized.[54] The subjectivist claims "that some of these relations, or indeed all, are determinations not only of men, but of being itself."[55] Duration, process, life, are all examples, according to Meillassoux, of some aspect of human access to the world that is then projected onto the world itself. That "life" is absolutized in Deleuze and Guattari's case is precisely the subjectivization of metaphysics that Meillassoux finds suspect: they project "onto the things themselves a correlation which might be perception, intellection, desire, etc., and makes it the absolute itself."[56]

What Thacker brings to our attention is the complexity that underwrites the vitalists' transgression of the correlational requirement—namely, that the failure to uphold the self-world correlation is a function of the concept of life itself. Why exactly life resists easy insertion into the correlational framework is beyond the scope of this essay, relying as it does on Thacker's illuminating account of the ontology of life from Aristotle to Kant through post-Aristotelian scholasticism. But suffice it to say that correlationism is insufficient for an ontology of life because

> life is at once an object of thought, an object of study, even, of the living "out there," and at the same time that which is lived "in here," within a conceptual framework of intuition and immediacy. These dual notions of life are at once mutually exclusive and reciprocally necessary to think life in one way or another (e.g., as biology or phenomenology, as natural or existential). For the vitalist correlation, then, what enables its absolutism is a *contradiction* at the heart of the *correlation*.[57]

Life poses a problem, then: what is once the most immediate, or "for-us," is also the most "out there," or "in-itself." Life resists the asymmetry of the correlational impasse. Thacker's marvelous study of the ontology of life therefore complicates the subjectivist critique of Deleuze and Guattari. The vitalist neither simply overcomes the correlational circle nor fails to appreciate it (i.e., as a bad correlationist), but absolutizes as a function of the complexity of the problem life poses. While for Thacker (via Bataille) this does not justify life's absolutization,[58] since an ontology of life is, at the end of the day, *nihil*[59]—which means that the vitalist disavows negativity—I part ways with this reading, not in order to critique his own "critique of life," as if to suggest that Deleuze and Guattari make the strong claim that life exists *in-itself,* but in order to add a necessary layer of complexity to the latter's metaphysics of life through their notion of the philosophical concept.

To my mind, both Meillassoux's and Thacker's critique of Deleuze and Guattari's absolutization of life fails to appreciate the complexity of the relation between conceptual construction and immanence. As the latter write in *What is Philosophy?*, "immanence is immanent only to itself and consequently captures everything, absorbs All-One, and leaves nothing remaining to which it could be immanent."[60] What this means is that "whenever immanence is interrupted as immanent *to* something," like a subject who *thinks it through the concept,* "we can be sure that this Something reintroduces the transcendent,"[61] and that *a life,* in the context of Deleuze's last essay, becomes someone's life, or rather the "the organism . . . which life sets against itself in order to limit itself" (*ATP,* 503). The point is that immanence, as it is discussed in their *What is Philosophy?,* is a "One-All,"[62] which means that thought is a segment of it, in no way outside of it, or reflecting on it, but a part of it, weaving it. This is why they write that "the plane of immanence has two facets as Thought and as Nature, as *Nous* and as *Physis.*"[63] All philosophic thought, and its conceptual machinery, is rigorously a part of the Real, not only as an existential "fact" of the Real—or facticity in Meillassoux—but as that through which the Real is given.

But this means that the concept cannot be a representation of the Real, as if from outside of it. This is why Deleuze and Guattari claim that the concept "has no *reference:* it is self-referential; it posits itself and its object at the same time as it is created."[64] Thus, the concepts that populate Deleuze and Guattari's metaphysical scheme (virtual/actual, nomadic/striated, and so on) are not representations of thought-independent reality, but are productions of immanent reality itself, which is just to say that immanence is at once the ground of the concept and what is constructed in the concept. This is why Deleuze and Guattari will say that the presupposition of immanence does not entail its preexistence.[65] Immanence must be "instituted," or philosophically constructed, but as what is presupposed.

What this means, more precisely, is that presupposition is the way the plane is posed, namely, as presupposed: at once already there, and yet constructed philosophically (e.g., through the reversible asymmetry of virtual and actual in indi-different/ciation); it is presupposed only insofar as it is *constructed as presupposed* in the concept: "even the prephilosophical plane," write Deleuze and Guattari, "is only so called because it is laid out as presupposed and not because it pre-exists without being laid out."[66] With this, we are given the magnificent self-synthesizing apparatus at the heart of their immanent constructivism: the concept poses or constructs immanence, but as what must be presupposed in order that immanence may be posed in the concept. The necessity of the philosophic presupposition is generated in and through the concept constructing immanence; the latter constructs its own necessity in and through philosophy. Life is not a contradiction, then, but is the effect of immanence being "immanent only to itself" by means of its own self-generation in and through philosophic concepts.

My interest in the absolutization of life is of course not limited to the status of Deleuze and Guattari's constructivism within contemporary speculative philosophy, but extends to what this constructivism means for the science of wet-life synthesis. Opening up the space for nomadicism within this science demands that we inquire into its metaphysics. It is not enough simply to indicate that there is a nomadic dimension to wet-life synthesis;[67] rather, this new dimension requires that we articulate what is speculatively at stake. And what is at stake is not life in-itself, but a construction of life through the philosophic concept. In this view, philosophic construction is not divorced from royal science, but is rather its intimate presupposition.

It is precisely this point, however—namely, that the Real is *given* solely through philosophic construction—that François Laruelle finds objectionable. Laruelle, known primarily in the English-speaking world through the work of Ray Brassier, though now becoming popular in his own right thanks to an abundance of English translations, is in many ways Deleuze and Guattari's ally in their quest for immanence.[68] Much as they do, Laruelle claims that philosophy is incapable of representing the Real, since it is immanent to it; but unlike them, he in no way privileges philosophy's relation to the Real; the latter is already "given-without-givenness," the "phenomena-without-phenomenality," or that by which we "have already been gripped," and so does not require being given through philosophic intellection (qua immanence that must be given *to* itself).[69] Without getting into the details of Laruelle's own elaborate invention of non-philosophy (or more recently, non-standard philosophy),[70] the point to appreciate is that for Laruelle, Deleuze and Guattari fall victim to what the former identifies as the "principle of sufficient philosophy," or the authority of philosophy over the Real, by instantiating the invariant threefold structure of all philosophical thinking, or what he calls the "philosophical decision."[71] This decision is what Laruelle refers to as the "essence" of philosophy, which makes use of three terms—namely, immanence, transcendence, and the transcendental—but in such a way that immanence figures twice.[72] According to Laruelle, all philosophy is an operation of dyadic splitting of immanent datum and transcendent factum, or conditioned and condition (which can take any manner of forms in the history of philosophy—e.g., beings and Being in Heidegger), whose sufficiency (philosophy needs to know that its concepts are real conditions of intelligibility) is guaranteed by a third term that unites condition and conditioned in a transcendental immanence that must already be supposed or given (ensuring the unification of the dyad— e.g., "horizontal *ekstasis*" in Heidegger), but only given by way of the philosophic division into condition and conditioned—hence guaranteeing the necessity of philosophic thought for producing the synthetic unity of experience.

In his "Response to Deleuze," Laruelle finds in the self-generating logic of the plane of immanence—in which immanence is only immanent *to* itself through the concept—an instantiation of the decisional structure. What Laruelle suggests is that instead of immanence being *given-without-givenness,* Deleuze proposes that immanence gives itself "to" itself through (the agency of) philosophical concepts (virtual/actual, nomadic/striated, and so on) that reinstate an "unobjectifiable" transcendence. More precisely, the philosophic splitting of condition and conditioned or factum and datum is instantiated in the virtual and actual pair, but their sufficiency is guaranteed by the production of their immanence (via a reversible asymmetry through indi-different/ciation) that is presupposed for their very construction, but given only in and through their construction. Immanence is therefore the "One," in Laruelle's terms, that is the unity presupposed by and only attained through the separation and synthesis of condition and conditioned in philosophy. So for Laruelle, there is a hierarchy of philosophy over all other forms of knowledge:

> we find here the distinction between man and philosopher, their hierarchy despite it all. The philosopher who constructs the system and the idiot to which he refers and certainly stumbles over the detours of the system are no longer adequately distinguished. Or once again the philosopher does not truly want stupidity, he limits it.[73]

What is relevant for us is not only how this critique flags the "sufficiency" of philosophy in Deleuze and Guattari, but also how science would have to become philosophic if its materials were to testify to the immanent life of the universe. There may of course be an easy rejoinder to this: in *What is Philosophy?* and in various other texts, Deleuze and Guattari certainly leave room for philosophy, science, and art to enter into "zones of indiscernibility" (this is especially the case with literature and philosophy, since their materials are language,[74] but no less so with nomad science), so that science and art, just as much as philosophy, may be capable of constructing a plane of immanence. Even so, the real force of Laruelle's challenge, I think, is that these zones of contamination—whether philosophy *becomes* literature or science *becomes* philosophy—still have "authority" over the Real through their idealization in the decisional structure.

In this view, even if Deleuze and Guattari escape Meillassoux's criticism of subjectivism by means of their immanent constructivism, they nevertheless risk idealizing immanence through the decision, which means that our central proposition—that the scientist is a "cosmic artisan" who, in following "the matter flow as pure productivity" testifies to the "prodigious idea of *Nonorganic Life*"—is in *no way* sufficient unto the Real through its very production. And yet just because the construction of nonorganic life is not exhaustive does not mean, I want to stress, that it is not immanent to the Real, that it is not a part of its production. While Laruelle, for his part, posits the radical "identity" of all decisions vis-à-vis the Real (since the One is equally indifferent to all decisions), what is useful for us is not so much his own non-philosophical practice, but how his insights prompt us to ask how nonorganic life is itself a construction that, while not sufficient vis-à-vis the Real, is nevertheless an immanent part of it and so has a *pragmatic* value.

It is in this perspective that Deleuze and Guattari experience a new convergence with the philosophy of Alfred North Whitehead. In what follows, I read into the latter's metaphysics a speculative pragmatics that offers a way through "the prodigious idea of *Nonorganic Life*" that does not fall prey to the idealization of the Real. In this way, I see deep affinities between the metaphysical systems of Whitehead and of Deleuze and Guattari, but extract a pragmatic strategy in the former for valuing nonorganic life: the construction is an immanent part of the Real that is philosophically valuable insofar as it generates an experience indissociable from a problem posed by human thought. And it is under these pragmatic constraints that we witness the conditions under which the practice of wet-life synthesis makes nonorganic life matter.

Constructing with Whitehead

The great service Isabelle Stengers has done for the work of Alfred North Whitehead in her magnificent *Thinking with Whitehead: A Free and Wild Creation of Concepts* cannot be overemphasized.[75] Not only does she rehabilitate his work from the charge of being a precritical anachronism (from analytical and Continental philosophers alike), but she is also attentive to the passions that animate Whitehead, the mathematician who dares to ask speculative philosophical questions. We can never forget that reading with Whitehead, Stengers insists, "means accepting to commit oneself to an adventure whose starting point is always the formulation of a problem" (*TWW*, 10)—a problem posed by a mathematician who dares "to 'trust' in the possibility of a solution that remains to be created. Without this trust in a possible solution, mathematics would not exist" (*TWW*, 15). Reading with Whitehead does not so much mean accepting his solutions as the final resolutions, but understanding the problem that forced him to think, the problem that animated his thought, and forced him to create a solution space.

Of course, Deleuze and Guattari say something decidedly similar when they write that "all concepts are connected to problems without which they have no meaning and which can themselves only be isolated or understood as their solution emerges."[76] The philosophical concept, according to the Deleuze and Guattari of *What is Philosophy?*, is a solution that at once cannot be without its problem "found on the plane of immanence presupposed by the concept,"[77] and is also required by the problem to complete itself. What we must ask with regard to Whitehead, then, is: What is the problem that animates his thought?

As early as *The Concept of Nature,* before Whitehead's "official turn" to metaphysics in *Science and the Modern World,* he pronounced that his problem was to construct a concept of nature that accounts for "what we are aware of in perception" (*CN,* 28). By "awareness" Whitehead is not limiting himself to "sense perception," the latter accounting for so many of the epistemological problems in modern philosophy (discussed below). But his problem is to construct a concept that accounts for all that human awareness offers (of which sense perception is a component), including the visions of the poet, the turquoise color of the ocean water, and even the atomic and molecular interactions that are supposed to cause this perception. Such is the challenge Whitehead gives himself: to construct a concept of nature that does not resort to a theory of "psychic additions." The color of water is not a *mere* act of the mind, a "psychic addition furnished by the perceiving mind, . . . [that] would leave to nature merely the molecules" (*CN,* 29–30). The problem Whitehead therefore gives himself is to construct a concept that does not let nature bifurcate into "primary" and "secondary" qualities, wherein there is an objective nature in-itself (primary) and a nature for-us (secondary), relative to human perception; rather, *they are equally a part of the Real.* In other words, his challenge is to resist all those theories that allow the Real to bifurcate "into two systems of reality, which, insofar as they are real, are real in different senses" (*CN,* 30), so that "all we know of nature is in the same boat, to sink or swim together" (*CN,* 148, see 44).

Right away we can see not only the difference between the problem that animates Whitehead's thought and many of the contemporary speculative projects that try to revitalize the distinction between primary and secondary qualities (following Meillassoux),[78] but also, and much more specifically, how any theory of "life in-itself" or "life for-us" bifurcates nature. Whether you isolate the chemical conditions of life or relegate it to what is merely for-us, you equally bifurcate nature according to Whitehead.

This is not to say, however, that "life" is an inherent trap, something that will always produce a bifurcation, and so we should launch a "critique of life" (as per Thacker). Life does not drop out of Whitehead's conceptual scheme; in fact, it takes on a great deal of importance in *Process and Reality* and *Modes of Thought* ("The doctrine I am maintaining is that neither physical nature nor life can be understood unless we fuse them together" [*MT,* 150]). By the time of *Science and the Modern World* and *Process and Reality,* Whitehead's problem transforms somewhat though. Emphasis falls more on the transformation of our habits of thought, our abstractions: "we cannot think without abstractions," explains Whitehead, so we must be "vigilant in critically revising . . . abstractions" (*SMW,* 59). We must "re-engineer" them[79] so that any one abstraction is not be overstated, becoming all-important;[80] when it does, it becomes an instance of what he comes to call "the fallacy of misplaced concreteness," or "the accidental error of mistaking the abstract for the concrete" (*SMW,* 51). What is at stake, then, is determining the conditions under which our abstractions may be revised so that they transform our habits of thought. If life is one such abstraction, we must get clear on: (1) Whitehead's method for revising our abstractions; (2) his criteria for determining the success of such revisions; and (3) how life meets this criteria, and does not therefore become another instance of the "fallacy of misplaced concreteness."[81] If Whitehead revises our conception of life so that it becomes "the name of originality," and has strong resonances with Deleuze and Guattari's conception of nonorganic life, this cannot be understood apart from the problem that animates its construction: to transform our experience such that all is "in the same boat."

It is with this in mind that we need to approach the daunting first pages of *Process and Reality,* where Whitehead articulates the demands of speculative philosophy: "the endeavor to frame a coherent, logical, and necessary system of general ideas in terms of which every element of our experience can be interpreted" (*PR,* 3). This means that all aspects of experience, "everything of which we are conscious, as enjoyed, perceived, willed or thought" (*PR,* 3), will therefore be included within a system of general notions, which must themselves be "coherent, logical, and necessary." Each experience "shall have the character," Whitehead continues, "of a particular instance of a general scheme" (*PR,* 3).

For Whitehead, "every element of experience" must be included within the system; if some element is unaccounted for, is deemed inessential, nature bifurcates, and "philosophy destroys its usefulness [by] indulg[ing] in brilliant feats of explaining away" (*PR,* 17). In *Adventure of Ideas* he explains that

> in order to discover some of the major categories under which we classify the infinitely various components of experience . . . [we] must appeal to evidence relating to every variety of occasion. Nothing can be omitted, experience drunk and experience sober, experience sleeping and experience waking. (*AI,* 226)

The problem Whitehead identifies with modern epistemology, from Descartes to Kant, is that it has used clear and distinct perception as the basis for disclosing the nature of reality, according to the mode of "presentational immediacy." This is the present world that is contemporaneous with the perceiver, where contemporaneity means that experiences do not enter into the constitution of each other (experiences are radically isolated), and its privilege has resulted in a host of problems, culminating in the phenomena-noumena distinction in Kant. This is to the neglect of those vague experiences of the past that enter into the constitution of the present and prepare for a future; this is the felt solidarity of the world. This vague, though equally constitutive, mode is known as "perception in the mode of causal efficacy" (cf. *PR,* 61–65, 168–83; *MT,* 65–85), and its neglect has resulted in conceiving of process as a derivative of substance, and is exemplary of "The Fallacy of Misplaced Concreteness" (cf. *SMW,* 51).

Thus all experiences, "drunk and sober," must be interpreted within the system. But by "interpret" Whitehead cannot mean that he is instituting a hierarchical system whereby all items are "accounted for" in terms of a few privileged notions, such as subatomic particles in physics. Once again, this would bifurcate nature by making some notions essential, or primary, while others inessential, or secondary. Rather, to put "all in the same boat" means devising a way to account for what holds experiences together, "drunk and sober," what makes it so that there is a solidarity between the cosmic artisan's and the physicist's view of inorganic matter, that there is something that draws them together in a non-bifurcating abstraction. Neither view is more essential, or Real; they are different exemplifications of a common scheme. It is in this sense that Whitehead seeks to find what is general, or generic, to all experience, so that every experience "shall have the character of a particular instance of a general scheme" (*PR,* 3).

Coherence is therefore what Whitehead demands of his system; it is a constraint requiring "that what is identifiable in one such notion cannot be abstracted from its relevance to the other notions. It is the ideal of speculative philosophy that its fundamental notions shall not be capable of abstraction from each other" (*PR,* 3). To interpret experience, then, is to render it coherent so that no one notion is necessary and sufficient unto itself. This means that no metaphysical principle derives its necessity or authority from privileged cases, allowing it to be "abstracted" out from the rest of the system. In other words, metaphysical notions must exhibit the fact that "no entity can be conceived in complete abstraction from the system of the universe, and it is the business of speculative philosophy to exhibit this truth. This character is its coherence" (*PR,* 3).

But to interpret experience according to ultimate generalizations does not mean that such generalizations are ordinarily experienced—that we experience, for example, the exemplification of a generic notion as much in the synthetic biologist's experimentation on molecules as in the child's dream of becoming a biologist. Where such instances are most often regarded as in conflict—one is objective, the other subjective, a mere childish fantasy—coherence demands that they be thought together. Such generalizations cannot be discovered or even derived from the analysis of our specialized experiences or interests; nor can they be "intuited" by means of Bergson's "method of intuition."[82] It is not as if, for example, we will one day discover actual occasions via intuition, derivation, or some other method, to be the new ultimate bits of reality, to be a substitution for Bergson's duration even; this would make the system radically incoherent, and Whitehead's speculative project a failure.

What we must remember here is that for Whitehead, these general notions are what are required of his thought according to the problem he has posed for himself—namely, that we may experience our practices without letting nature bifurcate. But also, and equally important, is that this is a distinctly human adventure of thought. In *Modes of Thought,* Whitehead asks, "What are we appealing to in the development of philosophic thought? What is our evidence?" To which he responds: "human experience as shared by civilized intercommunication" (*MT,* 70). Experiential evidence is human; it is not a turtle's, it is not a rock's, or any other nonhuman experience; so what is generic in human, turtle, and rock experiences is therefore limited by human abstraction. "Speculative philosophy," explains Whitehead in *Adventure of Ideas,* "embodies the method of the 'working hypothesis.' The purpose of this working hypothesis for philosophy is to coordinate the current human experience" (*AI,* 222).

To experience without bifurcating nature requires that human thought be coordinated into a larger system of generalities so that the former is only an instance of the latter; but the system itself is a product of human abstraction, using human "tools," namely, language, that guarantee its insufficiency. "The great difficulty of philosophy," explains Whitehead, "is the failure of language" (*MT,* 49), which is why "philosophy is akin to poetry. Philosophy is the endeavor to find a conventional phraseology for the vivid suggestiveness of the poet. It is the endeavor to reduce Milton's 'Lycidas' to prose" (*MT,* 49–50). That there is a poetics of speculative philosophy is not a casual remark, however; it is a full-scale method, detectable as early as *Science and the Modern World,* when Whitehead notes that one must be "vigilant in critically revising . . . abstractions" (*SMW,* 59), and rigorously developed by the time of *Process and Reality* by means of his method of "imaginative rationalization." It is a method that "must be rigidly adhered to," and whose reason for success, according to Whitehead, "is that, when the method of difference fails, factors which are constantly present may yet be observed under the influence of imaginative thought" (*PR,* 5).

"Imaginative rationalization" is the means by which human thought abstracts from its own specializations, interests, knowledges, and so on, so that they may become "particular instance[s] of a general scheme" (*PR,* 3) that is inherently fallible, limited by the human capacity to imagine such universality: "the aim of generalization is sound," insists Whitehead, "but the estimate of success is exaggerated" (*PR,* 7). Speculative systematization is *a* perspective *in* the Real, not *the* final perspective *on* the Real. This is why Whitehead's comments on speculative propositions are so important, since they provide a rigorous account for how it is that a proposition may be metaphysical without representing the world *as it is.*[83] Suffice it to say that the proposition is of metaphysical value, not because it characterizes the world as it is in-itself, but because it proposes *a way* the world *could be* felt as relating to all occasions within the human's finite perspective (cf. *PR,* 197). "It is more important," according to Whitehead, "that a proposition be interesting than true" (*PR,* 259).

There are certainly some resemblances between Whitehead's theory of the proposition and Deleuze and Guattari's concept of the concept, the most striking of which is perhaps the fact that speculative metaphysics does not entail a realist epistemology: metaphysics is through-and-through constructivist. Much as it does in Deleuze and Guattari, a speculative proposition proposes, or brings into being, a universe instead of merely representing a preexisting one; it proposes "the general character of the universe required for that fact" (*PR,* 11). Coherence demands that the metaphysical proposition is not isolated, a "self-sustained fact," and so must presuppose the universe that is required for it to exist. "Life is novelty" is a construction that is generative of its own ground, or "image of thought," in the language of Deleuze and Guattari, which is necessary for it to be meaningful as a speculative proposition. "Speculative propositions," as Stengers puts it, "do not designate a world that exists prior to them, but, quite the contrary, they bring into existence what Deleuze and Guattari call an 'image of thought'" (*TWW*, 267).

And yet underwriting this convergence between the register of Whitehead and that of Deleuze and Guattari is an important divergence: while for the latter, a philosophic concept constructs an image of thought as its required ground, this image is *imageless*, without a human, subject, object, or any reference at all; it is the preconceptual "earth or deterritorialization" that must be presupposed as the Real ground of thought.[84] Whitehead's plane, by contrast, is not a preconceptual, or an un-abstracted Real, but rather the set of *abstractions* that requires invention in order to realize a particular perspective. For Whitehead, there is no going behind abstractions; there is no unmediated experience.[85] "We cannot think without abstractions," he tells us *Science and the Modern World*, and so there is no pure or uninterpreted experience (cf. *PR*, 15). What is brought into being, therefore, is a general system of abstractions, a scheme of notions neutral vis-à-vis specialized interests; but this ultimate neutrality is human thought's imaginative construction of a world that is neutral with respect to its own interests. There is no pretension, then, concerning metaphysical descriptions exhausting the Real, or even ever getting the latter partially "right"—as in the accumulative epistemology so prevalent in the technosciences.[86] In the preface to *Process and Reality*, Whitehead writes that "there remains the final reflection, how shallow, puny, and imperfect are efforts to sound the depths in the nature of things. In philosophical discussion, the merest hint of dogmatic certainty as to finality of statement is an exhibition of folly" (*PR*, xiv).

Critically, however, Whitehead's speculative abstractions do not warrant the critique of "mere" construction, in which they would be abstractions that somehow obfuscate the Real, and be in need of "Critique." Although the speculative proposition does not represent the Real, proposing a "view-from-nowhere," it is no less a part of it: "a proposition is a new kind of entity," in Whitehead's thought; "it is a hybrid between pure potentialities and actualities," and has an existence that is irreducible to representation (*PR*, 185–86). In this way, the proposition is an immanent abstraction in the Real that proposes a new way of experiencing; it is a "lure for feeling" the world differently, a new habit of thought, without "the merest hint of dogmatic certainty."

It is in this perspective that two of the most unlikely thinkers, namely, Whitehead and Laruelle, experience a convergence over philosophy's materials: they are segments *in* the Real without being final perspectives *on* the Real. With this, we also get a better sense of how Whitehead's proposed "perspective on perspectivelessness" is not Deleuze and Guattari's preconceptual immanence given through the concept. This is a point worth emphasizing because Whitehead's image of thought is not Deleuze and Guattari's. Philosophy is a real "adventure," but an *abstract* one, whose success can be measured only against its ability to transform experience according to the human problem it poses for itself, and not against its sufficiency for the construction of a preconceptual Real. The speculative proposition has pragmatic value.

Thus, "life is novelty" is a proposition that embodies the "hypothetical" character of speculative philosophy (cf. *AI,* 222). That "life" is not empirically verifiable, that it cannot be measured according the standard biological or even emergentist criteria—as something "out-there"—means that it requires some other means of verification to guarantee that its construction is adequate. We must measure its success according to the task it was given.

This is why Whitehead will insist that corresponding to a system's "coherence" is its "adequacy" and "applicability," or what provides the justification of rational systematization. These two requirements correspond to the "empirical side" of the philosophic method, where applicability "means that some items of experience are thus interpretable, and [adequacy] means that there are no items incapable of such interpretation" (*PR,* 3). What this means is that particular observations (applicability) may be celebrated in terms that are relevant to all observations (adequacy). As Whitehead explains,

> Whatever is found in "practice" must lie within the scope of metaphysical description. When the description fails to include the 'practice' the metaphysics is inadequate and requires revision. There can be no appeal to practice to supplement metaphysics, so long as we remain contented with our metaphysical doctrines. Metaphysics is nothing but the description of the generalities which apply to all the details of practice. (*PR,* 13)

Suffice it to say that it is these empirical requirements, which determine whether practices are now interpretable in terms that include all other practices, provide the verification for imaginative rationalization. The rational requires the empirical for its verification; or rather, coherence is achieved to the extent that it is adequate and applicable. The rational and empirical are in mutual presupposition, requiring each other for their completion.

Hence Whitehead's well-known suggestion that the philosophic method is analogous to the flight of an airplane:

> The true method of discovery is like the flight of an aeroplane. It starts from the ground of a particular observation; it makes a flight into the thin air of imaginative generalization; and it again lands for renewed observation rendered acute by rational interpretation. (*PR*, 5)

Systematization is justified to the extent that it transforms experience, that it lands from the thin air of imaginative rationalization and produces within us an experience of our specialized practices in terms that are irreducible to such specialization.[87] Metaphysical concepts are what make it that the general, what is generic, may matter; they are what induce in us an experience that does not let nature bifurcate. Stengers reminds us of Whitehead's proclamation in *Modes of Thought:* "the aim of philosophy is sheer disclosure" (*MT*, 49) and not the concepts themselves: "the concepts are required by the transformation of experience, but it is this disclosure that has, and always will have, the last word" (*TWW*, 17).

The take-away point here is that Whitehead's perspective does not appear to be subject to the critique of "idealization" that Laruelle levels against Deleuze and Guattari. At least in the way I am reading Whitehead, his abstractions are finite perspectives on the process by which any one perspective is deprivileged; but they are not, nor do they purport to be, the final perspective. There are no illusions in this regard to concepts constructing their own preconceptual ground as *the* Real. Rather, the plane of neutrality constructed by Whitehead is a construction *in* the Real, but whose "efforts to sound the depths of the nature of things" is "shallow, puny, and imperfect" (*PR*, xiv). Philosophy's evidence is determined by the finitude of human experience, and so its abstractions are fallible; they are working hypotheses, abstractions, whose goal is "to coordinate the current human experience" in order to produce an experience that does not fall prey to habits of thought that overvalue any set of abstractions. In this view, abstractions, far from taking us away from experience, as Bergson once claimed, are actually generative of real experience, so that the measure of a good speculative concept is its ability to generate an experience so that all is "in the same boat, to sink or swim together" (*CN*, 148).

My hypothesis then is this: what Whitehead adds to our overall picture is far from another subjectivization or idealization of the Real; but rather he adds a speculative pragmatics to our account, so that what is testified to is the reality of the transformation of human experience by means of thought.

Life, What Does It Make Matter?

The goal of this essay all along has been to make life matter. This inquiry has been framed in terms of what may seem like an idiosyncratic field in speculative science, known variously as "bottom-up synthetic biology," "wet ALife," or even "wet-life synthesis." My claim is that it is significant for us precisely because it is an experimental science whose materials (molecules) arguably make the ontology of life a central question for itself; but it does so, as I have tried to stress, in such a way that obscures the most exciting metaphysical aspects of what their materials express. My suggestion is that their experimentation with molecules supports a much more radical notion of life, one that is expressive of *nonorganic life,* a vitality immanent to the material world that parallels the nomadic sciences of Deleuze and Guattari.

But as I have also tried to make clear, the validity of this proposition is undermined by recent speculative scholarship from Meillassoux, Thacker, Laruelle, among others, who all challenge the so-called neo-vitalist tradition for any number of sins, but most commonly for subjectivizing or idealizing matter in some form. While my retort is that some of these critiques fail to appreciate Deleuze and Guattari's constructivism, and that the latter's concepts are creative constructions, this still does not circumvent the problem that Laruelle identifies as an insidious form of transcendence that Deleuze and Guattari's immanence nevertheless maintains. The issue, then, is essentially this: there is a problem in identifying life with the Real, whether it be a preexistent Real, or a Real that must be given to itself. Either account produces a series of challenges.

My own suggestion is that we look to what I am calling the speculative pragmatics of Whitehead for promoting a notion of nonorganic life. As was indicated above, there are some important similarities between the concept of life in Whitehead and the nonorganic life of Deleuze and Guattari. And yet, my claim is that Whitehead's justification for this construction avoids the pitfalls that plague Deleuze and Guattari's construction. Whitehead stresses how life is a concept that can be justified only to the extent that it is generative of a particular kind of human experience—not a preexistent or preconceptual Real independent of human abstraction, but a *real* experience of the general within the particular, an event that is indissociable from the problem thought has posed for itself: experience without falling prey to the fallacy that bifurcates nature.

With this turn to Whitehead, however, I do not mean to suggest that he resolves the problem of how nonorganic life is connected to the wet synthesis of life once and for all—far from it. What I would suggest is that he articulates the conditions under which this practice would make the construction matter for it. As Whitehead insists, we always begin our speculative adventure somewhere: we begin in human experience; we "start from the ground of a particular observation . . . [make] a flight into the thin air of imaginative generalization . . . [and land] for renewed observation rendered acute by rational interpretation (*PR*, 5). We begin in an experience and return to that experience renewed. And so in this case, we ask whether the concept of life transforms the experience of wet-life synthesis according to the problem posed.

As we have seen, wet-life synthesis, as a practice, must define what life is, if only to oppose it to the nonlife that its materials supposedly overcome; but in so doing, it turns life into a "natural kind," or an "in-itself," with properties that hold irrespective of any cultural, historical, epistemic, and other variants, or what is merely "for us." The practice must therefore affirm certain abstractions, while relegating others to irrelevancy, thereby committing the fallacy of misplaced concreteness that bifurcates nature.

As I took pains to emphasize, however, through the excursion into Deleuze and Guattari's notions of metallurgy and nomadicism, the kinds of abstractions required for the existence of a scientific practice cover over experiences of creative indeterminacy that resonate throughout all experiences—molecular, metallurgical, technological, organic, and so on. What Whitehead adds here is how rigorous we must be when we say that these experiences testify to nonorganic life.

Life is not "out there," discoverable in molecular experiments; nor is it a concept that is purely "for us," a "mere" construction that neither participates in the Real nor has real effects. Rather, life is a real abstraction whose pragmatic value rests in its ability to generate a generic experience within the spheres of specialized practice. In this view, life is what makes it that nomadicism may matter in wet-life synthesis, so that the experiences of "pure productivity" are not covered over in a higher-order abstractions, but may be felt in solidarity with the rest of our experiences. To say that wet-life synthesis testifies to nonorganic life is to say that we have posed the Whiteheadian problem for ourselves: to experience experiments on the chemical universe nomadically through imaginative construction.

Notes

1. See *Protocells: Bridging Nonliving and Living Matter,* ed. Steen Rasmussen, Mark A. Bedau, Liaohai Chen, David Deamer, David C. Krakauer, Norman H. Packard, Peter F. Stadler (Cambridge, Mass.: MIT Press, 2009); and *The Ethics of Protocells: Moral and Social Implications of Creating Life in the Laboratory,* ed. Mark Bedau and Emily Parke (Cambridge, Mass.: MIT Press, 2009).

2. The generally agreed upon criteria of "minimal life" are that it have three operational functionalities within three interrelated chemical systems: (1) has identity over time; (2) uses resources from environment in order to grow, maintain, and reproduce; and (3) has inheritable information. See Rasmussen et al., *Protocells: Bridging Nonliving and Living Matter.*

3. See Martin M. Hanczyc, Taro Toyota, Takashi Ikegami, Norman Packard, and Tadashi Sugawara, "Fatty-Acid Chemistry at the Oil-Water Interface: Self-Propelled Oil Droplets," *Journal of the American Chemical Society* 129 (2007): 9386–91; and Takashi Ikegami and Martin Hanczyc, "The Search for a First Cell under the Maximalism Design Principle," *Technoetic Arts: A Journal of Speculative Research* 7, no. 2 (2009): 153–64.

4. See Mark Bedau, "Four Puzzles about Life," *Artifical Life* 4 (1998): 125–40; and Elliott Sober, "Learning from Functionalism: Prospects for Strong Artifical Life," *Artifical Life* 2 (2003): 749–65.

5. See Pier Luigi Luisi, Francesca Ferri, and Pasquale Stano, "Approaches to Semi-Synthetic Minimal Cells: A Review," *Naturwissenschaften* 93 (2006): 1–13; David Deamer, "A Giant Step towards Artificial Life," *Trends in Biotechnology* 23 (2005): 336–38; and Steen Rasmussen, Liaohai Chen, Martin Nilsson, Shigeaki Abe, "Bridging Nonliving and Living Matter," *Artifical Life* 9 (2003): 269–316.

6. See Carol Cleland and Christopher Chyba, "Does 'Life' Have a Definition?," *Planets and Life: The Emerging Science of Astrobiology,* ed. Woodruff T. Sullivan III and John Baross (Cambridge: Cambridge University Press, 2007).

7. See Steven Benner, Alonso Ricardo, and Mathew Carrigan, "Is There a Common Chemical Model for Life in the Universe?," *Current Opinion in Chemical Biology* 8 (2004): 672–89.

8. See G. J. T. Cooper, P. J. Kitson, R. S. Winter, M. Zagnoni, D. L. Long, and L. Cronin, "Modular Redox-Active Inorganic Chemical Cells: iCHELLs," *Angewandte Chemie International Edition* 50, no. 44 (October 2011): 10373–76; and Leroy Cronin, "Defining New Architectural Design Principles with 'Living' Inorganic Materials," *Architectural Design* 81, no. 2 (March–April 2011): 34–43.

9. In *After Life* (Chicago, Ill.: University of Chicago Press, 2010), Eugene Thacker notes that "Aristotle is confronted with a challenge, which is to articulate a concept that is adequate to the diversity of what counts as 'life.' Such a concept must account for the characteristics of life. . . . It must account for the conditions in which life is possible at all, as well as for the ends of life. . . . But this means that such a concept cannot itself be a part of life, or one among many instances of life" (10).

10. In *Vibrant Matter: A Political Ecology of Things* (Durham, N.C.: Duke University Press, 2010), Jane Bennett notes that her goal "is to articulate a vibrant materiality that runs alongside and inside humans to see how analyses of political events might change if we gave the force of things more due" (viii).

11. Bennett draws heavily on Gilles Deleuze and Félix Guattari's critique of hylomorphism in *A Thousand Plateaus: Capitalism and Schizophrenia*, trans. Brian Massumi (Minneapolis: University of Minnesota Press, 1987), which they borrow from Gilbert Simondon: "a presumably passive, unorganized, or raw matter can be given organic 'form' only by the agency of something that is not itself material" (Bennett, *Vibrant Matter*, 56).

12. Deleuze and Guattari, *A Thousand Plateaus*, 411; hereafter, cited parenthetically in the text as *ATP*.

13. Thacker, *After Life*, 6.

14. See Gilbert Simondon, *L'individu et sa genèse physico-biologique* (Grenoble: Éditions Jérôme Millon, 1995).

15. Cyril S. Smith, "The Texture of Matter as Viewed by Artisan, Philosopher, and Scientist in the Seventeenth and Eighteenth Centuries," *Atoms, Blacksmiths, and Crystals: Practical and Theoretical Views of the Structure of Matter in the Seventeenth and Eighteenth Centuries*, ed. Cyril S. Smith and John Garrett Burke (Los Angeles, Calif.: Williams Andrews Clark Memorial Library, University of California Los Angeles, 1967), 8–9n; also see Cyril S. Smith *A History of Metallography* (Chicago, Ill.: University of Chicago Press, 1960).

16. Bennett, *Vibrant Matter*, 59.

17. Bennett wants to undo—via Deleuze and Guattari—the Classical assumption that metal is symbol for stasis: "Aeschylus presented Prometheus's chains as fixed matter. The chains are strong because their metal is uniform and homogeneous, devoid of any internal differences (variations in texture, ductility, rates of decay, etc.) that Prometheus might have exploited to break it apart. The chains are impregnable, we are told, because their matter does not vary across its own surface or depth" (*Vibrant Matter*, 58).

18. Steven Shaviro gestures toward the relation between Deleuze's and Whitehead's conceptions of "interstitial life" in *Without Criteria: Kant, Whitehead, Deleuze, and Aesthetics* (Cambridge, Mass.: MIT Press, 2009), 70–71, 94–95.

19. See Didier Debaise, "The Living and Its Environments," *Process Studies*, 37, no. 2 (Fall–Winter 2008): 127–39.

20. Igakami and Hanczyc propose that their protocell is not life but the first cell on the way to it. Cf. Igakami and Hanczyc, "The Search for a First Cell under the Maximalism Design Principle."

21. See Rasmussen et al., introduction to *Protocells*.

22. See Mark A. Bedau, "Weak Emergence," in *Philosophical Perspectives: Mind, Causation, and World*, vol. 11, ed. J. Tomberlin (Malden, Mass.: Blackwell, 1997); and Mark A. Bedau, "Downward Causation and Autonomy in Weak Emergence," in *Emergence: Contemporary Readings in Philosophy and Science*, ed. Mark A. Bedau and Paul Humphreys (Cambridge, Mass.: MIT Press, 2008).

23. See Mark A. Bedau, "Artificial Life," in *Handbook of the Philosophy of Biology*, ed. M. Matthen and C. Stephens (Amsterdam: Elsevier, 2007).

24. Please see Eric Alliez's *The Signature of the World: What is Deleuze and Guattari's Philosophy?*, trans. Eliot Ross Albert and Alberto Toscano (New York: Continuum,

2004) for what still remains, in my view, one of the most compelling commentaries on nomad science in Deleuze and Guattari. Alliez explains that the distinction between the royal and nomad sciences is far from absolute; it is "ideal" rather than "real"—there is no autonomy of the nomad from the royal and vice versa. According to Alliez, "nomad sciences refuse to lead science towards an autonomous power and development" (ibid., 48–49). Though much Deleuze secondary literature suggests otherwise, to suggest that there is a nomad science, such as differential calculus, dynamical systems theory, endosymbiosis, etc., that resists royalization misses the point of what Deleuze and Guattari mean by nomad science (cf. *A Thousand Plateaus,* 372). And yet, this also holds true for what are deemed "royal sciences": there is a nomadism, or becoming, immanent to physicists' practice, for example. For what this might look like, see Isabelle Stengers's *Cosmopolitics I,* trans. Robert Bononno (Minneapolis: University of Minnesota Press, 2010). This also seems to speak, if indirectly, to concerns that have grown among Deleuze scholars as to why Deleuze and Guattari distinguish between philosophy and science in *What is Philosophy?,* but use royal definitions of science that seem to conflict with the nomadism of *A Thousand Plateaus.* See Isabelle Stengers's "Deleuze and Guattari's Last Enigmatic Message," *Angelaki,* 10 no. 2 (2005): 151–67.

25. Alliez, *The Signature of the World,* 48.

26. Hanczyc et al., "Fatty Acid Chemistry at the Oil-Water Interface," 9389.

27. See Ikegami and Hanczyc, "The Search for a First Cell under the Maximalism Design Principle."

28. Hanczyc et al., "Fatty Acid Chemistry at the Oil-Water Interface," 9390.

29. Ibid., emphasis added.

30. Ibid., emphasis added.

31. See Ikegami and Hanczyc, "The Search for a First Cell under the Maximalism Design Principle."

32. Martin Hanczyc, "Structure and Synthesis of Life," *Architectural Design* 81, no. 2 (March–April 2011): 31.

33. In "Weak Emergence," Bedau notes that, "although strong emergence is logically possible, it is uncomfortably like magic. How does an irreducible but supervenient downward causal power arise, since by definition it cannot be due to the aggregation of the micro-level potentialities? Such causal powers would be quite unlike anything within our scientific ken. This not only indicates how they will discomfort reasonable forms of materialism. Their mysteriousness will only heighten the traditional worry that emergence entails illegitimately getting something from nothing" (377).

34. Bedau and Humphreys, introduction, 14.

35. Bedau, "Downward Causation and Autonomy in Weak Emergence," 160.

36. See David Chalmers, *The Conscious Mind: In Search of a Fundamental Theory* (New York: Oxford University Press, 1996); Brian P. McLaughlin "Emergence and Supervenience," *Intellectia* 25 (1997): 25–43; and Brian P. McLaughlin, "Varieties of Supervenience," in *Supervenience: New Essays,* ed. E. Savello and O. Yalcin (Cambridge: Cambridge University Press, 1995).

37. As Rasmussen et al. claim in their introduction to *Protocells: Bridging Nonliving and Living Matter,* it is taken as axiomatic that life is an emergent state, a functional some-thing that is generated out of nonliving materials. This is more or less consistent with the basic theses of emergence and self-organizing systems theorists, ranging from

Humberto Maturana and Francisco Varela's autopoietic systems theory in *Autopoiesis and Cognition: The Realization of the Living* (Berlin: Springer, 1991) and Evan Thomson's extension of autopoietic systems in *Mind in Life: Biology, Phenomenology, and the Sciences of Mind* (Cambridge, Mass.: Harvard University Press, 2007) to Susan Oyama's theories of developmental biology (Developmental Systems Theory or DST) in *The Ontogeny of Information: Developmental Systems and Evolution* (Durham, N.C.: Duke University Press, 2000) and Stuart Kaufmann's complex living systems in *Investigations* (New York: Oxford University Press, 2000). Life is defined by the emergence of centers of homeostatic equilibrium, poised at the "edge of chaos," but nevertheless they are organized centers. Shaviro has recently written about the concept of life and self-organizing systems, and suggests that despite the attention they have received in Deleuze scholarship, theories of self-organization are conservative theories of life. Cf. Shaviro, *Without Criteria*, and Shaviro, "Interstitial Life: Remarks on Causality and Purpose in Biology," in *The Force of the Virtual: Deleuze, Science, and Philosophy*, ed. Peter Gaffney (Minneapolis: University of Minnesota Press, 2010).

38. See Chris Langton *Artificial Life* (Redwood City, Calif.: Addison-Wesley, 1999); and Bedau "Artificial Life."

39. See Bedau, "Artificial Life."

40. Deleuze and Guattari write that "major science has the perpetual need for the inspiration of the minor; but the minor would be nothing if it did not confront and conform to the highest scientific requirements" (*A Thousand Plateaus*, 486).

41. It is important to note that there is perhaps a becoming, or nomadicism, immanent to even the most royal of sciences (Alain Badiou's axiomatic set-theory, for example), as was alluded to above. Isabelle Stengers, for her part, elaborates on this notion with her speculative "ecology of practices" in her two-volume *Cosmopolitics* and her earlier work, *The Invention of Modern Science*, trans. Daniel W Smith (Minneapolis: University of Minnesota Press, 2000). It is for this reason that it seems overzealous to single out wet-life synthesis as exemplary for its capacity to be deterritorialized. Rather, the nomadicism of this particular practice is important precisely because there is a becoming-metallurgical immanent to it.

42. Iain Hamilton Grant also suggests reading the productivity of Deleuze and Guattari's universe as a problem of (dark) chemistry, but does so by way of Schelling's *Naturphilosophie*. Cf. Grant, "The Chemistry of Darkness," *Pli: The Warwick Journal of Philosophy* 9 (2000): 36–52.

43. See. Quentin Meillassoux, *After Finitude: An Essay on the Necessity of Contingency*, trans. Ray Brassier (London: Continuum, 2008), 37; and Thacker, *After Life*, ch. 4–5.

44. There are many transformations worth noting: from Deleuze's early Bergsonian vitalism in *Bergsonism*, trans. Hugh Tomlinson and Barbara Habberjam (New York: Zone Books, 1991) to his distancing from the latter by means of his notion of indi-drama-different/citation exemplified in embryogenesis ("the world is an egg") in *Difference and Repetition*, trans. Paul Patton (New York: Columbia University Press, 1994), 251; and from Deleuze and Guattari's "profound life" or "desiring-production" in *Anti-Oedipus: Capitalism and Schizophrenia*, trans. Robert Hurley, Mark Seem, and Helen R. Lane, (Minneapolis: University of Minnesota Press, 1983) to their "Nonorganic Life" of *A Thousand Plateaus*, and finally to Deleuze's own "a life" in "Immanence: A Life" in *Pure Immanence: Essays on a Life*, trans. Anne Boyman (New York: Zone Books, 2001). And

this still doesn't take into account the way in which life figures prominently in *Expressionism in Philosophy: Spinoza*, trans. Martin Joughin (New York: Zone Books, 1990) and in *Nietzsche and Philosophy*, trans. Hugh Tomlinson (New York: Columbia University Press, 1983). The point is, there are many such transitions to note in Deleuze's single and coauthored texts, which are far from exhausted here. See John Protevi's "Deleuze and Life," in *The Cambridge Companion to Deleuze*, ed. Daniel W. Smith and Henry Somers-Hall (New York: Cambridge University Press, 2012), which magnificently charts the developments of Deleuze's and Deleuze and Guattari's concept of life.

45. Deleuze, "Immanence: A Life," 28.

46. Ibid., 27.

47. Deleuze, *Expressionism in Philosophy*, 81.

48. Thacker, *After Life*, 226.

49. See Alain Badiou, *Deleuze: The Clamor of Being*, trans. Louise Burchill (Minneapolis: University of Minnesota Press, 2000).

50. See Levi Bryant, Nick Srnicek, and Graham Harman's introduction to the *Speculative Turn: Continental Materialism and Realism*, ed. Levi Bryant, Nick Srnicek, and Graham Harman (Victoria, Australia: re.press, 2011) for a good overview of the emergence of speculative realism.

51. Immanuel Kant, *Critique of Pure Reason*, trans. Norman Kemp Smith (Boston: Bedford St. Martin's, 1965), A297/B354. While Kant explains that it is in very nature of our reason to search for the "unconditioned," or ultimate metaphysical explanations ("this is an *illusion* which can no more be prevented than we can prevent the sea appearing higher at the horizon than at the shore . . ." [ibid.]), this is nevertheless the locus of the transcendental illusion, since these metaphysical explanations issue from subjective interests. The limitations of knowledge therefore need to be characterized (as he does in the Transcendental Analytic) so that there can be a "critique" of pure reason in order that we do not misuse reason and draw erroneous metaphysical conclusions—that is, mistake phenomena for the thing-in-itself.

52. Meillassoux, *After Finitude*, 5.

53. See Meillassoux's *After Finitude*, ch. 1–2 for an overview of the concept of correlationism; also see Ray Brassier's *Nihil Unbound: Enlightenment and Extinction* (New York: Palgrave Macmillan, 2007), ch. 3, for a thorough commentary on Meillassoux's notion of correlationism.

54. Meillassoux, *After Finitude*, 37.

55. Ray Brassier, Iain Hamilton Grant, Graham Harman, and Quentin Meillassoux, "Speculative Realism," *Collapse* 3 (2007): 427.

56. Ibid.

57. Thacker, *After Life*, 257.

58. "To question life in terms of its ontological status," writes Thacker, "would seem ridiculous—questioning the existence, or, shall we say, the 'realism' of life would be tantamount to questioning existence itself" (ibid.).

59. "If Bataille does put forward an ontology of life, it would therefore have to be *an ontology of life that is coextensive with* nihil. At times Bataille calls this 'negative immanence'" (ibid., 266).

60. Gilles Deleuze and Félix Guattari, *What is Philosophy?*, trans. Hugh Tomlinson and Graham Burchell (New York: Columbia University Press, 1994), 45.

61. Ibid., 47.

62. Ibid., 39.
63. Ibid., 38.
64. Ibid., 22.
65. Cf. Ibid., 41.
66. Ibid., 78.

67. This has too often been the tendency with Deleuzian studies of science. That there is minorization of cognitive science in the work of Evan Thompson and Francisco Varela, for example, does not mean that we can forget its inseparability from the royal practices it insists within; in other words, there may be "ideal moments" of minorization within their practice, but they get recuperated into the norms of the practice. This is easy enough to see in wet-life synthesis. We must therefore be sensitive to how these minor or even philosophic moments within scientific practice cannot become the new ideal for the practice.

68. In a footnote to their *What is Philosophy?*, Deleuze and Guattari cite François Laruelle as "engaged in one of the most interesting undertakings of contemporary philosophy. He invokes a One-All that he qualifies as 'non-philosophical' and oddly, as 'scientific,' on which the philosophical decision takes root. This One-All seems close to Spinoza" (220). Of course it has been noted in various places that Spinoza's and Deleuze and Guattari's conception of immanence has many significant differences with Laruelle's. See François Laruelle, "Response to Deleuze," trans. Taylor Adkins, *Pli: The Warwick Journal of Philosophy* 20 (2009); and François Laruelle, *Laruelle and Non-Philosophy,* ed. John Mullarkey and Anthony Paul Smith (Edinburgh: University of Edinburgh Press, 2012).

69. See. Brassier, *Nihil Unbound,* 128; and François Laruelle, *Philosophie et non-philosophie* (Liege-Bruxelles: Mardaga, 1989), 41–45.

70. See François Laruelle, *Philosophie non-standard* (Paris: Kime, 2010).

71. See François Laruelle, *Dictionnaire de la non-philosophie* (Paris: Editions Kime, 1998).

72. See Brassier, *Nihil Unbound,* 122–24.

73. See Laruelle, "Response to Deleuze," 155.

74. See Gregory Flaxman, *Gilles Deleuze and the Fabulation of Philosophy: Powers of the False* (Minneapolis: University of Minnesota Press, 2012), vol. 1, ch. 4.

75. With the 2011 English translation of Isabelle Stengers's *Thinking with Whitehead: A Free and Wild Creation of Concepts,* trans. Michael Chase (Cambridge, Mass.: Harvard University Press, 2011; hereafter cited parenthetically in the text as *TWW*), the English-speaking world experienced what Gilles Deleuze might have meant when he claimed that "the conclusion of *A Thousand Plateaus* is a table of categories (but an incomplete, insufficient one). Not in the style of Kant, but in the style of Whitehead." Cf. Gilles Deleuze, "Responses to a Series of Questions," an exchange between Arnauld Villani and Gilles Deleuze, *Collapse* 3 (November 2007): 41.

76. Deleuze and Guattari, *What is Philosophy?*, 16.

77. Ibid., 81.

78. A good deal has been written on the relation between object-oriented ontology (a brand of speculative realism) and Whitehead's metaphysics. That Whitehead may be an "honorary" speculative realist seems to hinge, however, on the idea that there is an anti-correlational reality that his metaphysics is supposed to interpret. Of course, this disregards the problem his metaphysics is designed to resolve, which is the tendency to see a reality "in-itself" distinct from a reality "for-us." Cf. *The Speculative Turn,* chaps. 18, 19.

79. In *Science and the Modern World,* Whitehead compares philosophy to engineering, writing that "an active school of philosophy is quite as important for the locomotion of ideas, as is an active school of railway engineers for the locomotion of fuel" (59).

80. According to Whitehead, "the disadvantage of exclusive attention to a group of abstractions, however well-founded, is that, by nature of the case, you have abstracted from the remainder of things" (*SMW,* 59).

81. It's not hard to see how the concept of life in twentieth- and twenty-first century molecular biology is exemplary of the fallacy of misplaced concreteness. The DNA molecule is paradigmatic of our experience of living organisms (from personalized medicine and gene therapy to genetically engineered food). But reducing life to this molecule, which defined the hopes and dreams of so many twentieth-century molecular biologists, produces a whole series of exclusions in the form of "yes, but what about . . . ?"; but so does excluding DNA altogether from our contemporary experience of living environments. So how might we learn to celebrate the molecular experience of life without falling prey to the fallacy that bifurcates nature? The demands of Whitehead's empiricism make themselves felt here: it forces us to ask whether a given conceptual framework is robust enough to allow us to affirm the importance of this molecular experience—e.g., how genetic manipulation has taught us a great deal about what an organic system can endure—without falling into the trap of exaggerating its impact. Whitehead's challenge is therefore to "engineer" our abstractions such that they lure us into regarding our experiences in terms that do not "explain away" other experiences. Can DNA be placed in a wider system of coordinated experiences? And might life, with the appropriate re-engineering, be an abstraction capable of generating this experience? For more on DNA as a source of the bifurcation of nature (under the guise of "gene fetishism"), see Donna Haraway's *Modest_Witness @Second_Millennium. FemaleMan© Meets OncoMouse™* (New York: Routledge, 1997), 147.

82. See Didier Debaise's "The Emergence of a Speculative Empiricism: Whitehead Reading Bergson," in *Deleuze, Whitehead, Bergson: Rhizomatic Connections,* ed. Keith Robinson (New York: Palgrave Macmillan, 2009), for a compelling account of the relation between Bergson's method of intuition and Whitehead's method of abstraction.

83. While the proposition is often overlooked in the commentary, not only is it among the eight "categories of existence" but also, more importantly for us,—*pace* the thesis of bivalency established in the *Principia Mathematica,* coauthored with Bertrand Russell—Whitehead now objects to the idea that the proposition is merely "material for judgment," and those judged to be "non-conformal" to the actual world "are merely wrong, and therefore worse than useless" (*PR,* 187). Whitehead suggests that the proposition is neither formally true nor false, but a "lure for feeling," indicating a world that "might be." In terms of the general scheme, this experience designates the "could be" of an eternal object, or predicate, with a subject, or nexus, for a concrescing occasion; it is their "potential togetherness," and not their actual realization, that defines a proposition: "the germaneness of a certain set of eternal objects to a certain set of actual entities" (*PR,* 188). It is this togetherness of the logical subject and predicate, their proposed realization within a concrescing occasion, and not their actual exemplification, that characterizes a propositional entity. For a metaphysical proposition to obtain, what is required is that the predicative pattern, or eternal object, relates in a potential pattern, all possible occasions as its subjects: "that its predicate potentially relates any and every set of actual occasions." Additionally, the proposition must have a "'uniform' truth-value, in the sense that, by reason

of its form and scope, its truth-value is identical with the truth-value of each of its singular propositions to be obtained by restricting the application of the predicate to any one set of logical subjects" (PR 197).

84. Deleuze and Guattari, *What is Philosophy?*, 41.

85. This is why Whitehead, in *Symbolism: Its Meaning and Effect*, writes that "'objectification' itself is abstraction; since no actual thing is 'objectified' in its 'formal' completeness. Abstraction expresses nature's mode of interaction and is not merely mental" (25–26). There is no objectivity without abstraction. Human knowledge can only ever be one mode of abstraction.

86. See *TWW*, 12.

87. "The supreme verification of the speculative flight is that it issues in the establishment of a practical technique for well-attested ends, and that the speculative system maintains itself as the elucidation of that technique. In this way there is progress from thought to practice, and regress from practice to the same thought. This interplay of thought and practice is the supreme authority. It is the test by which the charlatanism of speculation is restrained" (*FR*, 64–65).

Contributors

JEFFREY A. BELL is professor of philosophy at Southeastern Louisiana University. He is the author of *Philosophy at the Edge of Chaos: Gilles Deleuze and the Philosophy of Difference* and *Deleuze's Hume: Philosophy, Culture, and the Scottish Enlightenment*, and a coeditor of *Deleuze and History*.

NATHAN BROWN is assistant professor of English at Concordia University, Montreal. He is the author of *The Limits of Fabrication: Materials Science, Materialist Poetics*.

PETER CANNING practices analysis in New York City and teaches at Pratt Institute. He co-assembles work groups (cartels) in topology and analysis, and is cofounder of the New York Schizoanalytic Society.

DIDIER DEBAISE is a member of the Faculté de Philosophie et Lettres at the Université Libre de Bruxelles. He is the author of *Un empiricisme spéculatif: Lecture de Procés et réalité de Whitehead*.

ROLAND FABER is professor of process theology at the Claremont School of Theology and professor of religion and philosophy at the Claremont Graduate School. He is the author of *God as Poet of the World: Exploring Process Theologies* and *The Divine Manifold* and coeditor of *Event and Decision: Ontology and Politics in Badiou, Deleuze, and Whitehead; Beyond Metaphysics: Explorations in Alfred North Whitehead's Late Thought; Secrets of Becoming: Negotiating Whitehead, Deleuze, and Butler; Butler on Whitehead: On the Occasion; Theopoetic Folds: Philosophizing Multifariousness;* and *Beyond Superlatives: Regenerating Whitehead's Philosophy of Experience*.

Nicholas Gaskill is assistant professor of English at Rutgers University, New Brunswick.

Michael Halewood is senior lecturer in sociology at the University of Essex. He is the author of *A. N. Whitehead and Social Theory: Tracing a Culture of Thought.*

Graham Harman is Distinguished University Professor at the American University in Cairo. He is the author of several books, including *Prince of Networks: Bruno Latour and Metaphysics; Circus Philosophicus; The Quadruple Object;* and *Quentin Meillassoux: Philosophy in the Making.* He is a coeditor of *The Speculative Turn: Continental Materialism and Realism.*

Bruno Latour is professor and vice president of research at the Institut d'Études Politiques de Paris. He is the author or coauthor of several books, including *Laboratory Life; Science in Action: How to Follow Scientists and Engineers through Society; We Have Never Been Modern; The Politics of Nature: How to Bring the Sciences into Democracy; Reassembling the Social: An Introduction to Actor-Network-Theory; On the Modern Cult of the Factish Gods;* and *An Inquiry into Modes of Existence: An Anthropology of the Moderns.*

Erin Manning is associate professor and research chair in relational art and philosophy and director of SenseLab at Concordia University, Montreal. She is the author of *Always More Than One: Individuation's Dance; Relationscapes: Movement, Art, Philosophy; Politics of Touch: Sense, Movement, Sovereignty* (Minnesota, 2007); and *Ephemeral Territories: Representing Nation, Home and Identity in Canada* (Minnesota, 2003).

Steven Meyer is associate professor of English at Washington University in St. Louis. He is the author of *Irresistible Dictation: Gertrude Stein and the Correlations of Writing and Science* and coeditor of the *Configurations* special issue "Whitehead Now."

A. J. Nocek is an instructor in the Comparative History of Ideas Program and a PhD candidate in comparative literature at the University of Washington, Seattle.

Luciana Parisi is reader, director of the PhD program in cultural studies, and codirector of the Digital Culture Unit at the Centre for Cultural Studies, Goldsmiths University of London. She is the author of *Abstract Sex: Philosophy, Bio-technology, and the Mutations of Desire* and *Contagious Architecture: Computation, Aesthetics, and Space.*

KEITH ROBINSON is assistant professor of philosophy at the University of Arkansas at Little Rock. He is the editor of *Deleuze, Whitehead, Bergson: Rhizomatic Connections.*

ISABELLE STENGERS is professor of philosophy at the Université Libre de Bruxelles. She is the author or coauthor of several books translated into English, including *Order Out of Chaos; The Invention of Modern Science* (Minnesota, 2000); *Cosmopolitics I* and *II* (Minnesota, 2010 and 2011); and *Thinking with Whitehead: A Free and Wild Creation of Concepts.*

JAMES WILLIAMS is professor of European philosophy at the University of Dundee. He is the author or coauthor of *Gilles Deleuze's Philosophy of Time: A Critical Introduction and Guide; Gilles Deleuze's Logic of Sense: A Critical Introduction and Guide; The Lyotard Reader and Guide;* and *Gilles Deleuze's Difference and Repetition: A Critical Introduction and Guide.* He is also coeditor of *Postanalytic and Metacontinental: Crossing Philosophical Divides.*

Index